LONGMAN

PREPARATION SERIES FOR THE NEW TOEIC® TEST

Intermediate Course

Fourth Edition

D0224968

Lin Lougheed

PEARSON
Longman

Longman Preparation Series for the New TOEIC® Test, Intermediate Course, Fourth Edition

Pearson Education, 10 Bank Street, White Plains, NY 10606

Staff credits: The people who made up the *Longman Preparation Series for the New TOEIC® Test, Intermediate Course* team, representing editorial, production, design, and manufacturing, are listed below:

Jennifer Adamec
Rhea Banker
Angela M. Castro
Dave Dickey
Pam Fishman
Patrice Fraccio
Margo Grant
Lise Minovitz
Michael Mone
Cover design: Barbara Sabella
Text design: Pat Wosczyk
Text composition: TSI Graphics
Text font: 11/15 Palatino

Library of Congress Cataloging-in-Publication Data

Lougheed, Lin, 1946-
   Longman preparation series for the new TOEIC test. Intermediate course / Lin Lougheed. — 4th ed.
      p. cm.
   Includes indexes.
   Rev. ed. of: Longman preparation series for the TOEIC test.
Intermediate course. 3rd ed. c2005.
   ISBN 0-13-199314-3 (textbook with answer key) — ISBN 0-13-199315-1 (textbook without answer key) 1. Test of English for International Communication—Study guides. 2. English language—Textbooks for foreign speakers. 3. English language—Examinations—Study guides.   I. Lougheed, Lin, 1946- Longman preparation series for the TOEIC test. Intermediate course. II. Title.
   PE1128.L6457 2006
   428.0076—dc22

2004019078   2006023383

Printed in the United States of America
   9 10 V001 12 11

LONGMAN ON THE **WEB**

Longman.com offers online resources for teachers and students. Access our Companion Websites, our online catalog, and our local offices around the world.

Visit us at **longman.com**.

CONTENTS

INTRODUCTION

LISTENING COMPREHENSION

READING

READING REVIEW   **270**

PRACTICE TESTS

ANSWER SHEETS

AUDIOSCRIPTS

ANSWER KEYS AND CONVERSION CHARTS

PHOTO CREDITS

INTRODUCTION

TO THE STUDENT: SELF-STUDY GUIDE

Examine the Book

Before you begin to study for the new TOEIC® test, you should look through this book from the first page to the last. You will learn how the book is organized and how it will help you. Notice the headphone symbol used throughout the book. This symbol means that you will need the appropriate audio for that section. Now read this Self-Study Guide completely.

General Information

This introduction has information about the new TOEIC (Test of English for International Communication™) test. Parts 1 through 7 of the test are described, and the test directions are given with the permission of Educational Testing Service (ETS).

Level

When you take the new TOEIC test, you may be surprised at how difficult the test is. The test measures the proficiency levels of beginning, intermediate, and advanced students of English. You will find some questions easy; you will find some questions difficult. When you become an advanced student, you will find questions on the new TOEIC test easy. As you become more proficient in English, your score will improve.

The materials in the book are written for intermediate-level students like you. Study these materials carefully and you will be able to get a good intermediate level score. Do not be discouraged that the exam is more difficult than this book. If you study more, the test will be easier and your score will be higher.

Table of Contents

By looking at the table of contents, you will be able to see what is taught in the book and where each part of the new TOEIC test can be found.

Parts 1–7

Each part of the book has directions and activities that match the corresponding part of the new TOEIC test. The introduction to each part gives the new TOEIC test directions and discusses learning strategies. It is followed by practice activities.

DIRECTIONS: You should read and understand all the test directions. They are reprinted here with permission from the company that makes the new TOEIC test, Educational Testing Service. Study the directions, and be sure you understand what you are going to do for each part of the test.

STRATEGIES AND ACTIVITIES: Study all the strategies given in the book and do all the activities. The more you practice for each part of the test, the more you will be able to improve your score. In each part you will find words and situations that will help you increase your command of English.

This book will show you common test errors and help you avoid them, although, of course, it is not possible to predict exactly what will be on the new TOEIC test. However, this book will show you common themes and help you recognize them. It will show you common patterns and help you understand them. It is your responsibility to study as much as you can.

Practice Tests

The Practice Tests are very important. They have two purposes. They are both diagnostic tests and measures of achievement.

DIAGNOSTIC TESTS: The Practice Tests and the Self-Study Charts can help you find out what you need to study next.

ACHIEVEMENT MEASURES: You can use the Practice Tests and the Self-Study Charts to see how well you learned strategies for the new TOEIC test.

TEST SCORES: This book prepares you for the kinds of questions you will find on the new TOEIC test. If your score is low, you need to go over the strategy and activity sections more thoroughly. If your score is high, you have made a good beginning in preparing for the new TOEIC test.

SPEED: The new TOEIC test is a timed test. You must learn how to read questions quickly and how to look for the answer quickly. Push yourself to work faster and faster. Record your reading times in the blanks provided in the reading sections so that you can see if you are increasing your reading speed.

Choose a Study Plan

In Study Plan One, do each section of the book in the order in which it is presented. In Study Plan Two, do one section of a Practice Test at a time, correct your answers, and then go to the correct section to study the material you got wrong. Choose a method and check (✓) each section as you finish it.

STUDY PLAN ONE	DONE

Begin with Part 1 on page 2.
    Read and learn the strategies on page 3.
    Practice the strategies for Part 1 on pages 4–38.	

Next do Part 2.
    Read and learn the strategies on page 39.
    Practice the strategies for Part 2 on pages 40–73.	

Next do Part 3.
    Read and learn the strategies on page 74.
    Practice the strategies for Part 3 on pages 75–110.	

Next do Part 4.
    Read and learn the strategies on page 111.
    Practice the strategies for Part 4 on pages 112–152.	

Do the Listening Comprehension Review, Parts 1–4, on pages 153–165.
    Use the Answer Key to correct your test.
    Mark your Self-Study Chart.
    Study the pages indicated on your Self-Study Chart for the
      questions you answered incorrectly.	

Continue with Part 5.
    Read and learn the strategies for each section.
    Practice the strategies for Part 5 on pages 170–195.	

Next do Part 6.
    Read and study the grammar boxes for each section.
    Practice the strategies for Part 6 on pages 197–226.	

Next do Part 7.
    Read and learn the strategies on pages 227–229.
    Practice the strategies for Part 7 on pages 230–269.	

Do the Reading Review, Parts 5–7, on pages 270–297.
    Use the Answer Key to correct your test.
    Mark your Self-Study Chart.
    Study the pages indicated on your Self-Study Chart for the
      questions you answered incorrectly.	

Take Practice Test One, Parts 1–7, on pages 299–339.
    Pretend you are taking the real TOEIC test.
    Use the Answer Key to correct your test.
    Mark your Self-Study Chart.
    Study the pages indicated on your Self-Study Chart for the
      questions you answered incorrectly.	

Take Practice Test Two, Parts 1–7, on pages 341–383.
    Pretend you are taking the real TOEIC test.
    Use the Answer Key to correct your test.
    Mark your Self-Study Chart.
    Study the pages indicated on your Self-Study Chart for the
      questions you answered incorrectly.	

STUDY PLAN TWO	DONE

Do the Listening Comprehension Review, Part 1, on pages 153–158.
    Use the Answer Key to correct your test.
    Mark your Self-Study Chart.
    Study the pages indicated on your Self-Study Chart for the
      questions you answered incorrectly.	

Do the Listening Comprehension Review, Part 2, on page 159.
    Use the Answer Key to correct your test.
    Mark your Self-Study Chart.
    Study the pages indicated on your Self-Study Chart for the
      questions you answered incorrectly.	

Do the Listening Comprehension Review, Part 3, on pages 160–162.
    Use the Answer Key to correct your test.
    Mark your Self-Study Chart.
    Study the pages indicated on your Self-Study Chart for the
      questions you answered incorrectly.	

Do the Listening Comprehension Review, Part 4, on pages 163–165.
    Use the Answer Key to correct your test.
    Mark your Self-Study Chart.
    Study the pages indicated on your Self-Study Chart for the
      questions you answered incorrectly.	

Do the Reading Review, Part 5, on pages 270–273.
    Use the Answer Key to correct your test.
    Mark your Self-Study Chart.
    Study the pages indicated on your Self-Study Chart for the
      questions you answered incorrectly.	

Do the Reading Review, Part 6, on pages 274–278.
    Use the Answer Key to correct your test.
    Mark your Self-Study Chart.
    Study the pages indicated on your Self-Study Chart for the
      questions you answered incorrectly.	

Do the Reading Review, Part 7, pages 279–297.
    Use the Answer Key to correct your test.
    Mark your Self-Study Chart.
    Study the pages indicated on your Self-Study Chart for the
      questions you answered incorrectly.	

Take Practice Test One, Parts 1–7, on pages 299–339.
    Pretend you are taking the real TOEIC test.
    Use the Answer Key to correct your test.
    Mark your Self-Study Chart.
    Study what you missed.	

Take Practice Test Two, Parts 1–7, on pages 341–383.
    Pretend you are taking the real TOEIC test.
    Use the Answer Key to correct your test.
    Mark your Self-Study Chart.
    Study what you missed.	

The Self-Study Chart

The Self-Study Chart on page xiii is your own personal record of what you know and what you do not know about English. When you look at the Answer Key to correct your Practice Tests, you will see something like the left column:

ANSWER KEY   **ANSWER SHEET**

Part 2

21. (C) *By noon* answers *when*. Choice (B)   Ⓐ Ⓑ ●
    answers *when did she arrive*. Choice (C)
    is incorrect because he hasn't arrived yet.

22. (B) *I went shopping* answers *what did you* Ⓐ ● Ⓒ
    do. Choice (A) answers *how do you get to*
    your destination. Choice (C) confuses the
    similar-sounding *play* and *day*.

23. (A) *The woman came before the others*   Ⓐ ● Ⓒ
    answers *who came first*. Choice (B) confuses
    the opposites *last* and *first*. Choice (C)
    confuses the opposites *left* and *came*.

When you compare your Answer Sheet (right column) with the Answer Key, you see that you missed question 23. The correct answer was (A). Put a mark for *Who* under Part 2 in the Self-Study Chart.

PART 2: QUESTION-RESPONSE	ERRORS	STUDY PAGES
Statements	0	40–43
Who	I	44–47
What	II	48–52
When	I	53–56
Where	0	57–60
Why	III	61–64
How	0	65–68
Auxiliaries	0	69–72

The completed Self-Study Chart tells you that in Part 2 of this Practice Test, you missed one question with *Who*, two questions with *What*, one question with *When*, and three questions with *Why*. You should first review Part 2 activities on *Why*, then review *What*, and then review *When*.

The Self-Study Chart will help you make your studying very efficient. You need to review only those sections you missed on the Practice Tests.

SELF-STUDY CHART	ERRORS Review	ERRORS Practice Test One	ERRORS Practice Test Two	STUDY PAGES
Part 1: Photos				2–38
Part 2: Question-Response				
Statements				40–43
Who				44–47
What				48–52
When				53–56
Where				57–60
Why				61–64
How				65–68
Auxiliaries				69–72
Part 3: Conversations				
Occupations				75–80
Activities				81–87
Time				88–93
Locations				94–99
Reasons				100–105
Part 4: Talks				
Advertisements				112–117
Weather				118–123
News				124–129
Recorded Announcements				130–136
Special Announcements				137–143
Business Announcements				144–149
Part 5: Incomplete Sentences				
Word Choice: Nouns				170–171
Word Choice: Verbs				172–173
Word Choice: Adjectives				174–175
Word Choice: Adverbs				176–177
Word Choice: Conjunctions				178–179
Word Choice: Prepositions				180–181
Word Form: Nouns				182–183
Word Form: Verbs				184–185
Word Form: Adjectives				186–187
Word Form: Adverbs				188–189
Word Form: Pronouns				190–191
Part 6: Text Completion				
Reference				197–198
Verb Tenses				
The Simple Present				200–201
The Present Continuous				200–201
The Present Perfect				200–201
The Present Perfect Continuous				200–201
The Simple Past				202–204
The Past Continuous				202–204
The Past Perfect				202–204
The Simple Future				205–207
The Future Perfect				205–207
Modal Auxiliaries				208–210
Modifiers				
Adjectives: Comparative and Superlative Forms				216–217
Adverbs of Frequency				218–219
Verbal Adjectives: Present and Past Participles				220–221
Part 7: Reading Comprehension				
Advertisements				229–236
Forms				237–244
Letters, E-mail, Faxes, and Memos				245–251
Tables, Indexes, and Charts				252–258
Instructions and Notices				259–265

Taking the Test

Here are some hints to help you do well on the new TOEIC® test.

- Be on time.
- Sit as close to the audio source as possible.
- Make yourself comfortable.
- Read all the directions.
- Read all the answer choices.
- Guess. Do not leave blanks on the answer sheet.
- One minute before the test time ends, look over your answer sheet and make sure there are no unanswered questions.
- Do the questions that are easy for you first.

TO THE TEACHER: CLASSROOM STUDY GUIDE

Planning Your Lesson

▨ Level

Often students with limited English proficiency are surprised at how difficult the new TOEIC® test is when they take it. This is because the test must measure a student's ability at all different levels. There are challenging questions to measure the proficiency level of students whose English is at a native-speaker level. There are easier questions to measure the proficiency of students with minimal English.

The materials in this book are designed for students at the intermediate proficiency level. These materials develop language skills as well as provide test-taking practice. Students at the intermediate level will find some questions on the new TOEIC test very challenging. As students study more and as they move up from the *Intermediate Course* to the *Advanced Course*, they will find it easier to answer all the questions on the TOEIC test.

▨ Sequence

Preparing for the new TOEIC test should easily fit into a 30-hour course. The class should work through each part in successive order as presented in the book. The strategies that a student learns in one part will be helpful in subsequent parts. Vocabulary learned in one part will be useful in another part.

▨ Questions

Help students learn to ask questions when they examine a picture, study grammar problems, or read a passage. The strategies are all designed as questions. These questions focus the student's attention on themes and patterns in English in general and on the new TOEIC test specifically.

▨ Speed

The new TOEIC test is a timed test. Therefore, students must learn how to read questions quickly and how to look for the answer quickly. Push students to work faster and faster.

▨ Atmosphere

Make the Practice Tests simulate a real TOEIC test. Take the whole class period for the test experience. Do not allow students to bring anything but a pencil to their desks. Time the activities.

▨ Advanced Activities

You can supplement the activities in this book with other TOEIC test preparation books in this series, including the *Introductory Course* and the *Advanced Course*, as well as *More Practice Tests*, available from Pearson Longman ELT.

If you do not have enough time to go through the entire book, you can use a Class Study Chart to help you make efficient use of your class periods. Have your students take Practice Test One as a diagnostic test; correct the tests and prepare a Class Study Chart. The chart will show what most students need to study first, what can be saved until the end, and what can be assigned as homework.

For example, you may find that, in general, your students need more work on listening and less on grammar. Specifically, you may find that most students need work on Part 2, Question-Response. Even more specifically, you may find that most of your students need work on the *When* section of Part 2, Question-Response.

To use the Class Study Chart, do the following:

■ Have your students take the Listening Comprehension Review, Parts 1–4.

■ Correct the test in class.

■ Read aloud each category on the Class Study Chart, and count the number of students who missed questions in a particular category.

■ Enter the results on the chart.

CLASS STUDY CHART	STUDENT ERRORS REVIEW	STUDY PAGES
Part 2		
Statements	0	40–43
Who	III	44–47
What	⊬⊬ I	48–52
When	⊬⊬ IIII	53–56
Where	⊬⊬	57–60
Why	⊬⊬ III	61–64
How	II	65–68
Auxiliaries	I	69–72

For example, if this were your class chart, you would begin by teaching Part 2, *When*, because in the class a total of nine errors were made in this category. Then you would teach the *Why* section, followed by the *What* and *Where* sections. The sections *Who, How,* and *Auxiliaries* were not problems for most of your students and could be assigned as individual homework.

CLASS STUDY CHART	STUDENT ERRORS *Review*	STUDENT ERRORS *Practice Test One*	STUDENT ERRORS *Practice Test Two*	STUDY PAGES
Part 1: Photos				2–38
Part 2: Question-Response				
Statements				42–43
Who				44–47
What				48–52
When				53–56
Where				59–60
Why				61–64
How				65–68
Auxiliaries				69–72
Part 3: Conversations				
Occupations				75–80
Activities				81–87
Time				88–93
Locations				94–99
Reasons				100–105
Part 4: Talks				
Advertisements				112–117
Weather				118–123
News				124–129
Recorded Announcements				130–136
Special Announcements				137–143
Business Announcements				144–149
Part 5: Incomplete Sentences				
Word Choice: Nouns				170–171
Word Choice: Verbs				172–173
Word Choice: Adjectives				174–175
Word Choice: Adverbs				176–177
Word Choice: Conjunctions				178–179
Word Choice: Prepositions				180–181
Word Form: Nouns				182–183
Word Form: Verbs				184–185
Word Form: Adjectives				186–187
Word Form: Adverbs				188–189
Word Form: Pronouns				190–191
Part 6: Text Completion				
Reference				197–198
Verb Tenses				
The Simple Present				200–201
The Present Continuous				200–201
The Present Perfect				200–201
The Present Perfect Continuous				200–201
The Simple Past				202–204
The Past Continuous				202–204
The Past Perfect				202–204
The Simple Future				205–207
The Future Perfect				205–207
Modal Auxiliaries				208–210
Modifiers				
Adjectives: Comparative and Superlative Forms				216–217
Adverbs of Frequency				218–219
Verbal Adjectives: Present and Past Participles				220–221
Part 7: Reading Comprehension				
Advertisements				229–236
Forms				237–244
Letters, E-mail, Faxes, and Memos				245–251
Tables, Indexes, and Charts				252–258
Instructions and Notices				259–265

QUESTIONS ABOUT THE NEW TOEIC® TEST

What is the new TOEIC test?

The Test of English for International Communication (TOEIC) is a multiple-choice test of English for adult, nonnative speakers of the language. It consists of two sections: Listening Comprehension and Reading. Each section contains 100 questions. There are four parts to the Listening Comprehension section.

		NUMBER OF QUESTIONS
Part 1:	Photos	10
Part 2:	Question-Response	30
Part 3:	Conversations	30
Part 4:	Talks	30
	TOTAL	100

There are three parts to the Reading section of the test.

		NUMBER OF QUESTIONS
Part 5:	Incomplete Sentences	40
Part 6:	Text Completion	12
Part 7:	Reading Comprehension	
	• Single Passages	28
	• Double Passages	20
	TOTAL	100

How long does the new TOEIC test last?

The actual time for the new TOEIC test is approximately two hours. Additional time is required to answer questions about yourself on the Answer Sheet. You should allow up to three hours to take the test.

LISTENING COMPREHENSION SECTION	45 minutes
READING SECTION	1 hour and 15 minutes

What does the new TOEIC test measure?

The new TOEIC test is designed to test your proficiency in English. The test covers the English language as it is used internationally in business, commerce, and industry. You do not need to have specialized knowledge or know specialized vocabulary for business situations.

How is the new TOEIC test scored?

The new TOEIC test is scored on a scale of 10 to 990. This is the total of the listening comprehension score and the reading score.

LISTENING COMPREHENSION	5 to 495
READING	5 to 495
	10 to 990

The score is a scaled score determined by the number of correct responses the student makes on a test.

Are some TOEIC tests more difficult than others?

People who take the new TOEIC test more than once may believe that one test was easier or more difficult than another. While every effort is made to develop tests that are of equal difficulty, it is not possible to develop tests that are exactly equivalent. For the new TOEIC test, any difference in difficulty between forms of the test is eliminated statistically. This means that a score on one form of the test is equivalent to the same score on any other form of the test.

GUIDELINES FOR PREPARING FOR AND TAKING THE NEW TOEIC® TEST

■ **Use English as often as possible.**

If you are planning to take the new TOEIC test, you should make every effort to use English as often as possible at work, as well as in social, travel, and other everyday situations.

■ **Read the directions carefully.**

Before beginning the test, you will read a set of general directions. You will also be given specific directions as to how to answer each part of the test. Study the directions and the sample questions in this book carefully so that you will be familiar with the test format.

■ **Work rapidly and carefully.**

When you take the test, do not spend too much time on any one question. Work as fast as you can.

■ **Do not take notes.**

While you are taking the exam, do not make any notes on your answer sheet or on any other piece of paper.

■ **Guess.**

There is no penalty for guessing. Try to answer every question. Some questions are more difficult than others. You may not know the answer to every question, so make a guess.

■ **Mark only one answer per question.**

Questions with more than one answer marked will be counted wrong even if one of the answers marked is correct.

■ **Follow the directions of the test examiners.**

If you do not follow the rules during the test, your score may not be counted.

GENERAL DIRECTIONS: The following general directions are provided by the Educational Testing Service (ETS®) and are reprinted here with permission. Read them and be sure you understand them.

Test of English for International Communication

General Directions

This test is designed to measure your English language ability. The test is divided into two sections: Listening and Reading.

You must mark all of your answers on the separate answer sheet. For each question, you should select the best answer from the answer choices given. Then, on your answer sheet, you should find the number of the question and fill in the space that corresponds to the letter of the answer that you have selected. If you decide to change an answer, completely erase your old answer and then mark your new answer.

SPECIFIC DIRECTIONS: Each part of the new TOEIC test begins with specific directions for that part. In this book you will find them at the beginning of each study section and in the Practice Tests. Read them and be sure you understand them.

Note that the items in the study sections may differ slightly from those described in the actual TOEIC test directions, but the directions are provided so you will become familiar with them.

NEW TOEIC® TEST ANSWER SHEETS

The Answer Sheets used in this book are similar to those used in the new TOEIC test. The precise format of the Answer Sheets varies from test site to test site.

To record a response to a test question, examinees should find the number on the answer sheet that corresponds to the test question and make a solid mark with their pencil, filling in the space that corresponds to the letter of the answer they have chosen. If you have purchased a book that includes an Answer Key, you will find a Conversion Chart in the Answer Key section. This Conversion Chart will give you an *approximation* of what your TOEIC test scores might be. Please note that this is an approximation, not an actual TOEIC test score.

LISTENING

COMPREHENSION

In the first section of the new TOEIC® test, you will have the chance to show how well you understand spoken English. There are four parts to this section:

Part 1	Photos
Part 2	Question-Response
Part 3	Conversations
Part 4	Talks

In this part of the *Longman Preparation Series for the New TOEIC® Test: Intermediate Course,* you will learn strategies to help you on the Listening Comprehension section. Each part begins with activities to help you develop these strategies. Each part ends with listening comprehension questions similar to those on the new TOEIC test.

You will need the appropriate new audio for the activities and for the Listening Comprehension Review.

NOTE: The TOEIC test directions for each part of the new TOEIC test will be given at the beginning of the section. Read the directions carefully to be sure you understand them.

PART 1: PHOTOS

LISTENING TEST

In the Listening test, you will be asked to demonstrate how well you understand spoken English. The entire Listening test will last approximately 45 minutes. There are four parts, and directions are given for each part. You must mark your answers on the separate answer sheet. Do not write your answers in the test book.

PART 1

Directions: For each question in this part, you will hear four statements about a picture in your test book. When you hear the statements, you must select the one statement that best describes what you see in the picture. Then find the number of the question on your answer sheet and mark your answer. The statements will not be printed in your test book and will be spoken only one time.

Example

Sample Answer

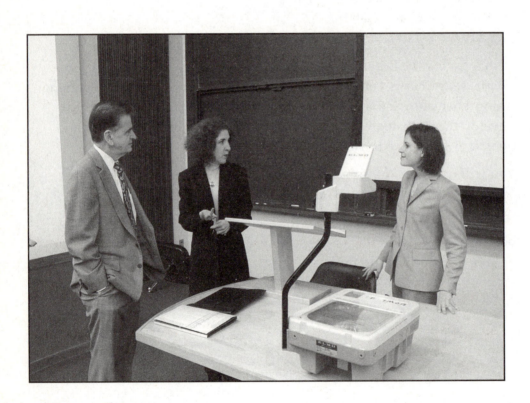

Statement (C), "They're standing near the table," is the best description of the picture, so you should select answer (C) and mark it on your answer sheet.

The next eight pictures will help you look at pictures and use these strategies. The exercises will help you improve your vocabulary, study more grammar, and sharpen your listening skills.

PHOTO STRATEGIES
WHEN STUDYING FOR THE NEW TOEIC TEST

- Look at the photo before you listen to the audio.

- Ask yourself some questions:

PHOTOS OF PEOPLE	**PHOTOS OF THINGS**
Who is in the photo?	*What* is in the photo?
Where are they?	*Where* is it?
What are they doing?	

- Give the photo a title.

- Tell yourself a story about the photo.

PHOTO STRATEGIES
WHEN TAKING THE NEW TOEIC TEST

- Quickly look at the photo before you hear the answer choices.

- Quickly ask yourself some *wh* questions:

Who	Who is in the photo?
What	What are they doing?
Where	Where was the photo taken?

You will have more opportunities to practice these strategies in the Photo Strategy Practice section. There are 12 photos similar to those on the new TOEIC test. You can then test yourself in the Review: Part 1 section, which has eight photos.

PHOTO 1: AT THE COMPUTER

The woman is working at the computer. She is sitting in a desk chair in front of the computer. Her left hand is on the keyboard. She is looking at the computer monitor. The screen is bright. On the screen, or display, you can see a software program. There is a printer beside the monitor. There is paper in the printer. There is probably a mouse attached to the keyboard, but we can't see it.

Vocabulary

DIRECTIONS: Find these items in the photo.

desk	monitor	screen	keyboard
printer	chair	cable	display

What Do You See?

A. DIRECTIONS: Read these statements about what you see in the photo. The statements may or may not be true. Put (Y) for *yes* beside the statements that match the photo. Put (N) for *no* beside the statements that do not match the photo. Correct the statements that are not true.

1. __N__ The man is sitting in front of the computer.

2. _____ The computer monitor is turned off.

3. _____ The woman has both hands on the keyboard.

4. _____ She is sitting in a chair in front of the desk.

5. _____ There is paper in the printer.

B. DIRECTIONS: You will be tested on what *is* in the photograph, not what *could be* in the photograph. Put (Y) beside the statements that are correct. Put (?) beside the statements that could be true, but you cannot be sure from the photo.

1. _?_ The woman has worked at the company for a long time.

2. _____ She is making the display brighter.

3. _____ The monitor is beside the printer.

4. _____ She is printing out a document.

5. _____ The keyboard is between the monitor and the worker.

Analyze This

DIRECTIONS: What do you think about the photo? Read each statement. Put (Y) for *yes*, (N) for *no*, or (?) for *maybe* next to each statement. Give reasons for your answers.

1. _____ It's a large office.

Reason: _____

2. _____ The woman works with computers a lot.

Reason: _____

3. _____ She knows how to use the software program.

Reason: _____

4. _____ The monitor is too far from the woman.

Reason: _____

5. _____ The display is too small.

Reason: _____

Prepositions

DIRECTIONS: Listen and complete the sentences with the prepositions you hear.

1. Her hand is _____ the keyboard.

2. The printer is _____ the monitor.

3. The monitor is _____ the desk.

4. She is sitting _____ the desk.

5. The clerk is looking at the display _____ the monitor.

Similar Sounds

A. DIRECTIONS: Listen. Which word or phrase do you hear first? Mark (A) or (B).

1. (A) print her   (B) printer   (A) (B)
2. (A) the play   (B) the display   (A) (B)
3. (A) monitor   (B) man or   (A) (B)
4. (A) keyboard   (B) employee is bored   (A) (B)
5. (A) her newspaper   (B) the printer paper   (A) (B)

B. DIRECTIONS: Listen. Which statement do you hear first? Mark (A) or (B).

1. (A) He prints her next document.   (A) (B)
   (B) Her printer is next to the documents.

2. (A) The display is not bright enough.   (A) (B)
   (B) This gray is not light enough.

3. (A) She put the monitor on the table.   (A) (B)
   (B) She may put the man or the woman at my table.

4. (A) The new employee is bored.   (A) (B)
   (B) The new employer has a keyboard.

5. (A) Her new paper is under the desk.   (A) (B)
   (B) Her newspaper is under the rest.

Extra Practice

DIRECTIONS: On a separate piece of paper, write about what is happening in the photo. Use the vocabulary in this section.

PHOTO 2: AT A RESTAURANT

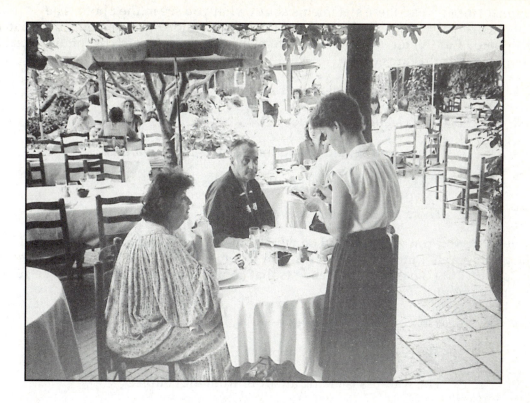

There are many tables in this restaurant. The restaurant is outside in a garden. There are some trees and plants in the garden. Some of the tables are covered with umbrellas. Some of the tables are under a tree. There are many empty tables.

At one of the tables, a waitress is taking an order. She is holding a pen and a small notebook or pad of paper. She writes the customers' orders on this pad. There are two customers, a man and a woman, at this table.

There is a tablecloth on the table. The table is set with glasses and plates. One knife is visible. There is a menu on the table by the man and an ashtray in the middle of the table.

Vocabulary

DIRECTIONS: Find these items in the photo.

table	umbrella	tablecloth	chair
customer	waitress	pad of paper	plate

What Do You See?

A. DIRECTIONS: Read these statements about what you see in the photo. The statements may or may not be true. Put (Y) for *yes* beside the statements that match the photo. Put (N) for *no* beside the statements that do not match the photo. Correct the statements that are not true.

1. _____ There are customers at every table.

2. _____ The restaurant is inside.

3. _____ The customers are giving their orders to the waitress.

4. _____ There are tablecloths on all the tables.

5. _____ There are umbrellas at every table.

B. DIRECTIONS: You will be tested on what *is* in the photograph, not what ***could be*** in the photograph. Put (Y) for yes beside the statements that describe what you see in the photo. Put (?) beside the statements that could be true, but you cannot be sure from the photo.

1. _____ The couple is ordering dessert.

2. _____ The restaurant is very popular.

3. _____ The waitress is taking an order from the couple.

4. _____ The waitress is standing.

5. _____ The restaurant is not full.

Analyze This

DIRECTIONS: What do you think about the photo? Put (Y) for *yes*, (N) for *no*, or (?) for *maybe* beside each statement. Give a reason for your answer.

1. _____ The restaurant is expensive.

Reason: _____

2. _____ It is lunchtime.

Reason: _____

3. _____ It is a hot day.

Reason: _____

4. _____ The tablecloth is clean.

Reason: _____

5. _____ The waitress is giving the customers menus.

Reason: _____

Prepositions

DIRECTIONS: Listen and complete the sentences with the prepositions you hear.

1. The couple is sitting _____ the table.

2. The restaurant is _____ the garden.

3. A tablecloth is _____ the table.

4. The waitress is standing _____ front _____ the customers.

5. The man and woman are _____ each other.

Similar Sounds

A. DIRECTIONS: Listen. Which word or phrase do you hear first? Mark (A) or (B).

1.	(A) cup of	(B) couple	Ⓐ	Ⓑ
2.	(A) talking together	(B) taking their order	Ⓐ	Ⓑ
3.	(A) waiter is setting	(B) waitress is sitting	Ⓐ	Ⓑ
4.	(A) a dress	(B) address	Ⓐ	Ⓑ
5.	(A) on the right	(B) wearing white	Ⓐ	Ⓑ

B. DIRECTIONS: Listen. Which statement do you hear first? Mark (A) or (B).

1. (A) The waitress is serving a cup of coffee.   Ⓐ Ⓑ
   (B) The waitress is serving the couple coffee.

2. (A) The waitress is taking their order.   Ⓐ Ⓑ
   (B) The waitresses are talking together.

3. (A) The waiter is setting the table.   Ⓐ Ⓑ
   (B) The waitress is sitting at the table.

4. (A) The woman is wearing a dress.   Ⓐ Ⓑ
   (B) The man is writing his address.

5. (A) The waiter is wearing white.   Ⓐ Ⓑ
   (B) The waitress is on the right.

Extra Practice

DIRECTIONS: On a separate piece of paper, write about what is happening in the photo. Use the vocabulary in this section.

PHOTO 3: IN THE OFFICE

There are two men sitting at a table. The table is very long. There are papers and books on the table. There are also two bottles. One bottle is not open. The other bottle is open. Its cap is on the table. There is a glass on a napkin.

Both men are wearing jackets. Both men are wearing ties. One man is wearing glasses. They are looking at each other. Both men have their hands on the table.

Vocabulary

DIRECTIONS: Find these items in the photo.

bottle	cap	glass	napkin
tie	glasses	shirt	hand

What Do You See?

A. DIRECTIONS: Read these statements about what you see in the photo. The statements may or may not be true. Put (Y) beside the statements that match the photo. Put (N) beside the statements that do not match the photo. Correct the statements that are not true.

1. _____ There are three bottles on the table.

2. _____ Only one man is wearing a tie.

3. _____ Both men are wearing glasses.

4. _____ There is a napkin under the glass.

5. _____ A bottle cap is on the table.

B. DIRECTIONS: You will be tested on what *is* in the photograph, not what *could be* in the photograph. Put (Y) beside the statements that describe what you see in the photo. Put (?) beside the statements that could be true, but you cannot be sure from the photo.

1. _____ The men are wearing jackets.

2. _____ The men are wearing suits.

3. _____ There is water in the bottle.

4. _____ Each man has a bottle beside him.

5. _____ Both men drink a lot of water.

Analyze This

DIRECTIONS: What do you think about the photo? Put (Y) for *yes*, (N) for *no*, or (?) for *maybe* beside each statement. Give reasons for your answers.

1. _____ It's night time.

Reason: _____

2. _____ The men are reading the newspaper.

Reason: _____

3. _____ It is an important meeting.

Reason: _____

4. _____ The men know each other very well.

Reason: _____

5. _____ They're discussing business.

Reason: _____

Prepositions

DIRECTIONS: Listen and complete the sentences with the prepositions you hear.

1. The glass is _____ top _____ the napkin.

2. The books are _____ front _____ the men.

3. The men are sitting _____ each other.

4. The cap is _____ the table.

5. A window is _____ them.

Similar Sounds

A. DIRECTIONS: Listen. Which word or phrase do you hear first? Mark (A) or (B).

1. (A) waiter   (B) water   Ⓐ   Ⓑ

2. (A) hurt   (B) shirt   Ⓐ   Ⓑ

3. (A) took a cap   (B) took a nap   Ⓐ   Ⓑ

4. (A) disc is in   (B) discussing   Ⓐ   Ⓑ

5. (A) Jack ate at   (B) jacket at   Ⓐ   Ⓑ

B. DIRECTIONS: Listen. Which statement do you hear first? Mark (A) or (B).

1. (A) The water is in the bottle.   Ⓐ   Ⓑ
   (B) The waiter has a bottle.

2. (A) He brought it himself.   Ⓐ   Ⓑ
   (B) He bought it himself.

3. (A) I took a cap from the table.   Ⓐ   Ⓑ
   (B) I took a nap at the table.

4. (A) They're discussing computers.   Ⓐ   Ⓑ
   (B) Their disk is in the computer.

5. (A) You know you need a jacket at the restaurant.   Ⓐ   Ⓑ
   (B) You know what Jack ate at the restaurant.

Extra Practice

DIRECTIONS: On a separate piece of paper, write about what is happening in the photo. Use the vocabulary in this section.

PHOTO 4: AT THE BUS STOP

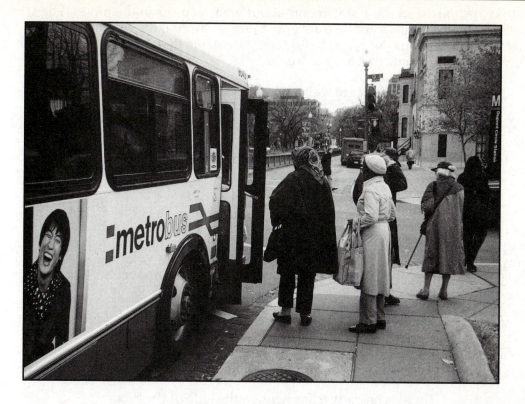

A bus is stopped at a bus stop. The bus stop is at the corner of the street. There is an advertisement on the side of the bus. The name of the bus company is on the side of the bus, too. Across the street from the bus stop, there is a street light, a traffic light, and a street sign.

There are several people standing at the corner. Two women are waiting to board the bus. The door is open. Other people are waiting to cross the street.

The woman closest to the bus has a scarf around her head. The woman behind her is wearing a hat. Both women are carrying bags. Both women are wearing pants and coats. One woman's coat is a dark color. The other woman's coat is a light color. They are dressed warmly.

Vocabulary

DIRECTIONS: Find these items in the photo.

| pants | advertisement | bag | scarf |
| hat | sidewalk | traffic light | street sign |

What Do You See?

A. DIRECTIONS: Read these statements about what you see in the photo. The statements may or may not be true. Put (Y) for *yes* beside the statements that match the photo. Put (N) for *no* beside the statements that do not match the photo. Correct the statements that are not true.

1. _____ Two women are waiting to board a bus.

2. _____ They are waiting for the movie to begin.

3. _____ The women are crossing the street.

4. _____ Two women are carrying bags.

5. _____ Both women are wearing scarves on their heads.

B. DIRECTIONS: You will be tested on what *is* in the photograph, not what *could be* in the photograph. Put (Y) beside the statements that describe what you see in the photo. Put (?) beside the statements that could be true, but you cannot be sure from the photo.

1. _____ The women at the corner just got off the bus.

2. _____ There are a lot of people on the bus.

3. _____ Only two people are getting on the bus.

4. _____ There is one advertisement on the side of the bus.

5. _____ The bus door is open.

Analyze This

DIRECTIONS: What do you think about the photo? Put (Y) for *yes,* (N) for *no,* or (?) for *maybe* beside each statement. Give reasons for your answers.

1. _____ The two women are going home after work.

Reason: _____

2. _____ The wind is very strong.

Reason: _____

3. _____ The weather is cold.

Reason: _____

4. _____ The bus windows are closed.

Reason: _____

5. _____ The women are carrying food for dinner.

Reason: _____

Prepositions

DIRECTIONS: Listen and complete the sentences with the prepositions you hear.

1. They're standing _____ the bus.

2. They're getting ready to get _____ the bus.

3. The bus is stopped _____ the bus stop.

4. The bus stop is _____ the corner.

5. She's tying a scarf _____ her head.

Similar Sounds

A. DIRECTIONS: Listen. Which word or phrase do you hear first? Mark (A) or (B).

1.	(A) woman	(B) women		Ⓐ	Ⓑ
2.	(A) handbags	(B) hand rags		Ⓐ	Ⓑ
3.	(A) tying	(B) trying		Ⓐ	Ⓑ
4.	(A) after work	(B) afterward		Ⓐ	Ⓑ
5.	(A) board a bus	(B) bored by us		Ⓐ	Ⓑ

B. DIRECTIONS: Listen. Which statement do you hear first? Mark (A) or (B).

1. (A) Did you talk to the woman at the bus stop?   Ⓐ Ⓑ
   (B) Did you walk the woman to the bus stop?

2. (A) Our handbags are in the closet with your coat.   Ⓐ Ⓑ
   (B) Your hand rags are in the cabinet with the soap.

3. (A) I've been trying to put this on this package   Ⓐ Ⓑ
       for ten minutes.
   (B) I've been tying a bow on this package for
       ten minutes.

4. (A) We went to the movie. Afterward we had dinner.   Ⓐ Ⓑ
   (B) We went to the movie after work. Then we
       had dinner.

5. (A) If you board the bus sooner, you can leave by 6.   Ⓐ Ⓑ
   (B) If you board the bus at 6, you won't have to leave
       so soon.

Extra Practice

DIRECTIONS: On a separate piece of paper, write about what is happening in the photo. Use the vocabulary in this section.

PHOTO 5: ON THE RUNWAY

A plane is on the tarmac of an airport. It is a jet plane. The name of the airline company is written on the side of the plane above the windows. On one side of the plane, you can see the wing, the jet engine, the tail, the windows, the door, and the cockpit. The pilots who fly the plane are in the cockpit.

The jet has just landed. The passengers get off using the steps on the plane itself. They walk from the jet onto the tarmac. After they get off the plane, they cross the tarmac to the terminal.

Many airline agents have come to meet the plane. The agents wear dark pants and white shirts. The shirts are short-sleeved shirts. Most have ties. Some are wearing caps.

There are two passengers getting off the plane. The man is wearing light pants and a dark shirt. His shirt has short sleeves. The woman has a short-sleeved shirt, too. It is white. Both are carrying bags over their shoulders.

Vocabulary

DIRECTIONS: Find these items in the photo.

jet	stairs	passengers	agents
tarmac	wing	short-sleeved shirt	tail

What Do You See?

A. **DIRECTIONS:** Read these statements about what you see in the photo. The statements may or may not be true. Put (Y) for *yes* beside the statements that match the photo. Put (N) for *no* beside the statements that do not match the photo. Correct the statements that are not true.

1. _____ Six passengers are on the steps.

2. _____ The agents are waiting in the terminal.

3. _____ The plane is on the tarmac.

4. _____ The crew is repairing the jet engine.

5. _____ The agents are checking passports.

B. **DIRECTIONS:** You will be tested on what *is* in the photograph, not what **could be** in the photograph. Put (Y) beside the statements that describe what you see in the photo. Put (?) beside the statements that could be true, but you cannot be sure from the photo.

1. _____ Tourists are arriving for a holiday.

2. _____ Two people are getting off the plane.

3. _____ The passengers are married.

4. _____ The agents are checking the tickets.

5. _____ The man and woman are getting off the plane.

Analyze This

DIRECTIONS: What do you think about the photo? Put (Y) for *yes*, (N) for *no*, or (?) for *maybe* beside each statement. Give reasons for your answers.

1. _____ The plane landed at a large international airport.

Reason: _____

2. _____ There are lots of tourists on the plane.

Reason: _____

3. _____ The agents are assisting the passengers.

Reason: _____

4. _____ The weather is very hot.

Reason: _____

5. _____ The tour bus is next to the terminal.

Reason: _____

Prepositions

🎧 DIRECTIONS: Listen and complete the sentences with the prepositions you hear.

1. The agents are _____ the plane.

2. The passengers are getting _____ the plane.

3. Several people are _____ the tarmac.

4. Two tourists are _____ the steps.

5. The plane is _____ its destination.

Similar Sounds

🎧 A. DIRECTIONS: Listen. Which word or phrase do you hear first? Mark (A) or (B).

1. (A) passenger is	(B) past hers	Ⓐ	Ⓑ
2. (A) plane	(B) train	Ⓐ	Ⓑ
3. (A) tour is	(B) tourist	Ⓐ	Ⓑ
4. (A) wing	(B) swing	Ⓐ	Ⓑ
5. (A) getting on	(B) getting off	Ⓐ	Ⓑ

🎧 B. DIRECTIONS: Listen. Which statement do you hear first? Mark (A) or (B).

1. (A) Go past hers to my counter. (B) The passenger is at the ticket counter.	Ⓐ	Ⓑ
2. (A) The plane's crew is to rest. (B) The train's new in the west.	Ⓐ	Ⓑ
3. (A) The tourist is going by bus. (B) The tour is going by bus.	Ⓐ	Ⓑ
4. (A) My seat is over the wing. (B) I like to sit on the swing.	Ⓐ	Ⓑ
5. (A) We're getting off the plane. (B) We're getting on the train.	Ⓐ	Ⓑ

Extra Practice

DIRECTIONS: On a separate piece of paper, write about what is happening in the photo. Use the vocabulary in this section.

PHOTO 6: AT PASSPORT CONTROL

There is a line of people. They are waiting in two lines to have their passports examined. The passengers are going through Passport Control. To get to the passport offices, the travelers pass through two entry points. A barrier separates the passport windows from the rest of the airport terminal. In front of the barrier, there are two luggage carts. People left these carts because they cannot take them through Passport Control.

Most of the passengers are male. A few are female. One of the women is pushing a baby stroller. There is a baby in the stroller. The woman is carrying a bag over her shoulder. Many of the passengers are also carrying shoulder bags. Some have suitcases in their hands. One man is wearing a cap. Most of the men are wearing sports jackets.

Vocabulary

DIRECTIONS: Find these items in the photo.

luggage	shoulder	luggage carts	barrier
shoulder bags	baby stroller	entry points	officer

What Do You See?

A. DIRECTIONS: Read these statements about what you see in the photo. The statements may or may not be true. Put (Y) for *yes* beside the statements that match the photo. Put (N) for *no* beside the statements that do not match the photo. Correct the statements that are not true.

1. _____ The woman with the stroller is at the front of the line.

2. _____ A man is pushing a luggage cart through Passport Control.

3. _____ There is only one entry point open.

4. _____ Two luggage carts are by the barrier.

5. _____ There are two lines open for Passport Control.

B. DIRECTIONS: You will be tested on what *is* in the photograph, not what **could be** in the photograph. Put (Y) beside the statements that describe what you see in the photo. Put (?) beside the statements that could be true, but you cannot be sure from the photo.

1. _____ Many of the men are wearing sports jackets.

2. _____ Their luggage is heavy.

3. _____ The luggage carts are empty.

4. _____ The baby stroller belongs to the airline.

5. _____ The woman with the baby is not in line yet.

Analyze This

DIRECTIONS: What do you think about the photo? Put (Y) for *yes*, (N) for *no*, or (?) for *maybe* beside each statement. Give reasons for your answers.

1. _____ The travelers were all on the same plane.

Reason: _____

2. _____ The people have been waiting a long time.

Reason: _____

3. _____ Everyone used the luggage carts.

Reason: _____

4. _____ The line on the left is shorter.

Reason: _____

5. _____ No one is wearing a hat indoors.

Reason: _____

Prepositions

DIRECTIONS: Listen and complete the sentences with the prepositions you hear.

1. The baby is _____ the stroller.

2. The passport officer is _____ the window.

3. The luggage carts are _____ front _____ the barrier.

4. The bags are _____ their shoulders.

5. The two Passport Control windows are side _____ side.

Similar Sounds

A. DIRECTIONS: Listen. Which word or phrase do you hear first? Mark (A) or (B).

1.	(A) stand in line	(B) and on line	(A)	(B)
2.	(A) carts	(B) cars	(A)	(B)
3.	(A) waited	(B) weight	(A)	(B)
4.	(A) passport	(B) past report	(A)	(B)
5.	(A) officer	(B) office or	(A)	(B)

B. DIRECTIONS: Listen. Which statement do you hear first? Mark (A) or (B).

1. (A) The traveler's waiting by the second barrier.   (A) (B)
   (B) The travelers are waiting for a second carrier.

2. (A) We put the luggage in the car.   (A) (B)
   (B) We put our bags on a luggage cart.

3. (A) She has a bag on her shoulder.   (A) (B)
   (B) She has a bug on her shoulder.

4. (A) He asked me for the past report.   (A) (B)
   (B) He wanted to see my passport.

5. (A) We can meet at our offices or yours.   (A) (B)
   (B) They can greet our officers and yours.

Extra Practice

DIRECTIONS: On a separate piece of paper, write about what is happening in the photo. Use the vocabulary in this section.

PHOTO 7: IN THE RAIN

Two men are walking in the rain. They are walking down the middle of a narrow street. On the left side of the photo are two trash cans. Behind the two men, you can see people with umbrellas.

Both men in the center of the photo have umbrellas. Their umbrellas are black. They are carrying umbrellas in their right hands. Both men are wearing jackets and ties. The man on the left is wearing a dark jacket and dark-striped tie. The man on the right is wearing a light jacket and tie. Their pants are also opposite colors. The man on the left is wearing a pair of light-colored pants.

Both men are carrying something in their left hands. The man on the left is carrying something to read. (Maybe it is a newspaper, a brochure, a flyer, or a restaurant guide.) The man on the right is carrying a briefcase.

The man on the right is wearing glasses. The man on the left is not.

Vocabulary

DIRECTIONS: Find these items in the photo.

trash cans	flyer	briefcase	right hand
left hand	light-colored pants	dark jacket	striped tie

What Do You See?

A. DIRECTIONS: Read these statements about what you see in the photo. The statements may or may not be true. Put (Y) for *yes* beside the statements that match the photo. Put (N) for *no* beside the statements that do not match the photo. Correct the statements that are not true.

1. _____ The men are both carrying white umbrellas.

2. _____ There are two trash cans on the left.

3. _____ Both men are carrying briefcases.

4. _____ The man on the left is wearing glasses.

5. _____ The man on the right has a dark jacket.

B. DIRECTIONS: You will be tested on what *is* in the photograph, not what **could be** in the photograph. Put (Y) beside the statements that describe what you see in the photo. Put (?) beside the statements that could be true, but you cannot be sure from the photo.

1. _____ The men are beside one another.

2. _____ It is raining.

3. _____ It is early in the morning.

4. _____ The briefcase is heavy.

5. _____ The men are walking quickly.

Analyze This

DIRECTIONS: What do you think about the photo? Put (Y) for *yes*, (N) for *no*, or (?) for *maybe* beside each statement. Give reasons for your answers.

1. _____ The men are going out to dinner.

Reason: _____

2. _____ The men are coming from work.

Reason: _____

3. _____ Both men have their jackets unbuttoned.

Reason: _____

4. _____ The men are brothers.

Reason: _____

5. _____ The men are catching a train.

Reason: _____

Prepositions

DIRECTIONS: Listen and complete the sentences with the prepositions you hear.

1. The men are carrying umbrellas _____ their right hands.

2. One man is carrying his briefcase _____ his left hand.

3. The trash cans are _____ the door.

4. The men are walking next _____ each other.

5. The man _____ the left is wearing a dark-colored jacket.

Similar Sounds

A. DIRECTIONS: Listen. Which word or phrase do you hear first? Mark (A) or (B).

1. (A) park   (B) dark   Ⓐ   Ⓑ
2. (A) jacket   (B) packet   Ⓐ   Ⓑ
3. (A) rain   (B) lane   Ⓐ   Ⓑ
4. (A) talking   (B) walking   Ⓐ   Ⓑ
5. (A) head   (B) bed   Ⓐ   Ⓑ

B. DIRECTIONS: Listen. Which statement do you hear first? Mark (A) or (B).

1. (A) The men are walking in the dark.   Ⓐ   Ⓑ
   (B) The men are walking in the park.

2. (A) He's wearing a light jacket.   Ⓐ   Ⓑ
   (B) He's carrying a light packet.

3. (A) The men are walking down the lane.   Ⓐ   Ⓑ
   (B) The men are walking in the rain.

4. (A) The people are talking on the train.   Ⓐ   Ⓑ
   (B) The people are walking in the rain.

5. (A) She holds an umbrella over her head.   Ⓐ   Ⓑ
   (B) She keeps an umbrella under her bed.

Extra Practice

DIRECTIONS: On a separate piece of paper, write about what is happening in the photo. Use the vocabulary in this section.

PHOTO 8: IN THE FACTORY

The setting of this photo is a factory. The factory is very large and clean. There are not many technicians on the factory floor.

We can see four technicians on the factory floor. The four technicians are wearing protective clothing. All of them are wearing protective caps. All of them are wearing a protective suit. Some of them are wearing protective gloves.

The four technicians are assembling a large piece of equipment. The equipment is suspended from the ceiling. It is being held by cables. It is being lowered and will be attached to the equipment below it. Some of the men are guiding the piece as it is lowered. They are guiding the piece with one hand. They are touching the equipment without gloves. One man is not touching the equipment. He is watching the process.

Vocabulary

DIRECTIONS: Find these items in the photo.

protective suit	ceiling	cables	equipment
technicians	factory floor	protective cap	gloves

What Do You See?

A. **DIRECTIONS:** Read these statements about what you see in the photo. The statements may or may not be true. Put (Y) for *yes* beside the statements that match the photo. Put (N) for *no* beside the statements that do not match the photo. Correct the statements that are not true.

1. _____ The technicians are on top of the equipment.

2. _____ All the technicians are wearing protective caps.

3. _____ The equipment is suspended by cables from the ceiling.

4. _____ No one is touching the equipment.

5. _____ The factory is big, crowded, and dirty.

B. **DIRECTIONS:** You will be tested on what *is* in the photograph, not what *could be* in the photograph. Put (Y) beside the statements that describe what you see in the photo. Put (?) beside the statements that could be true, but you cannot be sure from the photo.

1. _____ The technicians are lowering the equipment.

2. _____ The equipment is put together by robots.

3. _____ The workers are guiding the equipment with their hands.

4. _____ The equipment is part of the International Space Station.

5. _____ The technicians are going to add oil to the equipment.

Analyze This

DIRECTIONS: What do you think about the photo? Put (Y) for *yes*, (N) for *no*, or (?) for *maybe* beside each statement. Give reasons for your answers.

1. _____ The technicians are skilled at their jobs.

Reason: _____

2. _____ They need more workers to help.

Reason: _____

3. _____ They are raising the equipment to the ceiling.

Reason: _____

4. _____ They will move the equipment to another area.

Reason: _____

5. _____ The factory is clean and orderly.

Reason: _____

Prepositions

DIRECTIONS: Listen and complete the sentences with the prepositions you hear.

1. The technicians are monitoring the descent _____ the equipment.

2. The equipment will be tested _____ the technicians.

3. The cables are attached _____ the module.

4. There are four workers _____ the factory floor.

5. All _____ the technicians wear protective clothing.

Similar Sounds

A. DIRECTIONS: Listen. Which word or phrase do you hear first? Mark (A) or (B).

1. (A) component   (B) compartment   (A) (B)

2. (A) for four   (B) floor for   (A) (B)

3. (A) hiding   (B) guiding   (A) (B)

4. (A) international incident   (B) intentional or an accident   (A) (B)

5. (A) wearing   (B) where in   (A) (B)

B. DIRECTIONS: Listen. Which statement do you hear first? Mark (A) or (B).

1. (A) These are the last compartments to be walled.   (A) (B)
   (B) This is the first component to be installed.

2. (A) We've been searching the factory for hours.   (A) (B)
   (B) We've been researching the facts for four hours.

3. (A) She was guiding her supervisor.   (A) (B)
   (B) She was hiding from her supervisor.

4. (A) The explosion caused an international incident.   (A) (B)
   (B) The explosion was intentional or an accident.

5. (A) The caps that were in the sink are clean.   (A) (B)
   (B) The caps that we were wearing are green.

Extra Practice

DIRECTIONS: On a separate piece of paper, write about what is happening in the photo. Use the vocabulary in this section.

PHOTO STRATEGY PRACTICE

This section will give you more practice with photo strategies.

■ Look at the photo before you listen to the audio.

■ Ask yourself some questions:

PHOTOS OF PEOPLE
Who is in the photo?
Where are they?
What are they doing?

PHOTOS OF THINGS
What is in the photo?
Where is it?

■ Give the photo a title.

■ Tell yourself a story about the photo.

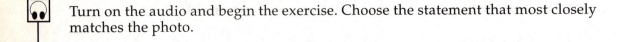 Turn on the audio and begin the exercise. Choose the statement that most closely matches the photo.

1. Ⓐ Ⓑ

2. Ⓐ Ⓑ

3. Ⓐ Ⓑ

4. Ⓐ Ⓑ

5. Ⓐ Ⓑ Ⓒ

6. Ⓐ Ⓑ Ⓒ

7.   Ⓐ   Ⓑ   Ⓒ

8.   Ⓐ   Ⓑ   Ⓒ

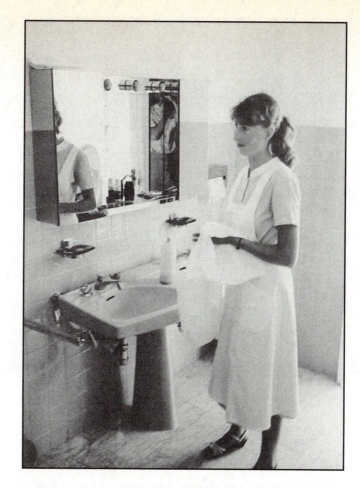

9. (A) (B) (C) (D)

10. (A) (B) (C) (D)

11. Ⓐ   Ⓑ   Ⓒ   Ⓓ

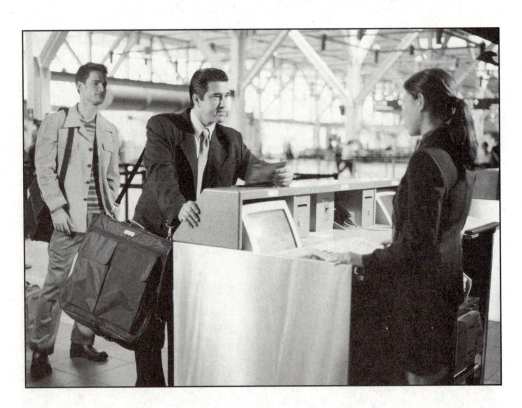

12. Ⓐ   Ⓑ   Ⓒ   Ⓓ

REVIEW: PART 1

DIRECTIONS: Listen. Choose the statement that best describes what you see in the photo.

1. Ⓐ   Ⓑ   Ⓒ   Ⓓ

2. Ⓐ   Ⓑ   Ⓒ   Ⓓ

3. (A) (B) (C) (D)

4. (A) (B) (C) (D)

5. Ⓐ Ⓑ Ⓒ Ⓓ

6. Ⓐ Ⓑ Ⓒ Ⓓ

7. Ⓐ Ⓑ Ⓒ Ⓓ

8. Ⓐ Ⓑ Ⓒ Ⓓ

PART 2: QUESTION-RESPONSE

PART 2

Directions: You will hear a question or statement and three responses spoken in English. They will not be printed in your test book and will be spoken only one time. Select the best response to the question or statement and mark the letter (A), (B), or (C) on your answer sheet.

Example

Sample Answer

You will hear: Where is the meeting room?

You will also hear: (A) To meet the new director.
(B) It's the first room on the right.
(C) Yes, at two o'clock.

Your best response to the question "Where is the meeting room?" is choice (B), "It's the first room on the right," so (B) is the correct answer. You should mark answer (B) on your answer sheet.

The following exercises will help you develop strategies for listening to the questions and choosing the best response. They will help you use context clues to guess what the question and response are about. The exercises will also help you improve your vocabulary in specific ways.

VOCABULARY STRATEGIES

- Listen for words that establish the context.

- Listen for words associated with these five topics.

Occupations	*Who?*
Activities	*What?*
Time	*When?*
Location	*Where?*
Reason	*Why?*

LISTENING STRATEGIES

- Listen to the intonation. Is it a question or a statement?

  > If it is a statement, match the topic with the response.
  > If it is a question, listen for the first word of the question.
  > Is it a question word? *who, what, when, where, why, how*
  > Is it an auxiliary? *is, are, was, were, can, will, etc.*

- Decide what kind of response will answer the question.

- Listen for a similar response on the audio source.

QUESTION-RESPONSE: STATEMENTS

Practice A

DIRECTIONS: Read the questions and the possible responses below. Mark the correct answer.

1. It's raining very hard.   Ⓐ Ⓑ Ⓒ
   (A) They're in the yard.
   (B) Then I'll take an umbrella.
   (C) This training course isn't easy.

2. I got new shoes.   Ⓐ Ⓑ Ⓒ
   (A) They look very nice.
   (B) The news I got was old.
   (C) Please help me choose.

3. This pen doesn't work.   Ⓐ Ⓑ Ⓒ
   (A) She doesn't work without a pencil.
   (B) Here, use mine.
   (C) He does it at work.

4. I haven't seen John all week.   Ⓐ Ⓑ Ⓒ
   (A) He's away on a trip.
   (B) You've seen John every day this week.
   (C) Yes, he seems weak.

5. Mary seems like a nice person.   Ⓐ Ⓑ Ⓒ
   (A) I like ice cream, too.
   (B) He personally doesn't like mice.
   (C) Yes, she's very friendly.

6. I can't find my keys.   Ⓐ Ⓑ Ⓒ
   (A) I can find the peas.
   (B) Yes, that's the right kind.
   (C) I saw them on your desk.

7. I love the food in this restaurant.   Ⓐ Ⓑ Ⓒ
   (A) I'm ready for a rest.
   (B) Really? I've never eaten here before.
   (C) You don't like a good meal.

8. I don't know how to swim.   (A)   (B)   (C)
    (A)   It's easy. I'll show you how.
    (B)   He doesn't know how to win.
    (C)   What a nice swimsuit.

9. Susan's plane doesn't get in until midnight.   (A)   (B)   (C)
    (A)   Please don't fight on the train.
    (B)   Susan does look plain at night.
    (C)   That's OK. I can pick her up.

10. That store is closed on Sunday.   (A)   (B)   (C)
    (A)   This is a really fun day at the shore.
    (B)   But it's open on Monday.
    (C)   Someday we'll store our clothes away.

Practice B

DIRECTIONS: Look at each of the statements and answer choices in Practice A.
In each one, circle all the words that are the same or are similar in meaning, if any.
Underline all the words that are opposite in meaning, if any. Cross out the words
that might sound similar, if any.

Not every conversation will have words that are the same, similar, opposite, or sound
similar.

Example:

I (came) to (the) office (first.)   SAME   I, I; the, the; first, first

    (A)   She spoke (first.)   SIMILAR   came, arrived

    (B)   (I) (arrived) after you.   OPPOSITE   first, last

    (C)   His name is last on (the) list.   SOUND SIMILAR   came, name

Practice C

DIRECTIONS: Match these statements with the correct responses.

1. _____ I came before noon.

2. _____ The meeting is either tomorrow or Friday.

3. _____ I bought two tickets to the concert.

4. _____ Our lease expires next month.

5. _____ I put the mail on your desk.

6. _____ The early morning flight is delayed.

7. _____ The product designer wants a blue box.

8. _____ My favorite restaurant is closed today.

9. _____ I'll rent a car if you want.

10. _____ The applicants aren't qualified for the job.

a. The plane must have a mechanical problem.

b. You'll enjoy the music, I'm sure.

c. Let's take taxis. It's easier than parking a car.

d. I'm sorry, but I had to leave at 11:30.

e. I'll open it later.

f. In that case, we'll have dinner in the cafeteria.

g. Actually, we met yesterday without you.

h. There must be someone with the qualifications.

i. We should renew it or find a new space.

j. I think red is a better choice.

Practice D

DIRECTIONS: Write possible responses to these statements.

1. My toothache is becoming really painful.

_____

2. We need someone to write a business plan.

_____

3. A computer virus shut down our network.

_____

4. In the summer, we don't wear coats or ties in the office.

_____

5. This letter should be sent overnight.

_____

6. The training program lasts all week.

_____

7. I think we're out of printer paper.

_____

8. Our expenses are greater than our revenues.

_____

9. The northbound train is on Track 1.

_____

10. The product warranty is only valid for a year.

_____

Practice E

DIRECTIONS: Listen to the statements, which are followed by three responses. They are not written out for you. You must listen carefully to understand what the speakers say. You are to choose the best response to each statement.

1. (A) (B) (C)   6. (A) (B) (C)
2. (A) (B) (C)   7. (A) (B) (C)
3. (A) (B) (C)   8. (A) (B) (C)
4. (A) (B) (C)   9. (A) (B) (C)
5. (A) (B) (C)   10. (A) (B) (C)

Practice F

DIRECTIONS: Listen to the statements, which are followed by three responses. They are not written out for you. You must listen carefully to understand what the speakers say. You are to choose the best response to each statement.

1. (A) (B) (C)   6. (A) (B) (C)
2. (A) (B) (C)   7. (A) (B) (C)
3. (A) (B) (C)   8. (A) (B) (C)
4. (A) (B) (C)   9. (A) (B) (C)
5. (A) (B) (C)   10. (A) (B) (C)

QUESTION-RESPONSE: WHO

Practice A

DIRECTIONS: Read the questions and the possible responses below. Mark the correct answer.

1. Who turned on the lights?　　　　　　　　　　　(A) (B) (C)
   (A) They are on all the time.
   (B) It isn't dark outside.
   (C) I'll turn them off.

2. Who makes the decisions in this office?　　　　(A) (B) (C)
   (A) We get new office supplies every week.
   (B) She decided on a desk for her office.
   (C) The office manager usually does.

3. Who ordered two boxes of copy paper?　　　　(A) (B) (C)
   (A) Mary read two newspapers every morning.
   (B) I asked for twenty-two cartons of wrapping paper.
   (C) John put in the order yesterday.

4. Who is in charge of advertising?　　　　　　　(A) (B) (C)
   (A) There was a charge for the ad.
   (B) The vice president of marketing.
   (C) He is very large.

5. Who is going to get this memo?　　　　　　　(A) (B) (C)
   (A) Everyone in the department.
   (B) I typed the memo myself.
   (C) They are going together.

6. Who sent you that package?　　　　　　　　　(A) (B) (C)
   (A) I'll mail it this afternoon.
   (B) The stamps cost fifty cents.
   (C) It came from the London office.

7. Who left these folders on my desk?　　　　　(A) (B) (C)
   (A) Martha's assistant put them there.
   (B) They're on your desk.
   (C) You can get more folders in the supply room.

8. Who will be at the meeting tomorrow?　　　　Ⓐ　Ⓑ　Ⓒ
　　(A)　The meeting's in the big conference room.
　　(B)　All the department heads will be there.
　　(C)　I'll be finished eating soon.

9. Who has read this article?　　　　　　　　　　Ⓐ　Ⓑ　Ⓒ
　　(A)　It was written by a marketing expert.
　　(B)　It's a very interesting article.
　　(C)　I have, and I thought it was interesting.

10. Who was the last person to leave the office?　Ⓐ　Ⓑ　Ⓒ
　　(A)　It lasted a long time.
　　(B)　I think Bob was here until 10:00.
　　(C)　It's the last office on the left.

Practice B

DIRECTIONS: Look at each of the questions and answer choices in Practice A. In each one, circle all the words that are the same or are similar in meaning, if any. Underline all the words that are opposite in meaning, if any. Cross out the words that might sound similar, if any.

Not every conversation will have words that are the same, similar, opposite, or sound similar.

Example:

I ⊘came⊘ to ⓣhe office ⓕirst.　　　　　SAME　I, I; the, the; first, first

　　(A)　She spoke ⓕirst.　　　　　　　　SIMILAR　came, arrived

　　(B)　I ⓐrrived after you.　　　　　　OPPOSITE　first, last

　　(C)　His ⊘name⊘ is last on ⓣhe list.　SOUND SIMILAR　came, name

Practice C

DIRECTIONS: Match these questions with the correct answers.

1. _____ Who left the copy machine on?

2. _____ Who was the winner of the lottery?

3. _____ Who did not receive a paycheck?

4. _____ Who came to work during the snowstorm?

5. _____ Who recommended the new lawyer?

6. _____ Who answered your e-mail message?

7. _____ Who rode the subway this morning?

8. _____ Who fixes your car?

9. _____ Who hired you?

10. _____ Who helped you write this report?

a. Ms. Marsden gave me this job.

b. Our legal office suggested her name.

c. I wrote all of it myself.

d. The boss never misses a day even in bad weather

e. The shipping clerk won $14 million.

f. I did not get one.

g. I think everybody drove today.

h. Mr. King sent me a very nice answer.

i. I did, but I'm still making copies.

j. I go to a very good mechanic on State Street.

Practice D

DIRECTIONS: Write possible answers to these questions.

1. Who designed this building?

_____

2. Who is working in the mailroom?

_____

3. Who is making coffee?

_____

4. Who typed this letter?

_____

5. Who is the new secretary?

_____

6. Who is going to the conference next week?

_____

7. Who took this telephone message?

_____

8. Who uses this desk?

_____

9. Who can fix the coffee machine?

_____

10. Who will be at the dinner tonight?

_____

Practice E

DIRECTIONS: Listen to the questions, which are followed by three responses. They are not written out for you. You must listen carefully to understand what the speakers say. You are to choose the best response to each question.

1. Ⓐ Ⓑ Ⓒ
2. Ⓐ Ⓑ Ⓒ
3. Ⓐ Ⓑ Ⓒ
4. Ⓐ Ⓑ Ⓒ
5. Ⓐ Ⓑ Ⓒ

6. Ⓐ Ⓑ Ⓒ
7. Ⓐ Ⓑ Ⓒ
8. Ⓐ Ⓑ Ⓒ
9. Ⓐ Ⓑ Ⓒ
10. Ⓐ Ⓑ Ⓒ

Practice F

DIRECTIONS: Listen to the questions, which are followed by three responses. They are not written out for you. You must listen carefully to understand what the speakers say. You are to choose the best response to each question.

1. Ⓐ Ⓑ Ⓒ
2. Ⓐ Ⓑ Ⓒ
3. Ⓐ Ⓑ Ⓒ
4. Ⓐ Ⓑ Ⓒ
5. Ⓐ Ⓑ Ⓒ

6. Ⓐ Ⓑ Ⓒ
7. Ⓐ Ⓑ Ⓒ
8. Ⓐ Ⓑ Ⓒ
9. Ⓐ Ⓑ Ⓒ
10. Ⓐ Ⓑ Ⓒ

QUESTION-RESPONSE: WHAT

Practice A

DIRECTIONS: Read the questions and the possible responses below. Mark the correct answer.

1. What do you see on his desk?   Ⓐ   Ⓑ   Ⓒ
   (A) There are papers and books on it.
   (B) His desk is in the corner.
   (C) It's on his desk.

2. What street do they live on?   Ⓐ   Ⓑ   Ⓒ
   (A) They live on New York Avenue.
   (B) That's where we live.
   (C) This is a busy street.

3. What did the printer do with our order?   Ⓐ   Ⓑ   Ⓒ
   (A) We ordered more envelopes.
   (B) The print has an odor.
   (C) He misplaced it.

4. What does this briefcase cost?   Ⓐ   Ⓑ   Ⓒ
   (A) He spoke briefly.
   (B) It's on sale for $150.
   (C) I lost my briefcase.

5. What are you doing after work?   Ⓐ   Ⓑ   Ⓒ
   (A) I'm going home.
   (B) I like my work very much.
   (C) We are late for work.

6. What did you buy at the store?   Ⓐ   Ⓑ   Ⓒ
   (A) It's not a big store.
   (B) It's right by my house.
   (C) I got some batteries.

7. What do you want for lunch?   Ⓐ   Ⓑ   Ⓒ
   (A) Just a sandwich.
   (B) Let's eat at 12:30.
   (C) It doesn't cost much.

8. What did your boss tell you?   Ⓐ   Ⓑ   Ⓒ
   (A) I don't want to sell it.
   (B) She asked me to help with the project.
   (C) Don't tell me about it.

9. What will we discuss at the meeting? Ⓐ Ⓑ Ⓒ
   (A) The meeting is at 10:00.
   (B) We'll talk about next year's budget.
   (C) Let's go by bus.

10. What is in that bag? Ⓐ Ⓑ Ⓒ
    (A) It's a new book I bought.
    (B) I'll take it back.
    (C) This bag is too heavy.

Practice B

DIRECTIONS: Look at each of the questions and answer choices in Practice A. In each one, circle all the words that are the same or are similar in meaning, if any. Underline all the words that are opposite in meaning, if any. Cross out the words that might sound similar, if any.

Not every conversation will have words that are the same, similar, opposite, or sound similar.

Example:

Ⓘ (came) to (the) office (first.)   SAME   I, I; the, the; first, first

   (A) She spoke (first.)   SIMILAR   came, arrived

   (B) (I) (arrived) after you.   OPPOSITE   first, last

   (C) His n̶a̶m̶e̶ is last on (the) list.   SOUND SIMILAR   came, name

Practice C

DIRECTIONS: Match these questions with the correct answers.

1. _____ What is this machine used for?

2. _____ What is your profession?

3. _____ What did your doctor tell you?

4. _____ What's for lunch?

5. _____ What is the best way to get there?

6. _____ What did they do last Saturday?

7. _____ What's on TV tonight?

8. _____ What's on that shelf?

9. _____ What do you like to read?

10. _____ What do you want a pen for?

a. Tuna fish sandwiches.

b. I'm an accountant.

c. The train is the cheapest and most comfortable.

d. To record my telephone calls.

e. To exercise more and eat less.

f. There's an interesting program about science.

g. I want to write down a phone number.

h. They went to the movies.

i. Paper and envelopes.

j. I enjoy novels.

DIRECTIONS: Write possible answers to these questions.

1. What did you put on my desk?

   _____

2. What is your favorite food?

   _____

3. What did you do last night?

   _____

4. What are you looking for?

   _____

5. What is the book about?

   _____

6. What do you do on your birthday?

   _____

7. What did she wear to the party?

   _____

8. What did you get in the mail?

   _____

9. What happened to your phone?

   _____

10. What did they do in New York?

    _____

Practice E

DIRECTIONS: Listen to the questions, which are followed by three responses. They are not written out for you. You must listen carefully to understand what the speakers say. You are to choose the best response to each question.

1. Ⓐ Ⓑ Ⓒ
2. Ⓐ Ⓑ Ⓒ
3. Ⓐ Ⓑ Ⓒ
4. Ⓐ Ⓑ Ⓒ
5. Ⓐ Ⓑ Ⓒ
6. Ⓐ Ⓑ Ⓒ
7. Ⓐ Ⓑ Ⓒ
8. Ⓐ Ⓑ Ⓒ
9. Ⓐ Ⓑ Ⓒ
10. Ⓐ Ⓑ Ⓒ

Practice F

DIRECTIONS: Listen to the questions, which are followed by three responses. They are not written out for you. You must listen carefully to understand what the speakers say. You are to choose the best response to each question.

1. Ⓐ Ⓑ Ⓒ
2. Ⓐ Ⓑ Ⓒ
3. Ⓐ Ⓑ Ⓒ
4. Ⓐ Ⓑ Ⓒ
5. Ⓐ Ⓑ Ⓒ
6. Ⓐ Ⓑ Ⓒ
7. Ⓐ Ⓑ Ⓒ
8. Ⓐ Ⓑ Ⓒ
9. Ⓐ Ⓑ Ⓒ
10. Ⓐ Ⓑ Ⓒ

QUESTION-RESPONSE: WHEN

Practice A

DIRECTIONS: Read the questions and the possible responses below. Mark the correct answer.

1. When are you leaving for France?　　　Ⓐ　Ⓑ　Ⓒ
   (A)　I like living in France.
   (B)　Not since 1945.
   (C)　My plane leaves at 7:45.

2. When will the meeting be over?　　　Ⓐ　Ⓑ　Ⓒ
   (A)　In about two hours.
   (B)　I'll meet you later.
   (C)　We talked it over.

3. When can we expect our check?　　　Ⓐ　Ⓑ　Ⓒ
   (A)　We did a thorough check already.
   (B)　We didn't expect him so soon.
   (C)　We will send your check out tomorrow.

4. When does the weather turn cold?　　　Ⓐ　Ⓑ　Ⓒ
   (A)　Usually not until December.
   (B)　We'll go whether you are there or not.
   (C)　The rain turned to snow yesterday.

5. When will the project be finished?　　　Ⓐ　Ⓑ　Ⓒ
   (A)　We finished the project on time.
   (B)　Next month, we hope.
   (C)　Yes, we predict it will be finished.

6. When will the plane arrive?　　　Ⓐ　Ⓑ　Ⓒ
   (A)　It'll be here in about 25 minutes.
   (B)　They plan to arrive.
   (C)　I never drive.

7. When did you call him?　　　Ⓐ　Ⓑ　Ⓒ
   (A)　You can call me tomorrow.
   (B)　Everyone calls him Bob.
   (C)　I spoke to him last night.

8. When do you have lunch? Ⓐ Ⓑ Ⓒ
   (A) I usually eat around noon.
   (B) I always go to the cafeteria downstairs.
   (C) I had a really big lunch.

9. When did Jane start her new job? Ⓐ Ⓑ Ⓒ
   (A) That job took a long time.
   (B) She began it last month.
   (C) She really likes her work.

10. When will the copy machine be fixed? Ⓐ Ⓑ Ⓒ
    (A) The machine is broken.
    (B) I made some copies this morning.
    (C) Someone will come to repair it tomorrow.

Practice B

DIRECTIONS: Look at each of the questions and answer choices in Practice A. In each one, circle all the words that are the same or are similar in meaning, if any. Underline all the words that are opposite in meaning, if any. Cross out the words that might sound similar, if any.

Not every conversation will have words that are the same, similar, opposite, or sound similar.

Example:

Ⓘ c̶a̶m̶e̶ to the office first.   SAME   I, I; the, the; first, first

(A) She spoke first.   SIMILAR   came, arrived

(B) I arrived after you.   OPPOSITE first, last

(C) His n̶a̶m̶e̶ is last on the list.   SOUND SIMILAR came, name

Practice C

DIRECTIONS: Match these questions with the correct answers.

1. _____ When are you leaving?
2. _____ When did you notice the problem?
3. _____ When do you think he will arrive?
4. _____ When are you taking the exam?
5. _____ When will you call your lawyer?
6. _____ When did you get the package?
7. _____ When did Mrs. Schmidt return from vacation?
8. _____ When can I see you?
9. _____ When did John send that e-mail message?
10. _____ When will you buy a new car?

a. She got back last week.
b. I'm leaving at noon.
c. I'll telephone him tomorrow.
d. After I study more, I'll take it.
e. I received it this morning.
f. He sent it yesterday.
g. He's expected on the 10:30 plane.
h. Let's get together tomorrow morning.
i. As soon as I have enough money.
j. I became aware of it last month.

Practice D

DIRECTIONS: Write possible answers to these questions.

1. When can you revise the report?

_____

2. When will the store be painted?

_____

3. When did they develop this new product?

_____

4. When did she join the firm?

_____

5. When are you going to go on vacation?

_____

6. When did you see Sally?

_____

7. When will the new computers arrive?

_____

8. When is the office party?

_____

9. When will your membership expire?

_____

10. When was this office last cleaned?

_____

Practice E

DIRECTIONS: Listen to the questions, which are followed by three responses. They are not written out for you. You must listen carefully to understand what the speakers say. You are to choose the best response to each question.

1. Ⓐ   Ⓑ   Ⓒ
2. Ⓐ   Ⓑ   Ⓒ
3. Ⓐ   Ⓑ   Ⓒ
4. Ⓐ   Ⓑ   Ⓒ
5. Ⓐ   Ⓑ   Ⓒ
6. Ⓐ   Ⓑ   Ⓒ
7. Ⓐ   Ⓑ   Ⓒ
8. Ⓐ   Ⓑ   Ⓒ
9. Ⓐ   Ⓑ   Ⓒ
10. Ⓐ   Ⓑ   Ⓒ

Practice F

DIRECTIONS: Listen to the questions, which are followed by three responses. They are not written out for you. You must listen carefully to understand what the speakers say. You are to choose the best response to each question.

1. Ⓐ   Ⓑ   Ⓒ
2. Ⓐ   Ⓑ   Ⓒ
3. Ⓐ   Ⓑ   Ⓒ
4. Ⓐ   Ⓑ   Ⓒ
5. Ⓐ   Ⓑ   Ⓒ
6. Ⓐ   Ⓑ   Ⓒ
7. Ⓐ   Ⓑ   Ⓒ
8. Ⓐ   Ⓑ   Ⓒ
9. Ⓐ   Ⓑ   Ⓒ
10. Ⓐ   Ⓑ   Ⓒ

QUESTION-RESPONSE: WHERE

Practice A

DIRECTIONS: Read the questions and the possible responses below. Mark the correct answer.

1. Where is the cafeteria? Ⓐ Ⓑ Ⓒ
   (A) Coffee usually keeps me awake.
   (B) In the basement of the next building.
   (C) It's open until midnight.

2. Where will you be waiting? Ⓐ Ⓑ Ⓒ
   (A) By the front door.
   (B) I weigh about 185 pounds.
   (C) This is the waiting room.

3. Where did you find your glasses? Ⓐ Ⓑ Ⓒ
   (A) On the floor of my car.
   (B) The glasses were dirty.
   (C) Yes, I would like a glass of water.

4. Where is the nearest phone? Ⓐ Ⓑ Ⓒ
   (A) I don't know her phone number.
   (B) My home is miles from here.
   (C) There is one in my office.

5. Where is the conference room? Ⓐ Ⓑ Ⓒ
   (A) The conference starts in ten minutes.
   (B) Turn left at the end of the hall.
   (C) We do not have individual rooms.

6. Where's the hotel? Ⓐ Ⓑ Ⓒ
   (A) It's near the airport.
   (B) I didn't tell anyone.
   (C) It's not an expensive hotel.

7. Where did you leave your cell phone? Ⓐ Ⓑ Ⓒ
   (A) Your phone is ringing.
   (B) He sells phones.
   (C) I think I left it on the bus.

8. Where does Lucy work? Ⓐ Ⓑ Ⓒ
    (A) Her office is downtown.
    (B) She works very hard.
    (C) Let's walk in the park.

9. Where did you go on your vacation? ⒶⒷ Ⓒ
    (A) The room is vacant.
    (B) We flew to Miami.
    (C) It was a great vacation.

10. Where's a good place to get dinner? Ⓐ Ⓑ Ⓒ
    (A) I think you're getting thinner.
    (B) I prefer a late dinner.
    (C) There's a nice restaurant on the corner.

Practice B

DIRECTIONS: Look at each of the questions and answer choices in Practice A. In each one, circle all the words that are the same or are similar in meaning, if any. Underline all the words that are opposite in meaning, if any. Cross out the words that might sound similar, if any.

Not every conversation will have words that are the same, similar, opposite, or sound similar.

Example:

I ⊘came to ⊙the office ⊙first.   **SAME**   I, I; the, the; first, first

    (A) She spoke ⊙first.   **SIMILAR**   came, arrived

    (B) ⒾI ⊙arrived after you.   **OPPOSITE**   first, last

    (C) His ⊗name is <u>last</u> on ⊙the list.   **SOUND SIMILAR**   came, name

Practice C

DIRECTIONS: Match these questions with the correct answers.

1. _____ Where will the bus stop?

2. _____ Where are you meeting your clients?

3. _____ Where did she study English?

4. _____ Where were you last night?

5. _____ Where can I buy a newspaper?

6. _____ Where did you grow up?

7. _____ Where is the magazine I lent you?

8. _____ Where is Ms. Salerian's office?

9. _____ Where can we park the car?

10. _____ Where is the bank?

a. There's a newsstand in the lobby.

b. It stops at the next corner.

c. She started in high school and then continued on her own.

d. They will meet me here.

e. I stayed at the office until midnight.

f. There's a garage in the building next door.

g. It's on my desk.

h. In a small town.

i. It's right across the street.

j. Down the hall to the left.

Practice D

DIRECTIONS: Write possible answers to these questions.

1. Where are you going to play golf?

_____

2. Where are the supplies kept?

_____

3. Where will the new employee sit?

_____

4. Where can I buy a used car?

_____

5. Where did you file the insurance policies?

_____

6. Where is the sugar?

_____

7. Where did you buy your new suit?

_____

8. Where will the party be?

_____

9. Where will you be tonight?

_____

10. Where can I put these books?

_____

Practice E

DIRECTIONS: Listen to the questions, which are followed by three responses. They are not written out for you. You must listen carefully to understand what the speakers say. You are to choose the best response to each question.

1. Ⓐ Ⓑ Ⓒ
2. Ⓐ Ⓑ Ⓒ
3. Ⓐ Ⓑ Ⓒ
4. Ⓐ Ⓑ Ⓒ
5. Ⓐ Ⓑ Ⓒ
6. Ⓐ Ⓑ Ⓒ
7. Ⓐ Ⓑ Ⓒ
8. Ⓐ Ⓑ Ⓒ
9. Ⓐ Ⓑ Ⓒ
10. Ⓐ Ⓑ Ⓒ

Practice F

DIRECTIONS: Listen to the questions, which are followed by three responses. They are not written out for you. You must listen carefully to understand what the speakers say. You are to choose the best response to each question.

1. Ⓐ Ⓑ Ⓒ
2. Ⓐ Ⓑ Ⓒ
3. Ⓐ Ⓑ Ⓒ
4. Ⓐ Ⓑ Ⓒ
5. Ⓐ Ⓑ Ⓒ
6. Ⓐ Ⓑ Ⓒ
7. Ⓐ Ⓑ Ⓒ
8. Ⓐ Ⓑ Ⓒ
9. Ⓐ Ⓑ Ⓒ
10. Ⓐ Ⓑ Ⓒ

QUESTION-RESPONSE: WHY

Practice A

DIRECTIONS: Read the questions and the possible responses below. Mark the correct answer.

1. Why were you late?　　　　　　　　　　　Ⓐ　Ⓑ　Ⓒ
   (A)　I overslept this morning.
   (B)　You ate very late last night.
   (C)　I'll be there at eight o'clock.

2. Why can't she come with us?　　　　　　Ⓐ　Ⓑ　Ⓒ
   (A)　She has too much work to do.
   (B)　We can't go with her.
   (C)　She came by bus.

3. Why do first-year students study economics?　Ⓐ　Ⓑ　Ⓒ
   (A)　They need the large, economy-size package.
   (B)　It's a college requirement.
   (C)　Yes, I caught the train at the station.

4. Why is the door closed?　　　　　　　　Ⓐ　Ⓑ　Ⓒ
   (A)　The wind blew it open.
   (B)　Because I want some peace and quiet.
   (C)　Her closet is full of clothes.

5. Why was the meeting postponed?　　　　Ⓐ　Ⓑ　Ⓒ
   (A)　Yes, we met today.
   (B)　Please post a notice about yesterday's meeting.
   (C)　The lawyers had not finished writing their reports.

6. Why did you stay late at the office?　　Ⓐ　Ⓑ　Ⓒ
   (A)　I had a lot of work to do.
   (B)　Please wait in my office.
   (C)　I'll spend the day at the office.

7. Why is Sam looking for a new job?　　　Ⓐ　Ⓑ　Ⓒ
   (A)　He knew about that job.
   (B)　He booked a flight for Japan.
   (C)　He wants to make more money.

8. Why hasn't that package arrived yet?　　　Ⓐ　Ⓑ　Ⓒ
   (A)　They'll arrive by jet.
   (B)　They just mailed it yesterday.
   (C)　I haven't learned how to drive yet.

9. Why isn't Mr. Lee here today?　　　Ⓐ　Ⓑ　Ⓒ
   (A)　He doesn't hear well.
   (B)　He's at a conference in New York.
   (C)　He usually sits here.

10. Why does it feel cold in here?　　　Ⓐ　Ⓑ　Ⓒ
   (A)　Yes, it's really old.
   (B)　It's not very near.
   (C)　Someone left the window open.

Practice B

DIRECTIONS: Look at each of the questions and answer choices in Practice A. In each one, circle all the words that are the same or are similar in meaning, if any. Underline all the words that are opposite in meaning, if any. Cross out the words that might sound similar, if any.

Not every conversation will have words that are the same, similar, opposite, or sound similar.

Example:

I came to the office first.

(A)　She spoke first.

(B)　I arrived after you.

(C)　His name is last on the list.

SAME	I, I; the, the; first, first
SIMILAR	came, arrived
OPPOSITE	first, last
SOUND SIMILAR	came, name

Practice C

DIRECTIONS: Match these questions with the correct answers.

1. _____ Why are you wearing a suit?

2. _____ Why isn't the water hot?

3. _____ Why has the meeting been delayed?

4. _____ Why did she move to Japan?

5. _____ Why is the window open?

6. _____ Why aren't there any envelopes?

7. _____ Why do you look so tired?

8. _____ Why did George leave after lunch?

9. _____ Why don't you take a vacation this month?

10. _____ Why did he send you those flowers?

a. No one was available to meet until this afternoon.

b. The air conditioner is broken.

c. It's my birthday today.

d. He had an appointment this afternoon.

e. There's no hot water heater.

f. I forgot to order the office supplies.

g. She wanted to study Japanese.

h. I'm too busy at work this month.

i. I always wear one to work.

j. I didn't sleep well last night.

Practice D

DIRECTIONS: Write possible answers to these questions.

1. Why are you smiling?

   _____

2. Why does she sit next to the window?

   _____

3. Why isn't this project finished yet?

   _____

4. Why won't the car start?

   _____

5. Why is the door closed?

   _____

6. Why didn't you make coffee?

   _____

7. Why did you bring an umbrella?

_____

8. Why can't John come to the party?

_____

9. Why do you always take the bus?

_____

10. Why aren't you hungry now?

_____

_____

Practice E

DIRECTIONS: Listen to the questions, which are followed by three responses. They are not written out for you. You must listen carefully to understand what the speakers say. You are to choose the best response to each question.

1. Ⓐ Ⓑ Ⓒ
2. Ⓐ Ⓑ Ⓒ
3. Ⓐ Ⓑ Ⓒ
4. Ⓐ Ⓑ Ⓒ
5. Ⓐ Ⓑ Ⓒ
6. Ⓐ Ⓑ Ⓒ
7. Ⓐ Ⓑ Ⓒ
8. Ⓐ Ⓑ Ⓒ
9. Ⓐ Ⓑ Ⓒ
10. Ⓐ Ⓑ Ⓒ

Practice F

DIRECTIONS: Listen to the questions, which are followed by three responses. They are not written out for you. You must listen carefully to understand what the speakers say. You are to choose the best response to each question.

1. Ⓐ Ⓑ Ⓒ
2. Ⓐ Ⓑ Ⓒ
3. Ⓐ Ⓑ Ⓒ
4. Ⓐ Ⓑ Ⓒ
5. Ⓐ Ⓑ Ⓒ
6. Ⓐ Ⓑ Ⓒ
7. Ⓐ Ⓑ Ⓒ
8. Ⓐ Ⓑ Ⓒ
9. Ⓐ Ⓑ Ⓒ
10. Ⓐ Ⓑ Ⓒ

Practice A

DIRECTIONS: Read the questions and the possible responses below. Mark the correct answer.

1. How much time do you have?   (A) (B) (C)
    (A) About ten o'clock.
    (B) I have another hour.
    (C) Just this watch.

2. How much does a new computer cost?   (A) (B) (C)
    (A) Without keyboard or monitor, it's about $500.
    (B) We have six new computers.
    (C) I bought it last month.

3. How will you get home?   (A) (B) (C)
    (A) I usually get home around 5 P.M.
    (B) As soon as it stops raining.
    (C) I'll probably walk.

4. How often does the bus come?   (A) (B) (C)
    (A) I always take the bus.
    (B) Every five minutes until six o'clock.
    (C) The bus stops in front of my house.

5. How many more file cabinets do you need?   (A) (B) (C)
    (A) We need five or six more.
    (B) I filed more than a hundred letters today.
    (C) Yes, I need to file my taxes soon.

6. How long did the meeting last?   (A) (B) (C)
    (A) It was the last meeting of the week.
    (B) Only about thirty minutes.
    (C) About fifteen people were there.

7. How soon can you finish this report?   (A) (B) (C)
    (A) I can have it for you by tomorrow morning.
    (B) I'm expecting an important call soon.
    (C) This is very big room.

8. How can I make copies? 　　　　　(A) (B) (C)
   (A) Take all the copies you need.
   (B) I need ten copies.
   (C) Use the copy machine in my office.

9. How long is that article you wrote? (A) (B) (C)
   (A) It took about a week.
   (B) It's fifteen pages.
   (C) It's about the economic situation.

10. How was your trip? 　　　　　　　(A) (B) (C)
   (A) I went there last week.
   (B) It was very pleasant and relaxing.
   (C) I read a tour book.

Practice B

DIRECTIONS: Look at each of the questions and answer choices in Practice A. In each one, circle all the words that are the same or are similar in meaning, if any. Underline all the words that are opposite in meaning, if any. Cross out the words that might sound similar, if any.

Not every conversation will have words that are the same, similar, opposite, or sound similar.

Example:

Ⓘ (came) to (the) office (first.) 　　　　　　**SAME**　　I, I; the, the; first, first

   (A) She spoke (first.) 　　　　　　　　　**SIMILAR**　came, arrived

   (B) Ⓘ (arrived) after you. 　　　　　　　**OPPOSITE**　first, last

   (C) His name is last on (the) list. 　　**SOUND SIMILAR**　came, name

Practice C

DIRECTIONS: Match these questions with the correct answers.

1. _____ How big is the conference room?
2. _____ How many people were at the meeting?
3. _____ How did you know my first name?
4. _____ How soon does the bank close?
5. _____ How far can you see without your glasses?
6. _____ How long does it take to get there?
7. _____ How often do you take a vacation?
8. _____ How much money do you need?
9. _____ How can I get in touch with you?
10. _____ How did you get here today?

a. It's bigger than the one we're in now.

b. Not very far—less than five meters.

c. About a dozen, if you count the officers.

d. In about an hour.

e. Your secretary told me.

f. Call me on my cell phone.

g. Just once a year.

h. About three hours by car.

i. Only a few dollars.

j. I drove my car.

Practice D

DIRECTIONS: Write possible answers to these questions.

1. How much is this table?

_____

2. How do you turn on the computer?

_____

3. How often do you play tennis?

_____

4. How old are his children now?

_____

5. How soon will you be leaving for your trip?

_____

6. How long is the movie?

_____

7. How far is the post office from here?

_____

8. How do you like your new job?

_____

9. How many envelopes do you need?

_____

10. How late did they arrive?

_____

Practice E

DIRECTIONS: Listen to the questions, which are followed by three responses. They are not written out for you. You must listen carefully to understand what the speakers say. You are to choose the best response to each question.

1. (A) (B) (C)
2. (A) (B) (C)
3. (A) (B) (C)
4. (A) (B) (C)
5. (A) (B) (C)
6. (A) (B) (C)
7. (A) (B) (C)
8. (A) (B) (C)
9. (A) (B) (C)
10. (A) (B) (C)

Practice F

DIRECTIONS: Listen to the questions, which are followed by three responses. They are not written out for you. You must listen carefully to understand what the speakers say. You are to choose the best response to each question.

1. (A) (B) (C)
2. (A) (B) (C)
3. (A) (B) (C)
4. (A) (B) (C)
5. (A) (B) (C)
6. (A) (B) (C)
7. (A) (B) (C)
8. (A) (B) (C)
9. (A) (B) (C)
10. (A) (B) (C)

QUESTION-RESPONSE: AUXILIARIES

Practice A

DIRECTIONS: Read the questions and the possible responses below. Mark the correct answer.

1. Have you used a word processing system before?   Ⓐ   Ⓑ   Ⓒ
   - (A) I processed it before I left yesterday.
   - (B) Yes, we were trained on them at school.
   - (C) It's a long process.

2. Did you send the report to the board members?   Ⓐ   Ⓑ   Ⓒ
   - (A) Yes, they reported to the board.
   - (B) No, I'm waiting for your signature on the report.
   - (C) They said the report was boring.

3. Can you take me to the train station?   Ⓐ   Ⓑ   Ⓒ
   - (A) Of course. I'll get my coat and we'll go.
   - (B) Yes, I caught the train at the station.
   - (C) We took a long time coming from the station.

4. Would you send this by overnight mail?   Ⓐ   Ⓑ   Ⓒ
   - (A) I'm sorry. It's too late for overnight service.
   - (B) I mailed this to you last night.
   - (C) No, overnight mail isn't too expensive.

5. Are the lawyers working on the new contracts?   Ⓐ   Ⓑ   Ⓒ
   - (A) My lawyer's name is Ramon Carerra.
   - (B) Yes, I contacted her by phone.
   - (C) I asked them to get started this morning.

6. Will we discuss the budget at tomorrow's meeting?   Ⓐ   Ⓑ   Ⓒ
   - (A) Yes, it's the first item on the agenda.
   - (B) Yes, the meeting is tomorrow.
   - (C) Yes, we'll take a bus to the meeting.

7. Do we need to order more office supplies?   Ⓐ   Ⓑ   Ⓒ
   - (A) I just ordered some yesterday.
   - (B) I wanted to give her a surprise.
   - (C) Yes, that machine is out of order.

8. Are you going to the office party tonight?   Ⓐ   Ⓑ   Ⓒ
   (A) I'll be there three nights.
   (B) Yes, I'm looking forward to it.
   (C) It's the last office on the right.

9. Can you take this check to the bank for me?   Ⓐ   Ⓑ   Ⓒ
   (A) I'll check on it right away.
   (B) Certainly. I'll take it there after lunch.
   (C) It's the bank across the street.

10. Have you worked here very long?   Ⓐ   Ⓑ   Ⓒ
   (A) It won't take long to finish.
   (B) No, it's not a long way from here.
   (C) I started this job just last month.

Practice B

DIRECTIONS: Look at each of the questions and answer choices in Practice A. In each one, circle all the words that are the same or are similar in meaning, if any. Underline all the words that are opposite in meaning, if any. Cross out the words that might sound similar, if any.

Not every conversation will have words that are the same, similar, opposite, or sound similar.

Example:

Ⓘ (came) to (the) office (first.)

(A) She spoke (first.)

(B) Ⓘ (arrived) after you.

(C) His name̶ is <u>last</u> on (the) list.

SAME	I, I; the, the; first, first
SIMILAR	came, arrived
OPPOSITE	first, last
SOUND SIMILAR	came, name

Practice C

DIRECTIONS: Match these questions with the correct answers.

1. _____ Can you work late this evening?

2. _____ Are they opening a branch office?

3. _____ Is there more paper in the supply room?

4. _____ Has the contract been signed?

5. _____ Will the chairperson resign?

6. _____ Did John get here on time today?

7. _____ Has the mail arrived yet?

8. _____ Were you calling about a package for me?

9. _____ Do you have my phone number?

10. _____ Do you know how to fix this fax machine?

a. She plans to resign tomorrow.

b. Yes, it's from Mr. Jones.

c. I'm sorry. I have another commitment.

d. Yes, I'm pretty sure it has been.

e. No, he was late again.

f. I think you should call a repair person.

g. Yes, I put your letters on your desk.

h. No, I'll order some more.

i. Yes, in Europe, I think.

j. No, please write it down for me.

Practice D

DIRECTIONS: Write possible answers to these questions.

1. Didn't you buy a new car?

   _____

2. Have you given the new clerk something to do?

   _____

3. Are you waiting for the express train?

   _____

4. Will we be able to start production on schedule?

   _____

5. Can they finish the chart by this afternoon?

   _____

6. Is the manager going to be here today?

   _____

7. Did you get the fax I sent you?

_____

8. Do you know how to speak French?

_____

9. Have you put the report on Martha's desk?

_____

10. Will everyone be at the meeting?

_____

Practice E

DIRECTIONS: Listen to the questions, which are followed by three responses. They are not written out for you. You must listen carefully to understand what the speakers say. You are to choose the best response to each question.

1. Ⓐ Ⓑ Ⓒ
2. Ⓐ Ⓑ Ⓒ
3. Ⓐ Ⓑ Ⓒ
4. Ⓐ Ⓑ Ⓒ
5. Ⓐ Ⓑ Ⓒ
6. Ⓐ Ⓑ Ⓒ
7. Ⓐ Ⓑ Ⓒ
8. Ⓐ Ⓑ Ⓒ
9. Ⓐ Ⓑ Ⓒ
10. Ⓐ Ⓑ Ⓒ

Practice F

DIRECTIONS: Listen to the questions, which are followed by three responses. They are not written out for you. You must listen carefully to understand what the speakers say. You are to choose the best response to each question.

1. Ⓐ Ⓑ Ⓒ
2. Ⓐ Ⓑ Ⓒ
3. Ⓐ Ⓑ Ⓒ
4. Ⓐ Ⓑ Ⓒ
5. Ⓐ Ⓑ Ⓒ
6. Ⓐ Ⓑ Ⓒ
7. Ⓐ Ⓑ Ⓒ
8. Ⓐ Ⓑ Ⓒ
9. Ⓐ Ⓑ Ⓒ
10. Ⓐ Ⓑ Ⓒ

REVIEW: PART 2

 DIRECTIONS: Listen and choose the appropriate response to the question or statement.

1. Ⓐ Ⓑ Ⓒ   6. Ⓐ Ⓑ Ⓒ
2. Ⓐ Ⓑ Ⓒ   7. Ⓐ Ⓑ Ⓒ
3. Ⓐ Ⓑ Ⓒ   8. Ⓐ Ⓑ Ⓒ
4. Ⓐ Ⓑ Ⓒ   9. Ⓐ Ⓑ Ⓒ
5. Ⓐ Ⓑ Ⓒ   10. Ⓐ Ⓑ Ⓒ

PART 3: CONVERSATIONS

The following exercises will help you develop strategies for listening to conversations and choosing the best response. They will help you use context clues to guess what the conversation is about. The exercises will also improve your vocabulary in specific ways.

VOCABULARY STRATEGIES

- From the questions and answer choices, try to guess what the conversation is about.

- Listen for words in the conversation associated with the five topics listed below.

OCCUPATIONS	*Who?*
ACTIVITIES	*What?*
TIME	*When?*
LOCATION	*Where?*
REASON	*Why?*

LISTENING STRATEGIES

- Read the question and answer choices before you hear the audio.

- Listen to get both the general idea and the specific answer to the question.

In this section, you are practicing listening strategies for the new TOEIC test. The questions in this section are focused on these strategies. Therefore, there is only one question for every conversation in the Strategy Practice exercises.

There are five TOEIC Test Practice exercises and one Review exercise. In these exercises, you will have three questions for each conversation, just like on the new TOEIC test. These reviews will help you to develop your memory skills. You must remember a lot of details to answer the questions correctly. You will be able to practice your listening strategies in these reviews.

CONVERSATIONS: OCCUPATIONS

Vocabulary Practice

DIRECTIONS: Certain words are associated with certain occupations. Look at the words below. Cross out the words that do not match the occupation. What occupation is associated with the crossed-out words? Look at the example, and then do the exercise.

OCCUPATION

ASSOCIATED WORDS

Example:

secretary

files, ~~singing~~, word processor, telephone, ~~song~~

singer

singing, song

1. cook

pots, kitchen, computer, knife, files

2. police officer

parking tickets, dessert, law, illegal, menu

3. teachers

class, mail, packages, exams, students

4. phone technician

telephone, novel, receiver, cord, write

5. computer programmer

files, software, memo, keyboard, monitor

6. bank teller

money, plane, deposit, withdrawal, fly

7. waiter

order, law, tip, customers, parking tickets

8. accountant

taxes, nails, receivables, wood, total

9. athlete

runner, training, sick, game, hospital

10. doctor   menu, medicine, nurse, tip, hospital

_____   _____

11. musician   instrument, orchestra, pills, notes, prescription

_____   _____

12. actor   engine, stage, drama, repair, theater

_____   _____

13. taxi driver   passenger, campaign, fare, election, tip

_____   _____

14. sales clerk   film, camera, cash register, change, receipt

_____   _____

15. journalist   write, newspaper, flowers, seeds, reports

_____   _____

Strategy Practice: Who

DIRECTIONS: Listen to the conversations on the audio and try to identify the occupation of the speakers. The words in the previous vocabulary exercise will be helpful to you. Remember to use the listening strategies described on page 74.

1. Who are the speakers talking about?   Ⓐ Ⓑ Ⓒ Ⓓ
   - (A)   A hairstylist.
   - (B)   A ticketseller.
   - (C)   A concert pianist.
   - (D)   A singer.

2. Who are the speakers waiting for?   Ⓐ Ⓑ Ⓒ Ⓓ
   - (A)   The delivery person with lunch.
   - (B)   The telephone technician.
   - (C)   The television salesman.
   - (D)   The computer programmer.

3. Who will the woman see next?   Ⓐ Ⓑ Ⓒ Ⓓ
   - (A)   A bank officer.
   - (B)   A police officer.
   - (C)   A cashier.
   - (D)   A foreman.

4. Who are the speakers? Ⓐ Ⓑ Ⓒ Ⓓ
   (A) Authors.
   (B) Librarians.
   (C) Booksellers.
   (D) Bookkeepers.

5. Who are the speakers waiting for? Ⓐ Ⓑ Ⓒ Ⓓ
   (A) A cab driver.
   (B) A friend.
   (C) A waitress.
   (D) A client.

6. Who is the man going to see? Ⓐ Ⓑ Ⓒ Ⓓ
   (A) A sales representative.
   (B) A tennis coach.
   (C) A repairperson.
   (D) A doctor.

7. Who are the speakers? Ⓐ Ⓑ Ⓒ Ⓓ
   (A) Teachers.
   (B) Police officers.
   (C) Accountants.
   (D) Travel agents.

8. Who is coming this afternoon? Ⓐ Ⓑ Ⓒ Ⓓ
   (A) An athlete.
   (B) An accountant.
   (C) A carpenter.
   (D) A math teacher.

9. Who is giving advice? Ⓐ Ⓑ Ⓒ Ⓓ
   (A) A doctor.
   (B) A waiter.
   (C) An exercise coach.
   (D) An athlete.

10. Who is waiting? Ⓐ Ⓑ Ⓒ Ⓓ
    (A) A gardener.
    (B) A taxi driver.
    (C) A mail carrier.
    (D) A musician.

11. Who is the man?   Ⓐ Ⓑ Ⓒ Ⓓ
    (A)   A baker.
    (B)   A gardener.
    (C)   A factory owner.
    (D)   An artist.

12. Who are the speakers?   Ⓐ Ⓑ Ⓒ Ⓓ
    (A)   Taxi drivers.
    (B)   Accountants.
    (C)   Pilots.
    (D)   Waiters.

13. Who left a phone message?   Ⓐ Ⓑ Ⓒ Ⓓ
    (A)   A taxi driver.
    (B)   A tennis coach.
    (C)   A telephone repairperson.
    (D)   An auto mechanic.

14. Who is Mr. Gomez?   Ⓐ Ⓑ Ⓒ Ⓓ
    (A)   A bookseller.
    (B)   A hotel manager.
    (C)   A travel agent.
    (D)   A banker.

15. Who is the woman talking to?   Ⓐ Ⓑ Ⓒ Ⓓ
    (A)   An athlete.
    (B)   A musician.
    (C)   A travel agent.
    (D)   A police officer.

TOEIC Test Practice

DIRECTIONS: On the TOEIC test, you will need to remember specific details from the conversation. You will have to improve your memory as well as your listening skills. Read the questions quickly before you listen to the conversation, and then listen for the answers.

CONVERSATION 1 (Questions 1–3)

1. Who is the woman talking to?   Ⓐ Ⓑ Ⓒ Ⓓ
    (A)   A hotel clerk.
    (B)   A waiter.
    (C)   A travel agent.
    (D)   An elevator operator.

2. What is her room number?   Ⓐ Ⓑ Ⓒ Ⓓ
   (A) 15.
   (B) 50.
   (C) 215.
   (D) 250.

3. Who recommended the restaurant to the woman?   Ⓐ Ⓑ Ⓒ Ⓓ
   (A) Her brother.
   (B) Her mother.
   (C) Her friend.
   (D) Her employer.

CONVERSATION 2 (Questions 4–6)

4. Who did the man have an appointment with?   Ⓐ Ⓑ Ⓒ Ⓓ
   (A) His dentist.
   (B) His secretary.
   (C) His hairstylist.
   (D) His rental agent.

5. Who missed the meeting?   Ⓐ Ⓑ Ⓒ Ⓓ
   (A) The manager.
   (B) The woman.
   (C) Everybody.
   (D) Bob.

6. When is the next meeting?   Ⓐ Ⓑ Ⓒ Ⓓ
   (A) Sunday.
   (B) Monday.
   (C) Tuesday.
   (D) Wednesday.

CONVERSATION 3 (Questions 7–9)

7. Who is the man talking to?   Ⓐ Ⓑ Ⓒ Ⓓ
   (A) A taxi driver.
   (B) A flight attendant.
   (C) A train conductor.
   (D) A box office clerk.

8. How much will the man pay?   Ⓐ Ⓑ Ⓒ Ⓓ
   (A) $10.00.
   (B) $17.00.
   (C) $30.00.
   (D) $70.00.

9. What time is it now?   Ⓐ Ⓑ Ⓒ Ⓓ
   (A) 11:13.
   (B) 11:30.
   (C) 12:15.
   (D) 12:45.

CONVERSATION 4 (Questions 10–12)

10. Who is the woman talking to?   Ⓐ Ⓑ Ⓒ Ⓓ
    (A) Her secretary.
    (B) Her accountant.
    (C) A garage attendant.
    (D) A meeting planner.

11. Who called this morning?   Ⓐ Ⓑ Ⓒ Ⓓ
    (A) The driver.
    (B) The mechanic.
    (C) The car rental agent.
    (D) The telephone repairperson.

12. What time will the woman pick up her car?   Ⓐ Ⓑ Ⓒ Ⓓ
    (A) 11:30.
    (B) 2:30.
    (C) 5:00.
    (D) 8:00.

CONVERSATION 5 (Questions 13–15)

13. Who is the woman waiting for?   Ⓐ Ⓑ Ⓒ Ⓓ
    (A) A customer service representative.
    (B) A printer salesperson.
    (C) A repairperson.
    (D) A doctor.

14. What day is this conversation taking place?   Ⓐ Ⓑ Ⓒ Ⓓ
    (A) Monday.
    (B) Tuesday.
    (C) Wednesday.
    (D) Thursday.

15. Who does the man want to see?   Ⓐ Ⓑ Ⓒ Ⓓ
    (A) A web site designer.
    (B) A receptionist.
    (C) A doctor.
    (D) A dentist.

CONVERSATIONS: ACTIVITIES

Vocabulary Practice A

DIRECTIONS: Certain words are associated with certain activities. Look at the verb phrases below. Write two or more words associated with each of the activities these phrases describe.

1. drinking coffee *cup, spoon, sugar, cream, coffee break*

2. watching a movie _____

3. opening the door _____

4. going to the post office _____

5. reading a book _____

6. making a phone call _____

7. using a computer _____

8. buying something from a vending machine _____

9. ordering food at a restaurant _____

10. buying clothes _____

Vocabulary Practice B

DIRECTIONS: Complete these sentences using the activities in Vocabulary Practice A.

1. Mr. Park is on his way to mail some letters and buy some stamps.

   He is _____

2. Ms. Kachi is in front of her house. She has the key in the lock.

   She is _____

3. Mr. Wu is putting cream and sugar in his coffee.

   _____

4. The Ransoms are sitting in a movie theater.

   _____

5. Mr. Teo is sitting in his chair with a book.

   _____

6. Kim is typing on a keyboard.

_____

7. George is asking the waitress a question.

_____

8. Ms. Cho is dialing a number.

_____

9. Mr. Wang is putting coins into the slot.

_____

10. Lily is trying on a suit in the dressing room.

_____

Vocabulary Practice C

DIRECTIONS: Complete the sentences below using the following verb phrases.

eating dinner	making a sandwich
waiting for a bus	parking the car
buying a newspaper	driving a car
copying a letter	washing the floor
leaving a friend's home ✓	riding a bus
moving furniture	paying the taxi fare
picking up the mail	riding an elevator
buying a plane ticket	paying the bus fare

1. I said good-bye to Mr. Ogato. I hope to visit him again soon.

   *I'm leaving a friend's home.*_____

2. I put paper in the photocopier.

   _____

3. The children are cold standing at the bus stop.

   _____

4. Mr. Imamura is putting his desk by the window and his table in the corner.

   _____

5. I usually drive around for ten minutes until I find a place to park.

   _____

6. When we get on a bus, the driver wants us to pay our fare.

   _____

7. This elevator stops at every floor. I want an express elevator to the sixtieth floor.

_____

8. She always pays attention to the traffic and wears her seat belt.

_____

9. The round-trip fare from Chicago to Tokyo is $950.

_____

10. We are sitting at a table. We have a lot of food on our plates.

_____

11. She put butter on the bread and now she's slicing a tomato.

_____

12. I take the letters out of the mailbox.

_____

13. I always give the driver a 15 percent tip.

_____

14. They have a mop and a bucket of water.

_____

15. She gives the man fifty cents and takes a paper from the counter.

_____

Strategy Practice: What

DIRECTIONS: Listen to the conversations on the audio and then answer the following questions. Remember to use the listening strategies described on page 74.

1. What are the speakers doing? Ⓐ Ⓑ Ⓒ Ⓓ
   (A) Typing a report.
   (B) Eating lunch.
   (C) Telling the time.
   (D) Cooking.

2. What are the speakers doing? Ⓐ Ⓑ Ⓒ Ⓓ
   (A) Getting on a bus.
   (B) Waiting for a bus.
   (C) Taking a taxi.
   (D) Paying a fare.

3. What are the speakers doing?   Ⓐ   Ⓑ   Ⓒ   Ⓓ
   - (A) Painting the office.
   - (B) Buying a chair.
   - (C) Opening the window.
   - (D) Moving furniture.

4. What are the speakers doing?   Ⓐ   Ⓑ   Ⓒ   Ⓓ
   - (A) Drinking coffee.
   - (B) Buying food.
   - (C) Sitting at a counter.
   - (D) Eating ice cream.

5. What is the woman doing?   Ⓐ   Ⓑ   Ⓒ   Ⓓ
   - (A) Paying her fare.
   - (B) Giving change.
   - (C) Going to the fair.
   - (D) Changing her hair.

6. What is the woman going to do?   Ⓐ   Ⓑ   Ⓒ   Ⓓ
   - (A) Drive a car.
   - (B) Take an elevator.
   - (C) Wait for a train.
   - (D) Walk up the stairs.

7. What are the speakers doing?   Ⓐ   Ⓑ   Ⓒ   Ⓓ
   - (A) Running in the park.
   - (B) Looking for parking.
   - (C) Walking across the street.
   - (D) Taking the car to the mechanic.

8. What is the woman doing?   Ⓐ   Ⓑ   Ⓒ   Ⓓ
   - (A) Buying a ticket.
   - (B) Giving directions.
   - (C) Going to the bank.
   - (D) Paying her taxes.

9. What are the speakers doing?   Ⓐ   Ⓑ   Ⓒ   Ⓓ
   - (A) Buying food.
   - (B) Getting married.
   - (C) Going to a restaurant.
   - (D) Eating dinner.

10. What is the woman doing?   Ⓐ   Ⓑ   Ⓒ   Ⓓ
   - (A) Having lunch.
   - (B) Comparing watches.
   - (C) Leaving for home.
   - (D) Arriving for a visit.

11. What is the man doing? (A) (B) (C) (D)
    (A) Making a sandwich.
    (B) Ordering food in a restaurant.
    (C) Shopping at a grocery store.
    (D) Gardening.

12. What are the speakers going to do? (A) (B) (C) (D)
    (A) Take a bath.
    (B) Do the laundry.
    (C) Put things away.
    (D) Wash the floor.

13. What is the woman doing? (A) (B) (C) (D)
    (A) Paying a bus fare.
    (B) Buying a newspaper.
    (C) Looking at a calendar.
    (D) Paying for office supplies.

14. What is the man going to do? (A) (B) (C) (D)
    (A) Buy a ladder.
    (B) Write a letter.
    (C) Send a package.
    (D) Pick up the mail.

15. What is the man doing? (A) (B) (C) (D)
    (A) Taking a taxi.
    (B) Asking for change.
    (C) Riding a bus.
    (D) Buying a train ticket.

TOEIC Test Practice

DIRECTIONS: On the TOEIC test, you will need to remember specific details from the conversation. You will have to improve your memory as well as your listening skills. Read the questions quickly before you listen to the conversation, and then listen for the answers.

CONVERSATION 1 (Questions 1–3)

1. Who is the man? (A) (B) (C) (D)
    (A) A waiter.
    (B) A financial adviser.
    (C) A restaurant manager.
    (D) A banker.

2. What is the woman doing?   (A) (B) (C) (D)
   (A) Cooking dinner.
   (B) Ordering a meal.
   (C) Paying her bill.
   (D) Eating something.

3. What is the man doing?   (A) (B) (C) (D)
   (A) Talking about the chef.
   (B) Hiring a chef.
   (C) Studying to become a chef.
   (D) Watching the chef.

CONVERSATION 2 (Questions 4–6)

4. Who are the speakers waiting for?   (A) (B) (C) (D)
   (A) A taxicab driver.
   (B) A pilot.
   (C) A train conductor.
   (D) A newspaper delivery person.

5. What did the man just do?   (A) (B) (C) (D)
   (A) He played a ball game.
   (B) He arrived at the airport.
   (C) He made a phone call.
   (D) He wrote an editorial.

6. What is the woman going to do?   (A) (B) (C) (D)
   (A) Read a book.
   (B) Eat something.
   (C) Read the newspaper.
   (D) Buy some paper.

CONVERSATION 3 (Questions 7–9)

7. Who is the woman?   (A) (B) (C) (D)
   (A) A pilot.
   (B) A flight attendant.
   (C) A waitress.
   (D) A journalist.

8. What is the woman about to do?   (A) (B) (C) (D)
   (A) Read a magazine.
   (B) Relax.
   (C) Serve lunch.
   (D) Show a movie.

9. What does the man want to do? Ⓐ Ⓑ Ⓒ Ⓓ
   (A) Eat lunch.
   (B) Watch a movie.
   (C) Read a magazine.
   (D) Tell jokes.

CONVERSATION 4 (Questions 10–12)

10. Who is the woman talking to? Ⓐ Ⓑ Ⓒ Ⓓ
    (A) An airline ticket agent.
    (B) A travel agent.
    (C) A hotel clerk.
    (D) A car driver.

11. What is the woman doing? Ⓐ Ⓑ Ⓒ Ⓓ
    (A) Making hotel reservations.
    (B) Buying plane tickets.
    (C) Choosing a book.
    (D) Renting a car.

12. What will the woman do on her trip? Ⓐ Ⓑ Ⓒ Ⓓ
    (A) Have a business meeting.
    (B) Get married.
    (C) Swim at the beach.
    (D) Attend a cousin's wedding.

CONVERSATION 5 (Questions 13–15)

13. Who is the woman waiting for? Ⓐ Ⓑ Ⓒ Ⓓ
    (A) An emergency technician.
    (B) The receptionist.
    (C) The dentist.
    (D) A patient.

14. What is the woman doing? Ⓐ Ⓑ Ⓒ Ⓓ
    (A) Complaining about waiting.
    (B) Discussing business.
    (C) Brushing her teeth.
    (D) Buying a watch.

15. What does the woman want to do? Ⓐ Ⓑ Ⓒ Ⓓ
    (A) Wait longer.
    (B) Find a new doctor.
    (C) Speak to her brother.
    (D) Reschedule her appointment.

CONVERSATIONS: TIME

Vocabulary Practice

DIRECTIONS: Time questions begin with *How long? How often? How soon? When?*
Write a question from each statement, using the question word or words provided.

1. The copy machine takes ten minutes to print a hundred pages.

   How long *does the copy machine take to print a hundred pages?*

2. Ms. Miller joined our staff in July.

   When _____

3. Mr. DeLorenzo has been in the hospital for two months.

   How long _____

4. The floors are cleaned every three months.

   How often _____

5. We are going to the reception at five o'clock.

   When _____

6. The mail usually comes before noon.

   When _____

7. It took all afternoon to fix the copy machine.

   How long _____

8. They tried to call him every night.

   How often _____

9. Mr. Gutfreund will be gone for two weeks.

   How long _____

10. She mailed the package last night.

    When _____

11. They've been working on this report all week.

How long _____

12. He sent the e-mail message this morning.

When _____

13. We have a staff meeting every Monday morning.

How often _____

14. Robert started his new job last week.

When _____

15. It will take about a week to paint all these offices.

How long _____

Strategy Practice: When

DIRECTIONS: Listen to the conversations on the audio and then answer the following questions. Remember to use the listening strategies described on page 74.

1. How often are the offices cleaned? Ⓐ Ⓑ Ⓒ Ⓓ
   (A) Two times a week.
   (B) Three times a week.
   (C) Once a day.
   (D) Twice a day.

2. How long did it take to fix the coffee machine? Ⓐ Ⓑ Ⓒ Ⓓ
   (A) All day.
   (B) Two hours.
   (C) All morning.
   (D) Four hours.

3. How long does it take to make eight copies? Ⓐ Ⓑ Ⓒ Ⓓ
   (A) One minute.
   (B) Five minutes.
   (C) Eight minutes.
   (D) One hour.

4. How often has the man tried to call? Ⓐ Ⓑ Ⓒ Ⓓ
   (A) Once.
   (B) One more time.
   (C) Every five minutes.
   (D) Every hour.

5. When does the mail come?   Ⓐ Ⓑ Ⓒ Ⓓ
   (A)   In the morning.
   (B)   At noon.
   (C)   In the afternoon.
   (D)   In the evening.

6. When was the check sent?   Ⓐ Ⓑ Ⓒ Ⓓ
   (A)   Last week.
   (B)   Yesterday.
   (C)   Today.
   (D)   On Friday.

7. When did Ms. Wallace join the company?   Ⓐ Ⓑ Ⓒ Ⓓ
   (A)   The same year as Mr. Chu.
   (B)   A month before Mr. Chu.
   (C)   A year after Mr. Chu.
   (D)   A month after Mr. Chu.

8. When are the speakers going?   Ⓐ Ⓑ Ⓒ Ⓓ
   (A)   Five o'clock.
   (B)   Six o'clock.
   (C)   Seven o'clock.
   (D)   Eight o'clock.

9. When did the woman visit her aunt?   Ⓐ Ⓑ Ⓒ Ⓓ
   (A)   A long time ago.
   (B)   Last week.
   (C)   Yesterday.
   (D)   This morning.

10. How long will Ms. Ono be away?   Ⓐ Ⓑ Ⓒ Ⓓ
    (A)   One week.
    (B)   Two weeks.
    (C)   Three weeks.
    (D)   Four weeks.

11. How long have they been working on the report?   Ⓐ Ⓑ Ⓒ Ⓓ
    (A)   For two days.
    (B)   For three days.
    (C)   All weekend.
    (D)   For a week.

12. When did Lucy start her new job?   Ⓐ Ⓑ Ⓒ Ⓓ
    (A) Four months ago.
    (B) One month ago.
    (C) Four weeks ago.
    (D) One week ago.

13. When did the woman read the e-mail message?   Ⓐ Ⓑ Ⓒ Ⓓ
    (A) Yesterday.
    (B) Last night.
    (C) This morning.
    (D) After lunch.

14. How long will it take to paint the house?   Ⓐ Ⓑ Ⓒ Ⓓ
    (A) Two days.
    (B) A weekend.
    (C) A week.
    (D) Two weeks.

15. How often do they have a staff meeting?   Ⓐ Ⓑ Ⓒ Ⓓ
    (A) Every day.
    (B) Every two days.
    (C) Every week.
    (D) Every month.

TOEIC Test Practice

DIRECTIONS: On the TOEIC test, you will need to remember specific details from the conversation. You will have to improve your memory as well as your listening skills. Read the questions quickly before you listen to the conversation, and then listen for the answers.

CONVERSATION 1 (Questions 1–3)

1. When did the woman return from her vacation?   Ⓐ Ⓑ Ⓒ Ⓓ
   (A) Today.
   (B) Last night.
   (C) Yesterday afternoon.
   (D) Last week.

2. Where will the man spend his vacation?   Ⓐ Ⓑ Ⓒ Ⓓ
   (A) In the mountains.
   (B) At the lake.
   (C) In Hong Kong.
   (D) At the beach.

3. When will the man take his vacation?   Ⓐ   Ⓑ   Ⓒ   Ⓓ
   (A) July.
   (B) August.
   (C) September.
   (D) December.

CONVERSATION 2 (Questions 4–6)

4. When will the meeting begin?   Ⓐ   Ⓑ   Ⓒ   Ⓓ
   (A) 8:00.
   (B) 8:30.
   (C) 9:30.
   (D) 10:00.

5. When will Sherry speak?   Ⓐ   Ⓑ   Ⓒ   Ⓓ
   (A) After the financial report.
   (B) After the coffee break.
   (C) Right after Tom's presentation.
   (D) Right before lunch.

6. What will happen after lunch?   Ⓐ   Ⓑ   Ⓒ   Ⓓ
   (A) Tom will speak.
   (B) Coffee will be served.
   (C) A committee will be organized.
   (D) The manager will give a presentation.

CONVERSATION 3 (Questions 7–9)

7. When did the man make his reservation?   Ⓐ   Ⓑ   Ⓒ   Ⓓ
   (A) Today.
   (B) Last night.
   (C) A week ago.
   (D) A month ago.

8. How long will he stay at the hotel?   Ⓐ   Ⓑ   Ⓒ   Ⓓ
   (A) Two nights.
   (B) Until Tuesday.
   (C) Until Wednesday.
   (D) Seven days.

9. What did the clerk offer the man?   Ⓐ   Ⓑ   Ⓒ   Ⓓ
   (A) A book.
   (B) Some free meals.
   (C) A couch.
   (D) Some movie tickets.

CONVERSATION 4 (Questions 10–12)

10. When will they leave the Natural History Museum? Ⓐ Ⓑ Ⓒ Ⓓ
    (A) 5:00.
    (B) 8:00.
    (C) 11:00.
    (D) 12:00.

11. How will they visit the monuments? Ⓐ Ⓑ Ⓒ Ⓓ
    (A) By car.
    (B) By bus.
    (C) By foot.
    (D) By train.

12. When will they see the monuments? Ⓐ Ⓑ Ⓒ Ⓓ
    (A) Right before lunch.
    (B) Right after lunch.
    (C) Before the Art Museum.
    (D) After shopping.

CONVERSATION 5 (Questions 13–15)

13. When did the woman call the man? Ⓐ Ⓑ Ⓒ Ⓓ
    (A) Yesterday morning.
    (B) Yesterday afternoon.
    (C) Last night.
    (D) This morning.

14. Where was the man last night? Ⓐ Ⓑ Ⓒ Ⓓ
    (A) At work.
    (B) At the movies.
    (C) At home.
    (D) At a friend's house.

15. When does the man want to see the play? Ⓐ Ⓑ Ⓒ Ⓓ
    (A) Tuesday.
    (B) Friday.
    (C) Saturday.
    (D) Sunday.

CONVERSATIONS: LOCATIONS

Vocabulary Practice

DIRECTIONS: Certain words are associated with certain locations. Look at the words below. Cross out the words that do not match the location. What location is associated with the crossed-out words? Look at the example and then do the exercise.

LOCATION	ASSOCIATED WORDS
Example:	
plane	flight, ~~bed~~, flight attendant, ~~double room~~, seat belt
hotel	*bed, double room*
1. restaurant	order, tip, teacher, waiter, lesson
2. airplane	seat belt, deposit, landing, bank officer, wings
3. hotel	single room, Thailand, lobby, reservation, Malaysia
4. gas station	car, gas, fill up, waitress, oil, menu
5. travel agency	package tours, library card, tickets, hotels, bookshelves
6. train station	track, double room, train, room service, platform
7. library	book, gas, card, fill up, overdue, shelves, periodicals
8. bank	waiter, checking account, teller, deposit, tip
9. car rental agency	patient, insurance, rent, cars, nurse, reservation

10.	import office	products, trade, export, engine, windshield
	_____	_____
11.	post office	stamps, art, package, mail, exhibit
	_____	_____
12.	clothing store	sand, dressing room, hanger, water, blouse
	_____	_____
13.	park	bench, path, can, box, garden, aisle
	_____	_____
14.	health club	cars, steam room, swimming pool, traffic light, exercise equipment
	_____	_____
15.	kitchen	stove, cabinets, screen, tickets, sink
	_____	_____

Strategy Practice: Where

DIRECTIONS: Listen to the conversations on the audio and then answer the following questions. Remember to use the listening strategies described on page 74.

1. Where are the speakers?   Ⓐ Ⓑ Ⓒ Ⓓ
   (A) At a gas station.
   (B) In an elevator.
   (C) In a kitchen.
   (D) In an office.

2. Where are the speakers?   Ⓐ Ⓑ Ⓒ Ⓓ
   (A) At a fish store.
   (B) At a restaurant.
   (C) At the beach.
   (D) At a party.

3. Where are the speakers?   Ⓐ Ⓑ Ⓒ Ⓓ
   (A) In a theater.
   (B) On a train.
   (C) In a plane.
   (D) In a grocery store.

4. Where will the woman return the book?   Ⓐ Ⓑ Ⓒ Ⓓ
   (A) To the bookstore.
   (B) To the library.
   (C) To her friend.
   (D) To the post office.

5. Where are the sweaters made?   Ⓐ Ⓑ Ⓒ Ⓓ
   (A) In the Philippines.
   (B) In Thailand.
   (C) In Hong Kong.
   (D) In Malaysia.

6. Where are the speakers?   Ⓐ Ⓑ Ⓒ Ⓓ
   (A) At an import company.
   (B) At a restaurant.
   (C) At a hotel.
   (D) At an airport.

7. Where is this conversation taking place?   Ⓐ Ⓑ Ⓒ Ⓓ
   (A) At a bank.
   (B) At a bookstore.
   (C) At a lost and found.
   (D) At a library.

8. Where are the speakers going?   Ⓐ Ⓑ Ⓒ Ⓓ
   (A) To the train station.
   (B) To the watch repair shop.
   (C) To a grocery store.
   (D) To a coffee shop.

9. Where is this conversation taking place?   Ⓐ Ⓑ Ⓒ Ⓓ
   (A) In Hawaii.
   (B) At a travel agency.
   (C) On a plane.
   (D) In a gift shop.

10. Where are the speakers?   Ⓐ Ⓑ Ⓒ Ⓓ
   (A) At a driving school.
   (B) At an insurance agency.
   (C) At a car rental agency.
   (D) At an automobile showroom.

11. Where is this conversation taking place?   Ⓐ Ⓑ Ⓒ Ⓓ
   (A) At a park.
   (B) In a garage.
   (C) On the street.
   (D) In a bus station.

12. Where are the speakers going? Ⓐ Ⓑ Ⓒ Ⓓ
    (A) To a movie theater.
    (B) To an airport.
    (C) To a TV store.
    (D) To a travel agency.

13. Where do the speakers like to go? Ⓐ Ⓑ Ⓒ Ⓓ
    (A) To a museum.
    (B) To the library.
    (C) To the street.
    (D) To a park.

14. Where does the man work? Ⓐ Ⓑ Ⓒ Ⓓ
    (A) At a paint store.
    (B) At an art museum.
    (C) At an airport.
    (D) At a restaurant.

15. Where is this conversation taking place? Ⓐ Ⓑ Ⓒ Ⓓ
    (A) At a restaurant.
    (B) In a kitchen.
    (C) In a grocery store.
    (D) On an airplane.

TOEIC Test Practice

DIRECTIONS: On the TOEIC test, you will need to remember specific details from the conversation. You will have to improve your memory as well as your listening skills. Read the questions quickly before you listen to the conversation, and then listen for the answers.

CONVERSATION 1 (Questions 1–3)

1. When will John arrive? Ⓐ Ⓑ Ⓒ Ⓓ
   (A) Noon.
   (B) 2:00.
   (C) 2:15.
   (D) 2:50.

2. How long has he been gone? Ⓐ Ⓑ Ⓒ Ⓓ
   (A) Four days.
   (B) Two weeks.
   (C) Three weeks.
   (D) One month.

3. Where will the woman take him?   Ⓐ Ⓑ Ⓒ Ⓓ
   (A) The train station.
   (B) The airport.
   (C) The office.
   (D) Home.

CONVERSATION 2 (Questions 4–6)

4. Where are these speakers now?   Ⓐ Ⓑ Ⓒ Ⓓ
   (A) In a waiting room.
   (B) At a restaurant.
   (C) At the beach.
   (D) At home.

5. How long have they been waiting?   Ⓐ Ⓑ Ⓒ Ⓓ
   (A) Five minutes.
   (B) Eight minutes.
   (C) Fifteen minutes.
   (D) One hour.

6. Where will they go later?   Ⓐ Ⓑ Ⓒ Ⓓ
   (A) Downtown.
   (B) To a theater.
   (C) To the movies.
   (D) To a ball game.

CONVERSATION 3 (Questions 7–9)

7. Where are the speakers?   Ⓐ Ⓑ Ⓒ Ⓓ
   (A) At the beach.
   (B) At a store.
   (C) At a pool.
   (D) On a boat.

8. How often does the man go there?   Ⓐ Ⓑ Ⓒ Ⓓ
   (A) Every three weeks.
   (B) Once a month.
   (C) Three times a year.
   (D) Once a year.

9. How long does the woman spend there?   Ⓐ Ⓑ Ⓒ Ⓓ
   (A) One week.
   (B) Two weeks.
   (C) Three weeks.
   (D) Four weeks.

CONVERSATION 4 (Questions 10–12)

10. Where are the speakers? (A) (B) (C) (D)
    (A) At the airport.
    (B) At the bus stop.
    (C) At the train station.
    (D) At the doctor's office.

11. When did the man get there? (A) (B) (C) (D)
    (A) 7:00.
    (B) 7:30.
    (C) 11:00.
    (D) 11:30.

12. How much longer will the speakers have to wait? (A) (B) (C) (D)
    (A) One minute.
    (B) Six minutes.
    (C) Nine minutes.
    (D) Ten minutes.

CONVERSATION 5 (Questions 13–15)

13. When is the meeting? (A) (B) (C) (D)
    (A) Today.
    (B) Tuesday.
    (C) Wednesday.
    (D) Friday.

14. Where will it take place? (A) (B) (C) (D)
    (A) In the conference room.
    (B) In Room 4.
    (C) In the cafeteria.
    (D) In a café.

15. What time will it start? (A) (B) (C) (D)
    (A) Noon.
    (B) 1:00.
    (C) 1:15.
    (D) 1:50.

CONVERSATIONS: REASONS

Vocabulary Practice A

DIRECTIONS: Match the reason with the activity in each section. Draw a line between the activity and the reason.

ACTIVITY

REASON

1. I prefer the train.
2. We'll need an umbrella.
3. I'll give you a raise.
4. I can't finish this book.
5. She borrowed my pencil.

a. You do extra work.
b. I don't like to drive.
c. Her pen was out of ink.
d. I don't have time now.
e. It's raining.

6. He can't read the newspaper.
7. She was late for work.
8. The car won't start.
9. I couldn't call you.
10. I bought bigger shoes.

f. We are out of gas.
g. He lost his glasses.
h. You were on the phone.
i. My feet hurt.
j. She missed her bus.

11. I couldn't make copies.
12. She didn't finish her dinner.
13. He returned the suit to the store.
14. She stayed at the office late.
15. We sent Jack a present.

k. She had a lot of work to finish.
l. The copier is broken.
m. It's his birthday.
n. It didn't fit.
o. She wasn't very hungry.

Vocabulary Practice B

DIRECTIONS: To complete each sentence, give a reason as an answer for the question.

1. She walked home in the snow.
   Why did she walk home in the snow?
   Because *she didn't want to drive.*

2. We will finish the report tomorrow.
   Why won't they finish the report today?
   Because _____

3. We used a pencil to sign the memo.
   Why didn't they use a pen?
   Because _____

4. My feet hurt.
   Why do your feet hurt?
   Because _____

5. She was late for work again.
    Why wasn't she on time?
    Because _____

6. Bob's clothes are wet.
    Why are Bob's clothes wet?
    Because _____

7. I tried to call you, but the line was busy.
    Why was the line busy?
    Because _____

8. Rita got a promotion at work.
    Why did Rita get a promotion?
    Because _____

9. She didn't eat anything for lunch.
    Why didn't she eat anything?
    Because _____

10. Please read this letter to me.
    Why don't you read the letter yourself?
    Because _____

Strategy Practice: Why

DIRECTIONS: Listen to the conversations on the audio and then answer the following questions. Remember to use the listening strategies described on page 74.

1. Why was Ms. Boggs late?   Ⓐ   Ⓑ   Ⓒ   Ⓓ
    (A)   She had car trouble.
    (B)   The bus broke down.
    (C)   The bus didn't stop.
    (D)   The train wasn't on time.

2. Why won't anyone come to the picnic?   Ⓐ   Ⓑ   Ⓒ   Ⓓ
    (A)   People work on Monday.
    (B)   It's raining.
    (C)   It starts at ten o'clock.
    (D)   It's not fun.

3. Why was the man pleased?   Ⓐ   Ⓑ   Ⓒ   Ⓓ
    (A)   The woman finished the memo.
    (B)   The woman is never late.
    (C)   He has a new desk.
    (D)   He likes to wait.

4. Why won't the speakers finish the letter today?   Ⓐ Ⓑ Ⓒ Ⓓ
   (A)   They need a new pen.
   (B)   They can't make it better.
   (C)   They need five stamps.
   (D)   There's not enough time.

5. Why can't the woman sign the memo?   Ⓐ Ⓑ Ⓒ Ⓓ
   (A)   She doesn't have time.
   (B)   It isn't typed yet.
   (C)   Her pen doesn't work.
   (D)   She can't think.

6. Why does the man want to be read to?   Ⓐ Ⓑ Ⓒ Ⓓ
   (A)   He broke his glasses.
   (B)   He forgot his glasses.
   (C)   He lost his glasses.
   (D)   He lent his glasses.

7. Why are the speakers taking the train?   Ⓐ Ⓑ Ⓒ Ⓓ
   (A)   The roads are covered with snow.
   (B)   They don't know how to drive.
   (C)   The roads are closed.
   (D)   It might rain.

8. Why will the speakers walk?   Ⓐ Ⓑ Ⓒ Ⓓ
   (A)   They prefer walking.
   (B)   They want to get some exercise.
   (C)   The bus was full.
   (D)   The car was out of gas.

9. Why didn't the man talk to the woman earlier?   Ⓐ Ⓑ Ⓒ Ⓓ
   (A)   Her line was busy.
   (B)   She went to the doctor's.
   (C)   He wasn't feeling well.
   (D)   Her phone was broken.

10. Why did the woman's shoes hurt her feet?   Ⓐ Ⓑ Ⓒ Ⓓ
   (A)   They were old.
   (B)   They were too big.
   (C)   They were new.
   (D)   They were too narrow.

11. Why can't the man make copies today?   Ⓐ Ⓑ Ⓒ Ⓓ
    (A)   The copier is broken.
    (B)   He doesn't have time.
    (C)   It's too late.
    (D)   It's before noon.

12. Why did they take Mr. Lee to dinner?   Ⓐ Ⓑ Ⓒ Ⓓ
    (A)   He was hungry.
    (B)   The restaurant is new.
    (C)   He doesn't have money.
    (D)   It was his birthday.

13. Why didn't Cindy join her friends for lunch?   Ⓐ Ⓑ Ⓒ Ⓓ
    (A)   She was at a meeting.
    (B)   She doesn't like sandwiches.
    (C)   She wasn't hungry.
    (D)   She was busy working.

14. Why did the man return the suit?   Ⓐ Ⓑ Ⓒ Ⓓ
    (A)   It was too expensive.
    (B)   It didn't fit well.
    (C)   He didn't like the color.
    (D)   The collar was too dark.

15. Why did Jack get a raise?   Ⓐ Ⓑ Ⓒ Ⓓ
    (A)   He's been working at the company for a long time.
    (B)   He's been a hard worker.
    (C)   He gave money to the company.
    (D)   He gets along well with everyone.

TOEIC Test Practice

DIRECTIONS: On the TOEIC test, you will need to remember specific details from the conversation. You will have to improve your memory as well as your listening skills. Read the questions quickly before you listen to the conversation and then listen for the answers.

CONVERSATION 1 (Questions 1–3)

1. Why did the woman miss the meeting?   Ⓐ Ⓑ Ⓒ Ⓓ
   (A)   She had a problem with her car.
   (B)   She didn't leave home on time.
   (C)   She was feeling tired.
   (D)   She was sick.

2. What time did the meeting start? Ⓐ Ⓑ Ⓒ Ⓓ
   (A) 1:00.
   (B) 8:00.
   (C) 9:00.
   (D) 10:00.

3. Why did the man leave his notes for his secretary? Ⓐ Ⓑ Ⓒ Ⓓ
   (A) She has to file them.
   (B) She wants to read them.
   (C) She will make copies of them.
   (D) She will rewrite them.

CONVERSATION 2 (Questions 4–6)

4. Where are the speakers going? Ⓐ Ⓑ Ⓒ Ⓓ
   (A) To a soccer game.
   (B) To the theater.
   (C) Out of town.
   (D) To a park.

5. Why doesn't the woman want to drive? Ⓐ Ⓑ Ⓒ Ⓓ
   (A) It's difficult to find parking.
   (B) Her car broke down.
   (C) The bus is faster.
   (D) The bus is free.

6. What time do they have to arrive? Ⓐ Ⓑ Ⓒ Ⓓ
   (A) 5:15.
   (B) 5:30.
   (C) 6:00.
   (D) 7:00.

CONVERSATION 3 (Questions 7–9)

7. Why does the woman want to borrow money? Ⓐ Ⓑ Ⓒ Ⓓ
   (A) To buy a wallet.
   (B) To buy lunch.
   (C) To buy coffee.
   (D) To buy a book.

8. When will the woman pay the money back? Ⓐ Ⓑ Ⓒ Ⓓ
   (A) This afternoon.
   (B) Tonight.
   (C) Tomorrow.
   (D) In two days.

9. How much does the man give her?   Ⓐ Ⓑ Ⓒ Ⓓ
    (A) $2.
    (B) $3.
    (C) $8.
    (D) $10.

CONVERSATION 4 (Questions 10–12)

10. Why doesn't the man want to go to the seafood restaurant?   Ⓐ Ⓑ Ⓒ Ⓓ
    (A) There are too many people.
    (B) The food isn't good.
    (C) It's too expensive.
    (D) It's closed tonight.

11. Where will the speakers go after dinner?   Ⓐ Ⓑ Ⓒ Ⓓ
    (A) To a play.
    (B) To the movies.
    (C) Shopping.
    (D) Home.

12. When do they have to leave?   Ⓐ Ⓑ Ⓒ Ⓓ
    (A) Right now.
    (B) In 15 minutes.
    (C) In 50 minutes.
    (D) In two hours.

CONVERSATION 5 (Questions 13–15)

13. Why was the meeting canceled?   Ⓐ Ⓑ Ⓒ Ⓓ
    (A) The boss is out of town.
    (B) The woman's presentation isn't ready.
    (C) Everyone has been working too hard.
    (D) The accountant is sick.

14. How did the woman hear about the canceled meeting?   Ⓐ Ⓑ Ⓒ Ⓓ
    (A) She got an e-mail.
    (B) The man called her.
    (C) Her boss told her.
    (D) She got a memo.

15. What day is the meeting rescheduled for?   Ⓐ Ⓑ Ⓒ Ⓓ
    (A) Tuesday.
    (B) Wednesday.
    (C) Thursday.
    (D) Friday.

REVIEW: PART 3

DIRECTIONS: Listen to the conversations and choose the appropriate answers to the questions. There will be three questions for each conversation.

1. When will the meeting be held?   Ⓐ Ⓑ Ⓒ Ⓓ
   (A)   Today.
   (B)   Tonight.
   (C)   Tomorrow morning.
   (D)   Tomorrow afternoon.

2. How many people will be at the meeting?   Ⓐ Ⓑ Ⓒ Ⓓ
   (A)   11.
   (B)   15.
   (C)   16.
   (D)   17.

3. Where does the woman want to have the meeting?   Ⓐ Ⓑ Ⓒ Ⓓ
   (A)   In the cafeteria.
   (B)   In the reading room.
   (C)   In the assistant's office.
   (D)   In the conference room.

4. How is the weather?   Ⓐ Ⓑ Ⓒ Ⓓ
   (A)   It's snowing.
   (B)   It's raining.
   (C)   It's sunny.
   (D)   It's hot.

5. When will Marina arrive?   Ⓐ Ⓑ Ⓒ Ⓓ
   (A)   9:00 A.M.
   (B)   10:00 A.M.
   (C)   11:30 A.M.
   (D)   2:30 P.M.

6. How is Marina traveling?   Ⓐ Ⓑ Ⓒ Ⓓ
   (A)   By bus.
   (B)   By car.
   (C)   By train.
   (D)   By plane.

7. When is the man leaving for his vacation? Ⓐ Ⓑ Ⓒ Ⓓ
   (A)   On Monday.
   (B)   On the weekend.
   (C)   In two weeks.
   (D)   In a month.

8. How often does he take a vacation? Ⓐ Ⓑ Ⓒ Ⓓ
   (A)   Once a month.
   (B)   Once a year.
   (C)   Twice a year.
   (D)   Three times a year.

9. Where will he spend his vacation? Ⓐ Ⓑ Ⓒ Ⓓ
   (A)   In the mountains.
   (B)   On a boat.
   (C)   At the beach.
   (D)   By a lake.

10. Why doesn't the man order shrimp? Ⓐ Ⓑ Ⓒ Ⓓ
    (A)   He doesn't like it.
    (B)   He has an allergy to it.
    (C)   It costs too much.
    (D)   It's not on the menu.

11. How much does the tuna special cost? Ⓐ Ⓑ Ⓒ Ⓓ
    (A) $7.50.
    (B) $11.00.
    (C) $17.00.
    (D) $17.50.

12. What will the man order? Ⓐ Ⓑ Ⓒ Ⓓ
    (A)   Shrimp.
    (B)   Tuna.
    (C)   Rice.
    (D)   Spaghetti.

13. Where is the woman going?   Ⓐ   Ⓑ   Ⓒ   Ⓓ
   (A)   The bank.
   (B)   The post office.
   (C)   The office supply store.
   (D)   The supply closet.

14. What does the man want?   Ⓐ   Ⓑ   Ⓒ   Ⓓ
   (A)   Paper.
   (B)   Folders.
   (C)   Pencils.
   (D)   Pens.

15. How much money does the man give the woman?   Ⓐ   Ⓑ   Ⓒ   Ⓓ
   (A) $10.00.
   (B) $15.00.
   (C) $20.00.
   (D) $25.00.

16. When is the meeting?   Ⓐ   Ⓑ   Ⓒ   Ⓓ
   (A)   Today.
   (B)   Tomorrow.
   (C)   Tuesday.
   (D)   Next week.

17. Where is the meeting?   Ⓐ   Ⓑ   Ⓒ   Ⓓ
   (A)   In a conference room.
   (B)   In the man's office.
   (C)   In New York.
   (D)   In a hotel.

18. Why can't the man attend the meeting?   Ⓐ   Ⓑ   Ⓒ   Ⓓ
   (A)   He will be at a conference.
   (B)   He will be away on a trip.
   (C)   His car broke down.
   (D)   He doesn't feel well.

19. Who is the woman talking to?   Ⓐ Ⓑ Ⓒ Ⓓ
    (A) Her doctor.
    (B) Her assistant.
    (C) A massage therapist.
    (D) A telephone operator.

20. Why was the woman late for her appointment?   Ⓐ Ⓑ Ⓒ Ⓓ
    (A) She had a hard time driving in the dark.
    (B) She couldn't find the doctor's office.
    (C) She had to make a phone call.
    (D) She couldn't park the car.

21. Where did the man put the messages?   Ⓐ Ⓑ Ⓒ Ⓓ
    (A) On the door.
    (B) In the desk.
    (C) On the floor.
    (D) In the apartment.

22. What is the woman's job?   Ⓐ Ⓑ Ⓒ Ⓓ
    (A) Bus driver.
    (B) Taxi driver.
    (C) Tour guide.
    (D) Train conductor.

23. Why is the fare higher than the man expected?   Ⓐ Ⓑ Ⓒ Ⓓ
    (A) It's snowing.
    (B) It's late at night.
    (C) He took a long trip.
    (D) All the prices have changed.

24. What is the man doing?   Ⓐ Ⓑ Ⓒ Ⓓ
    (A) Paying.
    (B) Asking directions.
    (C) Giving directions.
    (D) Asking the time.

25. Why are the speakers upset?   (A) (B) (C) (D)
    (A) The water is bad.
    (B) Their watches are broken.
    (C) The food doesn't taste good.
    (D) They've been waiting for a long time.

26. What time do they have to leave the restaurant?   (A) (B) (C) (D)
    (A) 3:00.
    (B) 4:00.
    (C) 8:00.
    (D) 9:00.

27. What will they do next?   (A) (B) (C) (D)
    (A) Go home.
    (B) Take a rest.
    (C) Hear some music.
    (D) Go to another restaurant.

28. Where are the speakers?   (A) (B) (C) (D)
    (A) At work.
    (B) At home.
    (C) At the garage.
    (D) At the bus stop.

29. Why does the woman take the bus?   (A) (B) (C) (D)
    (A) It's fast.
    (B) It's relaxing.
    (C) It's always on time.
    (D) It's cheaper than a taxi.

30. How long does the bus ride take?   (A) (B) (C) (D)
    (A) Half an hour.
    (B) Forty minutes.
    (C) Forty-five minutes.
    (D) An hour.

PART 4: TALKS

The following exercises will help you develop strategies for listening to talks and choosing the best response. They will also help you improve your vocabulary in specific ways.

VOCABULARY STRATEGIES

- From the questions and answer choices, try to guess what the talk is about.

- Listen for words in the conversation associated with the six topics listed below.

  Advertisements
  Weather
  News
  Recorded Announcements
  Special Announcements
  Business Announcements

LISTENING STRATEGIES

- Read the questions and answer choices before you hear the audio.

- Listen for the answers to the questions.

- Answer the questions quickly before the next talk begins.

- If you do not know an answer, guess. Do not try to work on a question after the next talk has started.

  Since each talk will be spoken only once, you must listen to each talk carefully to understand and remember what is being said.

TALKS: ADVERTISEMENTS

Vocabulary Practice A

DIRECTIONS: Match the type of advertisement with its usual location.

Type	Location
1. _____ print ads	a. streets, sides of buildings
2. _____ pop-up ads	b. radio, TV
3. _____ commercials	c. web sites
4. _____ billboards	d. magazines, newspapers

Vocabulary Practice B

DIRECTIONS: Write the correct form of the word in the sentence.

for sale   sale   selling

1. The used cars will not be _____ until they have been inspected.

2. The _____ lasts until Friday.

3. We're _____ our entire inventory.

to sell   sold   on sale

4. Hurry. This offer won't last. All stock _____ for only two more days!

5. The plan is _____ everything at 50 percent off.

6. Once a product is _____, we take it off the web site.

subscribes   subscriptions   subscribers

7. I have _____ for every major daily paper.

8. My office _____ to an e-newsletter.

9. Our magazine has over 3 million _____.

advertises advertisers advertisements

10. I want to block the pop-up _____ when I surf the Internet.

11. All _____ want to reach the largest market possible.

12. Our travel agent _____ the lowest fares to Europe.

TOEIC Test Practice

DIRECTIONS: You will hear ten advertisements. They will not be repeated. Below you will read three questions about each advertisement. After you listen to the advertisement, answer the questions.

TALK 1 (Questions 1–3)

1. What is being sold?   Ⓐ Ⓑ Ⓒ Ⓓ
  (A) Used cars.
  (B) Ship models.
  (C) Used televisions.
  (D) Computers.

2. How much can a buyer save? Ⓐ Ⓑ Ⓒ Ⓓ
  (A) One thousand dollars.
  (B) Over one thousand dollars.
  (C) Five percent of the total.
  (D) Ten percent of the total.

3. When will the sale end?   Ⓐ Ⓑ Ⓒ Ⓓ
  (A) Today.
  (B) Tomorrow.
  (C) In five days.
  (D) In two weeks.

TALK 2 (Questions 4–6)

4. How long is the sale?   Ⓐ Ⓑ Ⓒ Ⓓ
  (A) One day.
  (B) Two days.
  (C) Five days.
  (D) One week.

5. What is on sale?   Ⓐ Ⓑ Ⓒ Ⓓ
  (A) Clothing.
  (B) Kitchen chairs.
  (C) Office furniture.
  (D) Computers.

6. What is the discount on chairs? Ⓐ Ⓑ Ⓒ Ⓓ
    (A) 15 percent.
    (B) 17 percent.
    (C) 50 percent.
    (D) 75 percent.

TALK 3 (Questions 7–9)

7. What kind of sale is it? Ⓐ Ⓑ Ⓒ Ⓓ
    (A) Holiday.
    (B) Back-to-school.
    (C) Damaged goods.
    (D) Weekend.

8. What is on sale? Ⓐ Ⓑ Ⓒ Ⓓ
    (A) Notebooks.
    (B) Pens.
    (C) Paper.
    (D) A store.

9. How can you get a free notebook? Ⓐ Ⓑ Ⓒ Ⓓ
    (A) Buy more than ten notebooks.
    (B) Buy more than ten pens.
    (C) Arrive before 10:00.
    (D) Bring ten friends.

TALK 4 (Questions 10–12)

10. What kind of insurance is being sold? Ⓐ Ⓑ Ⓒ Ⓓ
    (A) Car.
    (B) Life.
    (C) Fire.
    (D) Health.

11. What must one be to get this insurance? Ⓐ Ⓑ Ⓒ Ⓓ
    (A) Sixty years old or older.
    (B) In good health.
    (C) A doctor.
    (D) Married.

12. How can one get information about this insurance? Ⓐ Ⓑ Ⓒ Ⓓ
    (A) Send an e-mail.
    (B) Visit an office.
    (C) Write a letter.
    (D) Make a phone call.

TALK 5 (Questions 13–15)

13. What is being advertised?   Ⓐ Ⓑ Ⓒ Ⓓ
    (A) Calendars.
    (B) Sunglasses.
    (C) Airfares.
    (D) Vacations.

14. What is the longest package available?   Ⓐ Ⓑ Ⓒ Ⓓ
    (A) Five days.
    (B) One week.
    (C) 350 days.
    (D) One year.

15. What does the $350 NOT include?   Ⓐ Ⓑ Ⓒ Ⓓ
    (A) Hotel.
    (B) Meals.
    (C) Airfare.
    (D) Golf lessons.

TALK 6 (Questions 16–18)

16. What is being advertised?   Ⓐ Ⓑ Ⓒ Ⓓ
    (A) A bakery.
    (B) A seafood store.
    (C) A grocery store.
    (D) A restaurant.

17. When can you buy desserts?   Ⓐ Ⓑ Ⓒ Ⓓ
    (A) Today only.
    (B) On Friday.
    (C) Once a week.
    (D) Every day.

18. Who can get a discount?   Ⓐ Ⓑ Ⓒ Ⓓ
    (A) Groups of at least eight people.
    (B) People who buy food for a party.
    (C) People who arrive later than 8:00.
    (D) Anyone who calls a certain phone number.

TALK 7 (Questions 19–21)

19. When will the orchestra perform?   Ⓐ Ⓑ Ⓒ Ⓓ
    (A) Next Monday.
    (B) Next Thursday.
    (C) Next week.
    (D) Next month.

20. How much is the cheapest ticket? Ⓐ Ⓑ Ⓒ Ⓓ
    (A) $10.
    (B) $15.
    (C) $35.
    (D) $55.

21. Who can get a discount on tickets? Ⓐ Ⓑ Ⓒ Ⓓ
    (A) Students.
    (B) Groups.
    (C) Orchestra members.
    (D) Senior citizens.

TALK 8 (Questions 22–24)

22. What's on sale? Ⓐ Ⓑ Ⓒ Ⓓ
    (A) Business suits.
    (B) Summer clothes.
    (C) Sunday dresses.
    (D) School clothes.

23. When is the store open? Ⓐ Ⓑ Ⓒ Ⓓ
    (A) From 8:00 to 10:30.
    (B) From 10:00 to 10:00.
    (C) From 2:00 to 4:00.
    (D) From 2:00 to 5:00.

24. When is the sale over? Ⓐ Ⓑ Ⓒ Ⓓ
    (A) August 3rd.
    (B) August 13th.
    (C) August 30th.
    (D) August 31st.

TALK 9 (Questions 25–27)

25. Where does the bus go? Ⓐ Ⓑ Ⓒ Ⓓ
    (A) To the bus station.
    (B) To the park.
    (C) To the airport.
    (D) Downtown.

26. How often does the bus leave? Ⓐ Ⓑ Ⓒ Ⓓ
    (A) Every twenty minutes.
    (B) Every thirty minutes.
    (C) Every hour.
    (D) Every other day.

27. How much do the tickets cost?   Ⓐ Ⓑ Ⓒ Ⓓ
    (A) $9.00.
    (B) $10.00.
    (C) $12.00.
    (D) $20.00.

TALK 10 (Questions 28–30)

28. What is the magazine about?   Ⓐ Ⓑ Ⓒ Ⓓ
    (A) Gardening.
    (B) Cooking.
    (C) Factories.
    (D) Computers.

29. How often is the magazine published?   Ⓐ Ⓑ Ⓒ Ⓓ
    (A) Daily.
    (B) Weekly.
    (C) Monthly.
    (D) Yearly.

30. How can subscribers get a 25 percent discount?   Ⓐ Ⓑ Ⓒ Ⓓ
    (A) Order a subscription online.
    (B) Order a two-year subscription.
    (C) Order a subscription by mail.
    (D) Order a subscription this week.

TALKS: WEATHER

Vocabulary Practice A

DIRECTIONS: Match the synonyms.

1. _____ cool   **a.** snowstorm

2. _____ very breezy   **b.** showers

3. _____ mild   **c.** sunny skies

4. _____ hot   **d.** comfortable

5. _____ freezing   **e.** windy

6. _____ rain   **f.** tropical windstorm

7. _____ clear   **g.** chilly

8. _____ cloudy   **h.** very warm

9. _____ typhoon   **i.** not clear

10. _____ blizzard   **j.** very cold

Vocabulary Practice B

DIRECTIONS: Use the words from the lists above to complete these sentences. (There may be more than one option.)

1. It's _____ outside, so I need to dress warmly.

2. I'll take my umbrella because it looks like _____.

3. It's getting _____ out, so we should close the windows in case it rains.

4. It's too _____ to play tennis.

5. When the sky is _____, it's good weather to fly.

6. It's not too hot and it's not too cold; the weather is nice and _____ for this time of year.

7. It's colder than cold. It's _____!

8. The light snowstorm turned into a heavy _____, and now all the roads are icy.

9. I want to go to the beach when the skies are _____, not when the skies are cloudy.

10. Hurricanes, also known as _____ in Asia, can cause lots of damage to buildings and homes.

TOEIC Test Practice

DIRECTIONS: You will hear ten weather reports. They will not be repeated. Below you will read three questions about each report. After you listen to the weather report, answer the questions.

TALK 1 (Questions 1–3)

1. What is today's weather?   Ⓐ Ⓑ Ⓒ Ⓓ
   - (A) Snowy.
   - (B) Cloudy.
   - (C) Rainy.
   - (D) Sunny.

2. What will the temperature be tomorrow?   Ⓐ Ⓑ Ⓒ Ⓓ
   - (A) Warm.
   - (B) Hot.
   - (C) Mild.
   - (D) Cold.

3. When will it rain?   Ⓐ Ⓑ Ⓒ Ⓓ
   - (A) Tomorrow.
   - (B) On the weekend.
   - (C) Next week.
   - (D) Wednesday or Thursday.

TALK 2 (Questions 4–6)

4. When will the rain begin?   Ⓐ Ⓑ Ⓒ Ⓓ
   - (A) Tonight.
   - (B) Tomorrow morning.
   - (C) In the afternoon.
   - (D) By tomorrow night.

5. When will the showers stop?   Ⓐ Ⓑ Ⓒ Ⓓ
   - (A) By tonight.
   - (B) By tomorrow morning.
   - (C) By tomorrow afternoon.
   - (D) By late tomorrow evening.

6. How will the weather be on the weekend?   Ⓐ Ⓑ Ⓒ Ⓓ
   (A)   Warm.
   (B)   Misty.
   (C)   Rainy.
   (D)   Cold.

TALK 3 (Questions 7–9)

7. When might it rain?   Ⓐ Ⓑ Ⓒ Ⓓ
   (A)   This afternoon.
   (B)   Late tonight.
   (C)   Tomorrow morning.
   (D)   Tomorrow night.

8. What might follow the rain?   Ⓐ Ⓑ Ⓒ Ⓓ
   (A)   Sunny skies.
   (B)   Snow.
   (C)   Thundershowers.
   (D)   A typhoon.

9. What will the temperature be tomorrow?   Ⓐ Ⓑ Ⓒ Ⓓ
   (A)   Hot.
   (B)   Warm.
   (C)   Cool.
   (D)   Cold.

TALK 4 (Questions 10–12)

10. What was the temperature today?   Ⓐ Ⓑ Ⓒ Ⓓ
   (A)   Hot.
   (B)   Cool.
   (C)   Mild.
   (D)   Average.

11. How were the winds described?   Ⓐ Ⓑ Ⓒ Ⓓ
   (A)   Cool.
   (B)   Light.
   (C)   Warm.
   (D)   Strong.

12. What is the season?   Ⓐ Ⓑ Ⓒ Ⓓ
   (A)   Spring.
   (B)   Summer.
   (C)   Fall.
   (D)   Winter.

TALK 5 (Questions 13–15)

13. When was the temperature measured? Ⓐ Ⓑ Ⓒ Ⓓ
    (A) In the morning.
    (B) At noon.
    (C) In the afternoon.
    (D) In the evening.

14. Where was the temperature measured? Ⓐ Ⓑ Ⓒ Ⓓ
    (A) Downtown.
    (B) At the airport.
    (C) At school.
    (D) At the dock.

15. What was the temperature? Ⓐ Ⓑ Ⓒ Ⓓ
    (A) 12 degrees Fahrenheit.
    (B) 12 degrees Celsius.
    (C) 21 degrees Fahrenheit.
    (D) 21 degrees Celsius.

TALK 6 (Questions 16–18)

16. What will the temperature be like today? Ⓐ Ⓑ Ⓒ Ⓓ
    (A) Cold.
    (B) Warm.
    (C) Cool.
    (D) Freezing.

17. How was the weather yesterday? Ⓐ Ⓑ Ⓒ Ⓓ
    (A) Clear.
    (B) Rainy.
    (C) Snowy.
    (D) Warm.

18. When will it snow? Ⓐ Ⓑ Ⓒ Ⓓ
    (A) Today.
    (B) Tomorrow.
    (C) Tuesday.
    (D) Thursday.

TALK 7 (Questions 19-21)

19. How is the weather today? Ⓐ Ⓑ Ⓒ Ⓓ
    (A) Stormy.
    (B) Sunny.
    (C) Rainy.
    (D) Cloudy.

20. When will it rain again?

    (A) All week.

    (B) On the weekend.

    (C) Next week.

    (D) In two weeks.

Ⓐ Ⓑ Ⓒ Ⓓ

21. What will happen in the middle of the week?

    (A) The temperature will become pleasant.

    (B) Temperatures will increase.

    (C) It will be windy.

    (D) The rain will stop.

Ⓐ Ⓑ Ⓒ Ⓓ

TALK 8 (Questions 22–24)

22. Why are the beaches closed?

    (A) The water will freeze.

    (B) It will be very cold.

    (C) It might snow.

    (D) The winds are dangerous.

Ⓐ Ⓑ Ⓒ Ⓓ

23. How will the weather be during the weekend?

    (A) Freezing.

    (B) Cloudy.

    (C) Sunny.

    (D) Snowy.

Ⓐ Ⓑ Ⓒ Ⓓ

24. When might there be snow?

    (A) In the morning.

    (B) At midday.

    (C) After midnight.

    (D) On Monday.

Ⓐ Ⓑ Ⓒ Ⓓ

TALK 9 (Questions 25–27)

25. What was today's temperature?

    (A) 55 degrees.

    (B) 57 degrees.

    (C) 75 degrees.

    (D) 90 degrees.

Ⓐ Ⓑ Ⓒ Ⓓ

26. How was today's temperature described?   Ⓐ Ⓑ Ⓒ Ⓓ
    (A)   Too high.
    (B)   Average.
    (C)   Above average.
    (D)   Unusual.

27. How was today's weather?   Ⓐ Ⓑ Ⓒ Ⓓ
    (A)   Cloudy.
    (B)   Sunny.
    (C)   Rainy.
    (D)   Windy.

TALK 10 (Questions 28–30)

28. What season is it?   Ⓐ Ⓑ Ⓒ Ⓓ
    (A)   Spring.
    (B)   Winter.
    (C)   Summer.
    (D)   Fall.

29. What is the weather today?   Ⓐ Ⓑ Ⓒ Ⓓ
    (A)   Rainy.
    (B)   Sunny.
    (C)   Clear.
    (D)   Snowy.

30. When will the skies be cloudy?   Ⓐ Ⓑ Ⓒ Ⓓ
    (A)   Next weekend.
    (B)   Next week.
    (C)   Next spring.
    (D)   Next summer.

TALKS: NEWS

Vocabulary Practice A

DIRECTIONS: Cross out the word that does not belong.

1. political   government   election   vote   game

2. cultural   math   art   concert   play

3. economic   finance   realtor   money   fiscal

4. tour   travel   trip   vacation   street

5. month   day   week   year   pound

6. high-speed   fast   convenient   quick   accelerated

Vocabulary Practice B

DIRECTIONS: Complete the sentences below using the following reasons.

because it hasn't rained

in order to see the parade

because of the snowstorm

because of the increase in the sales tax

because of the holiday

because it is so light

because they finally signed the agreement

1. The laptop computer is useful for business travelers _____.

2. The participants celebrated with a dinner _____.

3. We are experiencing a drought _____.

4. The town hall was closed _____.

5. The patients received gifts _____.

6. Everyone came downtown _____.

7. People will purchase less than before _____.

DIRECTIONS: You will hear ten news items. They will not be repeated. Below you will read three questions about each item. After you listen to the news item, answer the questions.

TALK 1 (Questions 1–3)

1. With what does the city have a problem? (A) (B) (C) (D)
   (A) Schools.
   (B) Crime.
   (C) Electricity.
   (D) Water.

2. When is rain expected? (A) (B) (C) (D)
   (A) In less than a week.
   (B) In a week.
   (C) Next week.
   (D) Not for several weeks.

3. How can residents get more information? (A) (B) (C) (D)
   (A) By visiting the web site of the Central Water Authority.
   (B) By calling the city government.
   (C) By visiting the city government web site.
   (D) By calling the radio station.

TALK 2 (Questions 4–6)

4. What word was used to describe the gifts? (A) (B) (C) (D)
   (A) Beautiful.
   (B) Expensive.
   (C) Useful.
   (D) Holiday.

5. Who distributed presents? (A) (B) (C) (D)
   (A) Children.
   (B) Doctors.
   (C) Nurses.
   (D) Patients.

6. When will there be a party for hospital patients? (A) (B) (C) (D)
   (A) Sunday.
   (B) Monday.
   (C) Tuesday.
   (D) Wednesday.

TALK 3 (Questions 7–9)

7. What is the advantage of this computer?   Ⓐ Ⓑ Ⓒ Ⓓ
   (A) Large memory.
   (B) Small size.
   (C) Sturdy construction.
   (D) Low price.

8. Who will find the computer most useful?   Ⓐ Ⓑ Ⓒ Ⓓ
   (A) Business travelers.
   (B) Stock market brokers.
   (C) Secretaries.
   (D) Travel agents.

9. When will the new computer arrive in stores?   Ⓐ Ⓑ Ⓒ Ⓓ
   (A) Today.
   (B) On Tuesday.
   (C) In two weeks.
   (D) In two months.

TALK 4 (Questions 10–12)

10. Why were public offices closed?   Ⓐ Ⓑ Ⓒ Ⓓ
    (A) Because of the heavy snowfall.
    (B) Because of the holiday.
    (C) Because it was lunchtime.
    (D) Because it was a weekend.

11. When will schools reopen?   Ⓐ Ⓑ Ⓒ Ⓓ
    (A) Tomorrow.
    (B) Next week.
    (C) Next month.
    (D) In the fall.

12. What are residents advised to do?   Ⓐ Ⓑ Ⓒ Ⓓ
    (A) Run for public office.
    (B) Go to school.
    (C) Stay at home.
    (D) Repair the roads.

TALK 5 (Questions 13–15)

13. What kind of agreement was signed? Ⓐ Ⓑ Ⓒ Ⓓ
    (A) Political.
    (B) Cultural.
    (C) Economic.
    (D) Trade.

14. What took place after the signing? Ⓐ Ⓑ Ⓒ Ⓓ
    (A) A concert.
    (B) A dinner.
    (C) A play.
    (D) A dance.

15. Which of the following groups is Ⓐ Ⓑ Ⓒ Ⓓ
    NOT part of the agreement?
    (A) Artists.
    (B) Drama.
    (C) Orchestras.
    (D) Ballet.

TALK 6 (Questions 16–18)

16. How long will the tour last? Ⓐ Ⓑ Ⓒ Ⓓ
    (A) One week.
    (B) Two weeks.
    (C) Five weeks.
    (D) Twelve weeks.

17. Where did the president go? Ⓐ Ⓑ Ⓒ Ⓓ
    (A) To Asia.
    (B) To Malaysia.
    (C) To Indonesia.
    (D) To Australia.

18. Who is traveling with the president? Ⓐ Ⓑ Ⓒ Ⓓ
    (A) His wife.
    (B) Office workers.
    (C) A tour guide.
    (D) The foreign minister.

TALK 7 (Questions 19–21)

19. What happened to Marisol's employees? Ⓐ Ⓑ Ⓒ Ⓓ
    - (A) They were terminated.
    - (B) They were promoted.
    - (C) They were transferred.
    - (D) They were given reduced pensions.

20. How many workers were affected? Ⓐ Ⓑ Ⓒ Ⓓ
    - (A) Two.
    - (B) Ten.
    - (C) A hundred.
    - (D) All of them.

21. What will happen to Marisol within two years? Ⓐ Ⓑ Ⓒ Ⓓ
    - (A) It will stay in Miami.
    - (B) It will move to Santo Domingo.
    - (C) It will hire back the workers.
    - (D) It will be bought by RTV Satellite.

TALK 8 (Questions 22–24)

22. What happened yesterday? Ⓐ Ⓑ Ⓒ Ⓓ
    - (A) There was free parking downtown.
    - (B) It rained.
    - (C) There was a parade.
    - (D) A new mayor was elected.

23. What did people do in the afternoon? Ⓐ Ⓑ Ⓒ Ⓓ
    - (A) They went to a concert in the park.
    - (B) They went home early.
    - (C) They followed the parade.
    - (D) They played ball.

24. How was the weather? Ⓐ Ⓑ Ⓒ Ⓓ
    - (A) Pleasant.
    - (B) Icy.
    - (C) Windy.
    - (D) Not nice.

TALK 9 (Questions 25–27)

25. How much is the new sales tax? Ⓐ Ⓑ Ⓒ Ⓓ
    - (A) 5 percent.
    - (B) 7 percent.
    - (C) 52 percent.
    - (D) 57 percent.

26. What might be a result of the new sales tax? Ⓐ Ⓑ Ⓒ Ⓓ
    - (A) People will buy new clothes.
    - (B) Some stores will have big sales.
    - (C) People will buy fewer things.
    - (D) Some new stores will open next month.

27. When will the new sales tax go into effect? Ⓐ Ⓑ Ⓒ Ⓓ
    - (A) Today.
    - (B) Next Monday.
    - (C) In two weeks.
    - (D) Next month.

TALK 10 (Questions 28–30)

28. When did high-speed train service begin? Ⓐ Ⓑ Ⓒ Ⓓ
    - (A) Last month.
    - (B) Last week.
    - (C) Yesterday.
    - (D) Last night.

29. Why do people like the train? Ⓐ Ⓑ Ⓒ Ⓓ
    - (A) It's faster than the plane.
    - (B) It's new.
    - (C) It's convenient.
    - (D) It takes a long time.

30. How long is the plane trip to the capital? Ⓐ Ⓑ Ⓒ Ⓓ
    - (A) 1 hour.
    - (B) 2 hours and 45 minutes.
    - (C) 3 hours.
    - (D) 3 hours and 45 minutes.

TALKS: RECORDED ANNOUNCEMENTS

Vocabulary Practice A

DIRECTIONS: Where do you call to find out certain information? Write the source.

You want to know:

1. the temperature _____

2. the time a film starts _____

3. the hours a reference desk is open _____

4. why you're having computer trouble _____

5. about job vacancies _____

6. how to get a driver's license _____

7. features about different office products _____

You call this source:

a. motor vehicles department

b. technical support

c. weather information

d. cinema hotline

e. library

f. employment helpline

g. customer service

Vocabulary Practice B

DIRECTIONS: Read the answer and write the question.

1. The museum will close at 9 P.M. on Sunday.

   When _____

2. All applicants should send an e-mail with their résumés.

   What _____

3. Guests are not permitted to play on Sunday or Monday.

   On what _____

4. The library is closed for a staff meeting.

   Why _____

5. All calls will be answered in the order they are received.

   How _____

6. A caller would contact this office for information on a product.

   Why _____

7. An adult ticket costs $9.00.

   How much _____

8. In an emergency, you should hang up and dial 911.

   What _____

9. You should bring a photo and proof of citizenship when you apply for a license.

   What _____

10. The store will close early because of the storm.

    Why _____

TOEIC Test Practice

DIRECTIONS: You will hear ten recorded announcements. They will not be repeated. Below you will read three questions about each announcement. After you listen to the announcement, answer the questions.

TALK 1 (Questions 1–3)

1. What time does the museum close on Tuesday?   Ⓐ Ⓑ Ⓒ Ⓓ
   (A) 4 P.M.
   (B) 6 P.M.
   (C) 7 P.M.
   (D) 9 P.M.

2. What day is the museum closed?   Ⓐ Ⓑ Ⓒ Ⓓ
   (A) Sunday.
   (B) Monday.
   (C) Thursday.
   (D) Friday.

3. Where should museum visitors put their coats?   Ⓐ Ⓑ Ⓒ Ⓓ
   (A) Near the back door.
   (B) On the ground floor.
   (C) In the bag room.
   (D) On the fourth floor.

TALK 2 (Questions 4–6)

4. In which of these occupations does Pacific Electronics   Ⓐ Ⓑ Ⓒ Ⓓ
   NOT have openings?
   (A) Electricians.
   (B) Plumbers.
   (C) Bricklayers.
   (D) Secretaries.

5. What should applicants do?   Ⓐ Ⓑ Ⓒ Ⓓ
 (A) Go in person.
 (B) Send references.
 (C) Request a job application.
 (D) Write a letter to the company.

6. When can people apply for a job?   Ⓐ Ⓑ Ⓒ Ⓓ
 (A) Any day.
 (B) Monday through Friday.
 (C) Monday and Friday only.
 (D) Monday, Thursday, and Friday.

TALK 3 (Questions 7–9)

7. Between what hours may only parties   Ⓐ Ⓑ Ⓒ Ⓓ
 of four people play?
 (A) 5 A.M. and 8 P.M.
 (B) 8 A.M. and 12 P.M.
 (C) 12 P.M. and 7 P.M.
 (D) 5 P.M. and 8 P.M.

8. On what days may guests NOT play?   Ⓐ Ⓑ Ⓒ Ⓓ
 (A) Monday and Tuesday.
 (B) Tuesday and Wednesday.
 (C) Thursday and Sunday.
 (D) Saturday and Sunday.

9. How often does the Senior Tournament take place?   Ⓐ Ⓑ Ⓒ Ⓓ
 (A) Every day.
 (B) Every week.
 (C) Every month.
 (D) Every year.

TALK 4 (Questions 10–12)

10. When will the library be closed?   Ⓐ Ⓑ Ⓒ Ⓓ
 (A) In 15 minutes.
 (B) Tomorrow.
 (C) During the holiday season.
 (D) January 7th.

11. What day does the library reopen?   Ⓐ Ⓑ Ⓒ Ⓓ
    (A) Monday.
    (B) Wednesday.
    (C) Friday.
    (D) Saturday.

12. When may books be returned?   Ⓐ Ⓑ Ⓒ Ⓓ
    (A) On or after January 7th.
    (B) During the holidays.
    (C) Only in the mornings.
    (D) On Saturdays.

TALK 5 (Questions 13–15)

13. Why would a caller contact this office?   Ⓐ Ⓑ Ⓒ Ⓓ
    (A) To make a complaint.
    (B) To order a product.
    (C) To get a job.
    (D) To talk to a consumer.

14. How will calls be answered?   Ⓐ Ⓑ Ⓒ Ⓓ
    (A) Patiently.
    (B) Promptly.
    (C) In the order received.
    (D) In the order of importance.

15. What is the caller advised to do?   Ⓐ Ⓑ Ⓒ Ⓓ
    (A) Hang up and try again.
    (B) Place an order.
    (C) Wait for an agent.
    (D) Talk to another agent.

TALK 6 (Questions 16–18)

16. What are the tickets for?   Ⓐ Ⓑ Ⓒ Ⓓ
    (A) A movie.
    (B) A concert.
    (C) A museum.
    (D) A fashion show.

17. How much is a ticket to the 8:00 show?   Ⓐ Ⓑ Ⓒ Ⓓ
   (A) $4.00.
   (B) $6.00.
   (C) $5.75.
   (D) $8.50.

18. Why should people get there early?   Ⓐ Ⓑ Ⓒ Ⓓ
   (A) To make a reservation.
   (B) Because tickets sell out quickly.
   (C) So that the workers can leave early.
   (D) Because the tickets are cheaper.

TALK 7 (Questions 19–21)

19. What should you do in an emergency?   Ⓐ Ⓑ Ⓒ Ⓓ
   (A) Call to make an appointment.
   (B) Call after 5:00 P.M.
   (C) Call tomorrow.
   (D) Call another phone number.

20. What should you do to speak with a nurse?   Ⓐ Ⓑ Ⓒ Ⓓ
   (A) Hang up.
   (B) Make an appointment.
   (C) Call between 9:00 A.M. and 5:00 P.M.
   (D) Visit the office tomorrow.

21. Why is Dr. Sato out of the office?   Ⓐ Ⓑ Ⓒ Ⓓ
   (A) He's on vacation.
   (B) He has an emergency.
   (C) He's at a conference.
   (D) He's sick.

TALK 8 (Questions 22–24)

22. What time does the License Office open?   Ⓐ Ⓑ Ⓒ Ⓓ
   (A) 8:00.
   (B) 8:30.
   (C) 4:00.
   (D) 4:30.

23. What do you have to bring to the License Office?   Ⓐ Ⓑ Ⓒ Ⓓ
    (A) An application.
    (B) A driver's license.
    (C) A test.
    (D) Identification.

24. How much does it cost to get a license?   Ⓐ Ⓑ Ⓒ Ⓓ
    (A) $43.
    (B) $45.
    (C) $83.
    (D) $85.

TALK 9 (Questions 25–27)

25. Where is Ms. Lee this week?   Ⓐ Ⓑ Ⓒ Ⓓ
    (A) On vacation.
    (B) In her office.
    (C) At a conference.
    (D) Visiting Mr. Roberts.

26. What is Ms. Lee's job?   Ⓐ Ⓑ Ⓒ Ⓓ
    (A) Journalist.
    (B) Office assistant.
    (C) Telephone operator.
    (D) Mail carrier.

27. What is Mr. Roberts' extension number?   Ⓐ Ⓑ Ⓒ Ⓓ
    (A) 57.
    (B) 157.
    (C) 507.
    (D) 1507.

TALK 10 (Questions 28–30)

28. What does the store sell?   Ⓐ Ⓑ Ⓒ Ⓓ
    (A) Office supplies.
    (B) Office furniture.
    (C) Office clothes.
    (D) Office telephones.

29. What day of the week is the store usually closed?   Ⓐ   Ⓑ   Ⓒ   Ⓓ

    (A)   Sunday.

    (B)   Monday.

    (C)   Tuesday.

    (D)   Friday.

30. Why will the store close early this Friday?   Ⓐ   Ⓑ   Ⓒ   Ⓓ

    (A)   For a meeting.

    (B)   Because it's the weekend.

    (C)   Because it's a holiday.

    (D)   For inventory.

TALKS: SPECIAL ANNOUNCEMENTS

Vocabulary Practice A

DIRECTIONS: Complete these sentences using these words.

main	chemistry
attentive	reviews
specialty	express
platform	guide
security guard	freight

1. I study history, but my _____ is history of ancient civilizations.

2. When I studied _____, I learned that H_2O means two parts hydrogen for one part oxygen.

3. The local train stops at every station, but the _____ train makes only one station stop.

4. Wait on _____ 9 for the train.

5. We shipped the goods with a reliable _____ company.

6. If you are not _____, you will miss important information.

7. I always read the _____ before I choose which movie to see.

8. The best _____ is one that likes people and loves to give tours.

9. You will have to show your ID to the _____ at the gate before you can be admitted.

10. Our branch office is in Miami, but our _____ office is in Madrid.

Vocabulary Practice B

DIRECTIONS: Read each sentence. Then write a new sentence using one of the following verb phrases.

taking a tour

working in the garden

getting on a plane

filling the car with gas

waiting for the express train

filling out a lost-article form

getting off at the next stop

playing golf

attending a concert

lining up for tickets

1. I enjoy planting flowers and growing vegetables.

   I'm working in the garden.

2. There will be a lot of people wanting to see this play, so I'll be at the box office early.

   _____

3. I gave my boarding pass to the gate agent and am now looking for my seat in economy class.

   _____

4. I'm new in this city, so I want to be taken to all the important sites.

   _____

5. My car is low on fuel, so I stopped at a service station.

   _____

6. I'm moving toward the door of the train so I will be ready to disembark.

   _____

7. I don't want to take the local since I'm in a hurry.

   _____

8. I enjoy all kinds of sports, especially one that keeps me outside.

   _____

9. I love watching an orchestra play.

   _____

10. I'm writing my name and address and describing what I can't find.

    _____

DIRECTIONS: You will hear ten special announcements. They will not be repeated. Below you will read three questions about each announcement. After you listen to the announcement, answer the questions.

TALK 1 (Questions 1–3)

1. Who is listening to this announcement?   Ⓐ Ⓑ Ⓒ Ⓓ
   (A) Students.
   (B) Politicians.
   (C) Reporters.
   (D) Teachers.

2. What is Professor Tran's specialty?   Ⓐ Ⓑ Ⓒ Ⓓ
   (A) Chemistry.
   (B) Biology.
   (C) Physics.
   (D) Geometry.

3. What will Professor Tran talk about tonight?   Ⓐ Ⓑ Ⓒ Ⓓ
   (A) Famous scientists.
   (B) Teaching methods.
   (C) The scientific method.
   (D) Majoring in science.

TALK 2 (Questions 4–6)

4. Who is listening to this announcement?   Ⓐ Ⓑ Ⓒ Ⓓ
   (A) Gas station attendants.
   (B) Exercise students.
   (C) Hospital patients.
   (D) Airline passengers.

5. What is NOT allowed?   Ⓐ Ⓑ Ⓒ Ⓓ
   (A) Smoking.
   (B) Sitting.
   (C) Boarding.
   (D) Eating.

6. When will the movie begin?   Ⓐ Ⓑ Ⓒ Ⓓ
   (A) In 13 minutes.
   (B) In half an hour.
   (C) At noon.
   (D) At 3:00.

TALK 3 (Questions 7–9)

7. Who is listening to this announcement?   (A) (B) (C) (D)
   (A) Children in school.
   (B) Men on a bus.
   (C) Women on a tour.
   (D) People working in the garden.

8. How long will the stop last?   (A) (B) (C) (D)
   (A) 15 minutes.
   (B) 16 minutes.
   (C) 50 minutes.
   (D) 60 minutes.

9. What time of day is this announcement being made?   (A) (B) (C) (D)
   (A) Before lunch.
   (B) After lunch.
   (C) In the evening.
   (D) At night.

TALK 4 (Questions 10–12)

10. On what kind of train is this announcement being made?   (A) (B) (C) (D)
    (A) Mail.
    (B) Freight.
    (C) Local.
    (D) Express.

11. What is across the platform?   (A) (B) (C) (D)
    (A) A cafeteria.
    (B) The local train.
    (C) The exit doors.
    (D) Some steps.

12. Where is the next stop?   (A) (B) (C) (D)
    (A) New York.
    (B) Tokyo.
    (C) Newark.
    (D) London.

TALK 5 (Questions 13–15)

13. Where is this announcement being heard?   (A) (B) (C) (D)
    (A) At a school.
    (B) At a golf course.
    (C) In a hospital.
    (D) In a theater.

14. At what time of day is this announcement being made? Ⓐ Ⓑ Ⓒ Ⓓ
- (A) In the morning.
- (B) At noon.
- (C) In the afternoon.
- (D) In the evening.

15. What is the problem being described? Ⓐ Ⓑ Ⓒ Ⓓ
- (A) Someone is sick.
- (B) There are no more rolls.
- (C) People are not attentive.
- (D) Children are playing on the stairs.

TALK 6 (Questions 16–18)

16. Where is the blue car now? Ⓐ Ⓑ Ⓒ Ⓓ
- (A) On the corner.
- (B) In the park.
- (C) In the garage.
- (D) Near the front door.

17. What should the driver of the blue car do? Ⓐ Ⓑ Ⓒ Ⓓ
- (A) Make a delivery.
- (B) Move the car.
- (C) Close the door.
- (D) Pay a parking fee.

18. What is done to cars that are NOT parked legally? Ⓐ Ⓑ Ⓒ Ⓓ
- (A) They are fined.
- (B) They are towed.
- (C) They are ticketed.
- (D) They are reparked.

TALK 7 (Questions 19–21)

19. When will the tour begin? Ⓐ Ⓑ Ⓒ Ⓓ
- (A) In 15 minutes.
- (B) In 30 minutes.
- (C) At 3:00.
- (D) At 10:00.

20. What should you do if you have a ticket? Ⓐ Ⓑ Ⓒ Ⓓ
- (A) Line up at the end of the hall.
- (B) Go to the front desk.
- (C) Tell the guide.
- (D) Wait at the front door.

21. How much are the tickets? Ⓐ Ⓑ Ⓒ Ⓓ
    (A) They're $15.00.
    (B) They're free.
    (C) They're three for the price of one.
    (D) They're $10.50.

TALK 8 (Questions 22–24)

22. Who is making the announcement? Ⓐ Ⓑ Ⓒ Ⓓ
    (A) An airplane pilot.
    (B) A ship's captain.
    (C) A flight attendant.
    (D) A passenger.

23. What does the announcer want people to do? Ⓐ Ⓑ Ⓒ Ⓓ
    (A) Sit on the other side.
    (B) Check the weather.
    (C) Look at the view.
    (D) Go swimming in the lake.

24. How is the weather? Ⓐ Ⓑ Ⓒ Ⓓ
    (A) Snowy.
    (B) Rainy.
    (C) Clear.
    (D) Cloudy.

TALK 9 (Questions 25–27)

25. What can you hear before the weather report? Ⓐ Ⓑ Ⓒ Ⓓ
    (A) A movie review.
    (B) An interview.
    (C) Music.
    (D) The news.

26. Who is Lucinda Park? Ⓐ Ⓑ Ⓒ Ⓓ
    (A) A reporter.
    (B) A musician.
    (C) A teacher.
    (D) A tour guide.

27. What will Lucinda Park talk about? Ⓐ Ⓑ Ⓒ Ⓓ
    (A) How to become famous.
    (B) Music classes.
    (C) A concert tour.
    (D) Violence around the world.

TALK 10 (Questions 28–30)

28. When were the keys found? Ⓐ Ⓑ Ⓒ Ⓓ
    (A) This morning.
    (B) Yesterday morning.
    (C) This Monday.
    (D) Last Tuesday.

29. Where are the keys now? Ⓐ Ⓑ Ⓒ Ⓓ
    (A) In the cafeteria.
    (B) At home.
    (C) In the main office.
    (D) By the front door.

30. What should the owner of the keys do? Ⓐ Ⓑ Ⓒ Ⓓ
    (A) Show identification.
    (B) Tell the security guard.
    (C) Fill out a form.
    (D) Speak to Mrs. Chang.

TALKS: BUSINESS ANNOUNCEMENTS

Vocabulary Practice A

DIRECTIONS: Certain words are associated with certain activities. Look at the verb phrases below. Write two or more words associated with each of the activities these phrases describe.

1. having a company picnic *food, activities*

2. buying new computers _____

3. hiring new employees _____

4. attending a conference _____

5. ordering supplies _____

6. taking a vacation _____

7. using a drinking fountain _____

8. starting a small business _____

9. parking near the door _____

10. writing a list _____

Vocabulary Practice B

DIRECTIONS: Read the sentences. Then write new sentences using the activities in Vocabulary Practice A.

1. Ms. Wilson is filling out a purchase order for more pens, pencils, and paper.
   She's ordering supplies.

2. The Human Resources officer is reviewing the qualifications of job applicants.

   _____

3. The president himself drove his workers to the park for their annual outing.

   _____

4. We shopped for bigger monitors and faster operating systems.

   _____

5. We are looking forward to hearing presentations and participating in seminars.

_____

6. I put everyone's name and their job on a piece of paper and posted it on our company's web site.

_____

7. She's thirsty and wants some water.

_____

8. She's reading a travel guide to find some places to visit.

_____

9. He's looking for a space large enough for his car by the main entrance.

_____

10. We're writing a business plan and getting financial backing before we can open our doors to our customers.

_____

TOEIC Test Practice

DIRECTIONS: You will hear ten business announcements. They will not be repeated. Below you will read three questions about each announcement. After you listen to the announcement, answer the questions.

TALK 1 (Questions 1–3)

1. When is this announcement being made?   Ⓐ Ⓑ Ⓒ Ⓓ
   (A)   In the morning.
   (B)   At noon.
   (C)   In the afternoon.
   (D)   In the evening.

2. At what event is this announcement being heard?   Ⓐ Ⓑ Ⓒ Ⓓ
   (A)   A company picnic.
   (B)   A school football game.
   (C)   An awards dinner.
   (D)   An honor society dance.

3. What will happen first?   Ⓐ Ⓑ Ⓒ Ⓓ
   (A)   Dinner will be served.
   (B)   An award will be given.
   (C)   A speech will be made.
   (D)   A life will be saved.

TALK 2 (Questions 4–6)

4. Where is this announcement being made? (A) (B) (C) (D)
   (A) At the office.
   (B) At a clubhouse.
   (C) In a schoolyard.
   (D) In a church.

5. What is the announcement about? (A) (B) (C) (D)
   (A) Proper clothing.
   (B) The dinner menu.
   (C) Clothes on sale.
   (D) Dining room hours.

6. What will happen tonight? (A) (B) (C) (D)
   (A) There will be a dance.
   (B) There will be a special dinner.
   (C) The dining room will be closed.
   (D) No one will be allowed inside.

TALK 3 (Questions 7–9)

7. What will be discussed at the meeting? (A) (B) (C) (D)
   (A) The budget.
   (B) Vacation policy.
   (C) Buying new computers.
   (D) Firing employees.

8. What is Mrs. Lopez's job? (A) (B) (C) (D)
   (A) Trainer.
   (B) Copywriter.
   (C) Accountant.
   (D) Meeting planner.

9. Why isn't Mrs. Lopez at the meeting? (A) (B) (C) (D)
   (A) She's on vacation.
   (B) She's sick.
   (C) She's out of town.
   (D) She's on the train.

TALK 4 (Questions 10–12)

10. What will be opened? (A) (B) (C) (D)
    (A) A store.
    (B) A factory.
    (C) A new company.
    (D) A management school.

11. What is this announcement about? Ⓐ Ⓑ Ⓒ Ⓓ
    (A) Food distribution.
    (B) Asia's economy.
    (C) Job openings.
    (D) Management styles.

12. What should applicants send? Ⓐ Ⓑ Ⓒ Ⓓ
    (A) Their financial statements.
    (B) Their college degrees.
    (C) A certified check.
    (D) A résumé.

TALK 5 (Questions 13–15)

13. Who is this announcement for? Ⓐ Ⓑ Ⓒ Ⓓ
    (A) People using the cafeteria.
    (B) People using the computers.
    (C) People using the drinking fountain.
    (D) People using the meeting rooms.

14. What are the listeners requested to do? Ⓐ Ⓑ Ⓒ Ⓓ
    (A) Turn off the computers.
    (B) Keep the fan on.
    (C) Smoke in the rooms.
    (D) Keep the door open.

15. When must the door be closed? Ⓐ Ⓑ Ⓒ Ⓓ
    (A) Only in the mornings.
    (B) During classes.
    (C) At all times.
    (D) During the weekends.

TALK 6 (Questions 16–18)

16. Who is Mr. Thompson? Ⓐ Ⓑ Ⓒ Ⓓ
    (A) A college professor.
    (B) An administrator.
    (C) An author.
    (D) An accountant.

17. What will Mr. Thompson talk about tonight? Ⓐ Ⓑ Ⓒ Ⓓ
    (A) Taxes.
    (B) Starting a small business.
    (C) Conferences.
    (D) His twenty years of experience.

18. What will happen after the talk? Ⓐ Ⓑ Ⓒ Ⓓ
    (A) Mr. Thompson will make a call.
    (B) Tea will be served.
    (C) Mr. Thompson will answer questions.
    (D) There will be a dinner.

TALK 7 (Questions 19–21)

19. What are employees asked not to use? Ⓐ Ⓑ Ⓒ Ⓓ
    (A) The north elevator.
    (B) The south elevator.
    (C) The stairs.
    (D) The building exits.

20. When will the repairs be finished? Ⓐ Ⓑ Ⓒ Ⓓ
    (A) Today.
    (B) This morning.
    (C) This afternoon.
    (D) Tomorrow morning.

21. What will happen next week? Ⓐ Ⓑ Ⓒ Ⓓ
    (A) The front parking lot will be paved.
    (B) The front door will be repaired.
    (C) The elevators will be painted.
    (D) The lobby will be painted.

TALK 8 (Questions 22–24)

22. How can someone become Employee of the Month? Ⓐ Ⓑ Ⓒ Ⓓ
    (A) Get along with co-workers.
    (B) Be efficient and dedicated.
    (C) Park near the front door.
    (D) Learn a new computer program.

23. What will the Employee of the Month receive? Ⓐ Ⓑ Ⓒ Ⓓ
    (A) A day off.
    (B) A new car.
    (C) Extra work.
    (D) Free lunches.

24. When will the name of the first Employee of Ⓐ Ⓑ Ⓒ Ⓓ
    the Month be announced?
    (A) At the end of the week.
    (B) After this weekend.
    (C) At the end of the month.
    (D) In ten weeks.

TALK 9 (Questions 25–27)

25. What is the problem?   Ⓐ Ⓑ Ⓒ Ⓓ
    - (A) People take supplies without permission.
    - (B) People have too many supplies.
    - (C) Mr. Lewis wants to give away supplies.
    - (D) Mr. Lewis lost the supply room key.

26. Who can enter the supply room?   Ⓐ Ⓑ Ⓒ Ⓓ
    - (A) No one.
    - (B) All employees.
    - (C) Only Mr. Lewis.
    - (D) Only company employees.

27. What must you do to get supplies?   Ⓐ Ⓑ Ⓒ Ⓓ
    - (A) Call Mr. Lewis on the phone.
    - (B) Ask for the key.
    - (C) Give Mr. Lewis a list.
    - (D) Tell your department head.

TALK 10 (Questions 28–30)

28. When will the conference take place?   Ⓐ Ⓑ Ⓒ Ⓓ
    - (A) At the end of the day.
    - (B) At the end of the week.
    - (C) At the end of the month.
    - (D) At the end of the year.

29. Where will the conference be?   Ⓐ Ⓑ Ⓒ Ⓓ
    - (A) In Canada.
    - (B) In California.
    - (C) In Colombia.
    - (D) In Korea.

30. How can you apply to attend the conference?   Ⓐ Ⓑ Ⓒ Ⓓ
    - (A) Go to the Human Resources office.
    - (B) Submit a list.
    - (C) Tell your department head.
    - (D) Send in your résumé.

REVIEW: PART 4

DIRECTIONS: Listen to the talks and choose the appropriate answers to the questions. There are three questions for each talk.

1. When will the snowfall begin?   Ⓐ   Ⓑ   Ⓒ   Ⓓ
   - (A) At midday.
   - (B) At 4:00.
   - (C) Before midnight.
   - (D) Tomorrow evening.

2. How much snow will fall?   Ⓐ   Ⓑ   Ⓒ   Ⓓ
   - (A) 3 centimeters.
   - (B) 13 centimeters.
   - (C) 30 centimeters.
   - (D) 33 centimeters.

3. What will the weather be like on Wednesday?   Ⓐ   Ⓑ   Ⓒ   Ⓓ
   - (A) Cold.
   - (B) Windy.
   - (C) Snowy.
   - (D) Cloudy.

4. Where is the shoe store?   Ⓐ   Ⓑ   Ⓒ   Ⓓ
   - (A) In the mall.
   - (B) On Maine Avenue.
   - (C) Near the train station.
   - (D) In the back of the school.

5. What is on sale this month?   Ⓐ   Ⓑ   Ⓒ   Ⓓ
   - (A) All styles of shoes.
   - (B) Men's shoes.
   - (C) Women's shoes.
   - (D) Children's shoes.

6. How much is the discount?   Ⓐ   Ⓑ   Ⓒ   Ⓓ
   - (A) 5 percent.
   - (B) 10 percent.
   - (C) 20 percent.
   - (D) 25 percent.

7. Where is Marlene Rich now? Ⓐ Ⓑ Ⓒ Ⓓ
   (A) In the director's office.
   (B) At a conference.
   (C) Talking to another employee.
   (D) Buying a desk.

8. When will she return? Ⓐ Ⓑ Ⓒ Ⓓ
   (A) On Sunday.
   (B) On Monday.
   (C) At the end of the week.
   (D) In two weeks.

9. What happens if callers press 1? Ⓐ Ⓑ Ⓒ Ⓓ
   (A) They can leave a message for Marlene.
   (B) They can speak with the director.
   (C) They can participate in a conference call.
   (D) They can hear a list of phone numbers.

10. What will be built? Ⓐ Ⓑ Ⓒ Ⓓ
    (A) A theater.
    (B) A bus station.
    (C) A concert hall.
    (D) A sports arena.

11. What will it have on the ground floor? Ⓐ Ⓑ Ⓒ Ⓓ
    (A) Restaurants.
    (B) A subway stop.
    (C) A concert hall.
    (D) A sports arena.

12. When will construction be finished? Ⓐ Ⓑ Ⓒ Ⓓ
    (A) Next month.
    (B) In two months.
    (C) Next year.
    (D) In two years.

13. What time is the first show?   Ⓐ Ⓑ Ⓒ Ⓓ
    (A) 7:00.
    (B) 7:30.
    (C) 8:00.
    (D) 9:30.

14. What is the price of a general admission ticket?   Ⓐ Ⓑ Ⓒ Ⓓ
    (A) $8.00.
    (B) $9.00.
    (C) $10.00.
    (D) $12.00.

15. Who is NOT allowed inside the theater?   Ⓐ Ⓑ Ⓒ Ⓓ
    (A) Children under 12.
    (B) Senior citizens.
    (C) People without an ID.
    (D) Candy sellers.

LISTENING COMPREHENSION REVIEW

You will find the Answer Sheet for the Listening Comprehension Review on page 387. Detach it from the book and use it to record your answers. Play the audio program for the Listening Comprehension Review when you are ready to begin.

LISTENING TEST

In the Listening test, you will be asked to demonstrate how well you understand spoken English. The entire Listening test will last approximately 45 minutes. There are four parts, and directions are given for each part. You must mark your answers on the separate answer sheet. Do not write your answers in the test book.

PART 1

Directions: For each question in this part, you will hear four statements about a picture in your test book. When you hear the statements, you must select the one statement that best describes what you see in the picture. Then find the number of the question on your answer sheet and mark your answer. The statements will not be printed in your test book and will be spoken only one time.

Example

Sample Answer

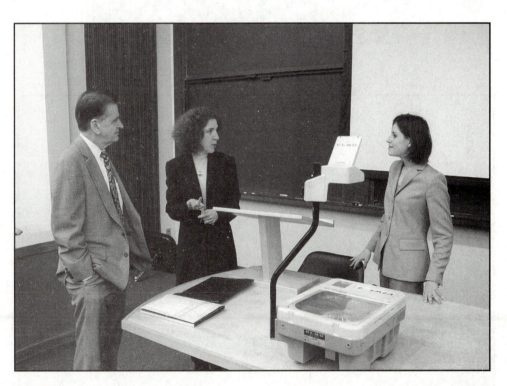

Statement (C), "They're standing near the table," is the best description of the picture, so you should select answer (C) and mark it on your answer sheet.

GO ON TO THE NEXT PAGE

1.

2.

3.

4.

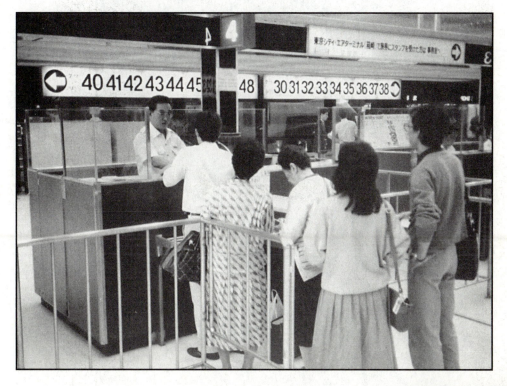

GO ON TO THE NEXT PAGE

5.

6.

7.

8.

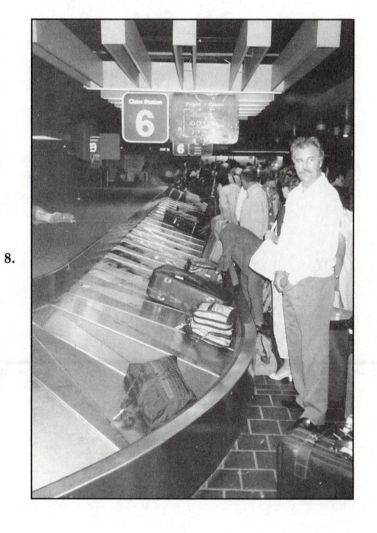

GO ON TO THE NEXT PAGE ➤

9.

10.

PART 2

 Directions: You will hear a question or statement and three responses spoken in English. They will not be printed in your test book and will be spoken only one time. Select the best response to the question or statement and mark the letter (A), (B), or (C) on your answer sheet.

Example

Sample Answer
Ⓐ ● Ⓒ

You will hear: Where is the meeting room?

You will also hear: (A) To meet the new director.
                      (B) It's the first room on the right.
                      (C) Yes, at two o'clock.

Your best response to the question "Where is the meeting room?" is choice (B), "It's the first room on the right," so (B) is the correct answer. You should mark answer (B) on your answer sheet.

---

11. Mark your answer on your answer sheet.

12. Mark your answer on your answer sheet.

13. Mark your answer on your answer sheet.

14. Mark your answer on your answer sheet.

15. Mark your answer on your answer sheet.

16. Mark your answer on your answer sheet.

17. Mark your answer on your answer sheet.

18. Mark your answer on your answer sheet.

19. Mark your answer on your answer sheet.

20. Mark your answer on your answer sheet.

21. Mark your answer on your answer sheet.

22. Mark your answer on your answer sheet.

23. Mark your answer on your answer sheet.

24. Mark your answer on your answer sheet.

25. Mark your answer on your answer sheet.

26. Mark your answer on your answer sheet.

27. Mark your answer on your answer sheet.

28. Mark your answer on your answer sheet.

29. Mark your answer on your answer sheet.

30. Mark your answer on your answer sheet.

31. Mark your answer on your answer sheet.

32. Mark your answer on your answer sheet.

33. Mark your answer on your answer sheet.

34. Mark your answer on your answer sheet.

35. Mark your answer on your answer sheet.

36. Mark your answer on your answer sheet.

37. Mark your answer on your answer sheet.

38. Mark your answer on your answer sheet.

39. Mark your answer on your answer sheet.

40. Mark your answer on your answer sheet.

GO ON TO THE NEXT PAGE ▶

Directions: You will hear some conversations between two people. You will be asked to answer three questions about what the speakers say in each conversation. Select the best response to each question and mark the letter (A), (B), (C), or (D) on your answer sheet. The conversations will not be printed in your test book and will be spoken only one time.

9/27

41. Why did the woman buy a new coat?
   (A) Her old coat was too small.
   (B) She wants to own two coats.
   (C) Her old coat wasn't a nice color.
   (D) The man didn't like his old coat.

42. What color is the new coat?
   (A) Gold.
   (B) Blue.
   (C) Green.
   (D) White.

43. How much did the new coat cost?
   (A) $70.
   (B) $700.
   (C) $740.
   (D) $1,100.

44. When will Mr. Kim's flight arrive?
   (A) At 3:00.
   (B) At 4:00.
   (C) At 5:00.
   (D) At 11:00.

45. How will Mr. Kim get downtown?
   (A) By car.
   (B) By bus.
   (C) By cab.
   (D) By subway.

46. Where will Mr. Kim probably meet the speakers tonight?
   (A) At his hotel.
   (B) At the airport.
   (C) At a restaurant.
   (D) At the subway station.

47. Where are the speakers?
   (A) At the beach.
   (B) At a fish store.
   (C) At a restaurant.
   (D) At an aquarium.

On the menu

48. How much does the tuna cost?
   (A) $13.
   (B) $30.
   (C) $35.
   (D) $40.

49. What will the man get?
   (A) Tuna.
   (B) Rice.
   (C) Shrimp.
   (D) Ice cream.

50. What are the speakers waiting for?
   (A) A bus.
   (B) A car.
   (C) A train.
   (D) A plane.

51. How long has the woman been waiting?
   (A) Thirty minutes.
   (B) An hour.
   (C) Since noon.
   (D) Since 5:00.

52. Where is the woman going?
   (A) To the store.
   (B) To the park.
   (C) To work.
   (D) Home.

53. When will the woman send the envelope?
    (A) Before lunch.
    (B) In the afternoon.
    (C) Tonight.
    (D) Tomorrow morning.

54. What is the woman doing now?
    (A) Reading a letter.
    (B) Typing a report.
    (C) Eating lunch.
    (D) Addressing envelopes.

55. What is in the envelope?
    (A) A book.
    (B) A form.
    (C) A letter.
    (D) A sweater.

56. Where will the speakers meet?
    (A) At the woman's office.
    (B) At the dentist's office.
    (C) In a conference room.
    (D) In a hotel.

57. When will the speakers meet?
    (A) Tuesday morning.
    (B) Tuesday afternoon.
    (C) Wednesday morning.
    (D) Thursday afternoon.

58. What will the secretary send to the woman?
    (A) Photocopies.
    (B) Photographs.
    (C) A book.
    (D) A conference report.

59. When will Mark start his new job?
    (A) Next week.
    (B) In two weeks.
    (C) Next month.
    (D) In two months.

60. Why did Mark leave his old job?
    (A) He retired.
    (B) He was fired.
    (C) He wasn't paid enough.
    (D) He didn't get enough vacations.

61. How long did he work at his old job?
    (A) 13 years.
    (B) 14 years.
    (C) 30 years.
    (D) 40 years.

62. Where are the speakers?
    (A) In a bank.
    (B) In a post office.
    (C) In a stationery store.
    (D) In a photographer's studio.

63. What is in the envelope?
    (A) Cash.
    (B) Jewelry.
    (C) Photographs.
    (D) Press releases.

64. How much will the woman have to pay?
    (A) $3.00.
    (B) $7.00.
    (C) $9.00.
    (D) $11.00.

65. Where are the speakers?
    (A) At home.
    (B) At a hotel.
    (C) At a restaurant.
    (D) At an exercise club.

66. What time does the man want to wake up?
    (A) 6:00.
    (B) 6:05.
    (C) 6:40.
    (D) 6:45.

67. What is the man going to do now?
    (A) Eat dinner.
    (B) Have breakfast.
    (C) Go swimming.
    (D) Attend a meeting.

68. When will Mrs. Davis arrive?
    (A) 1:00.
    (B) 7:00.
    (C) 8:00.
    (D) 11:00.

69. Why will Mrs. Davis be late?
    (A) Her plane is delayed.
    (B) It's raining hard.
    (C) Her train is late.
    (D) Her car won't start.

70. What does Mrs. Davis have to do this afternoon?
    (A) Write a letter.
    (B) Go to a meeting.
    (C) Read an article.
    (D) Eat lunch.

Directions: You will hear some talks given by a single speaker. You will be asked to answer three questions about what the speaker says in each talk. Select the best response to each question and mark the letter (A), (B), (C), or (D) on your answer sheet. The talks will not be printed in your test book and will be spoken only one time.

71. Who is speaking?
    (A) A college professor.
    (B) A book writer.
    (C) A student.
    (D) A doctor.

72. When is the exam?
    (A) Tuesday.
    (B) Wednesday.
    (C) Thursday.
    (D) Friday.

73. What should be brought to the exam?
    (A) Textbooks.
    (B) Pencils.
    (C) Notes.
    (D) Pens.

74. What will the low temperature be tonight?
    (A) 7 degrees.
    (B) 11 degrees.
    (C) 15 degrees.
    (D) 16 degrees.

75. What will the weather be like tomorrow?
    (A) Rainy.
    (B) Sunny.
    (C) Cloudy.
    (D) Windy.

76. When will the rain stop?
    (A) Saturday.
    (B) Sunday.
    (C) Monday.
    (D) Wednesday.

77. What happened at the zoo today?
    (A) New lions were bought.
    (B) Baby lions were born.
    (C) There were games for children.
    (D) A new director was hired.

78. Who made the announcement?
    (A) The lion specialist.
    (B) The zoo director.
    (C) The publicity agent.
    (D) The activities director.

79. When will there be special activities at the zoo?
    (A) In two days.
    (B) Next weekend.
    (C) Next week.
    (D) Next month.

80. Where is the speaker?
    (A) On a train.
    (B) On a boat.
    (C) On a plane.
    (D) On a tour bus.

81. When will they arrive in Los Angeles?
    (A) 5:00.
    (B) 5:30.
    (C) 12:00.
    (D) 12:30.

82. What will attendants bring to all the passengers?
    (A) Lunch.
    (B) Beverages.
    (C) Magazines.
    (D) Pillows and blankets.

GO ON TO THE NEXT PAGE ▶

83. What does the Beautiful Interiors store sell?
    (A) Office supplies.
    (B) Furniture.
    (C) Clothes.
    (D) Cars.

84. When is the last day of the sale?
    (A) Monday.
    (B) Thursday.
    (C) Friday.
    (D) Sunday.

85. Where is the store located?
    (A) In a shopping mall.
    (B) Down the street from a
         hotel.
    (C) In a subway station.
    (D) Next to City Hall.

86. What happens if callers press 2?
    (A) They can speak to a lawyer.
    (B) They can make an
         appointment.
    (C) They can speak with
         Ms. Stevenson.
    (D) They can find out the
         office hours.

87. Who can answer questions
    about bills?
    (A) Mr. Park.
    (B) Ms. Stevenson.
    (C) The office assistant.
    (D) The operator.

88. What should a caller do in case
    of an emergency when the office
    is closed?
    (A) Press 3.
    (B) Call back during office
         hours.
    (C) Dial a different phone
         number.
    (D) Ask for the office assistant.

89. Why was the bridge closed?
    (A) Because of an accident.
    (B) Because of the snow.
    (C) Because of heavy traffic.
    (D) Because of construction.

90. When will the bridge be
    reopened?
    (A) Today.
    (B) Tonight.
    (C) Tuesday.
    (D) Wednesday.

91. What will the weather be like
    on Tuesday?
    (A) Snowy.
    (B) Rainy.
    (C) Windy.
    (D) Sunny.

92. Who is James Jones?
    (A) A medical doctor.
    (B) A university professor.
    (C) A travel agent.
    (D) A florist.

93. What will James Jones talk
    about?
    (A) Chemistry.
    (B) University studies.
    (C) Hiking in the Amazon.
    (D) A train trip.

94. What will James Jones do after
    the talk?
    (A) He will answer questions.
    (B) He will take photographs.
    (C) He will display flowers.
    (D) He will sell photographs.

95. How much do tickets for the tour cost?
    (A) $7.00.
    (B) $8.00.
    (C) $10.00.
    (D) $11.00.

96. What will the tour participants see first?
    (A) Modern paintings.
    (B) Sculptures.
    (C) Prints.
    (D) Portraits.

97. Where are the works by local artists?
    (A) On the ground floor.
    (B) On the first floor.
    (C) On the second floor.
    (D) On the third floor.

98. Where are the passengers now?
    (A) On the train.
    (B) Waiting at the gate.
    (C) By the station exit.
    (D) At the baggage office.

99. When will the train arrive in the station?
    (A) In four minutes.
    (B) In five minutes.
    (C) In eight minutes.
    (D) In ten minutes.

100. What should passengers with checked baggage do?
    (A) Write a check to pay for it.
    (B) Wait for it by the gate.
    (C) Stay on the train.
    (D) Ask the conductor for help.

READING

In the second section of the new TOEIC test, you will have the chance to show how well you understand written English. There are three parts to this section, with special directions for each part:

Part 5   Incomplete Sentences
Part 6   Text Completion
Part 7   Reading Comprehension
• Single Passages
• Double Passages

In this part of the *Longman Preparation Series for the New TOEIC® Test: Intermediate Course,* you will learn strategies to help you on the Reading section. Each part begins with activities to help you develop these strategies. Each part ends with grammar or reading comprehension questions similar to those on the new TOEIC test.

PART 5: INCOMPLETE SENTENCES

In Part 5 of the new TOEIC test, you will be given a sentence that has a missing word or phrase. You are to choose the word or phrase that best completes the sentence.

One question type in this part focuses on WORD CHOICE; the other question type focuses on WORD FORM.

WORD CHOICE STRATEGIES

▪ In this section, we will look at new TOEIC questions that focus on these word choices.

Nouns	Adverbs
Verbs	Conjunctions
Adjectives	Prepositions

▪ You must understand the meaning of the whole sentence to choose the correct response.

Example

The speaker spoke _____ to be heard above the noise.

(A) unclearly
(B) loudly
(C) randomly
(D) certainly

If there is a lot of noise, the speaker must speak loudly to be heard above the noise. The correct answer is (B).

WORD FORM STRATEGIES

■ In this section, we will also look at new TOEIC test questions that focus on these word forms.

Nouns	Adverbs
Verbs	Pronouns
Adjectives	

■ You must understand the part of speech of the missing word to choose the correct response.

Example

The safety glasses will _____ your eyes.

(A) protective
(B) protection
(C) protector
(D) protect

In the sentence you can see that there is no verb, and the blank is preceded by the modal *will*. You should choose a verb. Option (A) *protective* is an adjective. Option B *protection* is a noun. Option (C) *protector* is another noun. Option (D) *protect* is a verb. The correct answer is (D).

WORD CHOICE: NOUNS

In these TOEIC test questions, you will have to choose the correct noun from four noun choices. You must understand the meaning of the sentence and the meaning of the noun choices.

Example

The _____ to the banquet were sent to all of our clients.

(A) requests
(B) invitations
(C) suggestions
(D) offers

The correct answer is (B) *invitations*. None of the other nouns fits the context of the sentence.

DIRECTIONS: Mark the choice that best completes the sentence.

1. Has anybody seen the _____ of toner that just arrived for the copy machine?
    (A) bags
    (B) envelopes
    (C) cans
    (D) boxes

    Ⓐ Ⓑ Ⓒ Ⓓ

2. There is a three-month probation _____ for all new employees.
    (A) timing
    (B) era
    (C) period
    (D) sequence

    Ⓐ Ⓑ Ⓒ Ⓓ

3. To call another company or other places, press 9 for an outside _____.
    (A) line
    (B) lane
    (C) land
    (D) lining

    Ⓐ Ⓑ Ⓒ Ⓓ

4. Your business card should have your contact _____.
    (A) information
    (B) report
    (C) announcement
    (D) figures

    Ⓐ Ⓑ Ⓒ Ⓓ

5. Tariffs are set by our federal _____ Department.
   (A) Business
   (B) Negotiation
   (C) Commerce
   (D) Deal

6. It's hard to read anything on your computer. You should get a new _____.
   (A) screen
   (B) television
   (C) monitor
   (D) viewer

7. Which _____ is Mr. Hashimoto arriving at when his plane lands?
   (A) terminal
   (B) building
   (C) house
   (D) place

8. The vending machines in the employee _____ are out of order again.
   (A) room
   (B) place
   (C) salon
   (D) lounge

9. To relieve work-related stress, our company provides free _____ for everyone.
   (A) messages
   (B) drugs
   (C) massages
   (D) sleep

10. Because Jack was injured at work, he's receiving workman's _____.
    (A) compensation
    (B) help
    (C) reimbursement
    (D) funds

WORD CHOICE: VERBS

In these TOEIC test questions, you will have to choose the correct verb from four verb choices. You must understand the meaning of the sentence and the meaning of the verb choices.

Example:

The meeting room _____ 40 people.
(A) gathers
(B) carries
(C) holds
(D) waits

The correct answer is (C) *holds*. None of the other verbs fit the context of the sentence.

DIRECTIONS: Mark the choice that best completes the sentence.

1. I'm sorry to be late for the meeting, but my new secretary _____ to tell me you had scheduled it earlier.
    (A) decided
    (B) neglected
    (C) refused
    (D) thought

    Ⓐ Ⓑ Ⓒ Ⓓ

2. When you get to our main entrance, _____ a left as you enter the parking lot.
    (A) make
    (B) turn
    (C) do
    (D) throw

    Ⓐ Ⓑ Ⓒ Ⓓ

3. It's a company custom to _____ to work in casual clothes on Fridays.
    (A) come
    (B) be
    (C) dress
    (D) attend

    Ⓐ Ⓑ Ⓒ Ⓓ

4. If you're _____ Ms. Rogers, you'll find her in the board room.
    (A) looking to
    (B) looking at
    (C) looking for
    (D) looking into

    Ⓐ Ⓑ Ⓒ Ⓓ

5. Most of us in this office _____ lunch at noon.   Ⓐ Ⓑ Ⓒ Ⓓ
   (A)   make
   (B)   have
   (C)   bring
   (D)   go to

6. The boss doesn't _____ (to) playing the radio at   Ⓐ Ⓑ Ⓒ Ⓓ
   your desk if the music is low.
   (A)   mind -ing
   (B)   refuse
   (C)   negate
   (D)   object 反対する

Noun   Verb
OBject / obJECT
              反的動後

7. If I criticize your work, you shouldn't ___ *take* ___ it   Ⓐ Ⓑ Ⓒ Ⓓ
   personally.
   (A)   make
   (B)   think
   (C)   believe
   (D)   take

take O personally
自分に向けられたものとして受け取る
女陛する

8. If you _____ long before leaving for the airport,   Ⓐ Ⓑ Ⓒ Ⓓ
   the hotel will keep your bags for you.
   (A)   exit
   (B)   depart   ·三相する
   (C)   check out 手続き ·朝いる
   (D)   move out

a room
Check out
             チェッ

9. I'm glad you enjoyed that appetizer, so I _____   Ⓐ Ⓑ Ⓒ Ⓓ
   the chicken for your entrée.
   (A)   feel
   (B)   recommend
   (C)   try
   (D)   refer

10. My daughter in college is _____ international   Ⓐ Ⓑ Ⓒ Ⓓ
   business.
   (A)   studying
   (B)   rehearsing
   (C)   revisiting
   (D)   inquiring

WORD CHOICE: ADJECTIVES

In these TOEIC test questions, you will have to choose the correct adjective from four adjective choices. You must understand the meaning of the sentence and the meaning of the adjective choices.

Example:

We want our employees to behave in the most _____ manner.
- (A) operational
- (B) expensive
- (C) awkward
- (D) professional

The correct answer is (D) *professional*. None of the other adjectives fit the context of the sentence.

DIRECTIONS: Mark the choice that best completes the sentence.

1. Did you know that in Western culture it can be considered _____ to stare at somebody?
   - (A) assertive
   - (B) rude
   - (C) silly
   - (D) funny

2. I still think that giving a presentation in front of many strangers is _____.
   - (A) energetic
   - (B) tepid
   - (C) scary
   - (D) famous

3. The new filing clerk's smile and cute way of speaking are completely _____.
   - (A) lovable
   - (B) loving
   - (C) beloved
   - (D) loved

4. It was not _____ to wear a T-shirt and jeans to the boss's retirement party.
   - (A) restful
   - (B) appropriate
   - (C) exciting
   - (D) friendly

5. If we don't meet those deadlines, we're going to be in _____ trouble.

   (A) heavy

   (B) big

   (C) large

   (D) great

   Ⓐ Ⓑ Ⓒ Ⓓ

6. It was very _____ finding Mr. Klein's cat sitting on his desk this morning.

   (A) satisfying

   (B) rewarding

   (C) intense

   (D) odd   奇妙

   Ⓐ Ⓑ Ⓒ Ⓓ

   even number 偶数
   odd number 奇数

7. Helen's typing, shorthand, and filing skills are simply _____.

   (A) amazing

   (B) outraged   憤慨した 激怒した.

   (C) novel

   (D) encouraging   激励の、励みとなる、好意的な.

   Ⓐ Ⓑ Ⓒ Ⓓ

   速記(法) ↔ longhand

8. I heard that the electrician says we should have a _____ overhaul of the wiring.

   (A) complete

   (B) fair

   (C) whole

   (D) round

   Ⓐ Ⓑ Ⓒ Ⓓ

9. My sales figures this quarter are much _____ than they've been for a long time.

   (A) grander

   (B) upper

   (C) higher

   (D) larger

   Ⓐ Ⓑ Ⓒ Ⓓ

   販売額、売上高

10. I hope the company has enough money to pay for these _____ renovations.   改装、修理.

    (A) needy

    (B) late

    (C) likely

    (D) costly

    Ⓐ Ⓑ Ⓒ Ⓓ

WORD CHOICE: ADVERBS

In these TOEIC test questions, you will have to choose the correct adverb from four adverb choices. You must understand the meaning of the sentence and the meaning of the adverb choices.

Example:

All the hotel rooms were _____ cleaned.
(A) anxiously
(B) thoroughly
(C) shortly
(D) firstly

The correct answer is (B) *thoroughly*. None of the other adverbs fit the context of the sentence.

DIRECTIONS: Mark the choice that best completes the sentence.

1. The company _____ accepts your resignation. (A) (B) (C) (D)
    (A) practically   事実上、実際には   辞職 辞任
    (B) sadly
    (C) stoically → STOIC   禁欲的な 冷静な
    (D) righteously   正しく 当然に

2. Al can copy documents so _____ that you can't (A) (B) (C) (D)
    tell the original from the copy.
    (A) intensely   激しく、感情的に (副)
    (B) directly   直接に いじかに (副)
    (C) acutely   鋭く、いたく、強く (副)
    (D) skillfully   上手に 巧練して (副)

3. We've sold _____ twice the amount of giftware (A) (B) (C) (D)
    this quarter than a year ago.   ギフト商品
    (A) roughly   おおよそ (副)
    (B) justly   正しく、公正に (副)
    (C) nicely   うまく、よく、立派に (副)
    (D) equally   等しく、同程度に、平等に

4. You _____ wouldn't object to a pay increase, (A) (B) (C) (D)
    would you?
    (A) happily   幸福に、楽しい、幸運に
    (B) obviously   明らかに 目に見えて
    (C) notably   → 形 著しい 卓越した、有名な
    (D) casually   → 副 偶然に、思いがけなく

5. _____, I'm so tired that I don't care if we're
   not offered any overtime.
   (A) Naturally
   (B) Critically
   (C) Frankly → very honestly
   (D) Bluntly

6. I was _____ pleased to be given such a
   generous pay increase.
   (A) extremely
   (B) willfully
   (C) sadly
   (D) barely

7. The supervisor _____ wanted to change our
   shifts, but he's changed his mind.
   (A) originally
   (B) awkwardly
   (C) principally
   (D) surely

8. The company _____ uses WordIt as our word
   processing program.
   (A) previously
   (B) currently
   (C) actively
   (D) tightly

9. Sheila has learned her job _____ well considering
   how new she is here.
   (A) purposely
   (B) reasonably
   (C) sincerely
   (D) neatly

10. Management has been thinking _____ of opening
    up two new branch offices.
    (A) additionally
    (B) abundantly
    (C) newly
    (D) seriously

WORD CHOICE: CONJUNCTIONS

In these TOEIC test questions, you will have to choose the correct conjunction from four conjunction choices. You must understand the meaning of the sentence and the meaning of the conjunction choices.

Example:

Both the secretary _____ the file clerk left early.

(A) nor
(B) either
(C) or
(D) and

The correct answer is (D) *and*. None of the other conjunctions fit the context of the sentence.

DIRECTIONS: Mark the choice that best completes the sentence.

1. We haven't seen that memo _____ it was first distributed.
   (A) since
   (B) when
   (C) while
   (D) as

   Ⓐ Ⓑ Ⓒ Ⓓ

2. Mr. Kendall will continue working _____ his replacement has been trained.
   (A) in order that
   (B) because
   (C) until
   (D) so

   Ⓐ Ⓑ Ⓒ Ⓓ

3. She got not only a substantial raise _____ a large bonus.
   (A) because
   (B) although
   (C) and
   (D) but also

   Ⓐ Ⓑ Ⓒ Ⓓ

4. _____ you come up with a better idea, let's try out my suggestion.
   (A) If
   (B) After
   (C) Neither
   (D) Unless

   Ⓐ Ⓑ Ⓒ Ⓓ

5. _____ Genji and I are being transferred to the Mumbai office.
   (A) Both
   (B) Either
   (C) And
   (D) Also

   Ⓐ Ⓑ Ⓒ Ⓓ

6. I'll go to the convention center _____ I've checked into the hotel.
   (A) since
   (B) as soon as
   (C) though
   (D) as

   Ⓐ Ⓑ Ⓒ Ⓓ

7. Mr. Romney didn't tell us _____ he'd decided to hire new people.
   (A) but
   (B) that
   (C) as
   (D) while

   Ⓐ Ⓑ Ⓒ Ⓓ

8. Neither the boss _____ his assistant were aware the deadline had passed.
   (A) or
   (B) but
   (C) nor
   (D) either

   Ⓐ Ⓑ Ⓒ Ⓓ

9. _____ Nora has finished this work, get her started on the Findlay account.
   (A) Once
   (B) While
   (C) As
   (D) So

   Ⓐ Ⓑ Ⓒ Ⓓ

10. I'll look for another restaurant _____ Chez Michel is fully booked.
    (A) although
    (B) before
    (C) not only
    (D) if

    Ⓐ Ⓑ Ⓒ Ⓓ

WORD CHOICE: PREPOSITIONS

In these TOEIC test questions, you will have to choose the correct preposition from four preposition choices. You must understand the meaning of the sentence and the meaning of the four preposition choices.

Example:

Put your coat _____ the closet.
(A) in
(B) next
(C) at
(D) to

The correct answer is (A) *in*. None of the other prepositions fit the context of the sentence.

DIRECTIONS: Mark the choice that best completes the sentence.

1. Please file these invoices _____ Payment Pending.
    (A) under
    (B) over
    (C) on
    (D) inside

    Ⓐ Ⓑ Ⓒ Ⓓ

2. When did you say you were leaving _____ London?
    (A) to
    (B) at
    (C) for
    (D) towards

    Ⓐ Ⓑ Ⓒ Ⓓ

3. In a business letter, you should put a colon _____ the greeting.
    (A) before
    (B) after
    (C) in
    (D) by

    Ⓐ Ⓑ Ⓒ Ⓓ

4. Wang is originally from Hong Kong, but he's lived in San Francisco _____ years.
    (A) for
    (B) in
    (C) through
    (D) over

    Ⓐ Ⓑ Ⓒ Ⓓ

5. What happened to the little memo I had attached
_____ this invoice?
(A) to
(B) on
(C) over
(D) at

6. _____ the time you read this message, I'll be
halfway across the Atlantic.
(A) In
(B) On
(C) By
(D) For

7. Now I'll never retrieve my ten-year pin because
it rolled _____ the refrigerator.
(A) below
(B) over
(C) around
(D) behind

8. I always get nervous driving _____ heavy
traffic on the way to work.
(A) on
(B) by
(C) in
(D) with

9. You can come _____ for an interview next
Monday at 9:30 A.M.
(A) through
(B) in
(C) out
(D) about

10. We were late because we had to drive _____
for twenty minutes looking for parking.
(A) around
(B) over
(C) up
(D) down

WORD FORM: NOUNS

In these TOEIC test questions, you will have to choose the noun form of a word from four choices. You must understand that a noun is missing from the sentence. You must also know which of the four choices is a noun.

Example:

The buffet table has a wide _____ of food items to choose from.
- (A) selectively
- (B) selective
- (C) select
- (D) selection

The correct answer is (D) *selection.* The missing word is a noun. None of the other choices is a noun.

DIRECTIONS: Mark the choice that best completes the sentence.

1. Your signature below will represent your _____ of this contract.
   - (A) accepted
   - (B) acceptance
   - (C) accept
   - (D) acceptable

   Ⓐ Ⓑ Ⓒ Ⓓ

2. The _____ on who could be hired for that position did not seem legal.
   - (A) restrictions
   - (B) restricted
   - (C) restricting
   - (D) restricted

   Ⓐ Ⓑ Ⓒ Ⓓ

3. Employee _____ in this company will prove beneficial for everyone.
   - (A) invest
   - (B) invested
   - (C) investments
   - (D) investing

   Ⓐ Ⓑ Ⓒ Ⓓ

4. The contract calls for a $1,000 _____ for every day we go over the deadline.
   - (A) penalize
   - (B) penalty
   - (C) penal
   - (D) penalizing

   Ⓐ Ⓑ Ⓒ Ⓓ

5. The manager's _____ for next year's
   profits is very optimistic.
   (A) projection
   (B) projecting
   (C) project
   (D) projected

6. We have no other _____ if we want to
   expand the company safely.
   (A) optimal
   (B) optimum
   (C) opt
   (D) option

7. I missed breakfast and lunch, so my _____
   right now is to get something to eat.
   (A) priority
   (B) prior
   (C) prioritize
   (D) priors

8. The restaurant is due for an _____ by the
   Health Department next week.
   (A) inspection
   (B) inspecting
   (C) inspect
   (D) inspected

9. Our success is based completely on the _____
   of our products.
   (A) rely
   (B) reliable
   (C) reliant
   (D) reliability

10. The low profits we've had over the last two quarters
    are due to the bad _____.
    (A) economical
    (B) economize
    (C) economic
    (D) economy

WORD FORM: VERBS

In these TOEIC test questions, you will have to choose the verb form of a word from four choices. You must understand that a verb is missing from the sentence. You must also know which of the four choices is a verb.

Example:

> We will _____ our operation and open two new branches.
> (A) expansion
> (B) expansive
> (C) expand
> (D) expansively

The correct answer is (C) *expand*. The missing word is a verb. None of the other choices is a verb.

DIRECTIONS: Mark the choice that best completes the sentence.

1. If you cannot _____ those accusations, I want to hear no more about it.   Ⓐ Ⓑ Ⓒ Ⓓ
    (A) substantial
    (B) substance
    (C) substantiate
    (D) substantially

2. Government experts _____ the stock market to do better in the coming months.   Ⓐ Ⓑ Ⓒ Ⓓ
    (A) expectable
    (B) expect
    (C) expectation
    (D) expectant

3. Do you _____ to increase employee benefits during the next open enrollment?   Ⓐ Ⓑ Ⓒ Ⓓ
    (A) intend
    (B) intent
    (C) intention
    (D) intently

4. Whenever out-of-town clients visit us, we do our best to _____ them.   Ⓐ Ⓑ Ⓒ Ⓓ
    (A) entertainment
    (B) entertaining
    (C) entertainer
    (D) entertain

5. The auditors _____ that the bookkeepers send them figures every two weeks.

    (A)   preference

    (B)   preferable

    (C)   preferential

    (D)   prefer

Ⓐ   Ⓑ   Ⓒ   Ⓓ

6. My boss's wife loves to _____ antique bottles and jars.

    (A)   collection

    (B)   collect

    (C)   collectible

    (D)   collector

Ⓐ   Ⓑ   Ⓒ   Ⓓ

7. I dislike radios playing in the office because they _____ me while I try to work.

    (A)   distraction

    (B)   distracter

    (C)   distract

    (D)   distracting

Ⓐ   Ⓑ   Ⓒ   Ⓓ

8. We would like to _____ that these bonuses are a one-time only thing.

    (A)   emphasize

    (B)   emphatic

    (C)   emphasis

    (D)   emphatically

Ⓐ   Ⓑ   Ⓒ   Ⓓ

9. Management likes employees who _____ to participate in company events.

    (A)   voluntary

    (B)   volunteerism

    (C)   volunteer

    (D)   voluntarily

Ⓐ   Ⓑ   Ⓒ   Ⓓ

10. By law, we must _____ how much federal income tax to deduct from your pay.

    (A)   calculable

    (B)   calculation

    (C)   calculate

    (D)   calculator

Ⓐ   Ⓑ   Ⓒ   Ⓓ

WORD FORM: ADJECTIVES

In these TOEIC test questions, you will have to choose the adjective form of a word from four choices. You must understand that an adjective is missing from the sentence. You must also know which of the four choices is an adjective.

Example:

Please sit down and make yourself _____.
(A) comfortable
(B) comfort
(C) comfortably
(D) comforter

The correct answer is (D) *comfortable*. The missing word is an adjective. None of the other choices is an adjective.

DIRECTIONS: Mark the choice that best completes the sentence.

1. All staff members are _____ for the accuracy of their time cards.
    (A) account
    (B) accountant
    (C) accountable
    (D) accountability

    Ⓐ Ⓑ Ⓒ Ⓓ

2. Everybody who works here has his/her _____ parking space in the garage.
    (A) own
    (B) owner
    (C) owe
    (D) owing

    Ⓐ Ⓑ Ⓒ Ⓓ

3. Some people say the _____ power in this company lies with the boss's brother.
    (A) reality
    (B) realism
    (C) really
    (D) real

    Ⓐ Ⓑ Ⓒ Ⓓ

4. We're all glad that the new CEO is a very _____ leader.
    (A) progressive
    (B) progress
    (C) progression
    (D) progressively

    Ⓐ Ⓑ Ⓒ Ⓓ

5. It's so nice that your assistant is such a
   _____ person.
   (A) friend
   (B) friendliness
   (C) friendly
   (D) friendship

6. The new line of cleaning products is still
   in the _____ stage of development.
   (A) experimenter
   (B) experiment
   (C) experimentation
   (D) experimental

7. The loyalty she has from her staff is _____
   of what a good manager she is.
   (A) indicate
   (B) indicative
   (C) indicator
   (D) indication

8. Jeanne's _____ approach to all of her work
   is what makes her so valuable to us.
   (A) methodical
   (B) methodology
   (C) method
   (D) methodically

9. Before you go abroad, make sure you have a
   _____ passport.
   (A) validity
   (B) validation
   (C) validate
   (D) valid

10. We are proud that our company has the most
    _____ health-care plan in the state.
    (A) comprehend
    (B) comprehensive
    (C) comprehensively
    (D) comprehension

WORD FORM: ADVERBS

In these TOEIC test questions, you will have to choose the adverb form of a word from four choices. You must understand that an adverb is missing from the sentence. You must also know which of the four choices is an adverb.

Example:

This form must be completed _____.
(A) accurate
(B) accuracy
(C) accurately
(D) accurateness

The correct answer is (C) *accurately.* The missing word is an adverb. None of the other choices is an adverb.

DIRECTIONS: Mark the choice that best completes the sentence.

1. When we plan out next year's budget, let's do   Ⓐ   Ⓑ   Ⓒ   Ⓓ
    it _____ this time.
    (A) really
    (B) reality
    (C) realistic
    (D) realistically

2. Our books are audited _____ by an   Ⓐ   Ⓑ   Ⓒ   Ⓓ
    outside agency.
    (A) periodical
    (B) period
    (C) periodically
    (D) periodic

3. Mr. Talbot is _____ awaiting the report   Ⓐ   Ⓑ   Ⓒ   Ⓓ
    on his yearly evaluation.
    (A) anxiously
    (B) anxious
    (C) anxiety
    (D) anxiousness

4. The CEO has been _____ advised by the   Ⓐ   Ⓑ   Ⓒ   Ⓓ
    board of directors.
    (A) reliably
    (B) reliable
    (C) reliability
    (D) rely

5. Ms. Yates surprised all of us at the conference with her _____ delivered speech.   Ⓐ Ⓑ Ⓒ Ⓓ
   (A) impressive
   (B) impression
   (C) impressively
   (D) impress

6. We've never seen a more _____ organized presentation than the one you gave.   Ⓐ Ⓑ Ⓒ Ⓓ
   (A) profess
   (B) professional
   (C) profession
   (D) professionally

7. _____ speaking, this hotel offers guests more amenities than most hotels.   Ⓐ Ⓑ Ⓒ Ⓓ
   (A) Generally
   (B) Generality
   (C) General
   (D) Generalize

8. All the candy produced in our factories is _____ wrapped for safety.   Ⓐ Ⓑ Ⓒ Ⓓ
   (A) individuality
   (B) individually
   (C) individual
   (D) individualize

9. The CEO's office is so _____ decorated that I feel it's embarrassing.   Ⓐ Ⓑ Ⓒ Ⓓ
   (A) expend
   (B) expensive
   (C) expensively
   (D) expense

10. From now on, any employee who is _____ late for work will be dismissed.   Ⓐ Ⓑ Ⓒ Ⓓ
    (A) habitually
    (B) habituate
    (C) habitual
    (D) habit

WORD FORM: PRONOUNS

In these TOEIC test questions, you will have to choose the correct form of a pronoun from four choices. You must understand what part of speech is missing. You must also know what part of speech the four pronouns are.

Example:

The customer called to cancel _____ order.
(A) it
(B) her
(C) hers
(D) she

The correct answer is (B) *her*. The missing pronoun is a possessive pronoun. None of the other choices is a possessive pronoun.

DIRECTIONS: Mark the choice that best completes the sentence.

1. The government has a responsibility to protect _____ citizens from inflation.
   (A) its
   (B) it's
   (C) it
   (D) their

   Ⓐ Ⓑ Ⓒ Ⓓ

2. I see you met my assistant. _____ and I go back many years.
   (A) Her
   (B) She
   (C) Hers
   (D) We

   Ⓐ Ⓑ Ⓒ Ⓓ

3. Instead of filling those orders now, take care of _____ tomorrow morning.
   (A) them
   (B) they
   (C) their
   (D) its

   Ⓐ Ⓑ Ⓒ Ⓓ

4. All of _____ have been invited to the boss's cocktail party this Friday evening.
   (A) we
   (B) our
   (C) us
   (D) ours

   Ⓐ Ⓑ Ⓒ Ⓓ

5. The idea for the new routing system wasn't Patterson's; it was _____. Ⓐ Ⓑ Ⓒ Ⓓ
   (A) me
   (B) mine
   (C) my
   (D) I

6. Telling somebody that _____ is laid off is a very unpleasant task. Ⓐ Ⓑ Ⓒ Ⓓ
   (A) him
   (B) his
   (C) he
   (D) they

7. My computer has a lot of memory, but _____ has more. Ⓐ Ⓑ Ⓒ Ⓓ
   (A) she
   (B) hers
   (C) her
   (D) it

8. _____ isn't good business practice to arrive late for meetings. Ⓐ Ⓑ Ⓒ Ⓓ
   (A) He
   (B) It
   (C) She
   (D) You

9. When _____ probation period is up, you'll be given the full benefits package. Ⓐ Ⓑ Ⓒ Ⓓ
   (A) you
   (B) your
   (C) yours
   (D) our

10. The police were right when _____ advised us to get a new security system. Ⓐ Ⓑ Ⓒ Ⓓ
    (A) it
    (B) she
    (C) them
    (D) they

REVIEW: PART 5

DIRECTIONS: Mark the choice that best completes the sentence.

1. Please call the _____ and find out if they
   have any more armchairs in stock.
   (A) storehouse
   (B) warehouse
   (C) outhouse
   (D) stock house

   Ⓐ Ⓑ Ⓒ Ⓓ

2. Hotel room _____ always go up during
   the tourist season.
   (A) tolls
   (B) invoices
   (C) monies
   (D) rates

   Ⓐ Ⓑ Ⓒ Ⓓ

3. You will be _____ for all your expenses
   on the trip.
   (A) reimbursed
   (B) recompensed
   (C) restituted
   (D) reprimanded

   Ⓐ Ⓑ Ⓒ Ⓓ

4. Because of family problems, he's _____
   a year's leave of absence.
   (A) taking
   (B) making
   (C) doing
   (D) fixing

   Ⓐ Ⓑ Ⓒ Ⓓ

5. Her speeches are much too _____ because
   she loves listening to herself speak.
   (A) bright
   (B) large
   (C) lengthy
   (D) interesting

   Ⓐ Ⓑ Ⓒ Ⓓ

6. If the lab test results are not _____, there could be dangerous consequences. Ⓐ Ⓑ Ⓒ Ⓓ
   (A) expected
   (B) accurate
   (C) acute
   (D) expelled

7. He handled that delicate matter very _____. Ⓐ Ⓑ Ⓒ Ⓓ
   (A) erroneously
   (B) factually
   (C) precisely
   (D) diplomatically

8. You can have a four-day work week _____ you stay two hours later each day. Ⓐ Ⓑ Ⓒ Ⓓ
   (A) whatever
   (B) as far as
   (C) considering
   (D) as long as

9. She's still coming into work _____ she has the flu. Ⓐ Ⓑ Ⓒ Ⓓ
   (A) however
   (B) even though
   (C) but
   (D) nonetheless

10. If you happen to drive _____ my house, stop in for a cup of coffee. Ⓐ Ⓑ Ⓒ Ⓓ
    (A) over
    (B) by
    (C) up to
    (D) around

11. The first records of an import/export business go back _____ 3500 B.C. Ⓐ Ⓑ Ⓒ Ⓓ
    (A) ago
    (B) for
    (C) at
    (D) to

12. Her _____ with accounting procedures should be good for our office.   Ⓐ   Ⓑ   Ⓒ   Ⓓ
   (A) familiarity
   (B) familiar
   (C) familiarize
   (D) familial

13. Your handwriting is so unclear that I can't read this _____ you made.   Ⓐ   Ⓑ   Ⓒ   Ⓓ
   (A) notate
   (B) noticeable
   (C) notation
   (D) notable

14. We need to _____ our expansion plans as soon as possible.   Ⓐ   Ⓑ   Ⓒ   Ⓓ
   (A) finale
   (B) finality
   (C) final
   (D) finalize

15. I hear the government is going to _____ some peculiar dealings on Wall Street.   Ⓐ   Ⓑ   Ⓒ   Ⓓ
   (A) investigation
   (B) investigate
   (C) investigational
   (D) investigative

16. Mr. Kaplowitz's _____ behavior is beginning to worry many of us.   Ⓐ   Ⓑ   Ⓒ   Ⓓ
   (A) oddity
   (B) oddly
   (C) odd
   (D) oddness

17. That was a _____ research job you did for the company!   Ⓐ   Ⓑ   Ⓒ   Ⓓ
   (A) fantastic
   (B) fantasy
   (C) fantasize
   (D) fantastical

18. Please remember to deal _____ with our competitors during the negotiations.   Ⓐ Ⓑ Ⓒ Ⓓ
    (A) cautious
    (B) caution
    (C) cautiously
    (D) cautiousness

19. My friend Bruno likes everybody _____ meets.   Ⓐ Ⓑ Ⓒ Ⓓ
    (A) it
    (B) him
    (C) he
    (D) its

20. I missed the news at 6:00, but I can watch _____ at 11:00.   Ⓐ Ⓑ Ⓒ Ⓓ
    (A) them
    (B) it
    (C) its
    (D) they

PART 6: TEXT COMPLETION

This section will introduce you to the new TOEIC test component Text Completion and to the important grammar that is tested in Part 6.

In Part 6 you will see text with three blanks. You will be asked to choose the word or phrase that best completes each blank. Much of the grammar that you studied for Part 5 will be useful here. In addition, you will need to understand these grammatical structures.

REFERENCE	VERBS	MODIFIERS
Number	Verb Tenses	Adjectives: Comparative and Superlative Forms
Part of Speech	Modal Auxillaries	Adverbs of Frequency
Pronoun		Verbal Adjectives: Present and Past Participles
Verb Tenses		

REFERENCE

Words do not stand alone. They depend on their context for meaning. When you complete the text in Part 6, you might have to read the whole passage to understand the context. You will need to understand how one word or phrase refers to another.

REFERENCE

NUMBER

A verb, a noun, or a pronoun must agree in number with its reference.

The director of all the schools _____ retiring.

The subject is *director*, a singular noun. You need the singular verb *is*.

PART OF SPEECH

A word must match the part of speech in a series.

The office runs smoothly and _____.

The adverb *efficiently* best follows the adverb *smoothly*.

PRONOUN

▦ A pronoun must match the gender and number of the noun and the part of speech required in the sentence.

My brother and I started this company while _____ were still in school.

The pronoun *we* refers to *My brother and I*. The plural verb *were* limits the choice to a plural pronoun.

VERB TENSE

▦ A verb must match time of the context of the passage.

Although we were unable to finish the report today, we _____ it tomorrow.

The time marker *tomorrow* indicates the blank requires a future verb *will finish*.

Practice

DIRECTIONS: Mark the choice that best completes the sentence.

1. We expect to finish renovations on the building by the end of the month. In fact, work on the first and second floor offices _____ completed

   (A) has been
   (B) have been
   (C) were
   (D) are

   Ⓐ Ⓑ Ⓒ Ⓓ

2. We hire only qualified individuals. All applicants must have a college degree and relevant _____.

   (A) experientially
   (B) experiential
   (C) experienced
   (D) experience

   Ⓐ Ⓑ Ⓒ Ⓓ

3. All our phone center employees are trained to provide top-quality customer service. We can rely on _____ to treat each customer with respect and patience.

   (A) us
   (B) him
   (C) them
   (D) you

   Ⓐ Ⓑ Ⓒ Ⓓ

4. We hope to finish the plans for the conference by Friday. We _____ on them for a month.

   (A) are working
   (B) were working
   (C) will be working
   (D) have been working

   Ⓐ Ⓑ Ⓒ Ⓓ

5. It is important that all your work be accurate. Please   Ⓐ Ⓑ Ⓒ Ⓓ
   check all documents for _____ before submitting
   the documents to your supervisor.
   (A) signatures
   (B) dates
   (C) errors
   (D) locations

6. You may have to go to other parts of the city on errands Ⓐ Ⓑ Ⓒ Ⓓ
   for the office. _____ for bus fare and other minor
   expenses is kept in the top file drawer.
   (A) Coins
   (B) Cash
   (C) Bills
   (D) Dollars

7. Our current office space is not comfortable for our   Ⓐ Ⓑ Ⓒ Ⓓ
   growing staff. It is too _____ and crowded.
   (A) furniture
   (B) rooms
   (C) small
   (D) size

8. My sister worked at this company for many years.   Ⓐ Ⓑ Ⓒ Ⓓ
   _____ often spoke of the friendly, cooperative
   work environment.
   (A) It
   (B) He
   (C) She
   (D) They

9. Mr. Park will speak at next month's conference.   Ⓐ Ⓑ Ⓒ Ⓓ
   He _____ to this when I communicated with
    him last week.
   (A) agrees
   (B) agreed
   (C) has agreed
   (D) will agree

10. More people than we expected are coming to the banquet.   Ⓐ Ⓑ Ⓒ Ⓓ
    We are not sure if the dining room can hold such a
    large _____.
    (A) menu
    (B) crowd
    (C) person
    (D) carpet

VERBS

VERB TENSES

Verb tenses in English indicate the time or state of the action in a sentence. Here we will review these verb tenses.

- Present Tense

    Simple Present and Present Continuous

    Present Perfect

    Present Perfect Continuous

- Past Tense

    Simple Past

    Past Continuous

    Past Perfect

- Future Tense

    Simple Future

    Future Perfect

THE SIMPLE PRESENT

- We form the simple present by using the basic verb (*I like*, *they need*). The only change is adding *-s* or *-es* for the third person singular (*he likes, she needs, it passes*).

- We use the simple present for two main reasons:
    - for a small group of verbs that deal with the senses (*see, taste, smell*, etc.) and the mind (*know, want, believe*, etc.);

        A: *Do you understand my point?*
        B: *Yes, now I know what you mean.*
    - to explain that something happens all the time, repeatedly, usually, or is a fact.

        A: *Where is Nobue?*
        B: *At home. She sleeps late on Saturday mornings.*

THE PRESENT CONTINUOUS

- We form the present continuous by using the auxiliary *be* in the present before the verb and adding *-ing* to the end of the verb.

- We use the present continuous with actions in the real present.

    A: *What are you doing?*
    B: *I'm getting dressed to go out.*

THE PRESENT PERFECT

■ We form the present perfect by using the auxiliary *have* or *has* and the past participle of the verb.

■ We use the present perfect to show that an action began in the past and continues to the general present.

> *Production in our factories <u>has increased</u> a lot since we installed the new machinery.*

THE PRESENT PERFECT CONTINUOUS

■ We form the present perfect continuous by using *have been* or *has been* before the verb and adding *-ing* to the end of the verb.

■ We use the present perfect continuous to show that an action began in the past and continues to <u>this moment</u> in the present.

> *I've been waiting for you for over an hour.*

In the following TOEIC test questions, you will have to choose the correct verb form from four verb choices. You must understand the meaning of the sentence and the meaning of the verb choices.

Practice A

DIRECTIONS: Mark the choice that best completes the sentence.

1. I only _____ to work on Monday. The rest of the week I work from home.   Ⓐ Ⓑ Ⓒ Ⓓ
   (A) go   (C) have gone
   (B) am going   (D) have been going

2. My boss _____ to Australia next month to open a new business.   Ⓐ Ⓑ Ⓒ Ⓓ
   (A) travels   (C) has traveled
   (B) is traveling   (D) has been traveling

3. My co-workers and I _____ at this restaurant once before.   Ⓐ Ⓑ Ⓒ Ⓓ
   (A) eat   (C) have eaten
   (B) is eating   (D) have been eating

4. Since June, Jake _____ rather than driving to the fitness center. He has more time now that he is retired.   Ⓐ Ⓑ Ⓒ Ⓓ
   (A) walking   (C) has walked
   (B) is walking   (D) has been walking

5. I always _____ to wish my boss a happy birthday.   Ⓐ Ⓑ Ⓒ Ⓓ
   (A) forget   (C) have forgotten
   (B) am forgetting   (D) have been forgetting

6. I _____ my suitcases already. You can put them   Ⓐ   Ⓑ   Ⓒ   Ⓓ
in the car now.
   (A)   pack   (C)   have packed
   (B)   am packing   (D)   have been packing

7. I'm sorry. I _____ to call you all week, but we   Ⓐ   Ⓑ   Ⓒ   Ⓓ
have been so busy at work.
   (A)   mean   (C)   have meant
   (B)   am meaning   (D)   have been meaning

attention
am going to → be   mean → plan to do   to do

8. First we _____ the forms. After that we sign   Ⓐ   Ⓑ   Ⓒ   Ⓓ
and mail them.
   (A)   print   (C)   have printed
   (B)   are printing   (D)   have been printing

9. I _____ your old telephone number, but I still   Ⓐ   Ⓑ   Ⓒ   Ⓓ
need to write your new one down.
   (A)   erase   (C)   have erased
   (B)   am erasing   (D)   have been erasing

10. We _____ the rose bushes all day. I apologize that   Ⓐ   Ⓑ   Ⓒ   Ⓓ
the front gardens are so messy.
   (A)   trim   (C)   have trimmed
   (B)   are trimming   (D)   have been trimming

THE SIMPLE PAST

▪ If a verb is regular, we form the simple past by putting *-ed* or *-d* on the end (*work, worked / type, typed*). If the verb is irregular, there are usually internal changes (*get, got*) or almost complete changes (*bring, brought*).

▪ We use the simple past for two main reasons:

> ➤ to show that an action happened in the past and is completely finished;
>
> *Columbus arrived in the New World in 1492.*
>
> ➤ to show which of two actions in the past lasted for a shorter time.
>
> *They were having dinner when I called.*

THE PAST CONTINUOUS

▪ We form the past continuous by using the auxiliary *was* or *were* before the verb and adding *-ing* to the end of the verb.

▪ We use the past continuous for two main reasons:

> ➤ to show that an action was in progress at a certain point in the past;
>
> *I was hoping to get a call from them before now.*
>
> ➤ to show which of two actions in the past was longer.
>
> *They were having dinner when I called.*

THE PAST PERFECT

▪ We form the past perfect by using the auxiliary *had* plus the past participle of the verb.

▪ We use the past perfect to show which of two actions in the past happened first. The past perfect represents what happened first; the simple past or past continuous represents what happened next.

> *He missed his appointment because his car had broken down.*

Practice B

DIRECTIONS: Mark the choice that best completes the sentence.

1. We _____ three new staff members last week. I'm happy with them so far.   Ⓐ Ⓑ Ⓒ Ⓓ
   (A) hired   (C) had hired
   (B) were hiring   (D) had been hiring

2. The old tenants _____ the property by the time we looked at it. There was no furniture left inside.   Ⓐ Ⓑ Ⓒ Ⓓ
   (A) vacated   (C) had vacated
   (B) were vacating (D) had been vacating

3. Sorry for not taking your call this afternoon. I _____ up some work for tonight's meeting.   Ⓐ Ⓑ Ⓒ Ⓓ
   (A) finished   (C) had finished
   (B) was finishing (D) had been finishing

4. We _____ from another supplier for three months 　Ⓐ　Ⓑ　Ⓒ　Ⓓ
   by the time James made his offer.
   (A)　ordered　　　　　　　　　(C)　had ordered
   (B)　ordering　　　　　　　　　(D)　had been ordering

5. The rent _____ by 5 percent this month. We might 　Ⓐ　Ⓑ　Ⓒ　Ⓓ
   need to close the shop.
   (A)　increased　　　　　　　　(C)　had increased
   (B)　was increasing　　　　　　(D)　had been increasing

6. The McKenzies almost _____ their house for less 　Ⓐ　Ⓑ　Ⓒ　Ⓓ
   than it was worth. A real estate agent helped them out.
   (A)　sold　　　　　　　　　　(C)　had sold
   (B)　were selling　　　　　　　(D)　had been selling

7. I _____ the bus by then. In fact, I was probably 　Ⓐ　Ⓑ　Ⓒ　Ⓓ
   at work by the time you arrived at my house.
   (A)　already caught　　　　　　(C)　had already caught
   (B)　was already catching　　　　(D)　had been already catching

8. Susan and I _____ you went home already. Do 　Ⓐ　Ⓑ　Ⓒ　Ⓓ
   you want to come to lunch with us?
   (A)　thought　　　　　　　　　(C)　had thought
   (B)　were thinking　　　　　　　(D)　had been thinking

9. The mayor forgot his main point while he _____ 　Ⓐ　Ⓑ　Ⓒ　Ⓓ
   the public.
   (A)　was addressed　　　　　　(C)　had addressed
   (B)　was addressing　　　　　　(D)　had been addressing

10. George and Jim _____ me to go to the conference 　Ⓐ　Ⓑ　Ⓒ　Ⓓ
    by the time I realized what it was about.
    (A)　convinced　　　　　　　　(C)　had convinced
    (B)　were convincing　　　　　(D)　had been convincing

THE SIMPLE FUTURE

■ With all verbs, both regular and irregular, we form the simple future by adding *will* before the verb.

■ We use the simple future for four main reasons:

➤ to show that an action will happen in the future

The office will close at 5:00 P.M. tonight.

➤ to make a prediction

We assume she'll quit her job.

➤ to make a promise

I'll mail the letters for you.

➤ to make a request

Will you close the door, please?

THE FUTURE PERFECT

■ We form the future perfect by using *will* plus the auxiliary *have* plus the past participle of the verb.

■ We use the future perfect for two main reasons:

➤ to show that an action will be completed before a time in the future;

I'll have read the article online before you find it in the newspaper.

➤ to make a prediction about actions that are now finished.

We will have to wait in the lobby because the performance will have started by now.

Practice C

DIRECTIONS: Mark the choice that best completes the sentence.

1. The new course —————— by the 5th of June. It's too
   bad that you don't get back on that date.   Ⓐ Ⓑ Ⓒ Ⓓ
   (A)   will start   (C)   will have started
   (B)   will be starting   (D)   will have been starting

2. Mr. Davidson —————— on the door when he is   Ⓐ Ⓑ Ⓒ Ⓓ
   ready to see you.
   (A)   will knock   (C)   will have knocked
   (B)   will be knocking   (D)   will have been knocking

3. Jenny will have lots of time to spend with her parents   Ⓐ Ⓑ Ⓒ Ⓓ
   in January. She _____ her job by then.
   (A)   is quitting   (C)   will have quit
   (B)   will be quitting   (D)   will have been quitting

4. _____ fax these documents to our client, please?   Ⓐ Ⓑ Ⓒ Ⓓ
   (A)   Will you   (C)   Will you have
   (B)   Will you be   (D)   Will you have been

5. We will have to stand at the back of the auditorium because the volunteers _____ all of the seats by now.

    (A) will take   (C) will have taken

    (B) will be taking   (D) will have been taking

6. Go home, Eric. I promise I _____ the lights before I leave the office.

    (A) will turn off   (C) will have turned off

    (B) will be turning off   (D) will have been turning off

7. I _____ the arrangements from home. I am sick today.

    (A) will be made   (C) will have made

    (B) will be making   (D) will have been making

8. The class _____ for three weeks by the time you join us. I'll fill you in at that time.

    (A) will run   (C) will have run

    (B) will be running   (D) will have been running

9. _____ you $20 that Jesse gets that raise when she asks for it.

    (A) I'll bet   (C) I'll have bet

    (B) I'll be betting   (D) I'll have been betting

10. I assume _____ to New York rather than drive.

    (A) you'll fly   (C) you'll have flown

    (B) you'll be flown   (D) you'll have been flying

MODAL AUXILIARIES

▪ The form of a modal does not change from first person to third person:

> *I can. / He can.*

▪ You never put *to* after a modal:

Incorrect:	*I can to type.*
Correct:	*I can type.*

▪ We use modals to help give verbs extra meaning. Here are the modals for this practice with their extra meanings:

- ➤ can = ability (*He can type 65 words per minute.*)
  - = permission [informal language] (*I can punch out early.*)
- ➤ could = possibility (*She could be late because of the heavy rain.*)
- ➤ will = future [usually for a promise or prediction] (*I'm sure they'll get raises.*)
- ➤ may = possibility (*She may be late because of the heavy rain.*)
  - permission [formal language] (*I may punch out early.*)
- ➤ might = possibility (*She might be late because of the heavy rain.*)
- ➤ shall = future [formal language, usually an offer or a suggestion] (*Shall we meet tomorrow afternoon to discuss the latest budget report?*)
- ➤ should = advice, suggestion, a good idea (*You should check the books again.*)
  - = expectation (*Because he works so hard, he should get promoted soon.*)
- ➤ ought to = should (*You ought to call her.*)
- ➤ must = necessity (*The bookkeeper must finish doing the payroll by Thursday.*)
  - = logical conclusion (*It must be very stressful being a CEO.*)
- ➤ would = possibility (*I would have gotten to work on time, but my train was late.*)
  - = intent (*He promised he would pick her up on time.*)

Practice D

DIRECTIONS: Mark the choice that best completes the sentence.

1. My receptionist ———— set you up with an appointment. Just go down the hall to your right.
   - (A) can
   - (B) might
   - (C) may
   - (D) ought to

   Ⓐ Ⓑ Ⓒ Ⓓ

2. ———— I hang your coat while you're removing your shoes?
   - (A) Shall
   - (B) Would
   - (C) Must
   - (D) Ought

   Ⓐ Ⓑ Ⓒ Ⓓ

3. We ———— finish this assignment by the deadline, but it's pretty unlikely.
   - (A) can
   - (B) might
   - (C) will
   - (D) would

   Ⓐ Ⓑ Ⓒ Ⓓ

4. You ——— bring your spouse if you wish. However, you'll have to pay for an extra ticket.

    (A) may   (C) ought to
    (B) might   (D) should

    Ⓐ   Ⓑ   Ⓒ   Ⓓ

5. He ——— take a taxi to the airport, but it makes more sense for me to just drop him off.

    (A) should   (C) ought to
    (B) could   (D) will

    Ⓐ   Ⓑ   Ⓒ   Ⓓ

6. I _____ have called you sooner, but our telephones weren't working.

    (A) will   (C) could
    (B) would   (D) must

    Ⓐ   Ⓑ   Ⓒ   Ⓓ

7. Is there a chance you _____ lose your job this winter?

    (A) can   (C) should
    (B) might   (D) must

    Ⓐ   Ⓑ   Ⓒ   Ⓓ

8. If you want, we _____ book you on an earlier flight.

    (A) should   (C) must
    (B) can   (D) may

    Ⓐ   Ⓑ   Ⓒ   Ⓓ

9. The office _____ close on the day before the holiday. It all depends how busy we are next week.

    (A) will   (C) might
    (B) must   (D) can

    Ⓐ   Ⓑ   Ⓒ   Ⓓ

10. _____ I take your order now, or are you still deciding?

    (A) May   (C) Would
    (B) Must   (D) Will

    Ⓐ   Ⓑ   Ⓒ   Ⓓ

REVIEW: VERBS AND REFERENCE

DIRECTIONS: Read the following passages and choose the word or phrase that best completes the blanks.

Questions 1–3 refer to the following letter.

May 18, 20____

To whom it may concern:

Jacob Rothman _____ for our company for the past five

    1.   (A)   works
           (B)   worked
           (C)   is working
           (D)   has worked

years. As my assistant, his duties include managing my travel and appointment schedule, typing and organizing documents, and answering the phone. He is a reliable and hardworking individual. He always _____ his assignments in a timely

    2.   (A)   completes
           (B)   will complete
           (C)   is completing
           (D)   had completed

and accurate manner. Because of _____ friendly manner

    3.   (A)   my
           (B)   its
           (C)   his
           (D)   our

and cooperative spirit, he is a pleasure to work with. We will miss him when he leaves our office to move to the West coast. I highly recommend him as a fine and promising employee for any company.

Sincerely,

Laurel Thornburg

Laurel Thornburg

Questions 4–6 refer to the following announcement.

Please welcome our newest _____, Claire Peterson. Ms. Peterson

4. (A) employ
    (B) employer
    (C) employee
    (D) employment

began working in the Accounting Department at the beginning of this week. Prior to joining our staff, she worked for the Simpson Group for eight years. While she _____ there, she wrote a

5. (A) is working
    (B) has worked
    (C) will work
    (D) was working

financial advice column for their monthly newsletter. We are very pleased that she has agreed to do the same for us. Ms. Peterson is enjoying her new position. "I _____ so many wonderful people

6. (A) have met
    (B) will have met
    (C) had met
    (D) meet

this week, " she says. "This seems like a fantastic place to work." We think so, too.

Questions 7–9 refer to the following memo.

To all employees:

As you know, we have a big anniversary coming up in a few weeks. As of the first of next month, this store _____ in operation for ten years. At the time my brothers and I

7. (A) is
   (B) was
   (C) will be
   (D) will have been

started Farnsworth Furniture, several other groups had attempted to operate a furniture outlet in this town and failed. We have shown them that _____ is possible. Of

8. (A) success
   (B) succeed
   (C) successful
   (D) successfully

course, we could not have done it without the hard work and dedication of each member of our staff. Therefore, we would like to invite all of you to an Employee Appreciation/Anniversary Celebration Banquet on Saturday, December 5. We hope that all of you _____ attend and celebrate with us.

9. (A) can
   (B) must
   (C) might
   (D) should

The Farnsworth Brothers

Questions 10–12 refer to the following e-mail.

To: Rita Marconi
From: Frank Howard
Subject: Company picnic

Rita,

The weather forecast for tomorrow is rain, so I think we _____

10. (A) can
     (B) might
     (C) would
     (D) should

postpone the company picnic. Of course, we could move it to an indoor location, but that wouldn't be the same. Please notify everyone that the picnic _____ place Friday of next week. Then call to change our picnic site

11. (A) will have taken
     (B) will take
     (C) takes
     (D) took

reservation. Mr. James, head of Park Reservations, has always been very helpful, so try to speak with him about it. When I _____ with him last time

12. (A) speak
     (B) spoke
     (C) was speaking
     (D) have spoken

about the possibilities of changing dates or locations, he was very accommodating, so I don't think there will be any problem. Thanks.

Frank

MODIFIERS

ADJECTIVES: COMPARATIVE AND SUPERLATIVE FORMS

COMPARATIVES

▨ We use comparatives when we talk about two things:

   Alexander of Macedonia was <u>greater than</u> Napoleon.

   Elizabeth I of England was <u>as great as</u> Catherine of Russia.

▨ We form comparatives four ways:
   ➢ If the adjective has one syllable (*great*), we add *-er* to it (*greater*) and follow the word with *than* (*greater than*).
   ➢ If the adjective has two syllables and ends in *-y* (*friendly*), we change the *y* to *i* and add *-er* (*friendlier*) and follow the word with *than* (*friendlier than*).
   ➢ If the adjective has two or more syllables (*interesting*), we put *more* before it (*more interesting*) and follow the word with *than* (*more interesting than*).
   ➢ If two or more things are the same, we put *as* before and after the adjective (*as great as*).

SUPERLATIVES

▨ We use superlatives when we talk about three or more things:

   Of the five bosses I've worked for in my career, Mr. Honeywell is <u>the friendliest</u>.

▨ We form superlatives in similar ways:
   ➢ If the adjective has one syllable (*great*), we put *the* before it and add *-est* to it (*the greatest*).
   ➢ If the adjective has two syllables and ends in *y* (*friendly*), we put *the* before it, change the *y* to *i*, and add *-est* to it (*the friendliest*).
   ➢ If the adjective has two or more syllables (*interesting*), we put *the most* before it (*the most interesting*).

▨ Some adjectives in English have irregular comparative and superlative forms:

good	*better*	*best*
bad	*worse*	*worst*
far	*farther/further*	*farthest/furthest*
little	*less (noncount)*	*least*
many/more	*more*	*most*
	few (count)	*fewest*

Practice A

DIRECTIONS: Mark the choice that best completes the sentence.

1. The size ten envelopes are _____ for sending documents than those small ones.
   (A) better
   (B) more better
   (C) best
   (D) the best

   Ⓐ Ⓑ Ⓒ Ⓓ

2. You can buy the slightly _____ pens this time. We don't need the most expensive ones.
   (A) cheap
   (B) cheaper
   (C) cheapest
   (D) the cheapest

   Ⓐ Ⓑ Ⓒ Ⓓ

3. Paul is _____ candidate for that position. He hates speaking in public.
   (A) the bad
   (B) worse
   (C) worst
   (D) the worst

   Ⓐ Ⓑ Ⓒ Ⓓ

4. Our new handbook is _____ than our old one.
   (A) interesting
   (B) more interesting
   (C) the interesting
   (D) the most interesting

   Ⓐ Ⓑ Ⓒ Ⓓ

5. _____ month of the year is usually January or February.
   (A) More slow
   (B) Slower
   (C) Slowest
   (D) The slowest

   Ⓐ Ⓑ Ⓒ Ⓓ

6. Please don't call us between noon and one. That is _____ time of day.
   (A) busy
   (B) a busier
   (C) busiest
   (D) the busiest

   Ⓐ Ⓑ Ⓒ Ⓓ

7. Which room is _____ one, Conference Room A or B? Ⓐ Ⓑ Ⓒ Ⓓ
   (A) more quiet
   (B) quieter
   (C) the quieter
   (D) quietest

8. The interior lights seem _____ than they usually do. Ⓐ Ⓑ Ⓒ Ⓓ
   (A) more bright
   (B) brighter
   (C) brightest
   (D) the brightest

9. You'll get _____ response if you call rather than e-mail the board members. Ⓐ Ⓑ Ⓒ Ⓓ
   (A) the quick
   (B) a quicker
   (C) quickest
   (D) the quickest

10. The flower bouquet was much _____ when it was delivered on Tuesday. Ⓐ Ⓑ Ⓒ Ⓓ
    (A) beautiful
    (B) more beautiful
    (C) the prettiest
    (D) more pretty

ADVERBS OF FREQUENCY

SINGLE WORDS

▧ Adverbs of frequency can be single words such as *always*, *seldom*, or *never*.

➤ We put adverbs of frequency after the verb *be*.

They are <u>rarely</u> late for meetings.

➤ We put adverbs of frequency between the subject and the verb.

She <u>never</u> acts rude, even when she has a lot of stress.

➤ We put adverbs of frequency after the first auxiliary.

She can <u>usually</u> be reached on her cell phone.

PHRASES

▧ Adverbs of frequency can also be phrases such as *on occasion* or *from time to time*.

<u>*On occasion*</u>, *the whole office likes having lunch together.*

The whole office likes having lunch together <u>from time to time</u>.

Practice B

DIRECTIONS: Mark the choice that best completes the sentence.

1. We _____ look at résumés sent by e-mail. You must deliver it by mail or in person.   Ⓐ Ⓑ Ⓒ Ⓓ
   - (A) sometimes
   - (B) rarely
   - (C) never
   - (D) always

2. I _____ buy a cup of coffee at work, but I usually bring one from home.   Ⓐ Ⓑ Ⓒ Ⓓ
   - (A) always
   - (B) sometimes
   - (C) usually
   - (D) often

3. It is our policy to give employees at least one warning. We _____ fire a person after only one minor mistake.   Ⓐ Ⓑ Ⓒ Ⓓ
   - (A) sometimes
   - (B) never
   - (C) rarely
   - (D) frequently

4. Jack _____ brings his dog Spot to work with him.   Ⓐ Ⓑ Ⓒ Ⓓ
   On most days, he leaves Spot in his backyard.
   (A) occasionally
   (B) frequently
   (C) almost always
   (D) often

5. I _____ forget to date forms. I must have been   Ⓐ Ⓑ Ⓒ Ⓓ
   really tired yesterday.
   (A) sometimes
   (B) frequently
   (C) often
   (D) rarely

6. We _____ invite students to come into the office   Ⓐ Ⓑ Ⓒ Ⓓ
   for a day. Ask our receptionist when our next session is.
   (A) never
   (B) rarely
   (C) frequently
   (D) almost never

7. The power _____ goes out in this building at   Ⓐ Ⓑ Ⓒ Ⓓ
   about this time. We should ask an electrician to look
   at the wiring.
   (A) seldom
   (B) often
   (C) rarely
   (D) sometimes

8. I _____ walk to work. When it's raining I take   Ⓐ Ⓑ Ⓒ Ⓓ
   the bus, though.
   (A) never
   (B) sometimes
   (C) almost always
   (D) occasionally

9. The boss _____ orders pizza for us on Fridays.   Ⓐ Ⓑ Ⓒ Ⓓ
   He's away today, so we'll have to go out to eat.
   (A) never
   (B) rarely
   (C) usually
   (D) occasionally

10. I _____ do my taxes on time. This is the first   Ⓐ Ⓑ Ⓒ Ⓓ
    year I sent them in late.
    (A) frequently
    (B) often
    (C) rarely
    (D) always

VERBAL ADJECTIVES: PRESENT AND PAST PARTICIPLES

PRESENT PARTICIPLE

- We use the present participle adjective to describe a person or thing that is responsible for doing an action or causing a feeling (*burning food / a frightening movie*).

- We form the present participle by adding *-ing* to a verb (*interesting*).

PAST PARTICIPLE

- We use the past participle adjective to describe a person or thing that receives an action or feeling (*the burned food / the frightened moviegoers*).

- We form the past participle in three ways:

  ➤ If the verb is regular, it looks just like the simple past: we add *-d* or *-ed* to it (*boiled*).

  ➤ If the verb ends in *-ay*, it looks like the simple past: we change the *y* to *i* and then add *-d* (*paid*).

  ➤ If the verb is irregular, it is the third form of that verb (*see, saw, seen*).

Practice C

DIRECTIONS: Mark the choice that best completes the sentence.

1. The _____ photocopier is sitting on the floor underneath the table.   Ⓐ Ⓑ Ⓒ Ⓓ
    - (A) break
    - (B) broken
    - (C) breaking
    - (D) broke

2. We're interested in the woman _____ in the last chair of the first row.   Ⓐ Ⓑ Ⓒ Ⓓ
    - (A) seat
    - (B) seated
    - (C) seating
    - (D) sat

3. I found this _____ piece of paper on your desk. Why did you destroy the document?   Ⓐ Ⓑ Ⓒ Ⓓ
    - (A) tearing
    - (B) tear
    - (C) torn
    - (D) to tear

4. Did you hear the _____ news? Anna is going to be the new manager!
   A B C D

   (A) surprise
   (B) surprised
   (C) surprising
   (D) to surprise

5. Our _____ candidate has at least three years of work experience.
   A B C D

   (A) preference
   (B) prefer
   (C) preferred
   (D) preferring

6. The speech that Mark delivered was well _____.
   A B C D

   (A) plan
   (B) planned
   (C) planning
   (D) planner

7. We can expect _____ costs in lumber this month.
   A B C D

   (A) rise
   (B) risen
   (C) rising
   (D) rose

8. The city finally removed the _____ tree from the sidewalk today. It's been in the way since the storm.
   A B C D

   (A) fall
   (B) falling
   (C) fall down
   (D) fallen

9. Please don't make me go to another _____ sales meeting.
   A B C D

   (A) boredom
   (B) boring
   (C) bored
   (D) bore

10. My eyes are sore from making these _____ calculations.
    A B C D

    (A) tired
    (B) tire
    (C) tiring
    (D) tire out

REVIEW: MODIFIERS AND REFERENCE

DIRECTIONS: Read the following passages and choose the word or phrase that best completes the blanks.

Questions 1–3 refer to the following e-mail.

From: G. Greengage
To: T. Margolies
Subject: New office

Tom,

Do you think we should go ahead and sign the lease on the State Street office? It is certainly _____ than our current office, but I am

1. (A) big
   (B) bigger
   (C) biggest
   (D) the biggest

concerned about the price. It is almost twice as much as what we're paying now. However, we may be able to find a way to pay for it if you really think this is the best space available. The main thing is, I want you to be _____ with it. Also, I know you are tired of looking at new offices

2. (A) satisfy
   (B) satisfied
   (C) satisfying
   (D) satisfaction

every day. I understand that this _____ chore has become a stress. So,

3. (A) daily
   (B) weekly
   (C) monthly
   (D) yearly

if you really believe this is our best option, call the landlord to make an appointment for sometime this week to go over the lease.

Gail

Questions 4–6 refer to the following memo.

To all employees:

Mr. Sachimoto of the Tokyo office will be visiting our offices next week. This will be his first visit with us. Since he has _____ been here before, please do all you can to make sure

    4. (A) never
          (B) often
          (C) seldom
          (D) occasionally

he leaves here with a good impression. While we plan to keep our guest very busy during the work day, we also want him to enjoy some _____ times with us. A reception is

    5. (A) relax
          (B) relaxed
          (C) relaxing
          (D) relaxation

planned for Friday evening, and all staff are strongly encouraged to attend. While each of you may have other occasions to meet and talk with Mr. Sachimoto during the week, we consider Friday's event _____ of his visit. We hope to see all of you there.

    6. (A) important
          (B) more important
          (C) the more important
          (D) the most important

Questions 7–9 refer to the following e-mail.

From: Luis Vasquez
To: Rosemary Hall
Subject: San Francisco Trip

Hi Rosemary,

I am traveling to San Francisco next week on company business, and I'd
like your advice. I know you _____ travel there; in

       7. (A)   never
            (B)   rarely
            (C)   occasionally
            (D)   often

fact, you were in San Francisco five or six times last year, weren't you? I
have a lot of recommendations for hotels and don't know how to choose.
Which do you think is _____ hotel? I'm looking for something

      8. (A)   good
            (B)   better than
            (C)   best
            (D)   the best

comfortable and affordable. It doesn't have to be right downtown. Also, I'm
thinking about taking the train instead of flying. Because of budget
restraints, I need to find the least _____ way to

      9. (A)   cheap
            (B)   price
            (C)   expensive
            (D)   cost

travel, and plane tickets cost a great deal more. Have you ever taken the
train? Is it comfortable? Reliable? Thanks for your help.

Luis

Andrew Witherspoon
Image Consultants, Inc.
360 Rosings Avenue, Suite 10
Roxbury, VA 23200

September 15, 20_

To whom it may concern:

_____ letter is to serve as a reference for Ms. Elizabeth

10. (A) Those
    (B) These
    (C) This
    (D) That

Rosen, who worked at Image Consultants, Inc. as my assistant
for five years. As her supervisor, I was able to closely observe
Ms. Rosen's skills on a daily basis. _____ was a

11. (A) I
    (B) She
    (C) He
    (D) It

responsible, reliable, and efficient employee. Ms. Rosen always
completed assignments in a timely manner and was willing to
take on extra work when circumstances required it. She always
had an upbeat attitude which contributed positively to the work
environment. We at Image Consultants, Inc. were sorry to lose
Ms. Rosen when she left us last year to move to London.
_____ office benefited greatly from having her on staff.

12. (A) Her
    (B) Our
    (C) Your
    (D) Their

Please don't hesitate to contact me if you have any further
questions about Ms. Rosen's work at Image Consultants, Inc.

Sincerely,

Andrew Witherspoon

Andrew Witherspoon

Questions 1–3 refer to the following article.

FINANCIAL DIFFICULTIES FOR GLOBAL AIRLINES

Because of financial difficulties, Global Airlines has announced a cutback on services. It will _____ the number of flights serving major cities and eliminate

1. (A) increase
   (B) reduce
   (C) maintain
   (D) expand

all flights to certain smaller destinations. The financially troubled airline also announced that it will lay _____ 1,000 employees, including 800 flight

2. (A) of
   (B) on
   (C) off
   (D) over

attendants and 200 pilots. The changes are planned _____ next month. These

3. (A) begin
   (B) begins
   (C) began
   (D) to begin

changes are necessary because of the $2 billion in losses experienced by the company over the past five years.

Sara Ramirez
180 Horseback Lane
Riverdale, NM 88449

April 1, 20__

Dear Ms. Ramirez:

Thank you for your letter expressing _____ in working

4. (A) interest
    (B) interested
    (C) interesting
    (D) interference

for our company. While I can see from your résumé that you are
highly qualified in your field, unfortunately we don't have any
openings for accountants right now. Sometimes when we have a
heavy workload, we hire accountants for _____ positions to

5. (A) full-time
    (B) temporary
    (C) permanent
    (D) supervisory

assist our regular staff. These positions usually involve 15–20
hours of work per week. They may last for one or two weeks or
for several months, depending on the situation. _____ you

6. (A) If
    (B) While
    (C) Because
    (D) Although

would like to be considered for such a position, please let me
know. Then I can contact you next time we have a need. Thank
you again for contacting us.

Sincerely,

Robert Wing

Robert Wing
Director of Human Resources

Questions 7–9 refer to the following e-mail.

From: R. Mitchell
To: L. Wang
Subject: Hong Kong Tickets

Mr. Wang,

I need to travel to Hong Kong next week. I want to depart on Monday and return on Friday, and I'd like to travel business class. Also, please _____ a hotel room for me for Monday through Thursday nights. I

7. (A)   loan
    (B)   hire
    (C)   book
    (D)   purchase

_____ with friends on Friday night. I liked the hotel you got for me last

8. (A)   stayed
    (B)   staying
    (C)   to stay
    (D)   will stay

time, and I would like to stay there _____. I don't remember the name

9. (A)   again
    (B)   over
    (C)   once
    (D)   yet

of the hotel, but you must have it in your files. Please let me know when you have the tickets. Thank you.

Rita Mitchell

Last night, the Mayor's Office _____ plans to start construction

    10. (A) announce
          (B) announces
          (C) announced
          (D) will announce

of a new soccer stadium early next year. "The condition of the current stadium is very dangerous," Mayor Wilson stated at last night's press conference. "The structure is falling apart, and renovation will be very costly. It's _____ to go ahead and build a new

    11. (A) efficient
          (B) more efficient
          (C) more efficient than
          (D) the most efficient

stadium than to try to repair the old one." The mayor said that construction of the new stadium should be completed in two years and expressed confidence that _____ would draw many new

    12. (A) it
          (B) he
          (C) they
          (D) we

businesses to the city.

PART 7:
READING COMPREHENSION

In this part, you will become familiar with the types of reading passages on the new TOEIC® test. In the first part of the Reading Comprehension section (Questions 153–180), you will read advertisements, forms, letters, e-mail, faxes, memos, tables, indexes, charts, instructions, or notices. You will have to answer two to five questions for each type.

In the second part (Questions 181–200), you will read a set of two of these passage types. You may read an e-mail and a memo, a form and a fax, a table and a letter, a letter and a letter. Each set of passages will be followed by five questions. In this last part of the Reading Comprehension section, these two passages relate to one another. You will need to understand both to answer the five questions for each set of double passages.

Your approach is the same in both the single-passage and the double-passage parts of Reading Comprehension. You will need to understand the facts and understand them quickly.

Good readers use strategies to help them understand what they read. These strategies include **skimming, scanning, using the context**, and **reading fast**. When using these strategies, readers ask themselves questions while reading. These questions help the reader understand better and faster. In this chapter, you will learn to ask yourself questions as you read. Don't forget to use these strategies when you take the new TOEIC test.

READING STRATEGIES

SKIMMING Good readers **skim** to find general information. When they skim, their eyes move quickly over the whole passage, looking for a general idea. For example, if you are reading a newspaper, you skim only the headlines of the paper to see generally what the news is that day. As you skim, you ask yourself:

Who did it?   *When* did they do it?
What did they do?   *Why* did they do it?
Where did they do it?

In the double-passage sets, skim over each passage and ask yourself the questions above. You also want to know how the passages are related. As you skim, you can ask yourself:

What do these two passages have in common?
How are they related?
What is different in the two passages?
Does the first passage present a problem and the second a solution?
Does the first passage state information that is revised in the second?

When you skim a passage on the new TOEIC test, move your eyes quickly over the whole passage; ask yourself the questions above to help you get a general idea of what the passage is about.

SCANNING Good readers **scan** to find specific information. When they scan, they move their eyes quickly to find specific information. For example, if you want a specific telephone number, you scan the pages of a telephone directory to find the name and number you want. As you scan, you ask yourself:

Where is the answer to my question?

When you scan a passage on the new TOEIC test, move your eyes quickly over the whole passage, looking for the specific answer to one of the reading comprehension questions.

In the double-passage sets, look for the key words in the questions and the answer choices. Then look for these key words or their synonyms or a paraphrase in both passages. As you scan, ask yourself:

Is the answer more likely in the first passage or second passage?
Is the answer found in information in both passages?

CONTEXT On the new TOEIC test you will find a new type of item: a vocabulary item. You will have to identify a synonym for a word. You will not be able to use a dictionary during the exam. You must learn to use the context to determine the meaning. You should look at other words in the sentence or even the whole paragraph to try to understand what the word means. Ask yourself:

How does the context help me understand a word?

Good readers guess the meanings of new words. They use the context to guess the meaning of a word so that they can read more quickly. This strategy works in both the single- and double-passage parts of Reading Comprehension.

READING FAST Good readers **read fast** to get the whole idea of the passage. This strategy works in both the single- and double-passage parts of Reading Comprehension. Reading faster will help you finish the passages faster, retain all the new information, and have more time to answer the questions.

ADVERTISEMENTS

Practice these reading strategies with the following advertisements. (Note that the short form of *advertisement* is *ad*.)

Sale! Sale! Sale!

McGruder's Department Store announces its biggest sale
of the year. You'll find fantastic savings throughout the store.

25% off all men's and women's business suits

25% off all men's and women's shoes

50% off all women's summer clothes

Don't miss out on this great opportunity to get
stylish designer items at bargain prices. With prices like these,
you can't afford not to shop.

Now through Saturday at all McGruder's locations:

**Park Avenue Mall   Springfield Center   Downtown
Manchester Depot**

Open Monday–Saturday, 8:30 A.M.–9:00 P.M.
Closed Sunday

SKIMMING Look quickly at the advertisement to answer these questions.

1. What is on sale?   Ⓐ **Ⓑ**
   (A) Business supplies
   (B) Clothes

2. Who is the sale for?   Ⓐ Ⓑ **Ⓒ**
   (A) Men
   (B) Women
   (C) Both men and women

SCANNING Mark the words that appear in the ad, and circle them in the ad.

3. (A) bathing suit   Ⓐ **Ⓑ**
   (B) business suit

4. (A) summer   **Ⓐ** Ⓑ
   (B) winter

5. (A) department   Ⓐ Ⓑ
   (B) apartment

6. Find and circle these days in the ad. Some may appear more than once.
   Monday   Saturday   Sunday

CONTEXT Find these words and phrases, and guess their meanings in this advertisement.

7. What does "25% off" mean?   Ⓐ **Ⓑ**
   (A) It costs $25.
   (B) It costs one quarter less than the usual price.

8. What does "Now through Saturday" mean?   Ⓐ Ⓑ
   (A) Beginning today and ending on Saturday
   (B) Beginning on Saturday

READING FAST

Read the ad as fast as you can. How long did it take?

_____ minutes _____ seconds

READING COMPREHENSION Mark the best answer.

9. What is not on sale?   Ⓐ Ⓑ Ⓒ Ⓓ
   (A) Men's shoes
   (B) Women's business suits
   (C) Men's summer clothes
   (D) Women's shoes

10. What is the first day of the sale?   Ⓐ Ⓑ Ⓒ Ⓓ
    (A) Today
    (B) On Saturday
    (C) On Sunday
    (D) Next week

11. How much do women's summer clothes cost?   Ⓐ Ⓑ Ⓒ Ⓓ
    (A) $50 each
    (B) $50 less than the usual price
    (C) Half the usual price
    (D) One quarter of the usual price

12. The word "Mall" in line 12 is closest in meaning to   Ⓐ Ⓑ Ⓒ Ⓓ
    (A) Shopping area
    (B) Parking lot
    (C) Food stall
    (D) Pedestrian track

Grand Opening!

For your convenience,

The State Street Bank

is opening a new full-service branch at the City Airport. Now it will be easier than ever to take care of all your banking needs as you leave or return from your trips.

Join us at our new location for our

Grand Opening

next

Saturday, September 15, from 1:00–4:00 P.M.

FOOD!

ENTERTAINMENT ACTIVITIES FOR THE WHOLE FAMILY

MUSIC

There will be food, music, and a variety of entertainment activities for the whole family. Representatives of local TV station WXYZ will be there to report on the event. So come on by and bring the whole family. Customer service specialists will be on hand to explain all the services our bank has to offer.

Find out about:
- The special benefits of opening a State Street checking or savings account
- How to qualify for our special low-interest loans
- State Street's custom-designed financial planning services

Prizes! Prizes! Prizes!

There will be prizes for the first 50 customers to open a checking or savings account at the new branch. In addition, all Grand Opening guests will be automatically entered in our Grand Prize Drawing. You could win a Caribbean Cruise for two!

See you there!

SKIMMING Look quickly at the advertisement to answer this question.

1. What kind of information does this advertisement give? Ⓐ Ⓑ
   (A)   A list of things for sale
   (B)   An explanation of an event ✓

SCANNING Look quickly at the advertisement to answer these questions.

2. What is the name of the bank? Ⓐ Ⓑ
   (A)   State Street Bank
   (B)   City Bank

3. What is the name of the airport? Ⓐ Ⓑ
   (A)   City Airport ✓
   (B)   Bank Street Airport

4. What hours do you see in the advertisement? Ⓐ Ⓑ
   (A)   1:00–4:00 A.M.
   (B)   1:00–4:00 P.M. ✓

CONTEXT Find these words and phrases, and guess their meanings in this advertisement.

5. branch Ⓐ Ⓑ
   (A)   part of a tree
   (B)   a business location

6. grand opening Ⓐ Ⓑ
   (A)   a special celebration for a new business
   (B)   the hours that a bank does business

READING FAST

Read the ad as fast as you can. How long did it take?

_____ minutes _____ seconds

READING COMPREHENSION Mark the best answer.

7. What is being advertised? Ⓐ Ⓑ Ⓒ Ⓓ
   (A)   A bank
   (B)   A restaurant
   (C)   A concert
   (D)   A travel agency

8. Where will the grand opening take place? Ⓐ Ⓑ Ⓒ Ⓓ
   (A)   On State Street
   (B)   At the airport ✓
   (C)   At a TV station
   (D)   In a park

9. The word "Representatives" in paragraph 2, line 2, is closest in meaning to
(A) Legislators
(B) Staff
(C) Siblings
(D) Specialists

10. When will the grand opening take place?
(A) In the morning
(B) In the afternoon
(C) In the evening
(D) At night

Advertisement 3

> Busy downtown law firm seeks administrative assistant with 3–5 years' experience working in a law office. Must be proficient in the use of word processing and database programs and be familiar with common legal documents. Must have a good telephone manner and a pleasant appearance. Working knowledge of Spanish a plus. Duties include word processing, management of client database, maintaining files, directing phone calls, and assisting clients who come to our office. We offer a competitive salary, health insurance, and paid vacation, as well as opportunity for advancement. To apply, call Ms. Ortiz, Director of Human Resources, between 10 and 4. Must be able to provide three references and proof of employment eligibility.

SKIMMING Look quickly at the advertisement to answer this question.

1. What is this advertisement for?
(A) A job opening
(B) An office for rent

SCANNING Look quickly at the advertisement to answer these questions.

2. Find and circle these numbers in the ad.
   3–5   10 and 4

3. What is 3–5?

    (A)   The number of people who work in the office

    (B)   The years of experience required for the job

4. What is 10 and 4?

    (A)   The daily hours of the job

    (B)   The hours to apply for the job

CONTEXT Find these words and phrases, and guess their meanings in this advertisement.

5. legal documents

    (A)   papers that lawyers write

    (B)   job application forms

6. telephone manner

    (A)   a way to speak on the phone

    (B)   a type of phone

7. paid vacation

    (A)   your job pays all your vacation expenses

    (B)   you continue to receive your salary while on vacation

8. firm

    (A)   hard

    (B)   a business or company

READING FAST

Read the ad as fast as you can. How long did it take?

_____ minutes _____ seconds

READING COMPREHENSION Mark the best answer.

9. What kind of position is advertised?

    (A)   Director of Human Resources

    (B)   Lawyer

    (C)   Administrative assistant

    (D)   Computer programmer

10. What is one skill required for this job?

    (A)   The ability to talk pleasantly on the telephone

    (B)   The ability to write legal documents

    (C)   The ability to develop computer programs

    (D)   The ability to find new clients

11. What is a benefit of this job?
    (A) They will pay for your vacation expenses.
    (B) You can make all the phone calls you want.
    (C) You only have to work from 10–4.
    (D) They will pay for your health insurance.

12. The word "Duties" in line 8 is closest in meaning to
    (A) Taxes
    (B) Benefits
    (C) Classes
    (D) Responsibilities

FORMS

READING STRATEGIES

▪ **Skimming** is an important strategy to use when you read different forms.

You want to know right away:

Who wrote it   *What* is it for?
Who is it for?   *Why* do I need to read it?
What kind of form is it?

▪ **Scanning** helps you look for specific information. Use the Reading Comprehension questions to guide your scanning.

▪ **Using context** is a way to find the meanings of new words. Look at the other words on the form. Then look at the new word in its context and try to guess what it means.

▪ **Reading fast** is very helpful. Just like advertisements, forms are often short readings. Good readers skim and scan quickly to learn the most important information on the form.

Practice these reading strategies with the forms on the following pages.

OUR TOWN SPORTS CLUB

Membership Application

Name _____

Address _____

_____

E-mail _____

Home phone _____ Work phone _____ Cell phone _____

Occupation _____

Type of membership (check one) Individual ($500) ___ Family ($1,200) ___

Student ($375) ___ Trial (one month only) ($100) ___

Method of payment (check one)   Cash ___   Check ___   Credit card ___

Credit card number _____ Expiration date _____

Signature (for credit card payments only) _____

Please check any of the following activities that you may wish to
participate in. We will forward the necessary information to you.

Teams:
___ Tennis   ___ Squash   ___ Swimming

Classes:
___ Aerobics   ___ Water Aerobics   ___ Swimming   ___ Squash
       ___ School vacation camps for kids

SKIMMING Mark the words you see at the top of the form.

1. (A) Membership application   (Ⓐ) Ⓑ
   (B) Job application

2. (A) Sports equipment   Ⓐ (Ⓑ)
   (B) Sports club

SCANNING Look quickly at the application to answer these questions.

3. Look at the form. Circle the names of the different types of membership.

4. Look at the form. Which type of payment is not mentioned?   Ⓐ Ⓑ (Ⓒ) Ⓓ
   (A) Cash
   (B) Credit card
   (C) Money order
   (D) Check

CONTEXT Find these words, and guess their meanings on this form.

5. occupation   (Ⓐ) Ⓑ
   (A) job or profession
   (B) an activity to pass the time

6. trial   (Ⓐ) (Ⓑ)
   (A) try doing something to see if you like it
   (B) a legal process

┌───┐
│   **READING FAST**   │
│   │
│ Read the form as fast as you can. How long did it take? │
│   │
│ _____ minutes _____ seconds   │
└───┘

READING COMPREHENSION Mark the best answer.

7. What is this form for?   Ⓐ (Ⓑ) Ⓒ Ⓓ
   (A) Getting a new telephone number
   (B) Joining a club
   (C) Applying for a job
   (D) Ordering sports equipment

8. Which is the least expensive type of membership?   Ⓐ Ⓑ Ⓒ (Ⓓ)
   (A) Individual
   (B) Family
   (C) Student
   (D) Trial

9. How many different types of payment are accepted?   Ⓐ Ⓑ   Ⓓ
   (A) One
   (B) Two
   (C) Three
   (D) Four

10. Who has to sign the form?   Ⓐ 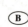 Ⓒ Ⓓ
   (A) Everybody
   (B) People who pay by credit card
   (C) People who pay by check
   (D) The whole family

11. The word "Method" in line 11 is closest in meaning to   Ⓐ Ⓑ
   (A) Technique
   (B) System
   (C) Process
   (D) Type

How did you enjoy your stay?

Help us serve you better by filling out this form and leaving it in your room.

	good	fair	poor
1. Your room			
Cleanliness of room	☐	☐	☐
Comfort of beds	☐	☐	☐
Maid service	☐	☐	☐
2. Room service			
Menu selection	☐	☐	☐
Speed of service	☐	☐	☐
Prices			
3. Front desk			
Helpfulness of staff	☐	☐	☐
4. Fitness room and pool			
Types of exercise machines	☐	☐	☐
Pool hours	☐	☐	☐
Cleanliness of lockers	☐	☐	☐

How can we improve? Please write your comments or suggestions here.

_____

_____

Thank you for your time.
We hope to see you again soon!

SKIMMING Look quickly at the form to answer this question.

1. What kind of form is this? (A) (B)
   - (A) An application
   - (B) A questionnaire

SCANNING Mark the words and phrases that appear in the form, and circle them on the form.

2. (A) men (A) (B)
   - (B) menu

3. (A) maid ⒶⒷ
(B) made

4. (A) front desk ⒶⒷ
(B) office desk

5. (A) customer service ⒶⒷ
(B) room service

CONTEXT Find these words and phrases, and guess their meanings on this form.

6. room service ⒶⒷ
(A) fixing broken things in a hotel room
(B) delivering meals to a hotel room

7. stay ⒶⒷ
(A) a visit to a hotel
(B) remain in one place

READING FAST

Read the form as fast as you can. How long did it take?

_____ minutes _____ seconds

READING COMPREHENSION Mark the best answer.

8. Where would you see this form? ⒶⒷⒸⒹ
(A) At a restaurant
(B) At an office
(C) At a furniture store
(D) At a hotel

9. What should you do with this form? ⒶⒷⒸⒹ
(A) Leave it in your room
(B) Put it on the front desk
(C) Give it to the maid
(D) Send it by mail

10. What is one thing that is not asked about? ⒶⒷⒸⒹ
(A) Menu selection
(B) Comfort of beds
(C) Cleanliness of front desk
(D) Speed of room service

11. The word "selection" in line 9 is closest in meaning to ⒶⒷⒸⒹ
(A) collection
(B) mixture
(C) selectivity
(D) choice

Form 3

Vacation Leave Request Form

TickTackSystems, Inc.

Vacation Leave Request Form

Date: *April 1*

Name: *Daniel Greenwood*

Position: *Research Assistant*

Department: *Marketing*

Supervisor: *Samantha Smith*

Dates you are requesting: *May 16-20*

Type of leave you are requesting: _X_ paid ___ unpaid

Please turn this form in to the Human Resources Director
at least 3 weeks before requested leave date.

SKIMMING Find and circle these words on the form. Some may appear more than once.

1. vacation   leave   request

SCANNING Find and circle the following.

2. Find and circle these names.
   Daniel Greenwood   Samantha Smith

3. Find and circle these job titles.
   Research Assistant   Human Resources Director

4. Find and circle these dates.
   April 1   May 16–20

CONTEXT Find these words, and guess their meanings on this form.

5. leave   Ⓐ   Ⓑ
   (A) exit a room
   (B) time off from work

6. request   Ⓐ   Ⓑ
   (A) ask for something
   (B) do something again

READING COMPREHENSION Mark the best answer.

7. What is this form for?   Ⓐ   Ⓑ   Ⓒ   Ⓓ
   (A) Asking for days off from work
   (B) Getting travel information
   (C) Making plane reservations
   (D) Paying for a trip

8. What is Mr. Greenwood's job?   Ⓐ   Ⓑ   Ⓒ   Ⓓ
   (A) Marketing supervisor
   (B) Human resources officer
   (C) Research assistant
   (D) Travel agent

9. When did Mr. Greenwood fill out this form?   Ⓐ   Ⓑ   Ⓒ   Ⓓ
   (A) Three weeks ago
   (B) Between May 16 and May 23
   (C) On April 1
   (D) On May 16

10. Who should Mr. Greenwood give this form to?   Ⓐ   Ⓑ   Ⓒ   Ⓓ
    (A) Samantha Smith
    (B) His assistant
    (C) A marketing researcher
    (D) The human resources director

11. The word "Leave" in line 1 is closest in meaning to   Ⓐ   Ⓑ   Ⓒ   Ⓓ
    (A) Exit
    (B) Time off
    (C) Removal
    (D) Project

LETTERS, E-MAIL, FAXES, AND MEMOS

READING STRATEGIES

▪ **Skimming** is the way to quickly find information.

> *Who* is the information for?　　*When* was it sent?
> *Who* sent it?

▪ **Scanning** helps you find specific information. Always check the Reading Comprehension questions and answer choices first. Scan for specific information.

> *Why* did they send the　　*What* do they want?
> information?

▪ **Using context** helps you find the meanings of new words by looking at the other words and sentences surrounding the words. Business letters may have more unfamiliar words than letters from friends.

▪ **Reading fast** is very helpful. Written forms of communication can be short and simple or long and complicated. When you practice the reading strategies, you will improve your speed and get the necessary information at the same time.

Practice these reading strategies with the letters, e-mail, faxes, and memos on the following pages.

Merry Marketing Company
244 Merry Way
Boston, MA 01106

July 17, 20___

To whom it may concern:

Alice Newbold has worked for the Merry Marketing Company for the past five years. She started as an administrative assistant and worked her way up to Assistant Director of Research, in which position she has been working for two years.

Ms. Newbold is a highly motivated and industrious worker. She is willing to put in long hours if necessary to get the job done. She is also a skilled manager and works well with those she supervises.

Ms. Newbold has contributed a great deal to this company. We will be sorry to lose her. I can highly recommend her for any position requiring independence, creativity, and supervisory skills.

Sincerely,

James Jones

James Jones, Director

SKIMMING Look quickly at the letter to answer these questions.

1. Who signed this letter? Ⓐ Ⓑ
   (A) Alice Newbold
   (B) James Jones

2. Who is the letter about? Ⓐ Ⓑ
   (A) Alice Newbold
   (B) James Jones

SCANNING Mark the words and phrases that appear in the form, and circle them on the form.

3. (A) nursing assistant Ⓐ Ⓑ
   (B) administrative assistant

4. (A) Assistant Director Ⓐ Ⓑ
   (B) Movie Director

5. (A) worker   (A)   (B)
    (B) walker

6. (A) request   (A)   (B)
    (B) recommend

CONTEXT Find these words and phrases, and guess their meanings in this letter.

7. To whom it may concern   (A)   (B)
    (A) This letter is for a specific person.
    (B) This letter is for any person who is interested in it.

8. worked her way up   (A)   (B)
    (A) She worked hard and got a higher job position.
    (B) She went upstairs.

9. contributed   (A)   (B)
    (A) given
    (B) taken

READING FAST

Read the letter as fast as you can. How long did it take?

_____ minutes _____ seconds

READING COMPREHENSION Mark the best answer.

10. What is the purpose of this letter?   (A)   (B)   (C)   (D)
    (A) To ask for a job
    (B) To describe a company
    (C) To recommend an employee for a new job
    (D) To advertise a position

11. The word "motivated" in paragraph 2, line 1, is   (A)   (B)   (C)   (D)
closest in meaning to
    (A) committed
    (B) irritated
    (C) intelligent
    (D) mobile

12. What has Alice Newbold done for the past five years?   (A)   (B)   (C)   (D)
    (A) She has been an administrative assistant.
    (B) She has worked for a marketing company.
    (C) She has looked for a job.
    (D) She has supervised James Jones.

To: Bob Smith
From: Joyce Miller
Subject: meeting change
Date: March 20, 20__

Bob,
The time for the meeting tomorrow has been changed from 9:00 to 12:30. I'm sorry about this, but it turns out it's the only time everyone can meet. I know you have another meeting later in the afternoon, but I expect ours won't last more than one hour, so it shouldn't interfere with that schedule. The good news is that since it's a lunchtime meeting, the office will provide sandwiches and coffee for everyone. I'll make sure that we order from the Garden House since I know that's your favorite sandwich shop. We'll meet in the training room on the fifth floor. Please don't forget to bring ten copies of your budget report. Thanks. See you tomorrow.

Joyce

SKIMMING Look quickly at the e-mail to answer these questions.

1. Who is the e-mail for?
   To: _____

2. Who sent the e-mail?
   From: _____

3. What is the e-mail about?
   Subject: _____

SCANNING Find these words and phrases about time in the e-mail, and circle them. Some may appear more than once.

4. March 20   tomorrow   9:00   12:30   one hour   lunchtime

CONTEXT Find these words, and guess their meanings in this e-mail.

5. change   Ⓐ   Ⓑ
   (A) make different
   (B) coins

6. last   Ⓐ   Ⓑ
   (A) opposite of first
   (B) take time

7. budget   Ⓐ   Ⓑ
   (A) a plan for spending money
   (B) a form of transportation

READING FAST

Read the letter as fast as you can. How long did it take?

_____ minutes _____ seconds

READING COMPREHENSION Mark the best answer.

8. When is the meeting?   Ⓐ   Ⓑ   Ⓒ   Ⓓ
   (A) On March 20 from 9–12:30
   (B) On March 20 at 12:30
   (C) On March 21 from 9–12:30
   (D) On March 21 from 12:30–1:30

9. What should Bob bring to the meeting?   Ⓐ   Ⓑ   Ⓒ   Ⓓ
   (A) Sandwiches
   (B) Coffee
   (C) Copies of his report
   (D) Training material

10. What will they probably discuss at the meeting?   Ⓐ   Ⓑ   Ⓒ   Ⓓ
    (A) The budget
    (B) Lunch
    (C) Training programs
    (D) Schedules

11. The word "provide" in paragraph 1, line 6, is closest in meaning to   Ⓐ   Ⓑ   Ⓒ   Ⓓ
    (A) warm
    (B) sell
    (C) make
    (D) supply

To: All staff
From: Sharon Lee, Office Manager
Re: Office supplies

In order to better manage the office supplies, I have developed a new system. From now on, the supply closet will remain locked at all times. The only people authorized to have keys to the closet are myself and my assistant, Mr. Whitehead. If you wish to request supplies, please get a supply request form from Mr. Whitehead. Please submit your form 24 hours in advance of when you need your supplies. We promise to get your supplies to you within 24 hours as long as we have them on hand. It may take up to a week to get supplies that need to be ordered.

I am sure you will understand the necessity of this new system. In the past we have run out of essential supplies too often. This system will help me keep track of our supplies, and I will know when to order more. By following this system, you will always have what you need when you need it. Thank you for your cooperation.

SKIMMING Look quickly at the memo to answer these questions.

1. Who is this memo for?   (A) (B)
    (A) All staff
    (B) Sharon Lee

2. Who is it from?   (A) (B)
    (A) The company director
    (B) The office manager

3. What is it about?   (A) (B)
    (A) Office supplies
    (B) Office schedules

SCANNING Mark the words and phrases that appear in the form, and circle them on the form. Some may appear more than once.

4. (A) resistant   (A) (B)
    (B) assistant

5. (A) myself   (A) (B)
    (B) yourself

6. (A) manage   (A) (B)
    (B) damage

7. (A) require   (A) (B)
    (B) request

Find these words and phrases, and guess their meanings in this memo.

8. authorized   Ⓐ Ⓑ
   (A) have permission
   (B) wrote a book

9. submit   Ⓐ Ⓑ
   (A) give
   (B) tell about

10. in advance   Ⓐ Ⓑ
    (A) very skilled
    (B) before

11. keep track of   Ⓐ Ⓑ
    (A) ride a train
    (B) know about

READING FAST

Read the message as fast as you can. How long did it take?

_____ minutes _____ seconds

READING COMPREHENSION Mark the best answer.

12. What is the purpose of this memo?   Ⓐ Ⓑ Ⓒ Ⓓ
    (A) To order new supplies
    (B) To explain a new system
    (C) To introduce Mr. Whitehead
    (D) To describe where supplies are kept

13. Who has keys to the supply closet?   Ⓐ Ⓑ Ⓒ Ⓓ
    (A) Only Ms. Lee
    (B) Only Mr. Whitehead
    (C) Both Ms. Lee and her assistant
    (D) All office staff

14. The word "essential" in paragraph 2, line 2,   Ⓐ Ⓑ Ⓒ Ⓓ
    is closest in meaning to
    (A) dispensable
    (B) expensive
    (C) forgotten
    (D) necessary

15. How can a staff member get office supplies?   Ⓐ Ⓑ Ⓒ Ⓓ
    (A) By filling out a form
    (B) By asking for the key to the supply closet
    (C) By ordering them from the supply company
    (D) By calling Ms. Lee

TABLES, INDEXES, AND CHARTS

Practice these reading strategies with the tables, indexes, and charts on the following pages.

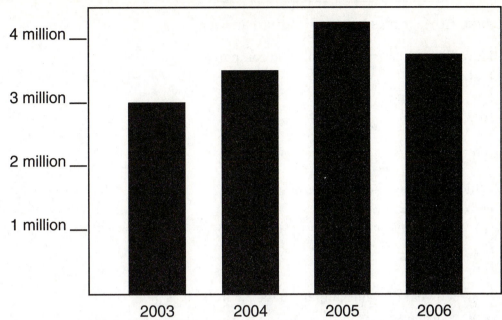

Acme Supply Company
Retail Sales 2003–2006

Please note: This chart represents domestic retail sales only. For figures regarding overseas retail sales for the years 2003–2006, please see page 12.

SKIMMING Look quickly at the graph to answer these questions.

1. What is this graph about?   Ⓐ   Ⓑ
   (A)   How much a company sold
   (B)   How much a company spent

2. How many years does it cover?   Ⓐ   Ⓑ   Ⓒ   Ⓓ
   (A)   One
   (B)   Two
   (C)   Three
   (D)   Four

SCANNING Find and circle the following.

3. Find and circle all the numbers that tell an amount of money.

4. Find and circle all the years.

CONTEXT Find this word, and guess its meaning in this graph.

5. retail   Ⓐ   Ⓑ
   (A)   sold in a store
   (B)   sold twice

READING FAST

Read the selection as fast as you can. How long did it take?

_____ minutes _____ seconds

▶ **READING COMPREHENSION** Mark the best answer.

6. How many dollars in sales did the company
    make in 2004?   Ⓐ   Ⓑ   Ⓒ   Ⓓ
    (A)   3 million
    (B)   3.5 million
    (C)   3.75 million
    (D)   4.25 million

7. Which year had the highest sales?   Ⓐ   Ⓑ   Ⓒ   Ⓓ
    (A)   2003
    (B)   2004
    (C)   2005
    (D)   2006

8. In which year did the company have 3.5 million
    dollars in sales?   Ⓐ   Ⓑ   Ⓒ   Ⓓ
    (A)   2003
    (B)   2004
    (C)   2005
    (D)   2006

Tables, Indexes, and Charts 2

FREEDONIA ISLAND

Average Temperatures (Fahrenheit)

You may find the following information useful when planning your trip to
Freedonia. Please keep in mind that these are average temperatures only
and that the weather can vary a great deal.

	January		July	
	high	low	high	low
Mountain region	32	18	75	51
Coast	70	55	85	61
Capital city	57	32	75	58

SKIMMING Look quickly at the chart to answer these questions.

1. What is the highest temperature you see? _____

2. What is the lowest temperature you see? _____

3. How many different places are mentioned? _____

SCANNING Find these words on the chart and circle them.

4. temperature   high   low   January   July

CONTEXT Find these words, and guess their meanings in this chart.

5. average   Ⓐ   Ⓑ
   (A) normal
   (B) something to drink

6. region   Ⓐ   Ⓑ
   (A) a type of church
   (B) an area

READING FAST

Read the index as fast as you can. How long did it take?

_____ minutes _____ seconds

READING COMPREHENSION Mark the best answer.

7. Where is the average high temperature 75 degrees
   in July?   Ⓐ   Ⓑ   Ⓒ   Ⓓ
   (A) In the mountain region only
   (B) On the coast only
   (C) In the capital city only
   (D) In both the mountains and the capital city

8. What is the average high temperature on the
   coast in January?   Ⓐ   Ⓑ   Ⓒ   Ⓓ
   (A) 55
   (B) 61
   (C) 70
   (D) 85

9. What is the coldest temperature in the
   mountain region?   Ⓐ   Ⓑ   Ⓒ   Ⓓ
   (A) 18
   (B) 32
   (C) 51
   (D) 55

10. Which is the warmest region of the island? (A) (B) (C) (D)
    (A) The mountains
    (B) The coast
    (C) The capital city
    (D) They are all the same

11. The word "Coast" in column 1, row 4, is closest in (A) (B) (C) (D)
    meaning to
    (A) Pond
    (B) Seaside
    (C) Rural
    (D) Riverbed

Tables, Indexes, and Charts 3

Emerald Airlines

Sale prices* between this city and:

Vancouver	$375
Los Angeles	$350
San Francisco	$225
Tokyo	$600
Seoul	$725
Honolulu	$525

*Prices are good until June 30 and are for one-way
economy class tickets. Round-trip tickets are twice
the one-way fare.

*Sale does not apply to business and first class tickets.
Make your reservation by visiting our web site. All major
credit cards are accepted. Tickets can also be reserved by
calling 1-800-555-9942. A 5% surcharge applies to all
reservations made by phone.*

SKIMMING Look quickly at the chart to answer these questions.

1. What are the numbers about? (A) (B) (C)
   (A) Distances
   (B) Prices
   (C) Time

2. What company's name is on the chart? _____

3. How many city names are on the chart? _____

4. Look for the asterisks (*) and circle them. There are two.

5. Find these different ticket types, and circle them.
   one-way   round-trip   economy class   business   first class

CONTEXT Find these words, and guess their meanings in this chart.

6. good   (A)   (B)
   (A) the opposite of bad
   (B) can be used

7. fare   (A)   (B)
   (A) price
   (B) food

8. apply   (A)   (B)
   (A) be related to
   (B) complete a form

READING FAST

Read the table as fast as you can. How long did it take?

_____ minutes _____ seconds

READING COMPREHENSION Mark the best answer.

9. What is on sale?   (A)   (B)   (C)   (D)
   (A) Economy class tickets only
   (B) Business class tickets only
   (C) Business and first class tickets
   (D) All classes of tickets

10. Which city has a fare of $725?   (A)   (B)   (C)   (D)
    (A) Los Angeles
    (B) Tokyo
    (C) Seoul
    (D) Honolulu

11. Which is the cheapest city to travel to?   (A)   (B)   (C)   (D)
    (A) Vancouver
    (B) Los Angeles
    (C) San Francisco
    (D) Honolulu

12. How much is a round-trip ticket to Tokyo?
    (A) $225
    (B) $600
    (C) $725
    (D) $1,200

    (A) (B) (C) (D)

13. The word "good" in line 9, is closest in
    meaning to
    (A) changing
    (B) valuable
    (C) excellent
    (D) valid

    (A) (B) (C) (D)

INSTRUCTIONS AND NOTICES

READING STRATEGIES

▪ **Skimming** is the way to find general information quickly.

What are the instructions or notices for?
How many steps are there in the instructions?
Do they seem easy or complicated? Could I follow them myself?
What kind of information do the notices give me?

▪ **Scanning** helps you find specific information quickly.

Will I need any tools to follow the instructions?
Are all the parts accounted for? Is anything missing?
What kinds of items or places do the notices mention?
What locations should I look for?

▪ **Using context** helps you find the meanings of new words by looking at them in context. Instructions and notices may have more unfamiliar words than letters from friends.

▪ **Reading fast** is very helpful. Instructions and notices can be short and simple or long and complicated. When you practice the reading strategies, you will improve your speed and get the necessary information at the same time.

Practice these reading strategies with the instructions and notices on the following pages.

The Acme Guarantee

Our products are fully guaranteed for one year from the date of purchase. If you are not satisfied for any reason, you can return the product directly to us for a complete refund. Simply mail it back to us at:

Acme Corporation
1500 State Street
Big Falls, CA 12345

Make sure you include the receipt with the date and place of purchase. You will receive a refund check in 8–12 weeks.
If you would like to exchange your product for another similar one of equal value, please contact our Customer Service office at 800-555-8765 for instructions. Customer Service representatives are available to serve you 24 hours a day.

SKIMMING Look quickly at the instructions to answer these questions.

1. Do these instructions include a street address? Ⓐ Ⓑ
   (A) Yes
   (B) No

2. Do these instructions include an e-mail address? Ⓐ Ⓑ
   (A) Yes
   (B) No

3. Do these instructions include a telephone number? Ⓐ Ⓑ
   (A) Yes
   (B) No

SCANNING Find the following.

4. Underline all the numbers you see in the instructions.

5. Find these words and phrases in the instructions, and circle them.
   mail   receive   check   Customer Service

CONTEXT Find these words, and guess their meanings in these instructions.

6. refund Ⓐ Ⓑ
   (A) repayment
   (B) gift

7. satisfied   Ⓐ   Ⓑ
   (A) happy with
   (B) not hungry

8. receipt   Ⓐ   Ⓑ
   (A) instructions for cooking
   (B) paper with information about a purchase

READING FAST

Read the instructions as fast as you can. How long did it take?

_____ minutes _____ seconds

READING COMPREHENSION Mark the best answer.

9. If a customer is not satisfied with the product, what   Ⓐ   Ⓑ   Ⓒ   Ⓓ
   should he or she do?
   (A) Return it to the place of purchase
   (B) Send it to the Acme Corporation
   (C) Call Customer Service
   (D) Write a letter to the Acme Corporation

10. What information has to be included on
    the receipt?   Ⓐ   Ⓑ   Ⓒ   Ⓓ
    (A) The customer's home address
    (B) The color and size of the product
    (C) The telephone number of the store
    (D) The name of the store where the product was bought

11. What will happen in 8 to 12 weeks?   Ⓐ   Ⓑ   Ⓒ   Ⓓ
    (A) You will get your money back.
    (B) A Customer Service representative will call you.
    (C) The Acme Corporation will send you a new product.
    (D) You will get a receipt.

12. The word "refund" in paragraph 1, line 4, is closest in
    meaning to   Ⓐ   Ⓑ   Ⓒ   Ⓓ
    (A) credit
    (B) new
    (C) reimbursement
    (D) blank

Tickets for all shows at the White River Theater may be ordered by calling the box office between 8:30 A.M. and 4:30 P.M. Tuesday through Saturday. Please have the following information ready when you call: the number of tickets you wish to purchase, the time and date of the performance you want to see, and your credit card number. Tickets ordered at least a week in advance of the performance can be mailed to your home. Otherwise, you can pick up your tickets in person at the box office one hour before the performance begins. A 15% discount is available on blocks of tickets for groups of ten or more when orders are made at least two weeks in advance of the performance date. Call the box office for details.

SKIMMING Look quickly at the instructions to answer this question.

1. Look at the first sentence of the instructions. What are the instructions about?　　　Ⓐ　Ⓑ
   (A) How to use tickets
   (B) How to buy tickets

SCANNING Find the following.

2. Find these times in the instructions, and circle them.
   8:30　　　4:30

Mark the words and phrases that appear in the notice, and circle them on the notice. Some may appear more than once.

3. (A) number　　　　　　　　　　Ⓐ　Ⓑ
   (B) numeral

4. (A) sailed　　　　　　　　　　Ⓐ　Ⓑ
   (B) mailed

5. (A) fall　　　　　　　　　　　Ⓐ　Ⓑ
   (B) call

6. (A) purchase　　　　　　　　　Ⓐ　Ⓑ
   (B) chase

7. box office   Ⓐ Ⓑ
   (A) a place that sells boxes
   (B) a place that sells theater tickets

8. performance   Ⓐ Ⓑ
   (A) a show in a theater
   (B) quality of work

READING FAST

Read the instructions as fast as you can. How long did it take?

_____ minutes _____ seconds

READING COMPREHENSION Mark the best answer.

9. What are these tickets for?   Ⓐ Ⓑ Ⓒ Ⓓ
   (A) A theater
   (B) An airplane trip
   (C) A museum
   (D) A boat ride

10. How can tickets be ordered?   Ⓐ Ⓑ Ⓒ Ⓓ
    (A) By going to the box office
    (B) By sending the order by mail
    (C) By calling the box office
    (D) By calling the credit card company

11. What information is required for
    ordering tickets?   Ⓐ Ⓑ Ⓒ Ⓓ
    (A) A telephone number
    (B) A credit card number
    (C) A house number
    (D) A fax number

12. When can tickets be picked up?   Ⓐ Ⓑ Ⓒ Ⓓ
    (A) Before 8:30
    (B) Between 8:30 and 4:30
    (C) After 4:30
    (D) One hour prior to the start of the event

13. The phrase "in person" in line 8 is closest in meaning to   Ⓐ Ⓑ Ⓒ Ⓓ
    (A) anyone
    (B) selfishly
    (C) one by one
    (D) personally

To all employees of the Rosings Company:

Please be advised that as part of the office remodeling project, all conference rooms are scheduled for painting this month. Conference rooms on the second floor will be painted next week, and conference rooms on the fourth floor will be painted the following week. During this time, the cafeteria will be available for meetings every morning before 12:00 and every afternoon after 2:00. Please see Ms. Smith in the engineering office to reserve your meeting times in the cafeteria. Since this is less meeting space than we usually have available, we will have to schedule carefully to make sure everyone's needs are met. To this end, we ask that you reserve your meeting time at least a week in advance and give Ms. Smith several alternative times if possible.

We apologize for the inconvenience and thank you in advance for your cooperation. Please see me if you have any questions.

Matilde Romero
Office Manager

SKIMMING Look quickly at the notice to answer this question.

1. Look at the first sentence of the notice. What will happen to the conference rooms?   Ⓐ   Ⓑ
   (A) They will be painted.
   (B) They will be scheduled for meetings.

SCANNING Find the following.

2. Underline all the numbers in the notice.

3. Find these time expressions, and underline them.
   this month   next week   the following week
   every morning   every afternoon

4. Find this name, and circle it.
   Ms. Smith

CONTEXT Find these words and phrases, and guess their meanings in this notice.

5. remodeling   Ⓐ   Ⓑ
   (A) taking away
   (B) improvement

6. available   Ⓐ   Ⓑ
   (A) open
   (B) closed

7. reserve   Ⓐ   Ⓑ
   (A) serve again
   (B) keep for a particular person or group

READING FAST

Read the instructions as fast as you can. How long did it take?

_____ minutes _____ seconds

▷ **READING COMPREHENSION** Mark the best answer.

8. When will conference rooms on the fourth floor
   be painted?   Ⓐ Ⓑ Ⓒ Ⓓ
   (A) Next week
   (B) Next month
   (C) In two weeks
   (D) In two months

9. Why should people see Ms. Smith?   Ⓐ Ⓑ Ⓒ Ⓓ
   (A) To plan lunch in the cafeteria
   (B) To schedule painting
   (C) To reserve the cafeteria for meetings
   (D) To plan a conference

10. When will the cafeteria be available for meetings? Ⓐ Ⓑ Ⓒ Ⓓ
    (A) Only in the mornings
    (B) Between 12:00 and 2:00
    (C) Every morning and afternoon
    (D) Only in the afternoon

11. Where does Ms. Smith work?   Ⓐ Ⓑ Ⓒ Ⓓ
    (A) On the second floor
    (B) In the conference department
    (C) In the cafeteria
    (D) In the engineering office

12. What word is closest in meaning to "scheduled"
    in paragraph 1, line 2?   Ⓐ Ⓑ Ⓒ Ⓓ
    (A) calendar
    (B) planned
    (C) timed
    (D) closed

Questions 1–5 refer to the following notice and e-mail.

Notice to all building staff

Next Tuesday, May 15, the elevators will be repaired. This means that they will be out of service between the hours of 9:00 and 5:00. During this time you will have to use the stairs. We are sorry for any inconvenience this may cause. Please don't hesitate to contact the Building Cleaning and Maintenance Office if you have any questions.

Jason Podryhula
Manager, Building Cleaning and Maintenance Staff

To: Lilya Yemchuk
From: Shirley Smith
Subject: Tuesday meeting

Lilya,

I assume you saw the notice about the repairs next Tuesday. This poses a problem for our lunch meeting. How can we get all that food up to the fifth floor conference room without an elevator? I think we'd do better to change the date. Please call the head of the cleaning and maintenance staff to see if the conference room is available for the next day. If he gives the OK, then go ahead and call the restaurant to change the day of our lunch order. Ask for Mr. Cho. He took our order last time.

You and I also need to get together to go over the Jones proposal before the lunch meeting. Let's meet first thing Tuesday. I plan to be here early enough to take the elevator up to the office. No stairs for me! I'll see you then.

Shirley

1. What will happen next Tuesday?
   (A) The elevators will be repaired.
   (B) The building will be cleaned.
   (C) The stairs will be painted.
   (D) The restaurant will be closed.

2. Why does Ms. Smith want to change the date of the meeting?
   (A) The conference room will not be available on Tuesday.
   (B) She doesn't want to carry food up the stairs.
   (C) Ms. Yemchuk can't attend on Tuesday.
   (D) The conference room won't be clean.

3. What day does Ms. Smith want to have the meeting?
   (A) Monday
   (B) Wednesday
   (C) Thursday
   (D) Friday

4. Who gives permission to use the conference room?
   (A) Ms. Smith
   (B) Ms. Yemchuk
   (C) Mr. Podryhula
   (D) Mr. Cho

5. What time does Ms. Smith plan to arrive on Tuesday?
   (A) Before 9:00
   (B) At 9:00
   (C) At 5:00
   (D) After 5:00

October 25, 20___

Mr. William Prince
1785 Honeycutt Boulevard
Marysville, IL 53028

Dear Mr. Prince:

We are pleased to offer you the position of Budget Assistant at Systems, Inc. We would like you to start work on Monday, November 10. You will report to your supervisor, Ms. Chen, in room 44. We are happy to offer you the salary that we discussed in your interview. Other benefits include health insurance for you and your family. We are sorry that we cannot offer life or dental insurance at this time, but we may be able to in the future. You will also get 20 vacation days and 5 sick days per year. Stock options and a pension plan are also available. I would suggest that you make an appointment to come in and speak with Emma Park, our benefits expert, very soon, and she can explain the full benefits package to you. At the same time you can fill out some paperwork for us.

Welcome to Systems, Inc. We look forward to working with you.

Sincerely,

Ivan Katz

Ivan Katz

October 31, 20___

Mr. Ivan Katz
Human Resources Director
Systems, Inc.
1700 Main Avenue
Chicago, IL 53147

Dear Mr. Katz:

Thank you for your offer of a position at Systems, Inc. Unfortunately, I have decided to take another position. I say this with real regret as I am sure that I would enjoy working at Systems, Inc., and the benefits are very attractive. However, I believe my new position at the Horizon Company will be better for me. Systems, Inc. has offered me a higher salary and twice as many vacation days as Horizon, but Horizon has offered me the same type of job and it's closer to my home. I find that location is very important. It would take me over an hour just to get to work if I had the job at Systems, Inc. Because of my family and other commitments, I cannot agree to put myself in such a situation. Thank you again for the offer.

Sincerely,

William Prince

William Prince

6. What insurance benefit does Systems, Inc. offer?
   (A) Life insurance
   (B) Health insurance
   (C) Dental insurance
   (D) Automobile insurance

7. Who is the benefits expert at Systems, Inc.?
   (A) Ms. Chen
   (B) Ms. Park
   (C) Mr. Katz
   (D) Mr. Prince

8. Why did Mr. Prince NOT accept a new position at Systems, Inc.?
   (A) The salary is too low.
   (B) The benefits are not good.
   (C) The location is inconvenient.
   (D) The job isn't interesting.

9. What job did Mr. Prince take with Horizon?
   (A) Budget Assistant
   (B) Human Resources Director
   (C) Budget Supervisor
   (D) Insurance Salesman

10. How many vacation days a year will he get at Horizon?
    (A) 5
    (B) 10
    (C) 20
    (D) 40

READING REVIEW

You will find the Answer Sheet for the Reading Review on page 387. Detach it from the book and use it to record your answers. On the new TOEIC test, you will have one hour and fifteen minutes to complete Parts 5, 6, and 7.

READING TEST

In the Reading test, you will read a variety of texts and answer several different types of reading comprehension questions. The entire Reading test will last 75 minutes. There are three parts, and directions are given for each part. You are encouraged to answer as many questions as possible within the time allowed.

You must mark your answers on the separate answer sheet. Do not write your answers in the test book.

PART 5

Directions: A word or phrase is missing in each of the sentences below. Four answer choices are given below each sentence. Select the best answer to complete the sentence. Then mark the letter (A), (B), (C), or (D) on your answer sheet.

---

101. If the client _____ dissatisfied, please have him write a letter.

    (A) am
    (B) is
    (C) are
    (D) be

102. My acquaintance with Mr. Broughton started as a business relationship and became a _____.

    (A) friends
    (B) friendly
    (C) friendless
    (D) friendship

103. The train from Osaka will be arriving _____ Tokyo in ten minutes.

    (A) before
    (B) in
    (C) around
    (D) at

104. The meeting was postponed because the typists weren't able to get the work _____ in time.

    (A) do
    (B) done
    (C) did
    (D) does

105. If the receptionist is unable to answer your question, Ms. Takai _____ help you.

    (A) can
    (B) did
    (C) could not
    (D) would not

106. We rely on Ms. Lee for her experience, sensitivity, and _____ advice.

    (A) wisdom
    (B) wisely
    (C) wise
    (D) wiser

107. Mr. Moore is doing very well at his job and expects to _____ over $100,000 next year.

   (A) salary
   (B) earn
   (C) worth
   (D) income

108. The secretary asked a clerk to check the report for typing _____.

   (A) errands
   (B) errs
   (C) errors
   (D) errant

109. Mr. Kim is considered one of the most honest _____ most hardworking members of the finance team.

   (A) but
   (B) or
   (C) and
   (D) with

110. The retirement luncheon has been changed from 12:00 _____ 12:30 because the speaker will arrive late.

   (A) at
   (B) to
   (C) until
   (D) by

111. The president of the company _____ to Korea for an important conference.

   (A) went
   (B) gone
   (C) go
   (D) going

112. Since Mr. Takahashi attends afternoon classes, he _____ the night shift.

   (A) will be always working
   (B) will always be working
   (C) will be working always
   (D) always will be working

113. We just bought a new copy machine and will install it _____ the two offices.

   (A) among
   (B) around
   (C) between
   (D) from

114. The student intern needs permission to take time off for a _____ interview.

   (A) job
   (B) worker
   (C) chore
   (D) golf

115. The employees at the factory eat lunch at that cafeteria at least _____.

   (A) often
   (B) sometimes
   (C) always
   (D) twice a week

116. Employees must turn off the lights _____ they leave the office.

   (A) afterward
   (B) before
   (C) while
   (D) because

117. _____ it was the office manager's birthday, the secretaries sent her roses.

   (A) But
   (B) Even though
   (C) Since
   (D) While

118. Employees of the Kita Corporation are encouraged to do exercises _____ during their breaks.

   (A) oftentimes
   (B) every day
   (C) monthly
   (D) day by day

119. The operator was not able to find the address _____ telephone number.

   (A) or
   (B) although
   (C) but
   (D) even though

120. Mrs. Gonzalez has been here for a long time, and she _____ one of the best workers we have.

   (A) always has considered been
   (B) has been always considered
   (C) has been considered always
   (D) has always been considered

GO ON TO THE NEXT PAGE

121. Do you know if the _____ for last week's order has been sent?

   (A) pay
   (B) payment
   (C) payable
   (D) pays

122. The board of directors proposed that an outside consultant be _____ in.

   (A) will be brought
   (B) bring
   (C) brought
   (D) will be bringing

123. The company requires that all employees have a physical examination _____.

   (A) rarely
   (B) never
   (C) annually
   (D) seldom

124. Files in the accounting department need to be _____ according to date.

   (A) organizing
   (B) organize
   (C) organization
   (D) organized

125. The elevators are located _____ the water fountain at the end of the hall.

   (A) into
   (B) across
   (C) near
   (D) between

126. The company policy states that when they _____ late, employees must be paid at the overtime rate.

   (A) working
   (B) worker
   (C) will work
   (D) work

127. The advertising manager is _____ that the telegram that just arrived will give him a new account.

   (A) hoping
   (B) hopeless
   (C) hopelessness
   (D) hope

128. Employees are reminded that the first parking space in each row of the lot _____ open for visitors.

   (A) left
   (B) leave
   (C) is left
   (D) is leaving

129. When Mr. Storer retires, the office is going to _____ a small party for him.

   (A) do
   (B) get
   (C) make
   (D) have

130. The company director has decided to hire an interior decorator to _____ the lobby.

   (A) decorating
   (B) decor
   (C) decorate
   (D) decoration

131. If our department _____ another typist, we'd get this report done quickly.

   (A) have
   (B) had
   (C) will have
   (D) have had

132. Mr. Johnson's daughter left home last year, and now she _____ in the city.

   (A) house
   (B) inhabits
   (C) lives
   (D) resident

133. If Mr. Wong arrives before noon, the committee members _____ very surprised.

   (A) would be
   (B) will be
   (C) is
   (D) was

134. Yesterday, a package for Mr. Chi was left _____ the receptionist's desk.

   (A) on
   (B) from
   (C) for
   (D) of

135. According to the ticket agent, the next plane for Rome _____ in two hours.

    (A) depart
    (B) departs
    (C) departed
    (D) departing

136. _____ Ms. Hogan was on the phone, her client could not see her right away.

    (A) Although
    (B) During
    (C) Before
    (D) Because

137. Unfortunately, the doctor was not able to see _____ without his glasses.

    (A) clearly
    (B) carefully
    (C) finely
    (D) nearly

138. We didn't notice that the package was already damaged when it _____.

    (A) arrived
    (B) has arrived
    (C) was arriving
    (D) had arrived

139. Ms. Smith was very _____ when she received the wrong letter.

    (A) confuse
    (B) confusing
    (C) confused
    (D) confuses

140. The store is open Monday through Saturday _____ not on Sunday.

    (A) either
    (B) or
    (C) but
    (D) so

GO ON TO THE NEXT PAGE

Directions: Read the texts that follow. A word or phrase is missing in some of the sentences. Four answer choices are given below each of the sentences. Select the best answer to complete the text. Then mark the letter (A), (B), (C), or (D) on your answer sheet.

Questions 141–143 refer to the following article.

Jan. 10

Coffee has become the most popular drink in offices. This information is the result of a recent _____ of office workers across the country. According to the results

141. (A) conference
(B) dismissal
(C) training
(D) survey

of the study, 55 percent of office workers choose coffee as their favorite beverage. The second most popular drink is tea, chosen by 30 percent of office workers in the study. The remaining 15 percent _____ soda, water, or other drinks.

142. (A) choose
(B) chosen
(C) choice
(D) choosing

preserve!

手法

During the workday, most coffee drinkers get their coffee from a machine in the office. In fact, 70 percent of coffee drinkers get their coffee in this way. Another 20 percent get their coffee "to go" at a coffee shop or restaurant. Ten percent make their coffee at home and take it to work in a thermos. The members of this last group, more than others, believe that there is nothing like the taste of _____ coffee.

143. (A) hot
(B) fresh
(C) sweet
(D) homemade

魔法瓶 vacuum flask の

(商)標か

GO ON TO THE NEXT PAGE

NOTICE
Skyline Telephone Company

Customer Account #: 05827716494-HJ0784922
Date: May 31, 20__

This is to notify you that your _____ of $155 for phone service during

144. (A) pay
(B) payer
(C) paying
(D) payment

the month of March is overdue. The amount owed must be paid in full by June 30
or your phone service may be _____.

145. (A) increased
(B) extended
(C) lowered
(D) cut off

If you have trouble paying your bill, please contact our customer service office to
find out if _____ qualify for financial assistance.

146. (A) he
(B) she
(C) you
(D) they

Spend the weekend in luxury at the Continental Hotel.

Take advantage of our special low weekend rates:

One night — $100
Two nights — $175

Prices include breakfast and _____ of the pool and exercise room.

147. (A) use
      (B) uses
      (C) user
      (D) using

_____! Call now. To take advantage of this offer, you must

148. (A) No wait
      (B) Don't wait
      (C) Can't wait
      (D) Doesn't wait

_____ your room two weeks in advance.

149. (A) prepare
      (B) inspect
      (C) reserve
      (D) consider

GO ON TO THE NEXT PAGE

Questions 150–152 refer to the following article.

Are you unhappy at work? _____ of sleep may be the reason. Recent studies

150.   (A)   Like
       (B)   Luck
       (C)   Lack
       (D)   Look

show that people who get fewer than six hours of sleep a night on average tend to feel less satisfied with their jobs. They report feeling angry, fatigued, unhappy, and irritable during the work day. Most of them also report difficulty in _____ their assignments. "Your coworker who always seems to be behind and

151.   (A)   completing
       (B)   completion
       (C)   completed
       (D)   complete

tends to have a large pile of undone projects on her desk may well be suffering from sleep deprivation," says Dr. Jocelyn Bush of the Sleep Studies Institute. "Naturally, there are many reasons why someone may not be able to keep _____ with a

152.   (A)   at
       (B)   of
       (C)   in
       (D)   up

normal workload," says Dr. Bush, "but until now we never considered that sleep, or not enough of it, could be a common cause for such problems." So, before sending your staff to expensive work efficiency training sessions, try suggesting that they get a little more sleep. Not on the job, of course.

Directions: In this part you will read a selection of texts, such as magazine and newspaper articles, letters, and advertisements. Each text is followed by several questions. Select the best answer for each question and mark the letter (A), (B), (C), or (D) on your answer sheet.

Questions 153–155 refer to the following e-mail message.

10:30— *Jan. 10*

To: George Young
From: Michelle Smith
Subject: Tokyo trip
Date: December 13, 20__

George,

I am going to have to make an emergency trip to the Tokyo office next week. Please arrange flights and hotels for me. I know this is last minute, but do the best that you can. I will have to leave Monday, and I would prefer an early morning flight if you can get me one. In Tokyo, I'd prefer to stay in a hotel near the airport rather than downtown, as that is actually a more convenient location for me. See if you can get one with a fitness room and a pool. I need to return here Saturday, or Sunday at the latest. Please make these arrangements before the end of today. E-mail a copy of the itinerary to Mr. Ono at the Tokyo office so that he can make arrangements to meet me at the hotel on Tuesday. Thank you.

Michelle

---

153. What does Michelle want George to do?
(A) Go to Tokyo with her
(B) Make plane and hotel reservations
(C) Give her travel advice
(D) Take her to the airport

154. When will Michelle begin her trip?
(A) Today
(B) Monday
(C) Saturday
(D) December 13

155. Where will Michelle stay in Tokyo?
(A) Downtown
(B) At the office
(C) Near the airport
(D) At George's house

READING REVIEW 281

A small computer software company seeking to expand into the Asian market seeks experienced sales representative. We are looking for an energetic self-starter with a minimum of three years' experience in sales, preferably with computer-related products. Must be able to work independently. Must be fluent in English and have good Japanese language skills. Must be familiar with most common office software packages. Job involves travel 1 to 2 weeks per month. We offer a competitive salary and excellent benefits, including 4 weeks paid vacation, health and life insurance, and computer training as needed. To apply, call Mr. Rogers at 555-6983 between 1 and 4. Or fax résumé and references to 555-6988. Closing date: March 31.

156. What kind of job is advertised?
   (A) Computer programmer
   (B) Salesperson
   (C) Software developer
   (D) Travel agent

157. How much experience is required?
   (A) No more than 3 years
   (B) 3 years or more
   (C) 1 to 4 years
   (D) At least 4 years

158. The word "involves" in line 9 is closest in meaning to
   (A) prohibits
   (B) includes
   (C) prevents
   (D) allows

159. How can you apply for the job?
   (A) Make a phone call
   (B) Take a computer training course
   (C) Send an e-mail
   (D) Write a letter

April 1, 20___

Ralph Johnson
President
Computers, Inc.
1334 Maple Avenue
Suite 10
Mapleville, MI 02148

Dear Mr. Johnson:

On behalf of Steven Reynolds, owner of the building at 1334 Maple Avenue, I am writing this letter to inform you that the rent on your office is overdue. As of today, April 1st, you owe three months' back rent. According to the lease agreement signed by you, we are permitted to request that you vacate the premises following three months of nonpayment of rent. Therefore, you are hereby notified that you are required to pay in full by April 15th, or we will have to ask you to leave the building at the end of the month. Payment must be made in the form of a cashier's check and must be received by this office on or before April 15th. We sincerely hope that we can resolve this matter in a manner satisfactory to all concerned. Please call me if you have any questions.

Sincerely,

Miriam Hopewell

Miriam Hopewell
Building Manager

160. Who wrote this letter?
  (A) A computer programmer
  (B) The president of a company
  (C) The building supervisor
  (D) The owner of the building

161. What does Mr. Johnson have to do by April 15th?
  (A) Pay rent for April only
  (B) Leave the building
  (C) Pay three months' rent
  (D) Call Miriam Hopewell

GO ON TO THE NEXT PAGE

Questions 162–165 refer to the following form.

SNYDER'S STORE
Mail Order Form

Name: *Richard Robles*

Address: *185 Broad Street, Apt. 212*

quantity	item	color	price
1	sweater	blue	$75
3	tennis shirts	white	$42
1	sweater	red	$90
5	pairs socks	black	$25
1	winter coat	green	$250
		add 5% tax	$24
		shipping	$15
		Total	$521

(Returns must be made within 30 days and will be charged a 15% handling fee.)

Method of payment: _X_ check ___ money order ___ credit card ___ gift certificate

To order by phone, dial 1-800-555-0983 Monday through Friday, 8:30 A.M. until 8:30 P.M. You can use this form to plan your order before calling. Please have your credit card ready when you call.

Fax your order by dialing 1-800-555-0977.

To order online and see our latest catalog listings, visit our web site.

162. What kind of store is Snyder's?
   (A) A tennis store
   (B) A shoe store
   (C) A sports store
   (D) A clothing store

163. What costs $15?
   (A) A blue sweater
   (B) Sending the order
   (C) Sales tax
   (D) Returning an item

164. How much does one pair of socks cost?
   (A) $2.50
   (B) $5.00
   (C) $25.00
   (D) $50.00

165. How will Mr. Robles pay for his order?
   (A) Check
   (B) Money order
   (C) Credit card
   (D) Gift certificate

Questions 166–169 refer to the following instructions.

To order by mail

Complete the form below and mail it to:

Garden Supply, Inc.
4869 Wilmer Avenue
Petersburg, VA 21278

Don't forget to enclose a check or money order with your order. Credit cards are not accepted when you order by mail. You will receive your order in 4–6 weeks.

- -

First Name: _____

Last Name: _____

Company/Organization: _____

Address: _____

_____

Telephone: _____

E-mail: _____

To order by phone: Call 800-555-9364   M–F   9–5
Please have the following information ready: the name, page number, and catalog number for all items you plan to order, and your credit card number. You will receive your order within 5 days.

To order online
Go to our web site and complete the form there. You must have a credit card to order online. You will receive your order in 1–2 weeks.

Substitutes
We do our best to fill each order as made. However, during the busy spring gardening season, we cannot avoid running out of items from time to time. In this case, if you would like us to select an alternate item of similar value for you, please check here: ___

---

166. When can someone order by phone?
(A) Anytime
(B) Monday through Friday only
(C) On the weekend
(D) In the evening

167. If someone wanted to pay by credit card, how would he or she order?
(A) By mail
(B) By phone only
(C) Online only
(D) Either by phone or online

168. To get an order the fastest, which way should one order?
(A) By mail
(B) By phone
(C) Online
(D) Either by phone or online

169. Which of the following is NOT needed for phone orders?
(A) A catalog number
(B) A page number
(C) A credit card
(D) An e-mail address

GO ON TO THE NEXT PAGE

NOTICE

All building visitors and tenants are hereby notified that smoking is prohibited in most areas of this office building by order of the City Chief of Police. Smoking is allowed only in the employee lounge on the second floor or on the sidewalk outside the building. Outside smokers must stand at least 10 feet away from all building entrances. Please report any violations to the Security Office in room 105. There is a $50 fine for violation of this order. Repeated violations may incur higher fines.

170. What is the punishment for people who smoke in the building?
(A) Pay $50
(B) Go to the police station
(C) Lose their employment
(D) Stay outside

171. Where is smoking allowed?
(A) On the entire second floor
(B) In most areas of the building
(C) In the office
(D) On the sidewalk

MEMORANDUM

To: All company personnel
From: Milton Freeman, Office Manager
Date: September 22, 20___
Re: Photocopier issues

The photocopier has broken down again. This is the third time this month. We are all frustrated by the loss of valuable time this causes, not to mention the costs of the repairs. Part of the problem results from attempts at repairs made by persons who don't completely understand the operation of the machine. Even a simple problem like a paper jam can become exacerbated if not dealt with properly. In order to avoid problems in the future, please observe the following guidelines:

1. If you are unsure how to operate the photocopy machine, please ask Sally Garfield, my assistant, to show you how to use it.

2. If you have any problem at all with the photocopy machine, do not attempt to fix it yourself.

3. Please report all problems with the photocopy machine to Ms. Garfield. She has been trained to fix most common problems with the machine and is always ready to assist you with all photocopier issues.

4. Do not call a repairperson yourself. This is the responsibility of Ms. Garfield.

Thank you for your patience and cooperation.

172. How many times has the photocopier been broken this month?
(A) One
(B) Two
(C) Three
(D) We don't know.

173. What should people do when the photocopier breaks?
(A) Fix it
(B) Call a repairperson
(C) Send a memo to the office manager
(D) Tell Sally Garfield

174. The word "observe" in paragraph 1, line 7, is closest in meaning to
(A) view
(B) state
(C) follow
(D) comment

GO ON TO THE NEXT PAGE

NORTHERN RAILROAD
Notice of Schedule Change

Date posted: March 28th

As of April 15th, there will be a new train schedule as follows.
Trains leaving for:

Marysville	10:00 A.M.	12:35 P.M.	2:50 P.M.	6:15 P.M.
Summerside	9:15 A.M.	11:45 A.M.	3:10 P.M.	5:50 P.M.
Woodmont	8:45 A.M.	12:15 P.M.	3:25 P.M.	6:40 P.M.

There will also be a fare increase starting April 15th:
Adult, one-way.........$15
Child, one-way............$9
Station office hours will remain the same (7 A.M.–8 P.M. daily)

The 15% surcharge on tickets purchased on board the train during hours
that the station is open remains in effect.

Monthly train passes are available for purchase at the station or online.

Please be advised that as of January of next year, there will be an increase
in station parking fees. The new fee schedule will be posted four weeks
in advance of the change.

---

175. When will the train schedule change?
(A) Today
(B) March 28th
(C) April 5th
(D) April 15th

176. What time will the latest train leave for
Woodmont?
(A) 8:45 A.M.
(B) 5:50 P.M.
(C) 6:15 P.M.
(D) 6:40 P.M.

177. What will NOT change?
(A) The price of adult tickets
(B) The train schedule
(C) The station office hours
(D) The fare for children

Questions 178–180 refer to the following e-mail.

To: Dan Reynolds
From: Cynthia See
Subject: Vacation schedule
Date: April 3, 20__

Dan,

I wanted to bring you up to date on the vacation schedule for next month since several people are requesting leave then. Lora Johnson wants to take off from the 1st through the 7th. Kyle Roberts asked for the following week, the 8th through the 14th. Both Sandy Greene and Tiffany Andrews asked to take off the week of the 22nd through the 28th. I have already approved all four of these requests. Do you think we could ask Philippa Conte to cover for Sandy and Tiffany during that week?

Kevin Kim also wants to take off during the last week of the month, but I haven't approved his request yet. If he's off then, we will be seriously understaffed. I don't think we can ask Philippa to cover for three people, do you? I will suggest to Kevin that he move his vacation to the first week of June. I don't want to approve any more vacations for next month. I will wait to take my vacation in July when, I hope, the schedule here will be back to normal. You were smart to plan your vacation for this month before everybody else starts taking off. You are leaving next week, right?

Let me know if you have any comments about next month's vacation schedule. Have a good time on your vacation, and I will see you when you return.
Cynthia

P196

answer

178. How many people want to take a vacation next month?
(A) One
(B) Two
(C) Four
(D) Five

179. Who will take a vacation during the last week of May?
(A) Philippa
(B) Kevin
(C) Sandy and Tiffany
(D) Sandy, Tiffany, and Kevin

180. When will Dan take his vacation?
(A) April
(B) May
(C) June
(D) July

Jan 10.

GO ON TO THE NEXT PAGE

Questions 181–185 refer to the following two e-mail messages.

To: Cheryl McLean
From: Lee Chang
Subject: My arrival

Hello Cheryl,

I will arrive in Springfield next Wednesday from Melbourne at 11:00 A.M. I will be staying at the Hotel Paris. It would be no problem for me to take a taxi to the hotel. I could meet you at your office in the early afternoon, let's say at 1:30. I understand that it is very close to the hotel, so I can just walk over. I will bring my computer with all the necessary files, but I still haven't seen a copy of the Petersen report. I'd like to look it over before I see you and would appreciate it if you'd send a copy to my hotel. I will have to leave for Hong Kong on Saturday afternoon, but I think we'll have plenty of time to complete our project before then. I look forward to meeting with you.

Lee Chang

To: Mark Robertson
From: Cheryl McLean
Subject: Fw: My arrival

Mark,

I am forwarding the details of Mr. Chang's arrival next week. Please use the company car to pick him up at the airport, and BE ON TIME. In fact, you should plan to arrive half an hour early to make sure. Also, you'll note that he asked me to send the Petersen information to his hotel room. Please don't forget to give it to him. It's very important. I'd like the staff to meet Mr. Chang, so please reserve the fourth floor conference room for Thursday morning. One more thing, I plan to take Mr. Chang to dinner on Wednesday evening, so we'll need reservations for 7:00 at the restaurant at his hotel. That's all for now. Thank you.

Cheryl

---

181. Where is Mr. Chang arriving from?
   (A) Springfield
   (B) Melbourne
   (C) Paris
   (D) Hong Kong

182. How will Mr. Chang get to his hotel?
   (A) By taxi
   (B) By car
   (C) By foot
   (D) By bus

183. What time should Mr. Robertson arrive at the airport?
   (A) 10:30 A.M.
   (B) 11:00 A.M.
   (C) 1:00 P.M.
   (D) 1:30 P.M.

184. What should Mr. Robertson give to Mr. Chang?
   (A) A computer
   (B) Some files
   (C) A report
   (D) His hotel room key

185. Where will Mr. Chang have dinner on Wednesday evening?
   (A) In Ms. McLean's office
   (B) In a conference room
   (C) In a restaurant
   (D) In his hotel room

GO ON TO THE NEXT PAGE

Questions 186–190 refer to the following article and letter.

The Playtime Corporation announced yesterday that Mai Le has been promoted to CEO of the company. Mai Le has been with Playtime for ten years. She formerly worked for the Trellis Mail Order Company and graduated from Western University School of Business 25 years ago. In her former capacity as Resource Director at Playtime, Ms. Le was noted for the innovative programs she brought to the company, including employee-of-the-month incentives and parent-friendly programs such as flexible scheduling and onsite daycare. Outgoing CEO Caroline Overall is retiring from the company and plans to open an executive consulting business.

May 15, 20___

Dear Mai,

I saw the article in today's newspaper and would like to extend my warmest congratulations to you. You deserve this more than anyone I know. From the moment I met you those many years ago on our first day of high school, I knew that you would go far. You were the smartest and most ambitious of all our classmates.

You deserve a special celebration, and I would like to invite you to dinner at the Spring Seasons Hotel. I've already spoken to your former boss, and she plans to join us. I asked some of your old coworkers, Violet Smith and Harry Wong, and I also called Lee Kim, but all three of them are out of town. So it will just be the three of us, but that will be fine. Let me know if this weekend or next weekend is better for you. I look forward to seeing you. It's been too long.

Your buddy,
Alice

186. Where does Mai Le currently work?
(A) At the Trellis Mail Order Company
(B) At the Playtime Corporation
(C) At the School of Business
(D) At Western University

187. When did Mai graduate from the university?
(A) 10 years ago
(B) 15 years ago
(C) 20 years ago
(D) 25 years ago

188. Why is Alice congratulating Mai?
(A) She got a promotion.
(B) She graduated from high school.
(C) She opened a consulting business.
(D) She won an employee-of-the-month award.

189. What is Alice's relationship to Mai?
(A) She is her boss.
(B) She is her parent.
(C) She is her employee.
(D) She is her former classmate.

190. Who will attend the dinner?
(A) Caroline Overall
(B) Violet Smith
(C) Harry Wong
(D) Lee Kim

GO ON TO THE NEXT PAGE

Questions 191–195 refer to the following memo and schedule.

To: Jeffrey Caldwell
From: Jose Amadeo
Re: Meeting follow-up

We agreed in our meeting that you need to improve your office skills in order to perform your job duties adequately. I have attached a schedule of classes from the Business Training Institute. A number of your co-workers have taken classes there, and it has a fine reputation. Take a look at the 105 courses. I think you should sign up for 105A. Even though you have a little experience here, it never hurts to start again from the beginning. Word Processing would also be useful, and I think you would qualify for the 101B course. Bookkeeping might be a good idea, too, but I'd prefer you sign up for just two courses now. There's no sense in overburdening yourself. So in addition to 105A, you can choose between 101B and 106A. The company will take care of the entire tuition for you, so you need have no worries there.

BUSINESS TRAINING INSTITUTE

Schedule of Classes

Course #	Course Title	Hours	Cost
101A	Word Processing—Beginning	Mon/Wed 7–9	$450
101B	Word Processing—Advanced	Tue/Thur 7–9	$450
105A	Introduction to Database Part I	Mon/Wed 5–7	$450
105B	Introduction to Database Part II	Mon/Wed 7–9	$450
105C	Advanced Database	Tue/Thur 5–7	$450
106A	Basic Bookkeeping	Tue/Thur 7–9	$450
106B	Intermediate Bookkeeping	Mon/Wed 7–9	$450
110A	Introduction to Business Writing	Tue 5:30–8:00	$425

191. Why does Mr. Caldwell need to take classes at the Business Training Institute?
    (A) To get a promotion
    (B) To earn a university degree
    (C) To be able to train his co-workers
    (D) To do better in his current position

192. Which database course does Mr. Amadeo recommend?
    (A) Introduction to Database Part I
    (B) Introduction to Database Part II
    (C) Intermediate Database
    (D) Advanced Database

193. How many nights a week will Mr. Caldwell study?
    (A) One
    (B) Two
    (C) Three
    (D) Four

194. What is the total amount Mr. Caldwell will pay for his classes?
    (A) $0
    (B) $450
    (C) $900
    (D) $1,350

195. How many business writing courses are offered at the Business Training Institute?
    (A) One
    (B) Two
    (C) Three
    (D) Four

GO ON TO THE NEXT PAGE

New Century Office Machines, Inc.
Product Guarantee

Your printer is completely guaranteed for one year from the date of purchase. If you are dissatisfied with your printer for any reason, you can return it for a complete refund within 30 days of the purchase date. After 30 days, please call our customer service number at 800-555-9927. If we cannot solve your problem over the phone, you will be asked to mail the printer back to us for repairs. For this purpose, please save the original box and packing material that your printer came with, as well as the return mailing label contained in the enclosed envelope. We are not responsible for the cost of postage.

To: Mary Jones
From: Peter Andrews
Subject: Printer

Mary,

It looks like we'll have to send the printer back to the factory. I spent two hours on the phone with customer service, but it still prints too light. Changing the ink cartridge didn't solve the problem. Unfortunately, it's too late for a complete refund. We've missed the last return date by just five days. Could you please pack up the printer and ship it to the company? I think you'll find everything you need in the storage closet. If you need money, take it out of petty cash. This is very annoying. This is the third New Century printer we've bought that's had problems. I won't buy anything from that company again. Their prices are great, but their products always break down.

Peter

196. When did they buy the printer?
(A) Five days ago
(B) Twenty-five days ago
(C) Thirty days ago
(D) Thirty-five days ago

197. What is the problem with the printer?
(A) It takes two hours to print something.
(B) It needs a new ink cartridge.
(C) The printing is too light.
(D) It's very old.

198. How will the company solve the problem?
(A) By fixing the printer
(B) By giving a complete refund
(C) By exchanging the old printer for a new one
(D) By sending a customer service representative to Peter's office

199. In order to return the printer, what will Mary have to pay for?
(A) A box
(B) Shipping
(C) An envelope
(D) Packing material

200. Why is Peter annoyed?
(A) The printer was too expensive.
(B) The company won't fix the printer.
(C) New Century printers always break down.
(D) It will cost a lot of money to return the printer.

PRACTICE TEST ONE

You will find the Answer Sheet for Practice Test One on page 389. Detach it from the book and use it to record your answers. Play the audio for Practice Test One when you are ready to begin.

LISTENING TEST

In the Listening test, you will be asked to demonstrate how well you understand spoken English. The entire Listening test will last approximately 45 minutes. There are four parts, and directions are given for each part. You must mark your answers on the separate answer sheet. Do not write your answers in the test book.

PART 1

Directions: For each question in this part, you will hear four statements about a picture in your test book. When you hear the statements, you must select the one statement that best describes what you see in the picture. Then find the number of the question on your answer sheet and mark your answer. The statements will not be printed in your test book and will be spoken only one time.

Example

Sample Answer

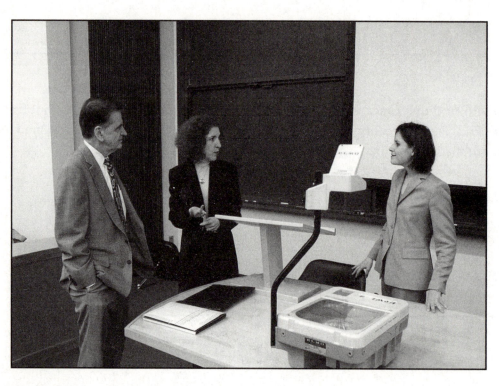

Statement (C), "They're standing near the table," is the best description of the picture, so you should select answer (C) and mark it on your answer sheet.

1.

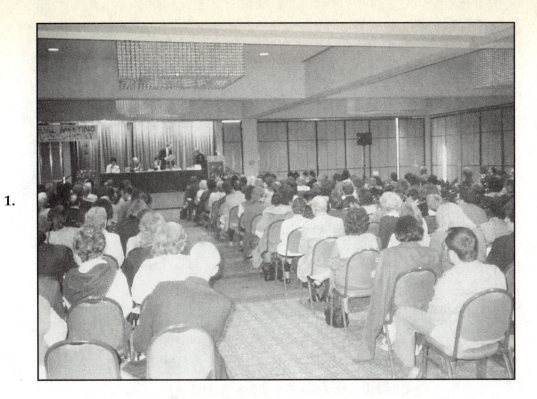

2.

GO ON TO THE NEXT PAGE

3.

4.

5.

6.

7.

8.

9.

10.

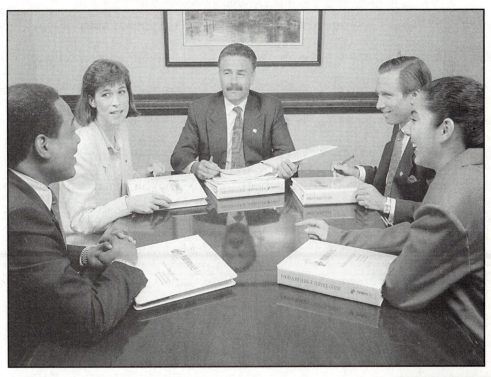

GO ON TO THE NEXT PAGE

PART 2

 Directions: You will hear a question or statement and three responses spoken in English. They will not be printed in your test book and will be spoken only one time. Select the best response to the question or statement and mark the letter (A), (B), or (C) on your answer sheet.

Example

Sample Answer
 (A) ● (C)

You will hear: Where is the meeting room?

You will also hear: (A) To meet the new director.
                        (B) It's the first room on the right.
                        (C) Yes, at two o'clock.

Your best response to the question "Where is the meeting room?" is choice (B), "It's the first room on the right," so (B) is the correct answer. You should mark answer (B) on your answer sheet.

11. Mark your answer on your answer sheet.   26. Mark your answer on your answer sheet.

12. Mark your answer on your answer sheet.   27. Mark your answer on your answer sheet.

13. Mark your answer on your answer sheet.   28. Mark your answer on your answer sheet.

14. Mark your answer on your answer sheet.   29. Mark your answer on your answer sheet.

15. Mark your answer on your answer sheet.   30. Mark your answer on your answer sheet.

16. Mark your answer on your answer sheet.   31. Mark your answer on your answer sheet.

17. Mark your answer on your answer sheet.   32. Mark your answer on your answer sheet.

18. Mark your answer on your answer sheet.   33. Mark your answer on your answer sheet.

19. Mark your answer on your answer sheet.   34. Mark your answer on your answer sheet.

20. Mark your answer on your answer sheet.   35. Mark your answer on your answer sheet.

21. Mark your answer on your answer sheet.   36. Mark your answer on your answer sheet.

22. Mark your answer on your answer sheet.   37. Mark your answer on your answer sheet.

23. Mark your answer on your answer sheet.   38. Mark your answer on your answer sheet.

24. Mark your answer on your answer sheet.   39. Mark your answer on your answer sheet.

25. Mark your answer on your answer sheet.   40. Mark your answer on your answer sheet.

Directions: You will hear some conversations between two people. You will be asked to answer three questions about what the speakers say in each conversation. Select the best response to each question and mark the letter (A), (B), (C), or (D) on your answer sheet. The conversations will not be printed in your test book and will be spoken only one time.

41. What is the man buying?

    (A) Shoes.
    (B) Pears.
    (C) A book.
    (D) A newspaper.

42. How much does he have to pay?

    (A) $7.75.
    (B) $17.75.
    (C) $70.75.
    (D) $75.

43. How will he pay?

    (A) With cash.
    (B) With a credit card.
    (C) With a traveler's check.
    (D) With a personal check.

44. How long will it take for the package to arrive?

    (A) Six days.
    (B) Eight days.
    (C) Ten days.
    (D) Twelve days.

45. What is inside the package?

    (A) China.
    (B) Checks.
    (C) Jewelry.
    (D) Class work.

46. How much will the man pay?

    (A) $6.00.
    (B) $9.00.
    (C) $15.00.
    (D) $1,000.00.

47. When will the repairperson come?

    (A) This morning.
    (B) Tomorrow.
    (C) At 4:00.
    (D) In four days.

48. What does the woman have to copy?

    (A) Reports.
    (B) Photographs.
    (C) A repair bill.
    (D) A meeting agenda.

49. Where is the photocopy store?

    (A) On the first floor.
    (B) On the fourth floor.
    (C) Across the street.
    (D) Next door.

50. What are the speakers waiting for?

    (A) A car.
    (B) A bus.
    (C) A train.
    (D) A plane.

51. What is the weather like?
    (A) It's raining.
    (B) It's cloudy.
    (C) It's cold.
    (D) It's hot.

52. How long has the man been waiting?
    (A) 15 minutes.
    (B) 16 minutes.
    (C) 50 minutes.
    (D) 60 minutes.

53. When does the woman's vacation begin?

  (A) On Monday.
  (B) On Tuesday.
  (C) On Wednesday.
  (D) On Thursday.

54. How long will her vacation last?

  (A) Two days.
  (B) One week.
  (C) Eight days.
  (D) Two weeks.

55. Where will she spend her vacation?

  (A) At a lake.
  (B) At the beach.
  (C) In the mountains.
  (D) In New York.

56. Why wasn't Mr. Kim at the meeting?

  (A) He is sick.
  (B) He went downtown.
  (C) He arrived too late.
  (D) He is away on a trip.

57. How many people were at the meeting?

  (A) Two.
  (B) Seven.
  (C) Eleven.
  (D) Fifteen.

58. When is the next meeting?

  (A) Tomorrow morning.
  (B) In two days.
  (C) Next week.
  (D) Next month.

59. Where are the speakers?

  (A) In a bank.
  (B) In a store.
  (C) In a doctor's office.
  (D) In an accountant's office.

60. How much money is the check for?

  (A) $400.
  (B) $500.
  (C) $800.
  (D) $900.

61. What does the woman have to sign?

  (A) A deposit slip.
  (B) A letter.
  (C) A check.
  (D) A form.

62. What is the weather like?

  (A) It's snowing.
  (B) It's raining.
  (C) It's hot.
  (D) It's windy.

63. How will the speakers get to work?

  (A) By car.
  (B) By train.
  (C) By walking.
  (D) By taxi.

64. What does the man have to do at 10:00?

  (A) Attend a meeting.
  (B) Clean the conference room.
  (C) Talk on the telephone.
  (D) Get on the train.

65. Where is the hotel?

    (A) On another street.
    (B) To the left.
    (C) Across the street.
    (D) To the right.

66. What is the woman buying?

    (A) A newspaper.
    (B) A magazine.
    (C) Candy.
    (D) Gum.

67. How much does the woman have to pay?

    (A) $4.15.
    (B) $4.16.
    (C) $4.50.
    (D) $4.60.

68. Where are the speakers?

    (A) At home.
    (B) At a bakery.
    (C) At a grocery store.
    (D) At a restaurant.

69. How often does the man go to this place?

    (A) Every day.
    (B) Every two days.
    (C) Once a week.
    (D) Once a month.

70. What will the man get?

    (A) Soup.
    (B) Rice.
    (C) Chicken.
    (D) Sandwiches.

GO ON TO THE NEXT PAGE

Directions: You will hear some talks given by a single speaker. You will be asked to answer three questions about what the speaker says in each talk. Select the best response to each question and mark the letter (A), (B), (C), or (D) on your answer sheet. The talks will not be printed in your test book and will be spoken only one time.

71. Who is listening to this announcement?

    (A) Company employees.
    (B) Doctors.
    (C) Parents of schoolchildren.
    (D) Police officers.

72. What has been revised?

    (A) Doctors' excuses.
    (B) Insurance regulations.
    (C) Company policy.
    (D) Employees' records.

73. When is a note required?

    (A) Within forty-eight hours.
    (B) After four days.
    (C) After a week.
    (D) Never.

74. What is happening?

    (A) Some people need a hotel room.
    (B) Some people are going home.
    (C) The personnel office is closing.
    (D) A building is on fire.

75. Who must get through?

    (A) Office personnel.
    (B) Emergency personnel.
    (C) Clerical workers.
    (D) File clerks.

76. Where should people stay?

    (A) Next to a room.
    (B) Across the street.
    (C) Beside the building.
    (D) In the emergency room.

77. What kind of program is mentioned?

    (A) Race.
    (B) Space.
    (C) Tasting.
    (D) Waste.

78. Which of the following animals is mentioned?

    (A) A dog.
    (B) A cat.
    (C) A sheep.
    (D) A rat.

79. How many times has this program been done before?

    (A) None.
    (B) Once.
    (C) Twice.
    (D) Several times.

80. How is the president described in the news report?

    (A) As a mother.
    (B) As a doctor.
    (C) As a father.
    (D) As a general.

81. How many children does the president have?

    (A) Two.
    (B) Three.
    (C) Four.
    (D) Five.

82. When did the event happen?

    (A) Yesterday.
    (B) This morning.
    (C) At noon.
    (D) In the early evening.

83. What is being sold?

   (A) A watch.
   (B) A television.
   (C) A calendar.
   (D) A guide.

84. How long does the subscription last?

   (A) Ten days.
   (B) One month.
   (C) Ten months.
   (D) One year.

85. How many people can get the special offer?

   (A) One.
   (B) The first ten.
   (C) The first one hundred.
   (D) There is no limit.

86. What is the problem?

   (A) No one is home.
   (B) The line is busy.
   (C) It's a nonworking number.
   (D) The caller hung up.

87. What is the listener advised to do?

   (A) Give up.
   (B) Get another job.
   (C) Not to hang up.
   (D) Try again.

88. What can a caller do by dialing 4-1-1?

   (A) Check the number he is dialing.
   (B) Ask for a refund check.
   (C) Get assistance with dialing the number.
   (D) Ask to have his phone number changed.

89. What is the weather like now?

   (A) Rainy.
   (B) Cool.
   (C) Warm.
   (D) Windy.

90. When will the weather change?

   (A) Sunday.
   (B) Monday.
   (C) Tuesday.
   (D) Friday.

91. How much rain is expected?

   (A) Two inches.
   (B) Three inches.
   (C) Four inches.
   (D) Twenty-four inches.

92. What is on sale?

   (A) Chairs.
   (B) Desks.
   (C) Paper.
   (D) Pencils.

93. What color is NOT available?

   (A) Blue.
   (B) Yellow.
   (C) Green.
   (D) White.

94. When will the sale end?

   (A) Sunday.
   (B) Tuesday.
   (C) Friday.
   (D) Saturday.

GO ON TO THE NEXT PAGE

95. What was robbed?

(A) A clothing store.
(B) A jewelry store.
(C) A computer store.
(D) A watch store.

96. What time did the robbery happen?

(A) 8:05.
(B) 8:15.
(C) 8:50.
(D) 8:55.

97. Who was in the store at the time of the robbery?

(A) Police.
(B) Customers.
(C) The store staff.
(D) The store owner.

98. When is the Sidewalk Café closed?

(A) Monday.
(B) Tuesday.
(C) Saturday.
(D) Sunday.

99. What can you get for $6.00 at the café?

(A) Birthday cake.
(B) Pancakes.
(C) Steak.
(D) Pans.

100. Where is the café located?

(A) By a river.
(B) In back of a park.
(C) Near a bus station.
(D) Close to a subway station.

This is the end of the Listening test. Turn to Part 5 in your test book.

In the Reading test, you will read a variety of texts and answer several different types of reading comprehension questions. The entire Reading test will last 75 minutes. There are three parts, and directions are given for each part. You are encouraged to answer as many questions as possible within the time allowed.

You must mark your answers on the separate answer sheet. Do not write your answers in the test book.

PART 5

Directions: A word or phrase is missing in each of the sentences below. Four answer choices are given below each sentence. Select the best answer to complete the sentence. Then mark the letter (A), (B), (C), or (D) on your answer sheet.

101. East Coast Airlines flight number 15 from New York _____ Chicago has been canceled.

    (A) to
    (B) in
    (C) by
    (D) at

102. Beginning the first of next month, lunch breaks will be _____ by fifteen minutes.

    (A) short
    (B) shortened
    (C) shortening
    (D) shortage

103. The computer programmer realized he had forgotten to turn off the office lights _____ he had left the premises.

    (A) after
    (B) because
    (C) since
    (D) and

104. Most employees have requested that their paychecks be _____ to their homes.

    (A) mail
    (B) mails
    (C) mailed
    (D) mailing

105. The error was noticed after Ms. Radice _____ the order to the supply company.

    (A) had sent in
    (B) sends in
    (C) has sent
    (D) is sending

106. Mr. Richards, the president of Capo Electronics, has had a very _____ year.

    (A) successfully
    (B) successful
    (C) success
    (D) successes

107. Since Dr. Yamoto is always busy, it is best to call _____ make an appointment before coming to her office.

    (A) while
    (B) before
    (C) nor
    (D) and

108. After working fifteen hours at the office, the new lawyer is finally putting away his papers and heading _____.

    (A) homely
    (B) homey
    (C) home
    (D) homeless

GO ON TO THE NEXT PAGE

109. The photographer that we hired to take pictures of the banquet will be accompanied _____ his assistant.

(A) with
(B) by
(C) to
(D) from

110. Ms. Ueki has never made any _____ decisions regarding the operation of her company.

(A) foolish
(B) fool
(C) foolishness
(D) fooled

111. Ten applications were filed _____ Monday morning for the receptionist position that we announced last week.

(A) at
(B) on
(C) until
(D) from

112. In order to provide her customers with the finest meals, the restaurant owner _____ her produce fresh daily.

(A) buy
(B) buys
(C) buying
(D) bought

113. The personnel manager needs someone to _____ her with the presentation to the board.

(A) attend
(B) assume
(C) assign
(D) assist

114. Our departmental staff meetings are held _____ in the conference room on the third floor.

(A) rarely
(B) every week
(C) always
(D) sometimes

115. The building is equipped with a sophisticated security system which turns on automatically _____ midnight.

(A) to
(B) from
(C) at
(D) for

116. The project _____ to require more time than the contractors have available.

(A) had seemed
(B) seems
(C) is seeming
(D) will seem

117. Staff members _____ ready to help out new employees and explain the office procedures.

(A) should always be
(B) being always should
(C) always be should
(D) always should being

118. The new schedules are _____ with the second shift workers at the factory.

(A) popularized
(B) popular
(C) populated
(D) popularity

119. It was agreed that the committee meet again _____ the tenth of April.

(A) for
(B) on
(C) to
(D) from

120. The travel agent said she would know the flight number and the precise arrival time _____ the airlines confirmed the reservation.

(A) during
(B) because
(C) when
(D) while

121. You will have to _____ an operator's manual from the library because I don't think we have one here.

(A) loan
(B) borrow
(C) lend
(D) send

122. There aren't any envelopes or file folders in the supply closet because they _____.

(A) have never been ordered
(B) never have ordered been
(C) have been never ordered
(D) have been ordered never

123. The assistant does not recall receiving a telex from the Mexico office _____ from the South American office.

(A) either
(B) and
(C) or
(D) but

124. _____ this kind of machine before, or should we call in a repairperson?

(A) Have ever you repaired
(B) Have you repaired ever
(C) Ever have you repaired
(D) Have you ever repaired

125. If our office _____ a coffee machine, Mr. Perkins said he would make coffee every morning.

(A) had
(B) have
(C) will have
(D) would have

126. The time sheets are to be filled out twice _____—in the morning when the staff arrives and in the evening when they leave.

(A) usually
(B) sometimes
(C) daily
(D) frequently

127. Boxes received from the print shop are not to be _____ unless marked otherwise.

(A) opening
(B) opened
(C) open
(D) opens

128. The goal of our meetings is to make the directors _____ our problem.

(A) understanding
(B) understood
(C) understand
(D) be understanding

129. _____ Mr. Park was the only one who knew the way to the conference, he drove the car.

(A) Although
(B) Since
(C) But
(D) Therefore

130. Ms. Wang did not want her check automatically _____ into her account.

(A) deposit
(B) deposits
(C) depositing
(D) deposited

131. If this package is sent by the express mail service, it _____ California by Friday.

(A) reaches
(B) will reach
(C) reached
(D) is reaching

132. All delivery persons are asked to use the side _____ to make their deliveries.

(A) enter
(B) entered
(C) entering
(D) entrance

GO ON TO THE NEXT PAGE

133. Hotel guests who _____ checking out after 1:00 P.M. should contact the front desk.

(A) will
(B) were
(C) are going
(D) will be

134. Mr. Davis, my lawyer, was a _____ by the time he was thirty.

(A) millions
(B) millionaire
(C) million
(D) millionfold

135. If the accountant _____ a mistake, she will not charge us for her time.

(A) makes
(B) will make
(C) had made
(D) make

136. Ms. Yuen is going to ask Human Resources how much vacation time she _____ left.

(A) shall have
(B) will have had
(C) is having
(D) has

137. We are fortunate to have a company president who is quite _____ about computers.

(A) knowing
(B) knowledge
(C) knowledgeable
(D) knows

138. Yasmin is one of our best employees and _____ working here for two years.

(A) has
(B) has been
(C) is
(D) will

139. The receptionist _____ the vice president if he knew where she was.

(A) will call
(B) call
(C) called
(D) would call

140. The conference participants arranged to have their suitcases _____ at the hotel before they left for the airport.

(A) picked up
(B) picking up
(C) pick up
(D) to be picked up

PART 6

Directions: Read the texts that follow. A word or phrase is missing in some of the sentences. Four answer choices are given below each of the sentences. Select the best answer to complete the text. Then mark the letter (A), (B), (C), or (D) on your answer sheet.

GO ON TO THE NEXT PAGE

February 22, 20___

Dear Samuel,

I have good news for you. I have taken a new job in Sydney. My family and I will move
_____ next month. Since you have lived in Sydney for so long, I would like to

141. (A) there
     (B) that
     (C) here
     (D) it

ask for your advice. We would like to rent a small house in a nice _____

                                                  142. (A) industrial
                                                          (B) residential
                                                          (C) influential
                                                          (D) commercial

neighborhood. My children are small, so we would like to be in a quiet place away from
businesses and traffic. We would like to live close to good schools, and I also want to be
near public transportation so that I can get to work easily. Can you recommend some
good neighborhoods to me?

I plan to visit your city in two weeks _____ for a house. Please send me your

                              143. (A) look
                                       (B) looking
                                       (C) to look
                                       (D) will look

recommendations before then if you can. I hope we can get together while I am in town.

Your friend,

Boris

Questions 144–146 refer to the following notice.

Welcome to the Sleepwell Motel. We hope _____ stay is a

144. (A) our
    (B) his
    (C) your
    (D) their

pleasant one. If you need assistance, please _____ 09 to speak to

145. (A) mark
    (B) dial
    (C) count
    (D) register

someone at the front desk.

Please take note of the following local services:

Transportation
Taxi   985-555-9965
City buses   985-555-0924
Airport   985-555-9321

Entertainment
Deluxe Movie Theater   985-555-9654
Restaurant Guide   985-555-8723
Black Cat Night Club   985-555-7342

Emergency
Police 985-555-9111
Fire   985-555-2233

A _____ breakfast is available to all motel guests in the lobby

146. (A) compliment
    (B) complimented
    (C) complimenting
    (D) complimentary

from 6:00 A.M. to 9:00 A.M.

GO ON TO THE NEXT PAGE

Office Works
544 Hudson Street
Boston, MA 03291

March 29, 20___

Mary Braddock
Banquet Director
Garden Hotel
219 Center Circle
Boston, MA 03299

Dear Ms. Braddock:

Office Works is seeking a place to host our first awards banquet.

The evening will include dinner, speeches and an awards presentation. The exact date is flexible, but we would like to hold it on a Friday or Saturday evening in June.

We expect approximately 200 guests. We would like a room with a good sound system so that the guests will be able to hear the speeches _____.

147. (A) ease
(B) easy
(C) easier
(D) easily

Also, we would like to have elegant decorations that are suitable for the occasion. Does your hotel provide assistance with decorating, or will we need _____ a separate decorator?

148. (A) hire
(B) hires
(C) to hire
(D) hiring

We would like to serve a simple but elegant meal with both a meat and a vegetarian choice.

Would the Garden Hotel be able to provide suitable accommodations for this event? If so, please send me a price list including rental _____ for

149. (A) fees
(B) dates
(C) leases
(D) agents

the room, menu choices and prices, and any other charges. Thank you for your help.

Sincerely,

Lynn Osaman

Events Coordinator

Questions 150–152 refer to the following advertisement.

Ready to buy a NEW CAR?
LOOK NO FURTHER

Cango Cars is holding the biggest sale in its history of selling cars. For over ten years, Cango has been the leading _____ of new and used cars in the Canmore area.

150. (A) retailer
     (B) insurer
     (C) automobiles
     (D) mechanic

That's because Cango has the best reputation for selling reliable, affordable vehicles in all of Alberta. We at Cango care about the drivers and passengers of Canmore. We pride _____ in doing all we can to prevent dangerous cars

151. (A) ourselves
     (B) yourself
     (C) yourselves
     (D) itself

from getting back onto our roads and making sure our customers feel secure with the cars they choose. There is nothing more important to us than _____.

152. (A) upholstery
     (B) safety
     (C) earnings
     (D) collision

Come to Cango Cars between August 5th and 10th, and enter to win a gently used 5-seat family sedan.

DON'T FORGET! Cango Cars is the home of the free one-year warranty. All of our vehicles, both new and used, come with a one-year money back guarantee for parts and labor.

PART 7

Directions: In this part, you will read a selection of texts, such as magazine and newspaper articles, letters, and advertisements. Each text is followed by several questions. Select the best answer for each question and mark the letter (A), (B), (C), or (D) on your answer sheet.

GO ON TO THE NEXT PAGE

Tomorrow, bus service on Orchard Road will be changed between the hours of 9 A.M. and 12:30 P.M. The Chingay Parade will take place from 10:00 A.M. to 12:00 P.M.

Number 7, 13, 14, 16, and 23 buses will turn left onto Scotts Road, right onto Clemenceau Avenue, and left onto Orchard Road below the parade route.

In the event of rain, the diversion will take place at 3:00 P.M. and the parade shortly after.

153. For whom is this report important?

(A) Weather reporters
(B) Bus riders
(C) City workers
(D) Bus repair people

154. At 10:00 A.M., what will happen to certain buses?

(A) They will be used in the parade.
(B) They will take a different route.
(C) They will have no riders.
(D) They will be taken out of service.

155. When will the parade take place if it rains?

(A) In the morning
(B) In the afternoon
(C) The next morning
(D) The following afternoon

To: All employees
From: R. Wettimuny
Re: Ordering Supplies

There has been a great deal of confusion regarding the correct procedures for ordering office supplies. Therefore, I will explain the proper steps to follow here. First, all requests for supplies must be typed and signed. Only typed requests will be accepted because I am tired of trying to decipher illegible handwriting. Second, all requests must be on my desk by the fifteenth of every month. I make out the order once each month and do not want to have to make addendums or extra orders. From now on, late requests will be put on hold until the following month. Requests that are received on time and approved by me will be sent on to the Accounting Department for processing.

Please be aware that it takes from two to six weeks for supplies to arrive once the order has been made, so it is important to plan ahead and make your requests accordingly.

Your cooperation is appreciated.

156. What does the memo concern?

(A) Overdue accounts
(B) Office furniture
(C) Supply requests
(D) Computers

157. What will happen to handwritten requests?

(A) They will not be accepted.
(B) They will be approved quickly.
(C) They will be read carefully.
(D) They will be sent to Accounting.

158. The word "approved" in paragraph 1, line 11, is closest in meaning to

(A) urgent
(B) valid
(C) signed
(D) accepted

159. What will happen to approved requests?

(A) They will be returned to the employee.
(B) They will be sent to Purchasing.
(C) They will be forwarded to Accounting.
(D) They will be returned to R. Wettimuny.

GO ON TO THE NEXT PAGE

Questions 160–162 refer to the following chart.

		Zone 1	Zone 2	Zone 3
Destination		Asia, Marshall Is., Guam, Midway, and others	North America, Central America, Oceania, Middle East, Europe	Africa, South America
Classification	Weight			
Letters*	Up to 25 g Up to 50 g	90 yen 160 yen	110 yen 190 yen	130 yen 230 yen
Postcard	Uniform rate of 70 yen to anywhere in the world			
Aerogramme	Uniform rate of 90 yen to anywhere in the world			
*Standard-sized item: 14–23.5 cm length, 9–12 cm width, thickness of within 1 cm				

160. What is the cost of sending a twelve-gram letter to South Africa?

    (A) ¥70
    (B) ¥90
    (C) ¥130
    (D) ¥230

161. How much would an aerogramme to Asia cost?

    (A) ¥70
    (B) ¥90
    (C) ¥110
    (D) ¥160

162. How much will a ¥110 letter to Europe weigh?

    (A) 25 grams or less
    (B) Between 25 and 50 grams
    (C) More than 50 grams
    (D) Unknown

Questions 163–166 refer to the following bulletin.

RESERVATIONS: Reservations are required for all first-class compartments. Second- and third-class coaches do not require reservations.

DINING: Trains that do not have first-class cars will not have a dining car. Sandwich and beverage carts will be on all trains.

BAGGAGE: Passengers may carry up to four pieces of luggage on the train. Additional baggage may be checked.

---

163. A passenger traveling in which of the following would read this bulletin?

(A) Plane
(B) Car
(C) Bus
(D) Train

164. For which of the following are reservations required?

(A) The dining car
(B) First-class car
(C) Second-class car
(D) Third-class car

165. According to the passage, which of the following have dining cars?

(A) All trains
(B) Trains with first-class cars
(C) Trains with second-class cars
(D) Trains with third-class cars

166. The word "Additional" in paragraph 3, line 2, is closest in meaning to

(A) Most
(B) Extra
(C) Overweight
(D) Large

GO ON TO THE NEXT PAGE

Lovely Lady Fashions
32 Elizabeth Bay Road
Sydney, Australia

December 15, 20__

Mrs. R.S.W. Mangala
Jewelry Export Ltd.
40 Galle Face Road
Colombo 1, Sri Lanka

Dear Mrs. Mangala:

I am interested in information regarding your company's new line of jewelry. I have seen the samples on your web site, and I am interested in the possibility of importing your jewelry into Australia. I think it would sell very well here, especially among the younger women who make up the majority of my company's clientele.

I will be making a trip to Malaysia, India, and Sri Lanka next summer. I would like to arrange to meet with you then to discuss setting up a business relationship. Please let me now when you will be available for a meeting. In the meantime, I would appreciate your sending a list of your wholesale prices and information about ordering and shipping.

My associates in London have been very pleased with the quality of the gems you have sent them, and they have had a great deal of success with them. I look forward to doing business with you in the near future.

Sincerely,

James Goodwin
James Goodwin
Import Manager

---

167. Where does Mr. Goodwin probably live?

(A) India
(B) Sri Lanka
(C) Australia
(D) Malaysia

168. What does Mrs. Mangala manufacture?

(A) Jewelry
(B) Fashions
(C) Textiles
(D) Toys

169. The word "line" in paragraph 1, line 1, is closest in meaning to

(A) bag
(B) straight
(C) design
(D) type

170. Where will the jewelry be exported from?

(A) India
(B) Australia
(C) Malaysia
(D) Sri Lanka

171. Which of the following best describes Mrs. Mangala's gems?

(A) High-quality
(B) Inexpensive
(C) Uncut
(D) Tax-free

TO WATERPROOF SHOES AND BOOTS:

Before applying, remove all dust, mud, and dirt from shoes. Make sure shoes are completely dry. Hold spray can 6–8 inches from clean, dry shoes. Let product saturate leather, covering all surfaces evenly. Allow to dry for one hour. Repeat application one more time. Allow to dry before use. The protection will last for six months under average climatic conditions. This product can also be used to protect leather handbags and briefcases. Do not use on suede. May cause discoloration of some leather products. Test on a small area first.

Caution

• Can cause damage to the respiratory system. Use in a well-ventilated area only, away from children and pets.

• Highly flammable. Use away from stoves, ovens, radiators, portable heaters, open flames, and other heat sources.

172. From what will this spray protect shoes?

(A) Dirt
(B) Dust
(C) Water
(D) Drying out

173. How many times must the shoes be sprayed?

(A) One time
(B) Two times
(C) Six times
(D) Eight times

174. How long will the application last?

(A) One hour
(B) One week
(C) A couple of months
(D) Half a year

GO ON TO THE NEXT PAGE

Questions 175–177 refer to the following table.

Introduction: While computer skills are becoming more and more necessary in everyday life, not enough children are receiving proper computer education in schools. This is the most serious educational issue facing our society today. A team of researchers looked into this issue in our local schools. See their results below.

SURVEY OF ELEMENTARY SCHOOL TEACHERS

Reasons for lack of computer education programs in public schools

	Respondents	
	Number	Percent
1. Not enough computers in school	14	32.6
2. Teachers fear computers	8	18.8
3. Not enough time in curriculum	14	32.6
4. Too expensive	20	46.5
5. Poor-quality software	16	37.2

Total Number of Teachers in Survey 43*
(* Some teachers responded to more than one reason.)

175. How many teachers responded to the survey?

(A) 20
(B) 40
(C) 43
(D) 76

176. What was the reason given most often for the lack of computer education in schools?

(A) Poor-quality software
(B) Not enough computers
(C) Fear of computers
(D) Expense

177. Which of the following do teachers consider the least problematic?

(A) Cost of computers
(B) Quality of software
(C) Fear of computers
(D) Time in curriculum

The Hotel Manager of the Year Award Essay Competition winner was announced last night by the County Association of Hotel Managers. The winning essay was written by Mr. Randolph Ng of the Henry Street Historic Hotel. Mr. Ng wins a prize of $2,500 for his essay titled "The Hotel Family." "I believe that a hotel manager must be like a parent to his or her staff," said Mr. Ng at the awards ceremony banquet last night. "A good manager concentrates on helping others to be successful." The second and third prize winners were Gina Becke of the Woodside Gardens Hotel and Yoko Lee of the Hotel at Riverton, respectively. The annual essay competition was started by the County Association of Hotel Managers six years ago as a means of recognizing the hard work of hotel managers and encouraging them to reflect on what they do and share it with their colleagues. "It has become a very popular contest," says Jim Wilkerson, president of the association. "We get hundreds of entries every year." Following the awards presentation at last night's ceremony, Mr. Wilkerson announced that he will be retiring from his position as association president next year. A replacement has not yet been announced.

178. What did Mr. Ng do?

(A) Wrote an essay
(B) Asked for more money
(C) Turned down a prize
(D) Announced his retirement

179. When was the award winner announced?

(A) Last year
(B) Last night
(C) This morning
(D) This afternoon

180. What is Mr. Ng's advice?

(A) Get your own promotion first
(B) Have more children
(C) Be a better parent
(D) Help others be successful

GO ON TO THE NEXT PAGE

The National Theater presents
a live performance of

Romeo and Juliet

the third in our Festival of Shakespeare series

March 12–29
Thursday, Friday, and Saturday evenings
Saturday and Sunday matinees

Ticket prices

Matinee:	orchestra—$45	balcony—$35
Evening:	orchestra—$75	balcony—$55

Special group discounts are available. Groups of 15 or more receive 10% off the regular price. Groups of 25 or more receive 20% off the regular price. Call the box office for details.

Getting there:
The National Theater is conveniently located downtown, within easy walking distance of the Center City subway station and near major bus lines. A parking garage is located near the theater.

To: Maya Berg
From: Morris Stein
Subject: Shakespeare tickets

Maya,
I'd like to get tickets for our entire department to see Romeo and Juliet. If everyone goes, there will be just enough people for a 10% discount on the ticket price. Call the box office to find out how to order the group discount tickets, and see if you can get tickets for opening night. Make sure they are orchestra seats. I think this will be an enjoyable and convenient outing for everyone. We can all take the subway to the theater together after work.
Thanks,
Morris

181. How many shows are there at the theater on Saturday?

(A) One
(B) Two
(C) Four
(D) Five

182. What does Mr. Stein want tickets for?

(A) A play
(B) A movie
(C) A lecture
(D) A concert

183. How many people work in Mr. Stein's department?

(A) 10
(B) 15
(C) 20
(D) 25

184. When does Mr. Stein want to go to the theater?

(A) March 12
(B) March 13
(C) March 21
(D) March 29

185. How does Mr. Stein plan to get to the theater?

(A) By bus
(B) By car
(C) By foot
(D) By subway

GO ON TO THE NEXT PAGE

Customer Service Office
Union Bank
135 Main Street
Home, AK 99999

Dear Customer Service:

I received a debit card from your bank last week, and I have some questions regarding its use. Specifically, I am concerned about liability. If a thief steals my card and makes charges to my account, am I responsible for paying for them, or do I have protection like I have with my credit card? I looked in the booklet *Rules for Personal Accounts at Union Bank,* but I didn't see the information there.

I have been a customer at your bank for over 15 years and have always been happy with the service I have received there. I hope you can answer my question satisfactorily.

Sincerely,

Arthur Schmidt

Arthur Schmidt

Mr. Arthur Schmidt
1705 Oak Boulevard
Home, AK 99999

Dear Mr. Schmidt:

You recently sent a letter to our office asking about the Union Bank debit card. You wanted to know about liability. Our policy is the following: If you report a lost or stolen card within 48 hours, you are not responsible for any charges made on it. If you report it after 48 hours, you will be responsible for charges up to $50. So you see, the debit card has similar protection to a credit card. The information is actually in the document you mentioned. It appears on page 39. I am enclosing a photocopy of it for your convenience. Please let me know if I can be of any further assistance to you.

Sincerely,

Elena Ugarte

Elena Ugarte

186. Why did Mr. Schmidt write the letter?

    (A) To open a new bank account
    (B) To report a stolen credit card
    (C) To find out his account balance
    (D) To get information about his debit card

187. How long has Mr. Schmidt been banking at Union Bank?

    (A) For 48 hours
    (B) For one week
    (C) For a little less than 15 years
    (D) For more than 15 years

188. Where can Mr. Schmidt find the information he needs?

    (A) On the back of his debit card
    (B) In a booklet of bank rules
    (C) On his account statement
    (D) In his checkbook

189. What is probably Elena Ugarte's job?

    (A) Customer service representative
    (B) Credit card specialist
    (C) Loan officer
    (D) Teller

190. What did Ms. Ugarte enclose in the letter?

    (A) A new debit card
    (B) A copy of a page
    (C) A bill for $50
    (D) A photograph

GO ON TO THE NEXT PAGE

Questions 191–195 refer to the following two e-mail messages.

To: M. Takubo
From: J. H. Choi
Subject: Office rental

Mr. Takubo,
As we discussed on the phone, I am interested in renting an office for my accounting firm. We are a small business, so the space doesn't need to be large, but a convenient location is important. We need to be downtown and close to subway and bus lines. I hope you can find something reasonably priced for us in that area. We hope to spend no more than $2,000 a month. We have to leave our current office soon, so we need something that will be available by the end of the month. Thank you for your help.
Jung Choi

To: J. H. Choi
From: M. Takubo
Subject: Downtown office

Ms. Choi,
I have an office to show you that I think you'll like. It is right downtown on State Street. Since it is on the small side, the rent is somewhat lower than other offices in the area, although it's $500 more than the price you mentioned. I don't think you'll find a better price in such a convenient location. The building is very clean, and the landlord keeps it well maintained. The office will be available by the time you need it. I would like to show it to you soon. Will tomorrow morning suit you? I can meet you at the office at 11:00. The address is 730 State Street, Suite 900. Please let me know if this works for you.
M. Takubo

191. What is Mr. Takubo's job?

   (A) Landlord
   (B) Accountant
   (C) Real estate agent
   (D) Personal assistant

192. What kind of office does Ms. Choi want?

   (A) Large
   (B) Quiet
   (C) Expensive
   (D) Convenient

193. What is the rent on the State Street office?

   (A) $500
   (B) $1,500
   (C) $2,000
   (D) $2,500

194. When will the State Street office be available?

   (A) Right now
   (B) Tomorrow
   (C) By the end of this month
   (D) At the end of next month

195. What time does Mr. Takubo want to meet with Ms. Choi?

   (A) 7:30
   (B) 9:00
   (C) 11:00
   (D) 11:30

Local cable television provider has an opening in its accounting department for a customer account representative. Responsibilities include answering customer telephone inquiries about billing and resolving billing disputes. Must have at least two years experience in customer service. Experience with accounting, billing, or collections desirable. Proficiency with word processing and spreadsheet software required. College degree in accounting or related field desirable. The right candidate will also have excellent communication and organization skills. Send résumé and cover letter to: Ms. Ahmad, Human Resources Director, Universal Cable Company, 1123 25th Street, Putnam, OH 44408.

June 25, 20__

Ms. Ahmad
Human Resources Director
Universal Cable Company
1123 25th Street
Putnam, OH 44408

Dear Ms. Ahmad:

I am interested in applying for the position you advertised in the Sunday edition of the Local Times. I have all the qualifications for the job, and more. I have worked for several years as a customer service representative for a mail order company—in fact, for three more years than you require. Prior to that, I worked for four years in the billing department of a local magazine. Though my college degree is in French, I took two semesters of accounting classes. I also have experience using the computer software your ad mentioned.

I hope you will consider me as a candidate for the position. I look forward to hearing from you.

Sincerely,

Joe Butler

Joe Butler

196. What kind of job is Joe applying for?

   (A) Accountant
   (B) Software engineer
   (C) Human resources director
   (D) Customer account representative

197. What should job applicants send to Ms. Ahmad?

   (A) A résumé
   (B) A billing statement
   (C) A letter of recommendation
   (D) A copy of their college diploma

198. Where does Joe work now?

   (A) For a magazine
   (B) For a French company
   (C) For a mail order company
   (D) For a cable television provider

199. How long has Joe had his current job?

   (A) Two years
   (B) Three years
   (C) Four years
   (D) Five years

200. What field is Joe's college degree in?

   (A) Computer science
   (B) Communications
   (C) Accounting
   (D) French

Stop! This is the end of the test. If you finish before time is called, you may go back to Parts 5, 6, and 7 and check your work.

PRACTICE TEST TWO

You will find the Answer Sheet for Practice Test Two on page 391. Detach it from the book and use it to record your answers. Play the audio program for Practice Test Two when you are ready to begin.

LISTENING TEST

In the Listening test, you will be asked to demonstrate how well you understand spoken English. The entire Listening test will last approximately 45 minutes. There are four parts, and directions are given for each part. You must mark your answers on the separate answer sheet. Do not write your answers in the test book.

PART 1

Directions: For each question in this part, you will hear four statements about a picture in your test book. When you hear the statements, you must select the one statement that best describes what you see in the picture. Then find the number of the question on your answer sheet and mark your answer. The statements will not be printed in your test book and will be spoken only one time.

Example

Sample Answer

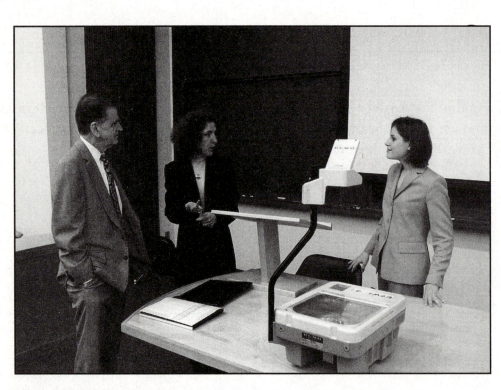

Statement (C), "They're standing near the table," is the best description of the picture, so you should select answer (C) and mark it on your answer sheet.

1.

2.

3.

4.

5.

6.

GO ON TO THE NEXT PAGE

7.

8.

9.

10.

PART 2

 Directions: You will hear a question or statement and three responses spoken in English. They will not be printed in your test book and will be spoken only one time. Select the best response to the question or statement and mark the letter (A), (B), or (C) on your answer sheet.

Example

Sample Answer

Ⓐ ● Ⓒ

You will hear: Where is the meeting room?

You will also hear: (A) To meet the new director.
                        (B) It's the first room on the right.
                        (C) Yes, at two o'clock.

Your best response to the question "Where is the meeting room?" is choice (B), "It's the first room on the right," so (B) is the correct answer. You should mark answer (B) on your answer sheet.

---

11. Mark your answer on your answer sheet.

12. Mark your answer on your answer sheet.

13. Mark your answer on your answer sheet.

14. Mark your answer on your answer sheet.

15. Mark your answer on your answer sheet.

16. Mark your answer on your answer sheet.

17. Mark your answer on your answer sheet.

18. Mark your answer on your answer sheet.

19. Mark your answer on your answer sheet.

20. Mark your answer on your answer sheet.

21. Mark your answer on your answer sheet.

22. Mark your answer on your answer sheet.

23. Mark your answer on your answer sheet.

24. Mark your answer on your answer sheet.

25. Mark your answer on your answer sheet.

26. Mark your answer on your answer sheet.

27. Mark your answer on your answer sheet.

28. Mark your answer on your answer sheet.

29. Mark your answer on your answer sheet.

30. Mark your answer on your answer sheet.

31. Mark your answer on your answer sheet.

32. Mark your answer on your answer sheet.

33. Mark your answer on your answer sheet.

34. Mark your answer on your answer sheet.

35. Mark your answer on your answer sheet.

36. Mark your answer on your answer sheet.

37. Mark your answer on your answer sheet.

38. Mark your answer on your answer sheet.

39. Mark your answer on your answer sheet.

40. Mark your answer on your answer sheet.

Directions: You will hear some conversations between two people. You will be asked to answer three questions about what the speakers say in each conversation. Select the best response to each question and mark the letter (A), (B), (C), or (D) on your answer sheet. The conversations will not be printed in your test book and will be spoken only one time.

41. What are the speakers planning to do?

    (A) Sightsee downtown.
    (B) Go to a movie.
    (C) See a play.
    (D) Tell jokes.

42. How does the man feel?

    (A) Sick.
    (B) Good.
    (C) Bored.
    (D) Worried.

43. What time will the speakers leave?

    (A) 6:15.
    (B) 6:30.
    (C) 7:00.
    (D) 11:00.

___

44. What is Mrs. Kowalski doing?

    (A) Eating.
    (B) Sleeping.
    (C) Reading a report.
    (D) Attending a meeting.

45. What is the receptionist NOT going to do?

    (A) Take a message.
    (B) Answer the telephone.
    (C) Answer the caller's questions.
    (D) Transfer the call to Mrs. Kowalski.

46. When will the caller call again?

    (A) At noon.
    (B) Later this afternoon.
    (C) Tomorrow morning.
    (D) Tomorrow afternoon.

___

47. According to the man, how many wedding guests will there be?

    (A) Less than 100.
    (B) At least 100.
    (C) 300.
    (D) More than 400.

48. What does the man ask the woman to do?

    (A) Invite more people to their wedding.
    (B) Marry him.
    (C) Cater his wedding.
    (D) Have the caterer plan for extra guests.

49. What kind of food does the man want at the wedding?

    (A) Fish.
    (B) Chicken.
    (C) Vegetarian.
    (D) Steak.

___

50. When will the woman return?

    (A) In one hour.
    (B) Before lunch.
    (C) In the afternoon.
    (D) Tomorrow.

51. What will she pick up?

    (A) Ice.
    (B) A suit.
    (C) A sweater.
    (D) Photographs.

52. How much does she have to pay?

    (A) $7.00.
    (B) $11.00.
    (C) $17.00.
    (D) $36.00.

___

GO ON TO THE NEXT PAGE

53. When did the woman go to the library?

(A) Sunday.
(B) Monday.
(C) Tuesday.
(D) Friday.

54. What did she do at the library?

(A) Wrote a report.
(B) Used the Internet.
(C) Searched for books.
(D) Read fashion magazines.

55. How does the man feel?

(A) Hot.
(B) Fine.
(C) Tired.
(D) Sorry.

56. What does the man tell the woman to do?

(A) Hurry.
(B) Get thinner.
(C) Put on boots.
(D) Change her dress.

57. How is the weather?

(A) It's snowing.
(B) It's raining.
(C) It's fine.
(D) It's hot.

58. Where are the speakers going?

(A) To work.
(B) To a show.
(C) To a dinner.
(D) To the shoe store.

59. Where are the speakers?

(A) In an office.
(B) In a clothes store.
(C) In a health club.
(D) In an exercise equipment store.

60. How long will the man stay?

(A) One hour.
(B) Four hours.
(C) Until 4:00.
(D) Until 8:00.

61. How can the man get more information?

(A) Call.
(B) Read a book.
(C) Ask the woman.
(D) Go online.

62. Where are the speakers?

(A) At a concert.
(B) At a lecture.
(C) At a movie.
(D) At a play.

63. How much did the tickets cost?

(A) $50 each.
(B) $100 each.
(C) $115 each.
(D) $150 each.

64. How does the man feel about the cost of the tickets?

(A) Sad.
(B) Glad.
(C) Angry.
(D) Comfortable.

65. What did the man order?

   (A) Pens.
   (B) Pencils.
   (C) Envelopes.
   (D) Notebooks.

66. How many did he order?

   (A) Four dozen.
   (B) Five dozen.
   (C) Four hundred.
   (D) Five hundred.

67. When will the order arrive?

   (A) Tuesday.
   (B) Wednesday.
   (C) On the weekend.
   (D) Next week.

68. Why does the man have to go to the office early?

   (A) To have breakfast there.
   (B) To attend a meeting.
   (C) To finish a report.
   (D) To get ready for a trip.

69. When will Mr. Park return to the office?

   (A) Tonight.
   (B) Tomorrow morning.
   (C) Tomorrow afternoon.
   (D) Tomorrow night.

70. When does the man plan to leave home?

   (A) 4:08.
   (B) 6:00.
   (C) 6:30.
   (D) 8:00.

GO ON TO THE NEXT PAGE

Directions: You will hear some talks given by a single speaker. You will be asked to answer three questions about what the speaker says in each talk. Select the best response to each question and mark the letter (A), (B), (C), or (D) on your answer sheet. The talks will not be printed in your test book and will be spoken only one time.

71. Where would one hear this announcement?

    (A) At a movie theater.
    (B) In a cafe.
    (C) In a phone booth.
    (D) At an airport.

72. Why is this message being broadcast?

    (A) Someone has a message.
    (B) Security is at risk.
    (C) No one is paying attention.
    (D) The air is polluted.

73. What does Mr. Bajarin have to do?

    (A) Sit at his desk.
    (B) Show his ticket.
    (C) Go to the courtesy desk.
    (D) Get some fresh air.

74. Why is this building important?

    (A) It is very old.
    (B) Its architecture is unusual.
    (C) It contains statues of kings.
    (D) It has been excavated.

75. How is it known that the whole statue was 7 meters high?

    (A) The statue was measured.
    (B) An architect's records were discovered.
    (C) It was estimated from the size of the head.
    (D) Another statue of Damatian was 7 meters high also.

76. Where would this announcement most likely be heard?

    (A) In a museum.
    (B) In a classroom.
    (C) On a tour bus.
    (D) At church.

77. Why is this message being played?

    (A) The receptionist is not in.
    (B) Randall Svetlanovich is not in.
    (C) The voice mail is being tested.
    (D) The receptionist is busy.

78. How can the caller contact Randall Svetlanovich?

    (A) Send him a present.
    (B) Leave a voice mail message.
    (C) Mail him a letter.
    (D) Call later.

79. What will happen if the caller waits?

    (A) Randall Svetlanovich will pick up the phone.
    (B) The caller will be able to speak to the receptionist.
    (C) The caller will hear Randall Svetlanovich's e-mail address.
    (D) A voice mail will be sent to the caller.

80. How is the sky described?

    (A) High.
    (B) Blue.
    (C) Cloudy.
    (D) Sunny.

81. What is covering the region?

    (A) A high pressure system.
    (B) Light clouds.
    (C) Sun.
    (D) Picnics.

82. How high will the temperature be?

    (A) Around 17.
    (B) In the high teens.
    (C) Just below 70.
    (D) In the 70s.

83. What crime was Mr. Robbins charged with?

    (A) Embezzlement.
    (B) Insider trading.
    (C) Tax evasion.
    (D) Gambling.

84. How did the Argentinean authorities find Ruiz?

    (A) They had a tip from a local merchant.
    (B) They obtained information from U.S. authorities.
    (C) They carried out extensive investigations.
    (D) They traced bogus tax statements.

85. What will happen to Mr. Robbins now?

    (A) He will change his name to Ruiz.
    (B) He will go to jail in Argentina.
    (C) He will work as a florist.
    (D) He will be returned to the United States.

---

86. What does this announcement concern?

    (A) Rainy weather.
    (B) Weekly duties.
    (C) Late employees.
    (D) Late buses.

87. How often are employees late?

    (A) Three times a week.
    (B) Five times a week.
    (C) Ten times a week.
    (D) Every day.

88. What problem do late employees cause?

    (A) The bus driver has to stand in the rain.
    (B) Employees at other stops wait longer for the bus.
    (C) The late employees lose their pay.
    (D) The punctual employees are on time.

---

89. What type of company is this?

    (A) Clothing store.
    (B) Restaurant.
    (C) Camping equipment store.
    (D) Baby furniture store.

90. How long is the sale?

    (A) Half a day.
    (B) Two days.
    (C) All spring.
    (D) All year.

91. How much are infants' clothes?

    (A) Half price.
    (B) $5.95.
    (C) $7.98.
    (D) $9.95.

---

92. What happened in downtown Riverdale?

    (A) A water pipe broke.
    (B) People were injured.
    (C) There was an accident.
    (D) People had to leave their homes.

93. How high did the water rise?

    (A) Half a meter.
    (B) A little less than one meter.
    (C) Just over one meter.
    (D) More than a meter and a half.

94. When did the rain stop?

    (A) Saturday afternoon.
    (B) Sunday evening.
    (C) Monday evening.
    (D) Wednesday morning.

GO ON TO THE NEXT PAGE

95. What type of company would leave this message?

    (A) An airline company.
    (B) A movie theater.
    (C) A travel company.
    (D) A phone company.

96. What happens if the caller presses 2?

    (A) The caller hears a movie schedule.
    (B) The caller can buy tickets.
    (C) The caller hears a flight schedule.
    (D) The caller can buy luggage.

97. How can the caller speak with a person?

    (A) Press 1.
    (B) Wait.
    (C) Call for a ticket agent.
    (D) Look for the number online.

98. Where will the concert be?

    (A) In a parking lot.
    (B) In City Hall.
    (C) In a library.
    (D) In a park.

99. When will the concert be held if the weather is bad?

    (A) Friday.
    (B) Saturday.
    (C) Sunday.
    (D) Monday

100. How much are the tickets?

    (A) Free.
    (B) $3.00.
    (C) $7.00.
    (D) $30.00.

This is the end of the Listening test. Turn to Part 5 in your test book.

READING TEST

In the Reading test, you will read a variety of texts and answer several different types of reading comprehension questions. The entire Reading test will last 75 minutes. There are three parts, and directions are given for each part. You are encouraged to answer as many questions as possible within the time allowed.

You must mark your answers on the separate answer sheet. Do not write your answers in the test book.

PART 5

Directions: A word or phrase is missing in each of the sentences below. Four answer choices are given below each sentence. Select the best answer to complete the sentence. Then mark the letter (A), (B), (C), or (D) on your answer sheet.

101. _____ is the biggest city in Brazil, it is not the capital.

   (A) São Paulo
   (B) If São Paulo
   (C) Although São Paulo
   (D) São Paulo, which

102. _____ direct link exists between acidic soil and tooth decay, according to public health officials.

   (A) There is a
   (B) A
   (C) That there is a
   (D) Because

103. Passengers are hereby notified that all luggage _____ one hour before the scheduled departure time.

   (A) will check
   (B) will be checked
   (C) checks
   (D) has checked

104. Did Mr. Moliere say that he _____ here only two weeks ago?

   (A) came
   (B) has come
   (C) has been coming
   (D) comes

105. _____ in large quantities is not necessarily an indication of its quality.

   (A) A product is sold
   (B) It is a product sold
   (C) That a product is sold
   (D) A product sells

106. The new security guard on the first floor is _____ person that everyone likes him.

   (A) a such nice
   (B) a so nice
   (C) such nice
   (D) such a nice

GO ON TO THE NEXT PAGE

107. I had to make so many international calls last month that now I am faced _____ a huge bill.

   (A) to
   (B) with
   (C) toward
   (D) at

108. The cost of the necklace depends _____ the quality of the gold.

   (A) to
   (B) on
   (C) of
   (D) about

109. It is an unfortunate fact that many forest fires are caused by cigarettes _____ out of car windows.

   (A) are throwing
   (B) have thrown
   (C) throw
   (D) thrown

110. I wish I _____ the answer to your question so I could help you.

   (A) would know
   (B) knew
   (C) know
   (D) have known

111. We ask that all important correspondence be sent by registered _____ certified mail.

   (A) or
   (B) however
   (C) but
   (D) yet

112. The assistant jumped up on a chair and screamed when he saw a mouse _____ across the lounge.

   (A) ran
   (B) run
   (C) runs
   (D) had run

113. _____ the plumber could repair the toilet, he still would not do it.

   (A) Therefore
   (B) However
   (C) So
   (D) Even if

114. The laborers were _____ with mud after spending all day digging the ditch.

   (A) covering
   (B) cover
   (C) covered
   (D) coverage

115. _____ his joining the group late, his manager is confident that he will fit right in.

   (A) Even though
   (B) Despite
   (C) If
   (D) However

116. I filed my report last week, but now I wish I _____.

   (A) have waited
   (B) waited
   (C) had waited
   (D) wait

117. The doctors will be ready to go home as soon as they _____ their rounds.

   (A) will finish
   (B) will have finished
   (C) are finishing
   (D) finish

118. Vice President D'Agostino had her driver _____ her husband at the airport.

   (A) picking up
   (B) to pick up
   (C) pick up
   (D) picked up

119. Mrs. Kurtoglu is a fast learner, and she has _____ mastered the drafting techniques.

    (A) already
    (B) ever
    (C) yet
    (D) still

120. We have to complete the project because we still have a _____ obligation.

    (A) contract
    (B) contractual
    (C) contracts
    (D) contracting

121. Who _____ how many of our clients can contact us at our new office?

    (A) knows
    (B) is knowing
    (C) has known
    (D) are knowing

122. The advertising staff has been working hard but has not finished the campaign _____.

    (A) still
    (B) yet
    (C) anymore
    (D) already

123. The high gross _____ product is an outcome of their work ethic.

    (A) nationally
    (B) nationwide
    (C) nation
    (D) national

124. Our company has chosen the Swedish vendor _____ they guarantee the best after-sales service.

    (A) and
    (B) because
    (C) but
    (D) so

125. After you go two kilometers, this road will turn _____ an interstate highway.

    (A) around
    (B) about
    (C) into
    (D) off

126. Most small business owners are required to file their taxes _____.

    (A) quarterly
    (B) usually
    (C) anymore
    (D) still

127. Our staff is smaller now because two people in our department _____ this year.

    (A) are terminated
    (B) terminate
    (C) had been terminated
    (D) have been terminated

128. Because of the strong economy, there has been an increase in exported _____ imported goods.

    (A) and
    (B) though
    (C) or
    (D) still

129. If Fujikin, Inc. _____ more available capital, they would have expanded their European operations.

    (A) has
    (B) had had
    (C) were having
    (D) has had

130. _____ the patient's condition get worse, the nurse will call in an internist.

    (A) Might
    (B) Unless
    (C) Should
    (D) If

GO ON TO THE NEXT PAGE

131. For reasons of public safety, the firefighters will not respond _____ the call is verified.

(A) and
(B) until
(C) even
(D) because

132. All shareholders must fill out a _____ slip in order to get money.

(A) withdraw
(B) withdrawing
(C) withdrawal
(D) withdrawn

133. The training staff does not have to attend the meeting, _____ they will anyway.

(A) but
(B) and
(C) or
(D) already

134. I will never forget _____ the beautiful country of Thailand during the summer after I graduated from college.

(A) to visit
(B) visited
(C) visiting
(D) visit

135. _____ president of the United States, but he also was a lawyer for a railroad company.

(A) Not only Lincoln was
(B) Although Lincoln was
(C) Lincoln, being
(D) Not only was Lincoln

136. Our friends offered _____ us some of their camping equipment for our trip to the mountains.

(A) lending
(B) to lend
(C) to have lent
(D) on lending

137. All trainees _____ eighty hours of instruction by the end of March.

(A) complete
(B) will have completed
(C) will be completing
(D) have completed

138. I think Ms. Chiu would not mind _____ so hard if only she had longer vacations.

(A) working
(B) to work
(C) works
(D) on working

139. I broke a tooth when I _____ into a piece of hard candy.

(A) bite
(B) had bitten
(C) have bitten
(D) bit

140. If Dr. Puri did not like jazz, he _____ to it so much.

(A) would listen
(B) would not listen
(C) would not have listened
(D) would be listening

Directions: Read the texts that follow. A word or phrase is missing in some of the sentences. Four answer choices are given below each of the sentences. Select the best answer to complete the text. Then mark the letter (A), (B), (C), or (D) on your answer sheet.

HTCD Bank
20 State Street
Trenton, New Jersey 08625

June 17, 20___

Ms. Nukket Topal
451 West Huron Drive
Chicago, Illinois 60239

Dear Ms. Topal:

We received your e-mail requesting to close your savings account. Unfortunately, we are unable to _____ with the request because it was sent by e-mail.

141. (A) comply
(B) compliant
(C) compliance
(D) complicate

To close your account, please mail us a letter stating that you wish to close your savings account. Don't forget to include your sixteen-digit account number and the mailing address where you would like to receive your remaining balance. You can also close your account by visiting our nearest branch.

We always strive to give our customers the best possible service. We hope that you have been happy with _____ and will consider using our bank again in the future. If you are

142. (A) me
(B) us
(C) him
(D) them

closing your account because you have had an _____ experience, please contact our

143. (A) adequate
(B) efficient
(C) interesting
(D) unsatisfactory

customer service representatives to discuss how we can serve you better.

If we may be of further assistance, please contact us any time. We look forward to working with you.

Sincerely,

Erich Gleisner

Erich Gleisner
Account Manager

From: Marika Fiehne
To: Astrid Anderson
Subject: New office equipment request

Thank you for welcoming me to Ontel. My first week working here has been wonderful.

You asked me to e-mail you about the _____ of my office. Overall, it is very

144. (A) color
       (B) location
       (C) condition
       (D) dimension

nice and suits most of my needs. However, I would like a few small changes. Could I get a different chair? The current chair is really too small for me. I'd also like a conference table for _____ with clients.

145. (A) meet
       (B) to meet
       (C) meeting
       (D) will meet

My office also needs some technology upgrades. The computer's Internet connection is slow and frequently freezes in the afternoons. It is very frustrating. Also, I don't have the ability to participate in video teleconferencing. Would it be possible for me to get this? I am expected to participate in weekly conferences with our partners in other countries.

I will need a visit from the IT specialist. I should have antivirus software installed on my computer. Maybe my current computer has it, but I _____ find it.

146. (A) should not
       (B) could not
       (C) must not
       (D) may not

Thank you.

GO ON TO THE NEXT PAGE

From: Sarah Spencer
To: Eduardo Allende
Re: Vacancy on Information Technology Committee

Maria Robles has _____ from her position on the IT Committee.

147. (A) reacted
     (B) resigned
     (C) rejoined
     (D) resisted

You have been recommended to fill the open spot. I hope that you want to participate on this important committee.

You time commitment would be minimal; however, the _____ is an

148. (A) respond
     (B) responsible
     (C) responsibly
     (D) responsiblity

important one. As you know, criminals have broken into our competitors' computer systems. These hackers have cost our industry millions in lost and compromised data. To prevent this electronic theft, we have installed anti-hacking measures on our company's computers. This is one of the IT Committee's best achievements.

Our company's sales _____ because news spread about our

149. (A) have stagnated
     (B) have increased
     (C) have declined
     (D) have stalled

anti-hacking devices. Customers trust us to protect their financial data.

The IT Committee agrees that you are our ideal new member. Please consider this invitation and get back to me within the next few days.

Thanks.

From: Sigmund Ferdinand
To: Mendel Wagner
Subject: Itinerary

Dear Mendel,

I wanted to let you know that I booked our train tickets for the upcoming business trip. The price of the tickets was higher than I expected. I don't know if the train is always so expensive or if this is considered a peak time of year for _____ travel.

150. (A) air
(B) road
(C) rail
(D) sea

In any case, Waterworks will cover the cost for us.

Since the conference is free _____ charge for all GBC members,

151. (A) at
(B) in
(C) by
(D) of

Waterworks has offered to put us up in a 5-star hotel. I booked us two single rooms at Champlain Manor. It has a spa, a heated indoor pool, tennis courts, and three restaurants. We definitely won't be _____ there.

152. (A) bore
(B) bored
(C) boring
(D) boredom

Let me know if you have any questions about these trip plans.

Yours,

Sigmund

Directions: In this part you will read a selection of texts, such as magazine and newspaper articles, letters, and advertisements. Each text is followed by several questions. Select the best answer for each question and mark the letter (A), (B), (C), or (D) on your answer sheet.

Yamitomo International continues to be a pioneer in the digital revolution. As one of the first companies to manufacture compact discs, we continue to develop and implement the latest techniques.

At Yamitomo we manufacture compact discs, analog and digital cassettes, and records, as well as CD-ROM, Video CD, CD-1, and we are ready to deliver the next generation of sound carriers. We have carefully built a reputation of excellence in quality and customer service, providing not only manufacturing but also printing, packaging, drop-shipping, marketing, and distribution of music and media products.

We are ready to provide you with complete factory-to-store shelf service. Our complete wholesale catalog can be viewed online. To order, create your customer account by clicking on "new accounts." In addition, new accounts can be created and orders made by calling our wholesale customer line at 1-800-555-9098. Online or on the phone, you can always count on the high quality of our products.

153. What kind of company is Yamitomo International?

(A) An electronics manufacturer
(B) A computer distributor
(C) A music company
(D) A moving company

154. What is the focus of this passage?

(A) Musical artists are given much freedom with Yamitomo.
(B) Analog cassettes were developed by Yamitomo.
(C) Music and media products are sold by Yamitomo.
(D) Yamitomo has a reputation of excellence, diversity, and innovation.

Choose the magazine that meets your sourcing needs better...
And get a FREE sample copy!!!

As a regular or potential importer of Japanese-made electronics, computer products, and components, you know how important the latest marketing information is. You must also be alert to **what, where,** and **how** to get the most competitive offers to maintain your competitive edge.

Each of these magazines, *Purchasing Components, Purchasing Computer Equipment,* and *Purchasing Electronics,* is published monthly and reports on the Japanese exporting industries in each of these specialized fields. In addition to advertisements, they also contain surveys of new products, corporate and technological developments, details on market changes, and other valuable information to help you in your purchasing decisions.

Fill out the **Request a Free Sample Copy** form on the next page to receive a complimentary copy of the magazine that is right for your business. You will receive your copy in two to four weeks. In order to serve you better, we also ask you to take a few minutes to complete the survey at the bottom of the form. As a thank-you gift, we will send you, absolutely free, a copy of our *Guide to Japanese Electronics Companies.* This is an exclusive offer made available only to our customers. This book is not available in stores or online.

155. Who is the audience for this advertisement?

(A) Japanese electronics manufacturers
(B) Security system installation companies
(C) Electronics wholesalers
(D) Magazine publishers

156. What is offered in this advertisement?

(A) Electronics components
(B) Corporate changes
(C) Magazines
(D) Computer products

Questions 157–159 refer to the following letter.

Dear 25-Year Club Members,

The massive changes taking place within Anderson Industries may be somewhat unsettling for our longer-term employees. Yet, as we pause to recognize our 25-Year Club members, it is appropriate that we also acknowledge the need to adapt and grow. For this, we need the knowledge and experience of you and of all our employees to guide us successfully through this journey.

Most of you will realize that the manufacturing processes that we utilize and the methods that we use to guide our business have changed very little over the years. In today's constantly changing world, it is the innovative companies with continuous improvement of flexible manufacturing systems and modern business practices that capture the attention of their customers. This is the kind of company that we are striving to become.

You are aware that we have been working over the past several months with a team of experts to discuss innovations in our manufacturing processes and business practices. I want to ensure that you are also aware that we have built into this discussion process numerous opportunities to consult with our 25-Year Club members. No one knows better than we do that the perspective gained from experience is an essential part of any innovation process.

Anderson Industries has a solid reputation in the automotive industry, thanks to the efforts of you, the 25-Year Club members. Now it is time for all of us to create the necessary changes in our company to ensure that our 25-Year Club will grow in membership for years to come.

Thank you all for your loyalty and commitment to the success of Anderson Industries.

Sincerely,

Karl Anderson

Karl Anderson
CEO

157. Why was this letter written?

   (A) To show appreciation to long-term employees
   (B) To explain the changes that have taken place
   (C) To explain that changes are necessary in the near future
   (D) To recruit new members

158. What does the writer of this letter hope for?

   (A) Innovation in the manufacturing process
   (B) Customers
   (C) A growth in club membership
   (D) A reputation in the automotive industry

159. Where would this letter be most likely to appear?

   (A) In a trade publication
   (B) In a company newsletter
   (C) In an executive memo
   (D) In a community newspaper

Flying over Venezuela's Lake Maracaibo, one is struck by the deep orange color of the water spewing from a river into the lake. This is not a natural phenomenon but the result of aggressive mining practices carried out in western Venezuela, where tons of earth and rock are flushed away every day in the search for valuable diamonds. As the river carries the earth and rock away from the mining areas, it carries it into other areas, most particularly to Lake Maracaibo. Tons of silt flow into the lake every day, with dire consequences for the natural environment and the people who live there. On the one hand, the silting of Lake Maracaibo increases the risk of flooding, thus endangering the lives and livelihoods of people living in the area. In addition, the mining is also destroying fishing grounds that have been a major source of protein food for the country, as well as an important part of the economy.

160. What is the most noticeable characteristic of the river?

(A) Its location
(B) Its direction
(C) Its rate of flow
(D) Its color

161. What has been the outcome of the silting of Lake Maracaibo?

(A) Fishing grounds have been increased.
(B) The loss of protein has been offset by the economic development of the mining.
(C) There has been an increase in the risk of flooding.
(D) Mining and flooding have been kept in check.

GO ON TO THE NEXT PAGE

The monthly luncheon meeting of the National Society of Fundraising Executives will be held at noon on Friday, May 5, in the Hall of World Cultures at the Knotty Pines Center, located at 4141 East State Street. The cost is $35 per person. Reservations are due by April 21 and should be sent directly to the Hall of World Cultures at the Knotty Pines Center. Following lunch, there will be a brief membership meeting with committee reports, then we will hear from our guest speaker. This month's speaker is Miranda Bottomley of Grantwriters, Inc., who will speak on the topic "Tapping into Old Money." Please note that this event is for members only. All those who are interested in joining the society in time to attend this month's meeting should contact our membership coordinator, Dr. Kamil Srivastava, at (312) 555-1298 before April 21.

162. Where should one send reservations?

(A) To Dr. Srivastava's office

(B) To the Hall of World Cultures of Knotty Pines

(C) To the luncheon hall

(D) To the National Society of Fundraising Executives' office

163. Who should contact Dr. Srivastava?

(A) Potential society members

(B) Current society members

(C) Any international representatives

(D) Fundraising experts

Questions 164–166 refer to the following chart.

Manufacturer's Value of Shipments of Selected Types of Mining Equipment in the Industry			
TYPE OF MACHINERY	$ AMOUNT IN MILLIONS	$ AMOUNT IN MILLIONS	% OF INCREASE OR DECREASE
Portable crushing, pulverizing, and screening machinery	63.7	85.1	+25
Stationary crushing, pulverizing, and screening machinery	160.3	132.1	–18
Underground mining machinery	381.8	318.8	–17
Mineral-processing equipment	90.2	86.6	–4
Portable drilling rigs	295.3	252.8	–14
Mine conveyors, hoists, and locomotives	56.6	82.8	+46

*Please note: For an analysis of the information on this chart, please see page 10 of this publication. The information on this chart presents shipment values from the past two years. For projected values for the next five years, please see the chart on page 15 of this publication.

164. What type of chart is this?

(A) An inventory list
(B) An industry report
(C) An advertisement
(D) A sales report

165. What was the decrease in mineral processing equipment?

(A) 3 percent
(B) 4 percent
(C) 14 percent
(D) 18 percent

166. Which product saw the largest increase in shipments?

(A) Portable crushing machinery
(B) Portable drilling rigs
(C) Mineral-processing equipment
(D) All mining machinery and related equipment

GO ON TO THE NEXT PAGE

```
═══════════════ NARTAGAZ ═══════════════

The 10th annual
International Trade Fair
for
Equipment for the Oil & Gas Industry
will take place at
Korbutt Andropov Park and Fairgrounds, Moscow, Russia
June 10–15, 20__


Sponsored by:
NGJ International GmbH
Stuttgart, Germany


Exhibitors and attendees should contact:
NGJ International
1151 Park Street
Baltimore, MD 22899
(410) 555-9292


Exhibitors:
Please ask for an application package.
Applications due: January 1, 20__


Attendees:
Visitors packages will be available February 1, including:
• A list of exhibit highlights
• Information on local accommodations
• Information on discounted travel and hotel packages
```

167. Who is sponsoring this event?

(A) U.S. Department of Commerce
(B) City of Moscow
(C) Oil & gas industry
(D) NGJ International

168. Where should one write for more information?

(A) Baltimore
(B) Moscow
(C) Stuttgart
(D) Washington, D.C.

169. Who will attend this trade fair?

(A) Politicians
(B) Oil and gas executives
(C) Environmentalists
(D) Trade negotiators

Questions 170–172 refer to the following advertisement.

DYNABOLD

Most European financial institutions agree that an ATM is not just a purchase, it is an investment. That is why more than 50 percent of banks that have ATMs have invested in ours.

At DynaBold we have always built our ATMs to last. But since we are continually developing new technologies, we have made them adaptable, too. Years ago we created the industry's first modular ATM that could be upgraded without changing the housing. Today these ATMs are still yielding dividends for their original investors.

However, we do much more than protect your investment. With more than 100 years of security expertise, we make sure your ATM is secure, too. Our service organization responds 24 hours a day, 365 days a year. Also, all our service engineers are trained to maintain everything from electronic components to security features.

It is no wonder that the majority of European financial institutions use our ATMs. They know their money is securely invested.

Shouldn't you invest your money wisely, too? Call DynaBold today to find out how. We will arrange to send a DynaBold representative to visit you at your place of business to discuss our complete line of products and show you how a DynaBold ATM system can save you valuable time and money in ways that other ATM systems cannot. Various maintenance and upgrade packages are available. Our representative will help you select the best system and packages to serve your needs. Call today.

---

170. What kind of company is DynaBold?

(A) An ATM manufacturer
(B) An investment firm
(C) A bank
(D) A security service

171. What did DynaBold develop?

(A) Modular homes
(B) New investment methods
(C) A chain of banks
(D) Upgradable ATMs

172. How does the company maintain its ATMs?

(A) By upgrading them often
(B) Through a 24-hour service program
(C) By making them secure
(D) By developing new technologies

GO ON TO THE NEXT PAGE

Drug advisory committees report to the Ministry of Health. It is the responsibility of these committees to protect consumers, most of whom have little chemical or biological knowledge with which to evaluate medications. Drug advisory committees provide the Ministry of Health with the necessary information for evaluating the proper degree of access to medications by the consumer. Drug advisory committees also oversee the preparation of materials that provide clearly explained information about commonly available drugs in a manner that is readily understandable to the layperson. Drug education may take the form of literature, advertisements, training of health care personnel, or other means as deemed appropriate by each committee. Drug advisory committees should be composed of physicians, registered nurses, epidemiologists, and pharmacologists. Members must posess specific scientific expertise and must have considerable experience working with consumers so that they can assess the impact of their decisions and projects on consumers. Each committee must have 10–15 members, who will be evaluated every two years by officials from the Ministry of Health.

173. Who is the audience for this passage?

(A) Nurses
(B) Medical doctors
(C) Lab workers
(D) Consumers

174. What is the purpose of these committees?

(A) To advise the Ministry of Health on the safety of drugs
(B) To sell drugs
(C) To serve as consumer advocates
(D) To evaluate the Ministry of Health

175. The word "advisory" in line 1 is closest in meaning to

(A) performance
(B) advocacy
(C) testing
(D) consulting

176. Which topic would a drug advisory committee discuss?

(A) Causes of cancer
(B) Availability of over-the-counter drugs
(C) Hospital drug-dispensing systems
(D) Ministry of Health budget cuts

Having the proper documentation when you travel abroad is very important. Remember that immigration and customs officials are very document-minded, so failing to obtain the proper paperwork before entering a country or losing your passport in a foreign city can cause many complications. When traveling, you should always know where your passport is. Always carry it in a safe place on your person or, if not going far, leave it in the hotel safe. Do not leave it lying about in your hotel room or easily visible in a pocket. If staying in a country for several weeks, it is worthwhile to register at your embassy or consulate. Then, if your passport is stolen, the process of replacing it is simpler and faster. It is also recommended to keep photocopies of essential documents as well as some additional passport-sized photographs.

Remember that it is your responsibility to ensure that your passport is stamped in and out when you cross borders. The absence of entry and exit stamps can cause serious difficulties and could invalidate your visa. Therefore, it is important to seek out the proper officials if the stamping process is not carried out as you cross the border. Also, do not lose your entry card. Replacing it can cause a lot of headaches and expense. Citizens of countries that require visas, such as France and Korea, can expect more delays and problems at border crossings.

177. Where would this advisory most likely appear?

(A) In a newspaper
(B) In an embassy pamphlet
(C) In an airline in-flight magazine
(D) In a travel guidebook

178. What should travelers do if staying in a country for a month?

(A) Register with their embassy
(B) Leave their passport in the hotel
(C) Find a good hotel
(D) Have extra passport photos taken

179. If border officials do not stamp the passport, what should a traveler do?

(A) Request that it be stamped as soon as possible
(B) Refrain from entering the country
(C) Go to the embassy
(D) Get help at the hotel

180. The word "ensure" in paragraph 2, line 1, is closest in meaning to

(A) fasten
(B) tighten
(C) make certain
(D) protect

GO ON TO THE NEXT PAGE

Questions 181–185 refer to the following letter and memo.

Lumpkin's Computer Center
88 Chestnut Street
Winterdale, MN 90480

July 26, 20___

Dear Neighborhood Business,

Lumpkin's Computer Center has just opened in your neighborhood. We offer all the computer supplies you need for your daily business. In addition, we do computer repair and sell refurbished computers. Best of all, we offer a convenient location close to your place of business. Please stop by and find out what we have to offer that will make your work easier. Our specials this week include brand-new printer ink cartridges @ $25 each and computer paper @ $7 for a package of 500 sheets. Show this letter for an additional 10% off your first purchase at Lumpkin's. See you soon!

Your neighbors,

Robert Oscar

Robert and Oscar Lumpkin

Holloway & Svenson
Attorneys-at-Law

Office Memorandum

From: Myra Holloway
To: Yoshi Phipps
Re: Computer Center

Please look at the attached letter. What a convenience to have a computer supply store on the same block as we are! Why don't you go today and pick up some things, let's say 5 ink cartridges and 10 packs of paper. Don't forget to take the letter with you for the discount. Then you can pop around the corner to Crawford's Stationery on Maple Avenue for some manila envelopes and anything else you think we need. Thanks.

181. Who probably received this letter?

   (A) Local attorneys only
   (B) Holloway & Svenson only
   (C) All neighborhood businesses
   (D) Businesses throughout the city

182. Who are Robert and Oscar Lumpkin?

   (A) Attorneys
   (B) Software trainers
   (C) Computer manufacturers
   (D) Owners of the Computer Center

183. According to the letter, what can you do at the Computer Center?

   (A) Buy a used computer
   (B) Learn to use a computer
   (C) Have your printer repaired
   (D) Recycle your ink cartridges

184. Where is the office of Holloway & Svenson located?

   (A) On Maple Avenue
   (B) On Chestnut Street
   (C) On Crawford Street
   (D) On Lumpkin Avenue

185. If Yoshi follows Myra's instructions, how much will he spend at the Computer Center?

   (A) $112.50
   (B) $125.00
   (C) $175.50
   (D) $195.00

September 9, 20___

Mr. T. Sachimoto
Human Resources Director
The Spindex Corporation
1809 35th Street
Mayfield, AL 20812

Dear Mr. Sachimoto:

I recently received my master's degree in Accounting from Pitt University and am currently seeking a position as an accountant. I graduated from Carson College with a bachelor's degree in Economics and worked for three years as a bookkeeper for Harrison Telemarketing, Inc. before I entered graduate school. I would be interested in applying for any opening you may have for an accountant. I am enclosing my résumé and two letters of reference. I also have copies of my college transcripts available if you are interested in seeing them.

Sincerely,

Gina Degenaro

Gina Degenaro

September 30, 20___

Ms. Gina Degenaro
71 Fern Lane
Mayfield, AL 20812

Dear Ms. Degenaro:

Thank you for your letter expressing interest in working for the Spindex Corporation. You have an impressive background. I was especially interested to see that you went to the same graduate school that I did.

We generally find that the best way to get a professional position in a large company like Spindex is to begin in one of the lower level jobs. Then you have the opportunity to show what you can do, and when an opening in your field comes up, you are well positioned to apply for it.

We currently have an opening in our Accounting Department, which you might be interested in applying for. It is for an administrative assistant. If you are interested in such a position, please call my assistant, Ms. Rogers, at 593-555-0954 to set up a time for an interview. When you come in, please bring the documents you mentioned in your letter. I look forward to meeting you.

Sincerely,

T. Sachimoto

T. Sachimoto

186. Why did Ms. Degenaro write the letter?

   (A) To ask for advice
   (B) To answer an ad
   (C) To apply for a job
   (D) To ask for a reference

187. What job does Mr. Sachimoto offer to Ms. Degenaro?

   (A) Accountant
   (B) Bookkeeper
   (C) Telemarketer
   (D) Administrative assistant

188. Where did Mr. Sachimoto go to graduate school?

   (A) Pitt University
   (B) Carson College
   (C) Harrison College
   (D) University of Mayfield

189. Who is Ms. Rogers?

   (A) Head of the Accounting Department
   (B) Ms. Degenaro's former employer
   (C) Mr. Sachimoto's assistant
   (D) Director of Spindex

190. What should Ms. Degenaro take with her to the interview?

   (A) Her résumé
   (B) Her phone number
   (C) Her college transcripts
   (D) Her letters of reference

GO ON TO THE NEXT PAGE

Trip Itinerary for Akiki Ono

Monday, May 12th	Sydney	Meeting with Mr. Andrews of BelAir Corp.
Tuesday, May 13th–Wednesday, May 14th	Melbourne	Visit to the offices of Holiday, Inc.
Thursday, May 15th–Sunday, May 18th	Darwin	Global Marketing Assoc. Conference
Monday, May 19th	Singapore	Meeting with Ms. Chang of World Market
Tuesday, May 20th	Hong Kong	Visit to Technomarket branch office
Wednesday, May 21st	Home	

To: Tamako Sato
From: Akiko Ono
Subject: My Trip
Attach: Itinerary

Hello Tamako,

I am attaching the itinerary for my upcoming trip. Please take care of the following for me:

1. I'll need the photos for the new ad campaign to show at the Global Marketing Conference, but I don't think they'll be ready before I leave. I'll be staying at the Hotel Internationale during the conference. Please send the photos to me there.
2. I will discuss with Ms. Chang the visit she plans to make here. It will be very soon. I'll call you from her office to let you know the exact dates so you can start getting ready for her.
3. Please note that Mr. Andrews no longer works for Holiday, Inc. Correct his contact information in our files.

Thanks.

191. How many days will Akiko stay in Melbourne?

(A) One
(B) Two
(C) Three
(D) Four

192. When will she be in Hong Kong?

(A) May 12th
(B) May 13th–14th
(C) May 15th–18th
(D) May 20th

193. What company does Mr. Andrews work for?

(A) BelAir Corporation
(B) Holiday, Inc.
(C) World Market
(D) Technomarket

194. Where will Akiko be when she receives the photos?

(A) Sydney
(B) Melbourne
(C) Darwin
(D) Singapore

195. When will Akiko call Tamako?

(A) May 18th
(B) May 19th
(C) May 20th
(D) May 21st

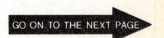
GO ON TO THE NEXT PAGE

October 17, 20___

Dear Roberto,

I have some interesting news for you. My company is sending me to Greendale to work on a project in our branch office there. I will spend about three months at that branch office. I wondered if you could give me some advice about housing. The office can arrange a hotel for me, but I'd rather find something more comfortable. Since my family won't be with me, I'll only need a small apartment. Our office is downtown, right across from Greendale Park, so I'll need to be able to get there easily by public transportation. I won't have a car. I would like to pay no more than $1,500 a month. Is that possible in Greendale? I would appreciate any advice you could give me.

I'm also looking forward to seeing you. I plan to stay two weeks after my assignment is finished to travel around the area. I plan to spend most of that time at the beach. Maybe you would like to join me on this vacation. I'll see you soon.

Your friend,

Luis

Luis Silva

October 31, 20___

Dear Luis,

I was very happy to receive your news. I know you'll enjoy your time in our wonderful city. I have a good recommendation for you. There are several hotels that have special suites that are like small apartments. They all have kitchens and are very comfortable to live in for a few months. They are also inexpensive— about $300 less than the price you said you could pay. All of these hotels are located in the North End of the city. There are hotels in the business district, close to your office, but they don't have these comfortable suites. I am enclosing some brochures so you can pick the hotel you like the best.

I look forward to seeing you and joining you on the vacation you have planned.

Your friend,

Roberto

Roberto Mendez

196. Why is Luis going to Greendale?

    (A) To take a vacation
    (B) To buy house
    (C) To visit Luis
    (D) To work

197. How long will Luis be in Greendale?

    (A) Two weeks
    (B) Three weeks
    (C) Two months
    (D) Three months

198. How much are the hotel suites that Roberto recommends?

    (A) $300
    (B) $1,200
    (C) $1,500
    (D) $1,800

199. Where are the hotel suites that Roberto recommends?

    (A) Downtown
    (B) Near a park
    (C) In the North End
    (D) In the business district

200. According to his letter, what will Roberto do during Luis's stay in Greendale?

    (A) Work with him
    (B) Take him to the park
    (C) Invite him to his house
    (D) Go to the beach with him

Stop! This is the end of the test. If you finish before time is called, you may go back to Parts 5, 6, and 7 and check your work.

ANSWER SHEETS

ANSWER SHEET: Listening Comprehension Review

Listening Comprehension

Part 1 **Part 2** **Part 3** **Part 4**

	Answer		Answer		Answer		Answer		Answer
	A B C D		A B C		A B C		A B C D		A B C D
1	Ⓐ Ⓑ Ⓒ Ⓓ	11	Ⓐ Ⓑ Ⓒ	31	Ⓐ Ⓑ Ⓒ	51	Ⓐ Ⓑ Ⓒ Ⓓ	71	Ⓐ Ⓑ Ⓒ Ⓓ
2	Ⓐ Ⓑ Ⓒ Ⓓ	12	Ⓐ Ⓑ Ⓒ	32	Ⓐ Ⓑ Ⓒ	52	Ⓐ Ⓑ Ⓒ Ⓓ	72	Ⓐ Ⓑ Ⓒ Ⓓ
3	Ⓐ Ⓑ Ⓒ Ⓓ	13	Ⓐ Ⓑ Ⓒ	33	Ⓐ Ⓑ Ⓒ	53	Ⓐ Ⓑ Ⓒ Ⓓ	73	Ⓐ Ⓑ Ⓒ Ⓓ
4	Ⓐ Ⓑ Ⓒ Ⓓ	14	Ⓐ Ⓑ Ⓒ	34	Ⓐ Ⓑ Ⓒ	54	Ⓐ Ⓑ Ⓒ Ⓓ	74	Ⓐ Ⓑ Ⓒ Ⓓ
5	Ⓐ Ⓑ Ⓒ Ⓓ	15	Ⓐ Ⓑ Ⓒ	35	Ⓐ Ⓑ Ⓒ	55	Ⓐ Ⓑ Ⓒ Ⓓ	75	Ⓐ Ⓑ Ⓒ Ⓓ
6	Ⓐ Ⓑ Ⓒ Ⓓ	16	Ⓐ Ⓑ Ⓒ	36	Ⓐ Ⓑ Ⓒ	56	Ⓐ Ⓑ Ⓒ Ⓓ	76	Ⓐ Ⓑ Ⓒ Ⓓ
7	Ⓐ Ⓑ Ⓒ Ⓓ	17	Ⓐ Ⓑ Ⓒ	37	Ⓐ Ⓑ Ⓒ	57	Ⓐ Ⓑ Ⓒ Ⓓ	77	Ⓐ Ⓑ Ⓒ Ⓓ
8	Ⓐ Ⓑ Ⓒ Ⓓ	18	Ⓐ Ⓑ Ⓒ	38	Ⓐ Ⓑ Ⓒ	58	Ⓐ Ⓑ Ⓒ Ⓓ	78	Ⓐ Ⓑ Ⓒ Ⓓ
9	Ⓐ Ⓑ Ⓒ Ⓓ	19	Ⓐ Ⓑ Ⓒ	39	Ⓐ Ⓑ Ⓒ	59	Ⓐ Ⓑ Ⓒ Ⓓ	79	Ⓐ Ⓑ Ⓒ Ⓓ
10	Ⓐ Ⓑ Ⓒ Ⓓ	20	Ⓐ Ⓑ Ⓒ	40	Ⓐ Ⓑ Ⓒ	60	Ⓐ Ⓑ Ⓒ Ⓓ	80	Ⓐ Ⓑ Ⓒ Ⓓ

	Answer		Answer
	A B C D		A B C D
81	Ⓐ Ⓑ Ⓒ Ⓓ	91	Ⓐ Ⓑ Ⓒ Ⓓ
82	Ⓐ Ⓑ Ⓒ Ⓓ	92	Ⓐ Ⓑ Ⓒ Ⓓ
83	Ⓐ Ⓑ Ⓒ Ⓓ	93	Ⓐ Ⓑ Ⓒ Ⓓ
84	Ⓐ Ⓑ Ⓒ Ⓓ	94	Ⓐ Ⓑ Ⓒ Ⓓ
85	Ⓐ Ⓑ Ⓒ Ⓓ	95	Ⓐ Ⓑ Ⓒ Ⓓ
86	Ⓐ Ⓑ Ⓒ Ⓓ	96	Ⓐ Ⓑ Ⓒ Ⓓ
87	Ⓐ Ⓑ Ⓒ Ⓓ	97	Ⓐ Ⓑ Ⓒ Ⓓ
88	Ⓐ Ⓑ Ⓒ Ⓓ	98	Ⓐ Ⓑ Ⓒ Ⓓ
89	Ⓐ Ⓑ Ⓒ Ⓓ	99	Ⓐ Ⓑ Ⓒ Ⓓ
90	Ⓐ Ⓑ Ⓒ Ⓓ	100	Ⓐ Ⓑ Ⓒ Ⓓ

ANSWER SHEET: Reading Review

Reading

Part 5 **Part 6** **Part 7**

	Answer		Answer		Answer		Answer		Answer
	A B C D		A B C D		A B C D		A B C D		A B C D
101	Ⓐ Ⓑ Ⓒ Ⓓ	111	Ⓐ Ⓑ Ⓒ Ⓓ	121	Ⓐ Ⓑ Ⓒ Ⓓ	131	Ⓐ Ⓑ Ⓒ Ⓓ	141	Ⓐ Ⓑ Ⓒ Ⓓ
102	Ⓐ Ⓑ Ⓒ Ⓓ	112	Ⓐ Ⓑ Ⓒ Ⓓ	122	Ⓐ Ⓑ Ⓒ Ⓓ	132	Ⓐ Ⓑ Ⓒ Ⓓ	142	Ⓐ Ⓑ Ⓒ Ⓓ
103	Ⓐ Ⓑ Ⓒ Ⓓ	113	Ⓐ Ⓑ Ⓒ Ⓓ	123	Ⓐ Ⓑ Ⓒ Ⓓ	133	Ⓐ Ⓑ Ⓒ Ⓓ	143	Ⓐ Ⓑ Ⓒ Ⓓ
104	Ⓐ Ⓑ Ⓒ Ⓓ	114	Ⓐ Ⓑ Ⓒ Ⓓ	124	Ⓐ Ⓑ Ⓒ Ⓓ	134	Ⓐ Ⓑ Ⓒ Ⓓ	144	Ⓐ Ⓑ Ⓒ Ⓓ
105	Ⓐ Ⓑ Ⓒ Ⓓ	115	Ⓐ Ⓑ Ⓒ Ⓓ	125	Ⓐ Ⓑ Ⓒ Ⓓ	135	Ⓐ Ⓑ Ⓒ Ⓓ	145	Ⓐ Ⓑ Ⓒ Ⓓ
106	Ⓐ Ⓑ Ⓒ Ⓓ	116	Ⓐ Ⓑ Ⓒ Ⓓ	126	Ⓐ Ⓑ Ⓒ Ⓓ	136	Ⓐ Ⓑ Ⓒ Ⓓ	146	Ⓐ Ⓑ Ⓒ Ⓓ
107	Ⓐ Ⓑ Ⓒ Ⓓ	117	Ⓐ Ⓑ Ⓒ Ⓓ	127	Ⓐ Ⓑ Ⓒ Ⓓ	137	Ⓐ Ⓑ Ⓒ Ⓓ	147	Ⓐ Ⓑ Ⓒ Ⓓ
108	Ⓐ Ⓑ Ⓒ Ⓓ	118	Ⓐ Ⓑ Ⓒ Ⓓ	128	Ⓐ Ⓑ Ⓒ Ⓓ	138	Ⓐ Ⓑ Ⓒ Ⓓ	148	Ⓐ Ⓑ Ⓒ Ⓓ
109	Ⓐ Ⓑ Ⓒ Ⓓ	119	Ⓐ Ⓑ Ⓒ Ⓓ	129	Ⓐ Ⓑ Ⓒ Ⓓ	139	Ⓐ Ⓑ Ⓒ Ⓓ	149	Ⓐ Ⓑ Ⓒ Ⓓ
110	Ⓐ Ⓑ Ⓒ Ⓓ	120	Ⓐ Ⓑ Ⓒ Ⓓ	130	Ⓐ Ⓑ Ⓒ Ⓓ	140	Ⓐ Ⓑ Ⓒ Ⓓ	150	Ⓐ Ⓑ Ⓒ Ⓓ

Part 7

	Answer		Answer		Answer		Answer		Answer
	A B C D		A B C D		A B C D		A B C D		A B C D
151	Ⓐ Ⓑ Ⓒ Ⓓ	161	Ⓐ Ⓑ Ⓒ Ⓓ	171	Ⓐ Ⓑ Ⓒ Ⓓ	181	Ⓐ Ⓑ Ⓒ Ⓓ	191	Ⓐ Ⓑ Ⓒ Ⓓ
152	Ⓐ Ⓑ Ⓒ Ⓓ	162	Ⓐ Ⓑ Ⓒ Ⓓ	172	Ⓐ Ⓑ Ⓒ Ⓓ	182	Ⓐ Ⓑ Ⓒ Ⓓ	192	Ⓐ Ⓑ Ⓒ Ⓓ
153	Ⓐ Ⓑ Ⓒ Ⓓ	163	Ⓐ Ⓑ Ⓒ Ⓓ	173	Ⓐ Ⓑ Ⓒ Ⓓ	183	Ⓐ Ⓑ Ⓒ Ⓓ	193	Ⓐ Ⓑ Ⓒ Ⓓ
154	Ⓐ Ⓑ Ⓒ Ⓓ	164	Ⓐ Ⓑ Ⓒ Ⓓ	174	Ⓐ Ⓑ Ⓒ Ⓓ	184	Ⓐ Ⓑ Ⓒ Ⓓ	194	Ⓐ Ⓑ Ⓒ Ⓓ
155	Ⓐ Ⓑ Ⓒ Ⓓ	165	Ⓐ Ⓑ Ⓒ Ⓓ	175	Ⓐ Ⓑ Ⓒ Ⓓ	185	Ⓐ Ⓑ Ⓒ Ⓓ	195	Ⓐ Ⓑ Ⓒ Ⓓ
156	Ⓐ Ⓑ Ⓒ Ⓓ	166	Ⓐ Ⓑ Ⓒ Ⓓ	176	Ⓐ Ⓑ Ⓒ Ⓓ	186	Ⓐ Ⓑ Ⓒ Ⓓ	196	Ⓐ Ⓑ Ⓒ Ⓓ
157	Ⓐ Ⓑ Ⓒ Ⓓ	167	Ⓐ Ⓑ Ⓒ Ⓓ	177	Ⓐ Ⓑ Ⓒ Ⓓ	187	Ⓐ Ⓑ Ⓒ Ⓓ	197	Ⓐ Ⓑ Ⓒ Ⓓ
158	Ⓐ Ⓑ Ⓒ Ⓓ	168	Ⓐ Ⓑ Ⓒ Ⓓ	178	Ⓐ Ⓑ Ⓒ Ⓓ	188	Ⓐ Ⓑ Ⓒ Ⓓ	198	Ⓐ Ⓑ Ⓒ Ⓓ
159	Ⓐ Ⓑ Ⓒ Ⓓ	169	Ⓐ Ⓑ Ⓒ Ⓓ	179	Ⓐ Ⓑ Ⓒ Ⓓ	189	Ⓐ Ⓑ Ⓒ Ⓓ	199	Ⓐ Ⓑ Ⓒ Ⓓ
160	Ⓐ Ⓑ Ⓒ Ⓓ	170	Ⓐ Ⓑ Ⓒ Ⓓ	180	Ⓐ Ⓑ Ⓒ Ⓓ	190	Ⓐ Ⓑ Ⓒ Ⓓ	200	Ⓐ Ⓑ Ⓒ Ⓓ

ANSWER SHEET: Practice Test One

Listening Comprehension

Part 1

No.	Answer (A B C D)
1	A B C D
2	A B C D
3	A B C D
4	A B C D
5	A B C D
6	A B C D
7	A B C D
8	A B C D
9	A B C D
10	A B C D

Part 2

No.	Answer (A B C)
11	A B C
12	A B C
13	A B C
14	A B C
15	A B C
16	A B C
17	A B C
18	A B C
19	A B C
20	A B C
21	A B C
22	A B C
23	A B C
24	A B C
25	A B C
26	A B C
27	A B C
28	A B C
29	A B C
30	A B C
31	A B C
32	A B C
33	A B C
34	A B C
35	A B C
36	A B C
37	A B C
38	A B C
39	A B C
40	A B C

Part 3

No.	Answer (A B C D)
41	A B C D
42	A B C D
43	A B C D
44	A B C D
45	A B C D
46	A B C D
47	A B C D
48	A B C D
49	A B C D
50	A B C D
51	A B C D
52	A B C D
53	A B C D
54	A B C D
55	A B C D
56	A B C D
57	A B C D
58	A B C D
59	A B C D
60	A B C D
61	A B C D
62	A B C D
63	A B C D
64	A B C D
65	A B C D
66	A B C D
67	A B C D
68	A B C D
69	A B C D
70	A B C D

Part 4

No.	Answer (A B C D)
71	A B C D
72	A B C D
73	A B C D
74	A B C D
75	A B C D
76	A B C D
77	A B C D
78	A B C D
79	A B C D
80	A B C D
81	A B C D
82	A B C D
83	A B C D
84	A B C D
85	A B C D
86	A B C D
87	A B C D
88	A B C D
89	A B C D
90	A B C D
91	A B C D
92	A B C D
93	A B C D
94	A B C D
95	A B C D
96	A B C D
97	A B C D
98	A B C D
99	A B C D
100	A B C D

Reading

Part 5

No.	Answer (A B C D)
101	A B C D
102	A B C D
103	A B C D
104	A B C D
105	A B C D
106	A B C D
107	A B C D
108	A B C D
109	A B C D
110	A B C D
111	A B C D
112	A B C D
113	A B C D
114	A B C D
115	A B C D
116	A B C D
117	A B C D
118	A B C D
119	A B C D
120	A B C D
121	A B C D
122	A B C D
123	A B C D
124	A B C D
125	A B C D
126	A B C D
127	A B C D
128	A B C D
129	A B C D
130	A B C D

Part 6

No.	Answer (A B C D)
131	A B C D
132	A B C D
133	A B C D
134	A B C D
135	A B C D
136	A B C D
137	A B C D
138	A B C D
139	A B C D
140	A B C D
141	A B C D
142	A B C D
143	A B C D
144	A B C D
145	A B C D
146	A B C D
147	A B C D
148	A B C D
149	A B C D
150	A B C D
151	A B C D
152	A B C D

Part 7

No.	Answer (A B C D)
153	A B C D
154	A B C D
155	A B C D
156	A B C D
157	A B C D
158	A B C D
159	A B C D
160	A B C D
161	A B C D
162	A B C D
163	A B C D
164	A B C D
165	A B C D
166	A B C D
167	A B C D
168	A B C D
169	A B C D
170	A B C D
171	A B C D
172	A B C D
173	A B C D
174	A B C D
175	A B C D
176	A B C D
177	A B C D
178	A B C D
179	A B C D
180	A B C D
181	A B C D
182	A B C D
183	A B C D
184	A B C D
185	A B C D
186	A B C D
187	A B C D
188	A B C D
189	A B C D
190	A B C D
191	A B C D
192	A B C D
193	A B C D
194	A B C D
195	A B C D
196	A B C D
197	A B C D
198	A B C D
199	A B C D
200	A B C D

ANSWER SHEET: Practice Test Two

Listening Comprehension

Part 1

	Answer			
	A	B	C	D
1	Ⓐ	Ⓑ	Ⓒ	Ⓓ
2	Ⓐ	Ⓑ	Ⓒ	Ⓓ
3	Ⓐ	Ⓑ	Ⓒ	Ⓓ
4	Ⓐ	Ⓑ	Ⓒ	Ⓓ
5	Ⓐ	Ⓑ	Ⓒ	Ⓓ
6	Ⓐ	Ⓑ	Ⓒ	Ⓓ
7	Ⓐ	Ⓑ	Ⓒ	Ⓓ
8	Ⓐ	Ⓑ	Ⓒ	Ⓓ
9	Ⓐ	Ⓑ	Ⓒ	Ⓓ
10	Ⓐ	Ⓑ	Ⓒ	Ⓓ

Part 2

	Answer		
	A	B	C
11	Ⓐ	Ⓑ	Ⓒ
12	Ⓐ	Ⓑ	Ⓒ
13	Ⓐ	Ⓑ	Ⓒ
14	Ⓐ	Ⓑ	Ⓒ
15	Ⓐ	Ⓑ	Ⓒ
16	Ⓐ	Ⓑ	Ⓒ
17	Ⓐ	Ⓑ	Ⓒ
18	Ⓐ	Ⓑ	Ⓒ
19	Ⓐ	Ⓑ	Ⓒ
20	Ⓐ	Ⓑ	Ⓒ

	Answer		
	A	B	C
21	Ⓐ	Ⓑ	Ⓒ
22	Ⓐ	Ⓑ	Ⓒ
23	Ⓐ	Ⓑ	Ⓒ
24	Ⓐ	Ⓑ	Ⓒ
25	Ⓐ	Ⓑ	Ⓒ
26	Ⓐ	Ⓑ	Ⓒ
27	Ⓐ	Ⓑ	Ⓒ
28	Ⓐ	Ⓑ	Ⓒ
29	Ⓐ	Ⓑ	Ⓒ
30	Ⓐ	Ⓑ	Ⓒ

Part 3

	Answer		
	A	B	C
31	Ⓐ	Ⓑ	Ⓒ
32	Ⓐ	Ⓑ	Ⓒ
33	Ⓐ	Ⓑ	Ⓒ
34	Ⓐ	Ⓑ	Ⓒ
35	Ⓐ	Ⓑ	Ⓒ
36	Ⓐ	Ⓑ	Ⓒ
37	Ⓐ	Ⓑ	Ⓒ
38	Ⓐ	Ⓑ	Ⓒ
39	Ⓐ	Ⓑ	Ⓒ
40	Ⓐ	Ⓑ	Ⓒ

	Answer			
	A	B	C	D
41	Ⓐ	Ⓑ	Ⓒ	Ⓓ
42	Ⓐ	Ⓑ	Ⓒ	Ⓓ
43	Ⓐ	Ⓑ	Ⓒ	Ⓓ
44	Ⓐ	Ⓑ	Ⓒ	Ⓓ
45	Ⓐ	Ⓑ	Ⓒ	Ⓓ
46	Ⓐ	Ⓑ	Ⓒ	Ⓓ
47	Ⓐ	Ⓑ	Ⓒ	Ⓓ
48	Ⓐ	Ⓑ	Ⓒ	Ⓓ
49	Ⓐ	Ⓑ	Ⓒ	Ⓓ
50	Ⓐ	Ⓑ	Ⓒ	Ⓓ

	Answer			
	A	B	C	D
51	Ⓐ	Ⓑ	Ⓒ	Ⓓ
52	Ⓐ	Ⓑ	Ⓒ	Ⓓ
53	Ⓐ	Ⓑ	Ⓒ	Ⓓ
54	Ⓐ	Ⓑ	Ⓒ	Ⓓ
55	Ⓐ	Ⓑ	Ⓒ	Ⓓ
56	Ⓐ	Ⓑ	Ⓒ	Ⓓ
57	Ⓐ	Ⓑ	Ⓒ	Ⓓ
58	Ⓐ	Ⓑ	Ⓒ	Ⓓ
59	Ⓐ	Ⓑ	Ⓒ	Ⓓ
60	Ⓐ	Ⓑ	Ⓒ	Ⓓ

	Answer			
	A	B	C	D
61	Ⓐ	Ⓑ	Ⓒ	Ⓓ
62	Ⓐ	Ⓑ	Ⓒ	Ⓓ
63	Ⓐ	Ⓑ	Ⓒ	Ⓓ
64	Ⓐ	Ⓑ	Ⓒ	Ⓓ
65	Ⓐ	Ⓑ	Ⓒ	Ⓓ
66	Ⓐ	Ⓑ	Ⓒ	Ⓓ
67	Ⓐ	Ⓑ	Ⓒ	Ⓓ
68	Ⓐ	Ⓑ	Ⓒ	Ⓓ
69	Ⓐ	Ⓑ	Ⓒ	Ⓓ
70	Ⓐ	Ⓑ	Ⓒ	Ⓓ

Part 4

	Answer			
	A	B	C	D
71	Ⓐ	Ⓑ	Ⓒ	Ⓓ
72	Ⓐ	Ⓑ	Ⓒ	Ⓓ
73	Ⓐ	Ⓑ	Ⓒ	Ⓓ
74	Ⓐ	Ⓑ	Ⓒ	Ⓓ
75	Ⓐ	Ⓑ	Ⓒ	Ⓓ
76	Ⓐ	Ⓑ	Ⓒ	Ⓓ
77	Ⓐ	Ⓑ	Ⓒ	Ⓓ
78	Ⓐ	Ⓑ	Ⓒ	Ⓓ
79	Ⓐ	Ⓑ	Ⓒ	Ⓓ
80	Ⓐ	Ⓑ	Ⓒ	Ⓓ

	Answer			
	A	B	C	D
81	Ⓐ	Ⓑ	Ⓒ	Ⓓ
82	Ⓐ	Ⓑ	Ⓒ	Ⓓ
83	Ⓐ	Ⓑ	Ⓒ	Ⓓ
84	Ⓐ	Ⓑ	Ⓒ	Ⓓ
85	Ⓐ	Ⓑ	Ⓒ	Ⓓ
86	Ⓐ	Ⓑ	Ⓒ	Ⓓ
87	Ⓐ	Ⓑ	Ⓒ	Ⓓ
88	Ⓐ	Ⓑ	Ⓒ	Ⓓ
89	Ⓐ	Ⓑ	Ⓒ	Ⓓ
90	Ⓐ	Ⓑ	Ⓒ	Ⓓ

	Answer			
	A	B	C	D
91	Ⓐ	Ⓑ	Ⓒ	Ⓓ
92	Ⓐ	Ⓑ	Ⓒ	Ⓓ
93	Ⓐ	Ⓑ	Ⓒ	Ⓓ
94	Ⓐ	Ⓑ	Ⓒ	Ⓓ
95	Ⓐ	Ⓑ	Ⓒ	Ⓓ
96	Ⓐ	Ⓑ	Ⓒ	Ⓓ
97	Ⓐ	Ⓑ	Ⓒ	Ⓓ
98	Ⓐ	Ⓑ	Ⓒ	Ⓓ
99	Ⓐ	Ⓑ	Ⓒ	Ⓓ
100	Ⓐ	Ⓑ	Ⓒ	Ⓓ

Reading

Part 5

	Answer			
	A	B	C	D
101	Ⓐ	Ⓑ	Ⓒ	Ⓓ
102	Ⓐ	Ⓑ	Ⓒ	Ⓓ
103	Ⓐ	Ⓑ	Ⓒ	Ⓓ
104	Ⓐ	Ⓑ	Ⓒ	Ⓓ
105	Ⓐ	Ⓑ	Ⓒ	Ⓓ
106	Ⓐ	Ⓑ	Ⓒ	Ⓓ
107	Ⓐ	Ⓑ	Ⓒ	Ⓓ
108	Ⓐ	Ⓑ	Ⓒ	Ⓓ
109	Ⓐ	Ⓑ	Ⓒ	Ⓓ
110	Ⓐ	Ⓑ	Ⓒ	Ⓓ

	Answer			
	A	B	C	D
111	Ⓐ	Ⓑ	Ⓒ	Ⓓ
112	Ⓐ	Ⓑ	Ⓒ	Ⓓ
113	Ⓐ	Ⓑ	Ⓒ	Ⓓ
114	Ⓐ	Ⓑ	Ⓒ	Ⓓ
115	Ⓐ	Ⓑ	Ⓒ	Ⓓ
116	Ⓐ	Ⓑ	Ⓒ	Ⓓ
117	Ⓐ	Ⓑ	Ⓒ	Ⓓ
118	Ⓐ	Ⓑ	Ⓒ	Ⓓ
119	Ⓐ	Ⓑ	Ⓒ	Ⓓ
120	Ⓐ	Ⓑ	Ⓒ	Ⓓ

Part 6

	Answer			
	A	B	C	D
121	Ⓐ	Ⓑ	Ⓒ	Ⓓ
122	Ⓐ	Ⓑ	Ⓒ	Ⓓ
123	Ⓐ	Ⓑ	Ⓒ	Ⓓ
124	Ⓐ	Ⓑ	Ⓒ	Ⓓ
125	Ⓐ	Ⓑ	Ⓒ	Ⓓ
126	Ⓐ	Ⓑ	Ⓒ	Ⓓ
127	Ⓐ	Ⓑ	Ⓒ	Ⓓ
128	Ⓐ	Ⓑ	Ⓒ	Ⓓ
129	Ⓐ	Ⓑ	Ⓒ	Ⓓ
130	Ⓐ	Ⓑ	Ⓒ	Ⓓ

	Answer			
	A	B	C	D
131	Ⓐ	Ⓑ	Ⓒ	Ⓓ
132	Ⓐ	Ⓑ	Ⓒ	Ⓓ
133	Ⓐ	Ⓑ	Ⓒ	Ⓓ
134	Ⓐ	Ⓑ	Ⓒ	Ⓓ
135	Ⓐ	Ⓑ	Ⓒ	Ⓓ
136	Ⓐ	Ⓑ	Ⓒ	Ⓓ
137	Ⓐ	Ⓑ	Ⓒ	Ⓓ
138	Ⓐ	Ⓑ	Ⓒ	Ⓓ
139	Ⓐ	Ⓑ	Ⓒ	Ⓓ
140	Ⓐ	Ⓑ	Ⓒ	Ⓓ

Part 7

	Answer			
	A	B	C	D
141	Ⓐ	Ⓑ	Ⓒ	Ⓓ
142	Ⓐ	Ⓑ	Ⓒ	Ⓓ
143	Ⓐ	Ⓑ	Ⓒ	Ⓓ
144	Ⓐ	Ⓑ	Ⓒ	Ⓓ
145	Ⓐ	Ⓑ	Ⓒ	Ⓓ
146	Ⓐ	Ⓑ	Ⓒ	Ⓓ
147	Ⓐ	Ⓑ	Ⓒ	Ⓓ
148	Ⓐ	Ⓑ	Ⓒ	Ⓓ
149	Ⓐ	Ⓑ	Ⓒ	Ⓓ
150	Ⓐ	Ⓑ	Ⓒ	Ⓓ

	Answer			
	A	B	C	D
151	Ⓐ	Ⓑ	Ⓒ	Ⓓ
152	Ⓐ	Ⓑ	Ⓒ	Ⓓ
153	Ⓐ	Ⓑ	Ⓒ	Ⓓ
154	Ⓐ	Ⓑ	Ⓒ	Ⓓ
155	Ⓐ	Ⓑ	Ⓒ	Ⓓ
156	Ⓐ	Ⓑ	Ⓒ	Ⓓ
157	Ⓐ	Ⓑ	Ⓒ	Ⓓ
158	Ⓐ	Ⓑ	Ⓒ	Ⓓ
159	Ⓐ	Ⓑ	Ⓒ	Ⓓ
160	Ⓐ	Ⓑ	Ⓒ	Ⓓ

	Answer			
	A	B	C	D
161	Ⓐ	Ⓑ	Ⓒ	Ⓓ
162	Ⓐ	Ⓑ	Ⓒ	Ⓓ
163	Ⓐ	Ⓑ	Ⓒ	Ⓓ
164	Ⓐ	Ⓑ	Ⓒ	Ⓓ
165	Ⓐ	Ⓑ	Ⓒ	Ⓓ
166	Ⓐ	Ⓑ	Ⓒ	Ⓓ
167	Ⓐ	Ⓑ	Ⓒ	Ⓓ
168	Ⓐ	Ⓑ	Ⓒ	Ⓓ
169	Ⓐ	Ⓑ	Ⓒ	Ⓓ
170	Ⓐ	Ⓑ	Ⓒ	Ⓓ

	Answer			
	A	B	C	D
171	Ⓐ	Ⓑ	Ⓒ	Ⓓ
172	Ⓐ	Ⓑ	Ⓒ	Ⓓ
173	Ⓐ	Ⓑ	Ⓒ	Ⓓ
174	Ⓐ	Ⓑ	Ⓒ	Ⓓ
175	Ⓐ	Ⓑ	Ⓒ	Ⓓ
176	Ⓐ	Ⓑ	Ⓒ	Ⓓ
177	Ⓐ	Ⓑ	Ⓒ	Ⓓ
178	Ⓐ	Ⓑ	Ⓒ	Ⓓ
179	Ⓐ	Ⓑ	Ⓒ	Ⓓ
180	Ⓐ	Ⓑ	Ⓒ	Ⓓ

	Answer			
	A	B	C	D
181	Ⓐ	Ⓑ	Ⓒ	Ⓓ
182	Ⓐ	Ⓑ	Ⓒ	Ⓓ
183	Ⓐ	Ⓑ	Ⓒ	Ⓓ
184	Ⓐ	Ⓑ	Ⓒ	Ⓓ
185	Ⓐ	Ⓑ	Ⓒ	Ⓓ
186	Ⓐ	Ⓑ	Ⓒ	Ⓓ
187	Ⓐ	Ⓑ	Ⓒ	Ⓓ
188	Ⓐ	Ⓑ	Ⓒ	Ⓓ
189	Ⓐ	Ⓑ	Ⓒ	Ⓓ
190	Ⓐ	Ⓑ	Ⓒ	Ⓓ

	Answer			
	A	B	C	D
191	Ⓐ	Ⓑ	Ⓒ	Ⓓ
192	Ⓐ	Ⓑ	Ⓒ	Ⓓ
193	Ⓐ	Ⓑ	Ⓒ	Ⓓ
194	Ⓐ	Ⓑ	Ⓒ	Ⓓ
195	Ⓐ	Ⓑ	Ⓒ	Ⓓ
196	Ⓐ	Ⓑ	Ⓒ	Ⓓ
197	Ⓐ	Ⓑ	Ⓒ	Ⓓ
198	Ⓐ	Ⓑ	Ⓒ	Ⓓ
199	Ⓐ	Ⓑ	Ⓒ	Ⓓ
200	Ⓐ	Ⓑ	Ⓒ	Ⓓ

AUDIOSCRIPTS

AUDIOSCRIPT
LISTENING COMPREHENSION

PART 1: PHOTOS

Photo 1 (page 4)

Prepositions

1. Her hand is on the keyboard.
2. The printer is next to the monitor.
3. The monitor is on the desk.
4. She's sitting at the desk.
5. The clerk is looking at the display on the monitor.

Similar Sounds

A. 1. print her
      printer
   2. the display
      the play
   3. monitor
      man or
   4. keyboard
      employee is bored
   5. the printer paper
      her newspaper

B. 1. He prints her next document.
      Her printer is next to the documents.
   2. This gray is not light enough.
      The display is not bright enough.
   3. She may put the man or woman at my table.
      She put the monitor on the table.
   4. The new employee is bored.
      The new employer has a keyboard.
   5. Her newspaper is under the rest.
      Her new paper is under her desk.

Photo 2 (page 7)

Prepositions

1. The couple is sitting at the table.
2. The restaurant is in the garden.
3. A tablecloth is on the table.
4. The waitress is standing in front of the customers.
5. The man and woman are next to each other.

Similar Sounds

A. 1. cup of
      couple
   2. talking together
      taking their order
   3. waitress is sitting
      waiter is setting
   4. address
      a dress
   5. on the right
      wearing white

B. 1. The waitress is serving the couple coffee.
      The waitress is serving a cup of coffee.
   2. The waitress is taking their order.
      The waitresses are talking together.
   3. The waitress is sitting at the table.
      The waiter is setting the table.
   4. The woman is wearing a dress.
      The man is writing his address.
   5. The waitress is on the right.
      The waiter is wearing white.

Photo 3 (page 10)

Prepositions

1. The glass is on top of the napkin.
2. The books are in front of the men.
3. The men are sitting near each other.
4. The cap is on the table.
5. A window is behind them.

Similar Sounds

A. 1. waiter
      water
   2. hurt
      shirt
   3. took a nap
      took a cap
   4. disc is in
      discussing
   5. jacket at
      Jack ate at

B.
1. The water is in the bottle.
   The waiter has a bottle.
2. He brought it himself.
   He bought it himself.
3. I took a nap at the table.
   I took a cap from the table.
4. They're discussing computers.
   Their disc is in the computer.
5. You know you need a jacket at the restaurant.
   You know what Jack ate at the restaurant.

Photo 4 (page 13)

Prepositions

1. They're standing next to the bus.
2. They're getting ready to get on the bus.
3. The bus is stopped at the bus stop.
4. The bus stop is on the corner.
5. She's tying a scarf around her head.

Similar Sounds

A.
1. woman
   women
2. hand rags
   handbags
3. trying
   tying
4. after work
   afterward
5. board a bus
   bored by us

B.
1. Did you talk to the woman at the bus stop?
   Did you walk the woman to the bus stop?
2. Our handbags are in the closet with your coat.
   Your hand rags are in the cabinet with the soap.
3. I've been tying a bow on this package for ten minutes.
   I've been trying to put this on this package for ten minutes.
4. We went to the movie. Afterward we had dinner.
   We went to the movie after work. Then we had dinner.
5. If you board the bus sooner, you can leave by 6.
   If you board the bus at 6, you won't have to leave so soon.

Photo 5 (page 16)

Prepositions

1. The agents are beside the plane.
2. The passengers are getting off the plane.
3. Several people are on the tarmac.
4. Two tourists are on the steps.
5. The plane is at its destination.

Similar Sounds

A.
1. past hers
   passenger is
2. plane
   train
3. tourist
   tour is
4. wing
   swing
5. getting on
   getting off

B.
1. The passenger is at the ticket counter.
   Go past hers to my counter.
2. The plane's crew is to rest.
   The train's new in the west.
3. The tourist is going by bus.
   The tour is going by bus.
4. I like to sit on the swing.
   My seat is over the wing.
5. We're getting off the plane.
   We're getting on the train.

Photo 6 (page 19)

Prepositions

1. The baby is in the stroller.
2. The passport officer is behind the window.
3. The luggage carts are in front of the barrier.
4. The bags are on their shoulders.
5. The two Passport Control windows are side by side.

Similar Sounds

A.
1. stand in line
   and on line
2. cars
   carts
3. waited
   weight
4. past report
   passport
5. officer
   office or

B. 1. The travelers are waiting for a second carrier.
   The traveler's waiting by the second barrier.
2. We put the luggage in the car.
   We put our bags on a luggage cart.
3. She has a bag on her shoulder.
   She has a bug on her shoulder.
4. He wanted to see my passport.
   He asked me for the past report.
5. We can meet at our offices or yours.
   They can greet our officers and yours.

Photo 7 (page 22)

Prepositions

1. The men are carrying umbrellas in their right hands.
2. One man is carrying his briefcase in his left hand.
3. The trash cans are by the door.
4. The men are walking next to each other.
5. The man on the left is wearing a dark-colored jacket.

Similar Sounds

A. 1. park
      dark
2. packet
   jacket
3. rain
   lane
4. talking
   walking
5. bed
   head

B. 1. The men are walking in the park.
      The men are walking in the dark.
2. He's wearing a light jacket.
   He's carrying a light packet.
3. The men are walking down the lane.
   The men are walking in the rain.
4. The people are walking in the rain.
   The people are talking on the train.
5. She holds an umbrella over her head.
   She keeps an umbrella under her bed.

Photo 8 (page 25)

Prepositions

1. The technicians are monitoring the descent of the equipment.
2. The equipment will be tested by the technicians.
3. The cables are attached to the module.
4. There are four workers on the factory floor.
5. All of the technicians wear protective clothing.

Similar Sounds

A. 1. compartment
      component
2. for four
   floor for
3. guiding
   hiding
4. intentional or an accident
   international incident
5. wearing
   where in

B. 1. These are the last compartments to be walled.
      This is the first component to be installed.
2. We've been researching the facts for four hours.
   We've been searching the factory for hours.
3. She was guiding her supervisor.
   She was hiding from her supervisor.
4. The explosion caused an international incident.
   The explosion was intentional or an accident.
5. The caps that we were wearing are green.
   The caps that were in the sink are clean.

Photo Strategy Practice (page 28)

1. (A) The passengers are boarding the plane.
   (B) The passengers are taking the train.
2. (A) The trainer is talking to the employees.
   (B) The gardener is watering the plants.
3. (A) They're getting on the bus.
   (B) They're getting off the bus.

4. (A) He's wearing a hard hat.
   (B) He's driving a taxicab.
5. (A) The paintings are hanging on the wall.
   (B) The pictures are resting on the floor.
   (C) The artists are painting a picture.
6. (A) The man is carrying the suitcase.
   (B) The woman is driving a cab.
   (C) The couple is polishing the car.
7. (A) He's holding a serving tray.
   (B) He's setting the table.
   (C) He's sitting down to eat.
8. (A) They're testing the equipment.
   (B) They're reading a newspaper.
   (C) They're buying a hat.
9. (A) She's cleaning the window.
   (B) She's taking a bath.
   (C) She's standing by the sink.
   (D) She's scrubbing the floor.
10. (A) The matches are on the counter.
    (B) The sales personnel are on time.
    (C) The clock strikes on the hour.
    (D) The watches are on display.
11. (A) They're standing in line to eat.
    (B) They're waiting to board the bus.
    (C) They're writing to us at home.
    (D) They're handing out receipts.
12. (A) He's checking in for a flight.
    (B) He's writing a check in the car.
    (C) He's preparing to fight.
    (D) He's touring the sites.

Review: Part 1 (page 35)

1. (A) She's adding paper to the printer.
   (B) She's touching the keyboard.
   (C) She's cleaning the monitor.
   (D) She's looking at her colleague.
2. (A) The waitress is taking the couple's order.
   (B) The waiter is ordering a new book.
   (C) The chef is cooking lunch.
   (D) The customers are eating a salad.
3. (A) The bottle is under the table.
   (B) The napkins are piled high on the table.
   (C) The table is covered with water.
   (D) The men are side by side.
4. (A) One woman is filling her bag.
   (B) The passengers are looking for their seats.
   (C) Two women are boarding the bus.
   (D) The shoppers are purchasing a scarf.

5. (A) Tourists are getting off the plane.
   (B) The crew is leaving the train.
   (C) The plumber is fixing the drain.
   (D) The guide is walking down the lane.
6. (A) They're waiting for a movie.
   (B) They're buying new luggage.
   (C) They're standing in line.
   (D) They're stepping over the barrier.
7. (A) They're carrying umbrellas.
   (B) They're emptying the trash.
   (C) They're starting to work.
   (D) They're walking through the train.
8. (A) The politicians are raising the taxes.
   (B) The operators are taking a break.
   (C) The technicians are lowering the equipment.
   (D) The drivers are starting their engines.

PART 2: QUESTION-RESPONSE

Statements

Practice E (page 43)

1. I didn't like that movie at all.
   (A) Me, neither. It was really boring.
   (B) They're moving next week.
   (C) Yes, he's very tall.
2. This photocopy machine is broken again.
   (A) You can use the machine downstairs.
   (B) We haven't spoken in a long time.
   (C) Those are lovely photos.
3. Let's take the bus.
   (A) The lettuce doesn't look fresh.
   (B) I'd rather walk.
   (C) They made such a fuss.
4. There's a big sale at the mall.
   (A) They look too small.
   (B) I love to sail.
   (C) Let's go shopping there after work.
5. This room is too cold.
   (A) No, you're not that old.
   (B) I'll turn up the heat.
   (C) There's enough room.
6. I put the message on your desk.
   (A) Yes, I saw it.
   (B) That one's my desk.
   (C) Would you like to leave a message?
7. What a lovely, sunny day.
   (A) Yes, he's very funny.
   (B) Yes, I hate to spend it inside.
   (C) Yes, they make a lovely couple.

8. I'll call you later.
    (A) OK. I'll be home around eight-thirty.
    (B) I read his letter.
    (C) They call me Bill.
9. I get off work at five-thirty.
    (A) I like to walk, too.
    (B) It never works.
    (C) Then I'll meet you at six.
10. I've decided to paint my office.
    (A) There's a post office on the corner.
    (B) Really? What color?
    (C) He went to the dentist's office.

Practice F (page 43)

1. I can't read this without my glasses.
    (A) He's taking some interesting classes.
    (B) Here. Let me read it to you.
    (C) Those are water glasses.
2. Let's take a walk in the park.
    (A) All right. I'll get my jacket.
    (B) We parked the car over there.
    (C) They talked until dark.
3. The train leaves at ten-thirty.
    (A) The rain makes everything dirty.
    (B) The leaves are pretty in the autumn.
    (C) Then we should be at the station at ten-fifteen.
4. I'm not earning enough money.
    (A) Maybe you should look for another job.
    (B) He's usually here on Monday.
    (C) I'm learning a lot in this class.
5. I'm going to the bank after lunch.
    (A) Thank you very much.
    (B) I'll go with you. I want to cash a check.
    (C) It's not a good idea to eat too much.
6. I need some stamps for these letters.
    (A) That's a very nice sweater.
    (B) I have some. How many do you want?
    (C) It's fun to camp out in the summer.
7. Lucy called in sick again today.
    (A) There are six of them.
    (B) They'll stick if you use glue.
    (C) She's been ill a lot this month.
8. Mr. Smith is on the phone for you.
    (A) Tell him I'll call him back later.
    (B) Yes, that's my cell phone.
    (C) They have a very nice home.

9. Actually, I prefer coffee.
    (A) I can't stop coughing.
    (B) No problem. I'll make you a cup.
    (C) Refer them to me.
10. Tomorrow will be warm and sunny.
    (A) Then we should go to the beach.
    (B) I warned you about him.
    (C) It doesn't cost much money.

Who

Practice E (page 47)

1. Who left the lights on?
    (A) I'm sure it's dark outside.
    (B) We always leave them on.
    (C) John turned them off.
2. Who wrote this memo?
    (A) The vice president.
    (B) She wrote a letter to me.
    (C) I had to memorize it.
3. Who's in charge of marketing?
    (A) The market closes at 5 P.M.
    (B) Charge it to my account.
    (C) The new manager.
4. Who won the lottery?
    (A) The secretary had the winning ticket.
    (B) The salesperson wanted a lot.
    (C) He'll leave later tonight.
5. Who uses the corner office?
    (A) It used to be on the corner.
    (B) It belongs to the office manager.
    (C) Yes, it's a big office.
6. Who repaired the copy machine?
    (A) Robert fixed it.
    (B) I made some copies.
    (C) It's an old machine.
7. Who gave you this job?
    (A) I really like my job.
    (B) He gave me some envelopes.
    (C) Mr. Rogers hired me.
8. Who went to the meeting?
    (A) It was an interesting meeting.
    (B) There wasn't enough seating.
    (C) Most people from this office were there.
9. Who helped you on this project?
    (A) He was very helpful.
    (B) Mr. Chang and Ms. Kim were my assistants.
    (C) It was a big project.

10. Who can make coffee?
    (A) I take milk in my coffee.
    (B) I can't stop coughing.
    (C) I'll make you a cup.

Practice F (page 47)

1. Who's making coffee?
    (A) No, thank you. I prefer tea.
    (B) I had a cup for breakfast.
    (C) I am. It'll be ready soon.
2. Who designed this building?
    (A) An architect designed it.
    (B) You can follow the signs.
    (C) I decided not to buy it.
3. Who typed this letter?
    (A) My secretary was late.
    (B) The new secretary typed it.
    (C) I don't know what type it is.
4. Who's working in the mailroom?
    (A) The mail is in my room.
    (B) The mail clerk is working there.
    (C) There isn't any room to work.
5. Who is the new secretary?
    (A) A secretarial school graduate.
    (B) The paper is full of news.
    (C) I have a new secretary.
6. Who took this phone message?
    (A) The phone is over there.
    (B) John took it.
    (C) I have a phone book.
7. Who uses this computer?
    (A) It's a brand new computer.
    (B) It's Susan's computer.
    (C) It's next to the computer.
8. Who sent you that e-mail message?
    (A) I mailed you a letter yesterday.
    (B) A stamp costs 45 cents.
    (C) The message was from my boss.
9. Who will you meet in New York?
    (A) I'll eat at a restaurant.
    (B) It will be a long meeting.
    (C) I'll see the director and her assistant.
10. Who put this package on my desk?
    (A) Mr. Kim put it there.
    (B) Your desk is next to the door.
    (C) I can mail it tomorrow.

What

Practice E (page 52)

1. What is your name?
    (A) I came at three.
    (B) Her name is Mary Lee.
    (C) My name is Mary Lee.

2. What did this desk cost?
    (A) It was only $125.
    (B) That's my desk.
    (C) The desk is next to the window.
3. What are you doing for dinner?
    (A) He's going to eat lunch at noon.
    (B) I'm eating with a client.
    (C) I'm having dinner.
4. What street is your office on?
    (A) I work on Thirteenth Street.
    (B) My office is in Suite 313.
    (C) It's a quiet street.
5. What did we order from the printer?
    (A) Five hundred envelopes and one thousand labels.
    (B) The order arrived late.
    (C) The printer cost 100 dollars.
6. What will you wear to the ceremony?
    (A) At eight o'clock.
    (B) An awards ceremony.
    (C) My new suit.
7. What does Bob do for a living?
    (A) He's a doctor.
    (B) He's leaving early.
    (C) He lives in a nice neighborhood.
8. What did you send to John?
    (A) I lent him some money.
    (B) I sent him a copy of the report.
    (C) I went there with him.
9. What do you want that newspaper for?
    (A) I got it at the newsstand.
    (B) There's an article I want to read.
    (C) It's today's paper.
10. What's the best place to eat lunch?
    (A) I usually don't eat much.
    (B) Twelve-thirty is a good time.
    (C) There's a great restaurant across the street.

Practice F (page 52)

1. What did you have for lunch?
    (A) At 12:30.
    (B) A tuna fish sandwich.
    (C) At the corner coffee shop.
2. What is his occupation?
    (A) He's a bookkeeper.
    (B) He uses public transportation.
    (C) This seat is occupied.
3. What did your doctor recommend?
    (A) I highly recommend my doctor.
    (B) He suggested I go on a diet.
    (C) My daughter recommends this restaurant.

4. What's in your briefcase?
   (A) Only some papers.
   (B) It's on the desk.
   (C) It won't take long.
5. What is the fastest way to go to the airport?
   (A) The plane is on time.
   (B) The airport is forty miles from the city.
   (C) At this hour, the subway is the fastest.
6. What did you get at the bookstore?
   (A) I bought some magazines.
   (B) I looked some more.
   (C) I went to the store.
7. What did you see on TV?
   (A) I got a new TV.
   (B) The picture is very clear.
   (C) I watched a news program.
8. What will you do after work tonight?
   (A) I work during the day.
   (B) I think I'll just go home.
   (C) I'll stay two nights.
9. What did you tell the manager?
   (A) Mr. Matsui is the manager.
   (B) I didn't sell my car.
   (C) I told him I would arrive later.
10. What's in that room?
    (A) The copy machine is there.
    (B) It's across the hall.
    (C) The room is too small.

When

Practice E (page 56)

1. When are you leaving for the meeting?
   (A) Shortly after 1950.
   (B) In about ten minutes.
   (C) It'll be over at ten.
2. When is the English exam?
   (A) At the end of August.
   (B) Before you enter the room.
   (C) In the classroom.
3. When did we send the check?
   (A) Last Friday.
   (B) Yes, I'll check on it.
   (C) To the bank.
4. When is the plane expected?
   (A) We expect the plane to be full.
   (B) It should arrive at 4:50.
   (C) I planned it carefully.
5. When will they finish the project?
   (A) Next week if they stay on schedule.
   (B) We need a new projector.
   (C) It was an expensive project.
6. When will they get here?
   (A) I expect them before lunch.
   (B) We got it yesterday.
   (C) Put them over here.
7. When will he begin work on the report?
   (A) He'll report it to the manager.
   (B) It's very important work.
   (C) He'll start on it next week.
8. When did the copy machine break down?
   (A) It was repaired last week.
   (B) It stopped working this morning.
   (C) I'll take those copies downstairs.
9. When did Jim receive the package?
   (A) It wasn't a big package.
   (B) It arrived yesterday.
   (C) He'll mail it tomorrow.
10. When can I see Dr. Park?
    (A) She'll sit over here.
    (B) She'll be in her office.
    (C) She'll be free this afternoon.

Practice F (page 56)

1. When did it snow?
   (A) I love the snow.
   (B) It'll snow all winter.
   (C) It snowed the last two days of December.
2. When did the lawyer first call you?
   (A) She called me early last week.
   (B) I will call the lawyer first.
   (C) Our lawyer is my best friend.
3. When will the product be ready?
   (A) This was our only product.
   (B) Sometime next week.
   (C) I'm not ready to talk.
4. When is the tenth anniversary of the firm?
   (A) No, not until next month.
   (B) We've been married for ten years.
   (C) It will be ten years old next May.
5. When was this letter mailed?
   (A) Last Friday, on the fifteenth.
   (B) In five more days.
   (C) The mail is very slow.
6. When will this office be cleaned?
   (A) The cleaners will be here on Friday.
   (B) They'll paint it green.
   (C) You can see it tomorrow.

7. When will your boss be back from the conference?
   (A) He'll return on Monday.
   (B) He has a bad back.
   (C) It's in the back of the closet.

8. When was the party over?
   (A) It was over there.
   (B) Everyone left around midnight.
   (C) I really enjoyed the party.

9. When do these tickets expire?
   (A) You can pick it up tomorrow.
   (B) They were expensive tickets.
   (C) They're good for one month.

10. When did they buy these computers?
    (A) They got them last year.
    (B) They bought them at that new store.
    (C) They got five new computers.

Where

Practice E (page 60)

1. Where can I buy a newspaper?
   (A) There's a newsstand on the corner.
   (B) The newspaper's on the step.
   (C) That's old paper.

2. Where was the conference held?
   (A) It held ten people comfortably.
   (B) It was held in a hotel this year.
   (C) It was well attended.

3. Where do you live?
   (A) Just across the street from the park.
   (B) I'll leave tomorrow.
   (C) No, I've lived here only a month.

4. Where did you wait for me?
   (A) I ate in a restaurant.
   (B) We waited in your office.
   (C) I weigh 150 pounds.

5. Where is a taxi stand?
   (A) You have to pay taxes.
   (B) There's one in front of the hotel.
   (C) I can't stand taxis.

6. Where did you find your keys?
   (A) They were on my desk.
   (B) Yes, please.
   (C) He didn't kiss her.

7. Where can I get a cup of coffee?
   (A) That cup is broken.
   (B) She's still coughing.
   (C) There's a cafeteria downstairs.

8. Where did they go last night?
   (A) It was their last night in town.
   (B) They went to the movies.
   (C) It's the last room on the right.

9. Where did he park the car?
   (A) The park isn't far.
   (B) It's a dark-colored car.
   (C) In the lot across the street.

10. Where will you go on vacation?
    (A) Probably to the beach.
    (B) The rooms are all vacant.
    (C) I have a two-week vacation.

Practice F (page 60)

1. Where are the envelopes kept?
   (A) She put the letters in large envelopes.
   (B) They can be kept here until Tuesday.
   (C) We keep them in the supply cabinet.

2. Where will the new secretary work?
   (A) He'll work in the morning.
   (B) His office will be across from mine.
   (C) The secretary is new.

3. Where are the company's insurance records?
   (A) My insurance company is in England.
   (B) Our firm broke a record.
   (C) The records are in the file cabinet.

4. Where is she going to play tennis?
   (A) The tennis court is closed.
   (B) Ten of us are going with them.
   (C) She's going to play at her health club.

5. Where can we buy used furniture?
   (A) There's a store on Twelfth Street.
   (B) My office has new furniture.
   (C) I never use my desk.

6. Where can I hang up my coat?
   (A) That's a very nice coat.
   (B) Put it in this closet.
   (C) I need a new coat.

7. Where will the meeting be?
   (A) We'll meet in Joe's office.
   (B) We need more seats.
   (C) It starts at three.

8. Where can I make copies?
   (A) Take just one copy apiece.
   (B) It's in the lobby.
   (C) There's a copy machine in that room.

9. Where's the manager's office?
   (A) He managed to finish the project.
   (B) He has a nice office.
   (C) It's right across the hall.

10. Where should I wait for the bus?
    (A) I waited for hours.
    (B) There's a bus stop on the corner.
    (C) There's nothing to discuss.

Why

Practice E (page 64)

1. Why is she happy?
   - (A) She got a new job this morning.
   - (B) Yes, I did notice that.
   - (C) Yes, it happened.
2. Why are you sitting next to the door?
   - (A) I may have to leave early.
   - (B) The doors are closed.
   - (C) They live next door.
3. Why won't this printer work?
   - (A) You have nice printing.
   - (B) It needs a new cartridge.
   - (C) It was a cold winter.
4. Why can't you finish this project on time?
   - (A) My watch is broken.
   - (B) I've been sick.
   - (C) It's time to go.
5. Why were you late?
   - (A) My car wouldn't start.
   - (B) I ate lunch already.
   - (C) He'll have to wait.
6. Why are you so hungry?
   - (A) He really made me angry.
   - (B) I didn't have time to eat lunch.
   - (C) I ordered a hundred envelopes.
7. Why did they come by bus?
   - (A) They didn't call us.
   - (B) Their car is broken.
   - (C) He's someone you can trust.
8. Why are you wearing that coat?
   - (A) It's really cold outside.
   - (B) I put it in the closet.
   - (C) He doesn't know where it is.
9. Why isn't Ms. Wilson here today?
   - (A) Her office is near mine.
   - (B) She didn't hear you.
   - (C) She's away on vacation.
10. Why is it so cold in this room?
    - (A) He told me to come here.
    - (B) This isn't the right room.
    - (C) The heating system doesn't work.

Practice F (page 64)

1. Why aren't they finished copying the reports?
   - (A) The copy machine is out of paper.
   - (B) They want a nice finish on the furniture.
   - (C) They are crossing the finish line.
2. Why are these bills overdue?
   - (A) We paid them last month.
   - (B) There's no money in our account.
   - (C) Bill is due here any minute.
3. Why is there no water?
   - (A) They're repairing the water pipe.
   - (B) It is always dry in the summer.
   - (C) You can build it anywhere.
4. Why does she speak Japanese?
   - (A) She studied the language in school.
   - (B) She loves Japanese food.
   - (C) She speaks Japanese quite well.
5. Why aren't you wearing a tie?
   - (A) I like wearing ties.
   - (B) They wear ties to work.
   - (C) I never wear ties on the weekend.
6. Why did you turn the computer on?
   - (A) It's on my desk.
   - (B) He turned the report in yesterday.
   - (C) I'm going to type a letter.
7. Why doesn't this phone work?
   - (A) It needs new batteries.
   - (B) You can call me at work.
   - (C) He works alone.
8. Why did you send Tom a card?
   - (A) To wish him a happy birthday.
   - (B) I've been working too hard.
   - (C) I bought a new car.
9. Why did he move to California?
   - (A) It was a very good movie.
   - (B) John helped me move it.
   - (C) He got a job there.
10. Why do you always open the window?
    - (A) The window is open.
    - (B) I like to breathe fresh air.
    - (C) He went downstairs.

How

Practice E (page 68)

1. How long is this letter?
   - (A) The letter is two pages long.
   - (B) She's five feet tall.
   - (C) It took two hours.
2. How many files are in the cabinet?
   - (A) It's a new filing cabinet.
   - (B) There are too many to count.
   - (C) There will be six cabs in the line.
3. How late will the bank be open?
   - (A) The banker ate at his desk.
   - (B) The bank will be open until 6 P.M.
   - (C) The bank is two blocks away.

4. How often do you take the bus?
   (A) A bus ride costs one dollar.
   (B) I ride the bus every day.
   (C) I go there quite often.
5. How much does a new computer cost?
   (A) She has ten different costumes.
   (B) A basic model costs about $800.
   (C) We need some new computers.
6. How long will it take to finish that report?
   (A) I'll report it to the manager.
   (B) It's about 20 pages long.
   (C) I'll have it finished by next week.
7. How did you get to New York?
   (A) I took a train.
   (B) It's a very interesting city.
   (C) I got it at a store.
8. How did you like the movie?
   (A) It lasted about two hours.
   (B) The next one starts at five o'clock.
   (C) I thought it was boring.
9. How soon will the meeting be over?
   (A) It's just upstairs.
   (B) We'll be finished in about thirty minutes.
   (C) The meeting was very interesting.
10. How much paper do you need?
   (A) I think five pieces will be enough.
   (B) A newspaper costs fifty cents.
   (C) I need it to write some letters.

Practice F (page 68)

1. How much time will we have to do the work?
   (A) We have until next week.
   (B) We worked all night.
   (C) I don't have a watch.
2. How long has it been raining?
   (A) It is raining from California to New York.
   (B) It's rained all afternoon.
   (C) Rain turns to snow in cold weather.
3. How much mail do you get every day?
   (A) I get about thirty letters a day.
   (B) The mail carrier earns one hundred dollars a day.
   (C) The mail was late today.
4. How well do you play golf?
   (A) I feel better when I play golf.
   (B) Golfing is a relaxing sport.
   (C) Not very well; I'm a beginner.

5. How many members are on the board of directors?
   (A) There are ten, counting the chairperson.
   (B) We all need direction sometimes.
   (C) No, I'm not a member.
6. How often do you take a business trip?
   (A) Our business didn't do well this year.
   (B) I always go by plane.
   (C) I travel about three times a year.
7. How old are these computers?
   (A) We bought them last year.
   (B) They work very well.
   (C) They weren't very expensive.
8. How can I get to the airport?
   (A) It's only five miles from here.
   (B) There's a bus that will take you there.
   (C) It's a very busy airport.
9. How can I contact Mr. Peterson?
   (A) He'll come back tomorrow.
   (B) They already signed the contract.
   (C) You can send him an e-mail message.
10. How far is your office from here?
   (A) This office is too small.
   (B) It's only two blocks away.
   (C) I come here everyday.

Auxiliaries

Practice E (page 72)

1. Is your company opening a branch office?
   (A) We plan to open one next year.
   (B) My office is open to the public.
   (C) Yes, I would like to have some company.
2. Did you find any pencils?
   (A) Yes, I lost my favorite pen.
   (B) Yes, in the supply cabinet.
   (C) Yes, those pants will fit you.
3. Has the order for the new chair gone out?
   (A) Yes, it was ordered yesterday.
   (B) We'll be out only a little while.
   (C) It's out of order.
4. Are you having lunch at your desk?
   (A) No, I'm going to the cafeteria.
   (B) No one had lunch today.
   (C) No, there's not much on my desk.
5. Is production on schedule?
   (A) Yes, we are even two weeks ahead of schedule.
   (B) We produce nothing but schedules.
   (C) He's not a productive worker.

6. Have you met the new director yet?
   (A) No, I don't have the directions.
   (B) No, I don't know how to get there.
   (C) No, I expect to meet him tomorrow.

7. Do you know how to start this computer?
   (A) Just press the green button.
   (B) He sells computer parts.
   (C) Yes, you're allowed to use that computer.

8. Did you send that fax to Mrs. Kim?
   (A) No, I'll send it right now.
   (B) I fixed it this morning.
   (C) I explained all the facts to him.

9. Can you come to the office early tomorrow?
   (A) Yes, he'll be there tomorrow.
   (B) I'm sorry. I can't arrive before nine.
   (C) The office will be open tomorrow.

10. Is this your desk?
    (A) There are four desks in there.
    (B) I need a computer disk.
    (C) No, mine is next to the door.

Practice F (page 72)

1. Can the accountant recalculate these figures?
   (A) Yes, my calculator is broken.
   (B) No, he can't draw a figure.
   (C) No, he won't be in for the rest of the day.

2. Will there be an interpreter at this meeting?
   (A) Yes, two people will help translate for us.
   (B) There will be two meetings this morning.
   (C) Yes, we will meet at intermission.

3. Isn't this conference open to the public?
   (A) We publicized the conference.
   (B) No, it's not open yet.
   (C) No, it's a closed session.

4. Have you given the workers their checks?
   (A) The workers checked their equipment.
   (B) Yes, they were paid this morning.
   (C) The workers have something to say.

5. Are there any messages for me?
   (A) No, there are none for you.
   (B) Yes, I'll give you a message.
   (C) I can take a message if you'd like.

6. Are there more envelopes in the supply room?
   (A) I need four envelopes.
   (B) Yes, there are two boxes left.
   (C) Yes, the supply room is downstairs.

7. Can this computer be fixed soon?
   (A) I'll see you at six this afternoon.
   (B) There's a computer in that room.
   (C) A repairperson will come tomorrow.

8. Will Dr. Stevens be at the conference?
   (A) It'll be in the big conference room.
   (B) Yes, she plans to be there.
   (C) It starts at three.

9. Has Carlos worked here very long?
   (A) He's been here about fifteen years.
   (B) It took about a month.
   (C) It's about ten meters long.

10. Is this package for Mr. Kovacs?
    (A) Yes, please put it on his desk.
    (B) Yes, I can pack it for you.
    (C) Yes, this is my baggage.

Review: Part 2 (page 73)

1. Who ordered lunch?
   (A) Mr. Kim ordered it.
   (B) May I take your order?
   (C) Everything's in order.

2. What did you do in New York?
   (A) New York is a very big city.
   (B) The work is very interesting.
   (C) I visited some museums.

3. When can we get together?
   (A) Yes, it's very nice weather.
   (B) I'm free tomorrow afternoon.
   (C) They look nice together.

4. It's really cold today.
   (A) I'd better wear a sweater.
   (B) You don't look really old.
   (C) Not today, but really soon.

5. Why isn't Jane here?
   (A) No, I can't hear.
   (B) It's very near.
   (C) She's sick today.

6. How can I get to the airport?
   (A) A taxi is the fastest way.
   (B) It's a very modern airport.
   (C) The plane arrives at 5:30.

7. How much is a newspaper?
   (A) We enjoyed it very much.
   (B) Fifty cents.
   (C) About 25 pages.

8. Have you met Mrs. Johnson?
   (A) I met her at the conference.
   (B) No, I don't have any pets.
   (C) She came by jet.
9. Will the report be finished this afternoon?
   (A) Yes, it will be ready by two o'clock.
   (B) Yes, the repairman will be here soon.
   (C) Yes, we'll stay at the same resort.
10. I can't find my car key.
   (A) McCarthy is my name.
   (B) You need my new card.
   (C) Let's take my car.

PART 3: CONVERSATIONS

Occupations

Strategy Practice: Who (page 76)

1. **Woman** I love the way she sings.
   Man Me, too. She has a beautiful voice. I have all her recordings.
   Woman I hope we can get tickets for her concert.
   Man It shouldn't be difficult. No one likes opera.

2. **Man** Did the telephone repair person come?
   Woman Not yet. He said he'd come after lunch.
   Man You mean we can't use our phones until then?
   Man You can always use your mobile phone.

3. **Woman** I'd like to apply for a loan, please.
   Man Please fill out this form and see one of our officers.
   Woman I hope I'll be able to get the money today.
   Man This is a loan department, not an ATM.

4. **Man** I read your new book and I think you're a great writer.
   Woman Thank you. Have you read all my books?
   Man Unfortunately, I haven't had time. I write novels, too.

5. **Woman** The service in this restaurant is very slow.
   Man I hope our waitress comes soon. I'm really hungry.
   Woman She didn't even bring us our drinks. I wouldn't give her a tip.
   Man Let's give her a chance.

6. **Man** I finally have an appointment with my doctor this afternoon.
   Woman You've had that cold all week, haven't you?
   Man Yes, and now I have a cough and my back hurts.
   Woman You'd better stay home from work.

7. **Man** I'm planning to give a test the first day of school.
   Woman I don't like giving tests. I don't think they accurately measure a student's performance.
   Man If my students hear that, they'll want to go to your class.

8. **Woman** What time is the accountant coming this afternoon?
   Man As soon as he finishes our tax forms.
   Woman I hope he adds the numbers correctly this time. Do you remember all the mistakes he made on our last tax filing?
   Man We should get a new tax accountant. We can't afford to keep this one.

9. **Man** I advise you to eat less and exercise more.
   Woman First you change my diet; now you want me to exercise.
   Man As your physician, I know what's best for you. I want you to be healthy.
   Woman Sorry, doctor. My body says eat and rest.

10. **Man** Hurry up. The taxi is here.
    Woman He can wait a few minutes. I'll be right there.
    Woman I hope the driver doesn't put the meter on. It's expensive enough to take a cab.

11. **Woman** These flowers are beautiful—so bright and colorful.

    Man Yes, I grew them myself from seeds.

    Woman I wish I could grow such pretty plants as yours.

    Man You could if you were more patient.

    Woman And more experienced. Every plant I touch dies.

12. **Man 1** I got a huge tip from my last passenger.

    Man 2 Really? How much?

    Man 1 The fare was only five dollars and she tipped me two dollars.

    Man 2 That's why I like to park my cab in front of the stock exchange.

    Man 1 Sure. If they can afford the cab, they can afford a big tip.

13. **Woman** Did I get any phone messages?

    Man Yes. The mechanic called to say he's finished the repairs on your car.

    Woman Great. I'll pick it up after my tennis lesson this afternoon.

    Man I can give you a ride to the garage.

14. **Man** This is Mr. Gomez. How can I help you?

    Woman I'd like to book a flight to Paris for next week.

    Man I can get you a good price on that. Would you like me to reserve a hotel room for you, too?

    Woman Yes and a rental car too please.

15. **Woman** You play with the City Orchestra, don't you?

    Man Yes, I play the violin.

    Woman I hear you're having a concert at the stadium next week. Could you get me some tickets?

    Man I think all of our performances are sold out.

TOEIC Test Practice (page 78)

Questions 1 through 3 refer to the following conversation.

Man Here's your room key, ma'am. You're in room 215, on the second floor at the end of the hall. The elevator's right over there. Oh, and by the way, checkout time is at noon.

Woman Thank you. Is there someone who can help me with my luggage?

Man Of course. I'll call someone right away. Is there anything else I can help you with?

Woman Yes, if it's not too much bother. My boss told me there's a good restaurant near here called Mama's House. Could you tell me how to get there?

Questions 4 through 6 refer to the following conversation.

Man I'm sorry I had to miss the meeting today. Did my secretary call you to tell you? I had an appointment to get my tooth repaired.

Woman Yes, she told me you had a dental problem. I'm sorry about that. Everyone else managed to get to the meeting except Bob.

Man Really? But he was supposed to give the budget report, wasn't he? That was really important.

Woman Yes, so we're having another meeting just for that on Monday. I hope you can make it for that one.

Questions 7 through 9 refer to the following conversation.

Woman The one-way fare to Shelburg is $17, and it's $30 for a round-trip ticket.

Man I'll take a round-trip ticket, then. How many more stops is it until Shelburg?

Woman	The next station is Williamstown, the station after that will be Shelburg. We should be there is about 45 minutes.
Man	It's 11:30 now, so it'll be 12:15 when we get there. This trip is a lot shorter that I thought it would be.

Questions 10 through 12 refer to the following conversation.

Woman	Did anyone call while I was in the meeting?
Man	Yes, George Powell.
Woman	Who?
Man	George, the guy who's fixing your car. You know, the guy from the Maple Street Garage. Well, he called at 11:30. He says the repairs on your car are done and you can pick it up any time today.
Woman	Great. Please call him back and tell him I'll be there at 5:00. What's my schedule for this afternoon?
Man	Not much. You have an appointment with your accountant at 2:30, and the office manager would like to go over a few things with you before you go home.

Questions 13 through 15 refer to the following conversation.

Man	Why are you sitting in here? Are you waiting for someone?
Woman	Yes, someone is supposed to come fix the printer today. I called the company, and the customer service representative said a repairperson would be here by 3 o'clock, but it's 3:30 already and no one is here.
Man	But didn't they say they'd send someone over on Wednesday?

Woman	Yes, they did, and today's...Oh, no! You're right. Tomorrow's Wednesday. I've been waiting here for nothing. I even canceled my doctor's appointment to be here. You know how hard they are to get.
Man	I know. I've been trying to make an appointment for my dentist, but the receptionist was always putting me on hold. Finally, I tried the dentist's web site. Who knew you could make an appointment on the Internet?

Activities

Strategy Practice: What (page 83)

1.	Woman	Do you need some help typing that report?
	Man	I sure do. It needs to be completed by one.
	Woman	We should be able to finish it before lunch.

2.	Man	I've been waiting here 15 minutes. How often do the buses come?
	Woman	One stops here every 20 minutes.
	Man	Good. We only have five minutes more to wait, then.
	Woman	It should be here any minute.

3.	Woman	Will you help me move my desk by the window?
	Man	Do you want the chair by the door?
	Woman	No, let's move it next to the desk.
	Man	Chair by the desk, desk by the window. Anything else to move?

4.	Woman	The coffee is still hot. Would you like some?
	Man	Yes, please. Is there any cream and sugar?
	Woman	Yes, over there on the counter.
	Man	I wish there was some cake to go with this coffee.

5. **Man** The fare's a dollar fifty.
   Woman Do I need the exact change?
   Man No, I can give you change.
   Woman I hope you can change a $100 bill.

6. **Woman** Does this elevator stop on the fourth floor?
   Man No, this car is an express to the tenth floor.
   Woman Then we'll wait for the next one.

7. **Woman** Turn right at the next corner. Then park the car and let's walk.
   Man Do you see a parking space?
   Woman No, but there's a parking garage on the next street.
   Man We could have parked in the lot we just passed.

8. **Man** Would you like a one-way or a round-trip ticket?
   Woman One-way, please.
   Man That'll be $495, including tax.
   Woman That's a coach ticket right, not first class?

9. **Man** It was very kind of you to invite me for dinner.
   Woman We always like to have company. Would you like more bread?
   Man Yes, and the butter, too, please.

10. **Man** I hope you'll come back and have lunch with us next time.
    Woman Yes, I will. I'm sorry I have to leave so soon.
    Man Call us when you get home.
    Woman I had a lovely time. Thank you for inviting me.

11. **Man** Do you want me to put mustard or butter on your sandwich?
    Woman Just a little butter, but I'd like lots of meat.
    Man OK, and I'll add some lettuce and tomato slices, too.
    Woman Yes, lots of tomatoes, please.

12. **Man** Here, fill this bucket with water and make sure it's hot.
    Woman OK. Here's the mop, but where's the soap?

Man It's in the closet on the top shelf.

13. **Woman** I'll take this. It's fifty cents, right?
    Man Yes, but I don't think you want that one. It's yesterday's.
    Woman Oh, of course. Here's today's paper. I'll take this one.
    Man Would you like any other papers?

14. **Woman** Did any letters come for me today?
    Man I don't know. I'm going to check the mailbox right now.
    Woman Let me know if there's anything for me. I'm expecting an important letter.

15. **Man** Does this bus stop at the train station?
    Woman No, you'll have to change buses downtown.
    Man Change buses? I guess I should have taken a taxi instead.
    Woman It's easy to change. The buses run very frequently.

TOEIC Test Practice (page 85)

Questions 1 through 3 refer to the following conversation.

   Man Your total comes to twenty-five dollars and sixty-five cents.
   Woman Here's thirty dollars.
   Man And here's your change—one, two, three, four dollars and thirty-five cents. Did you enjoy your meal?
   Woman It was delicious. I sent my compliments to the chef. He's very talented.
   Man Yes. He's new here. We all think the manager was very smart to hire him.

Questions 4 through 6 refer to the following conversation.
   Woman He'd better get here soon or we'll miss our plane. It takes at least 30 minutes to get to the airport from here.
   Man Relax. When I called the cab company, they said the driver would be here by 6 o'clock. That gives us plenty of time.

Woman	All right. I'll read the paper while we're waiting. That will distract me.	
Man	Good idea. Could you hand me the editorial section?	

Questions 7 through 9 refer to the following conversation.

Man	Excuse me. Will there be a movie on this flight?
Woman	Yes. We're getting ready to serve lunch now, and when that's done we'll show the movie.
Man	Good. I hope it's a funny movie. I get nervous on these long flights. Laughing helps me relax.
Woman	We have plenty of magazines on board if you'd like to read one while you're waiting for the movie.

Questions 10 through 12 refer to the following conversation.

Woman	I'd like to book a flight to Miami Beach for next weekend.
Man	Certainly. Will you also be needing a rental car and hotel reservations?
Woman	No, nothing like that. I'll be staying with relatives. My cousin's getting married.
Man	How nice. Much more fun than a business trip.

Questions 13 through 15 refer to the following conversation.

Man	The doctor will be with you shortly. She's still with her last patient.
Woman	But my appointment was for 2:15, and it's 2:30 already, and my tooth is really bothering me.
Man	I'm very sorry, but she's had a very busy day. There were several emergencies.
Woman	Well, I can't wait any longer. Toothache or no, I want to change my appointment to another day.

Time

Strategy Practice: When (page 89)

1.	*Woman*	Our offices are cleaned on Monday and Wednesday.
	Man	Do you think they should be cleaned on Friday, too?
	Woman	I think twice a week is enough.
	Man	Two times is hardly enough.
2.	*Woman*	Is the coffee machine working yet?
	Man	Yes, it took all morning to fix it.
	Woman	I'm sure it will be broken again before too long.
	Man	Well, enjoy your coffee while you can.
3.	*Man*	We need a new copy machine. It takes one minute just to copy eight pages.
	Woman	That's really slow. That's less than 500 pages an hour.
	Man	We'll never get it finished at this rate.
4.	*Man*	Every time I call this number, I get a busy signal.
	Woman	How often have you tried?
	Man	Every hour. I'll try one more time.
5.	*Woman*	When does the mail come?
	Man	It usually comes just before noon, but sometimes earlier.
	Woman	Good, I hope it's early today.
	Man	Expecting something important?
6.	*Woman*	Your check was put in the mail yesterday, Mr. Brennan.
	Man	Yesterday? That means it will arrive next week.
	Woman	If it doesn't arrive by Friday, give me a call.
	Man	You bet I will.
7.	*Man*	Mr. Chu joined the company in August.
	Woman	Didn't Ms. Wallace join in August, too?
	Man	Yes, but Mr. Chu joined the year before.
	Woman	How time flies.

8. Man   Are we going at five or six o'clock?

Woman   We're going at six. The show starts at seven.

Man   Good. I don't want to be late.

Woman   I know you'd rather wait for an hour than be late by five minutes.

9. Woman   I visited my aunt in the hospital last night.

Man   How long has she been sick?

Woman   She's been sick a long time, but she just went to the hospital last week.

Man   That's a long time to be in the hospital. I hope she gets well soon.

10. Man   I took Ms. Ono to the airport yesterday. We almost missed the plane—we got there with only a half hour to spare.

Woman   I hear she'll be gone for three weeks.

Man   No, only for two.

11. Man   We've been working on this report for three days now.

Woman   Do you think we'll have it done by the end of the week?

Man   No, but I hope we can finish it before the meeting next Tuesday.

12. Woman   How does Lucy like her new job?

Man   She loves it so far, but she's been there only a week.

Woman   Only a week? I thought she'd been there for at least a month.

Man   She had her first interview last month.

13. Man   Did you read that e-mail message that Bill sent to everyone?

Woman   Yes, I read it this morning and I plan to answer it after lunch.

Man   I sent him my answer last night.

Woman   What's your hurry?

14. Woman   Did you start painting your house today?

Man   Actually, we started last weekend. It'll probably take about two weeks to complete the job.

Woman   Two weeks to paint that huge house? You'll have to work night and day to finish that fast.

Man   I'll have lots of help.

15. Man   Are you ready for the weekly staff meeting today?

Woman   No. I worked on this report all day yesterday, but I'm still not ready.

Man   I know. We should have these meetings once a month, not once a week.

Woman   Once every four weeks. That's a good idea.

TOEIC Test Practice (page 91)

Questions 1 through 3 refer to the following conversation.

Woman   I'm really tired today. We didn't get back from our trip until late last night.

Man   That's right. You just spent a week skiing in the mountains. How was it?

Woman   It was fantastic. I can't remember the last time I had so much fun. Aren't you planning to take a vacation soon?

Man   No, not until after July. I have to wait until I return from my business trip to Hong Kong. I'm planning to rent a house at the beach for the first week of August.

Questions 4 through 6 refer to the following conversation.

Man   We need to plan tomorrow's meeting. It's scheduled to start at 8:30, and I think we'll have to have the financial report first.

Woman   That's fine with me. Sherry should speak second because she's going to introduce the New York project.

Man   That sounds good. Then I think it'll be time for a coffee break. Let's put Tom's presentation after the coffee break. That should take us to lunch.

Woman   Fine. After lunch we can go over the quarterly report and organize the planning committee. I think we can manage to cover everything before the end of the day.

Questions 7 through 9 refer to the following conversation.

Woman   I'm terribly sorry, sir, but I don't see your name anywhere on our reservation list.

Man   But I called to make this reservation four weeks ago. I reserved a single room for an entire week. Here's my reservation number.

Woman   We just don't seem to have a record of it here, but I can do this. I'll give you a double room for two nights and just charge you for a single. Then on Wednesday you can move into a single room for the rest of the week. And, look, I'll give you a voucher good for three dinners in our restaurant.

Man   OK, I think that'll work out, and thanks for the meal tickets.

Questions 10 through 12 refer to the following conversation.

Man   Welcome to the city tour. Our bus will be leaving in just five minutes for the Natural History Museum.

Woman   Great. I hope we can spend all morning there.

Man   Actually, we'll have to leave there by 11:00. Then, if it doesn't rain, we'll have a walking tour of some of the nearby monuments before arriving at our restaurant for lunch at 12. Then it's off to the Art Museum for the afternoon.

Woman   A walking tour? Well, I hope we don't have to walk too far. And I guess I'll have to wait until tomorrow to get to the shopping district.

Questions 13 through 15 refer to the following conversation.

Woman   I tried calling you last night, but you weren't home. Where were you?

Man   I went to the movies with some friends after work. I told you to call me this morning because I knew I'd be out all day yesterday.

Woman   Sorry. I forgot. So are you still interested in seeing the play? I want to buy the tickets today. I could get them for Friday or Saturday night, or Sunday afternoon.

Man   I'd rather go in the afternoon than at night, so see if you can get them for Sunday.

Locations

Strategy Practice: Where (page 95)

1. Man   Fill it up with unleaded gas, please.

    Woman   Would you like the oil checked, too?

    Man   Yes, and wash the windshield.

    Woman   I'll check the tire pressure, too, if you like.

2. Woman   I don't know what to order. I could eat everything on the menu.

    Man   Why don't you try the tuna?

    Woman   That sounds good. I love fish.

    Man   Save room for dessert though. They have great pies here.

3. Woman   I'm sorry, sir. This section of the plane is for business class travelers.

    Man   I thought this was Economy.

    Woman   No, on this flight, the Economy section begins at row 23.

    Man   That's why the seats were so comfortable.

4. **Woman** I need to return this book to the library. It's overdue.

   Man Could you check out a book for me?

   Woman Sure. Give me your library card.

   Man Ask if I can have a three-week loan rather than two.

5. **Woman** Most of our sweaters are imported from Hong Kong.

   Man Do you make any in the Philippines?

   Woman Not yet. But we are talking with their officials.

6. **Man** I have a reservation for a double room for two nights.

   Woman And your name, sir?

   Man Frank Jones, J-O-N-E-S, with the East Asia Import Company.

   Woman Yes, here it is. A non-smoking room on a high floor.

7. **Woman** I lost my checkbook. Do I apply for a new one here?

   Man Is your checking account at this bank?

   Woman Yes. My savings account is here, too.

   Man May I see some ID please?

8. **Woman** We'd better hurry or we'll miss our train.

   Man Relax. Have another cup of coffee. We can walk to the station in ten minutes.

   Woman I always like to be on the platform a few minutes before the train arrives.

   Man There are trains every ten minutes. Take it easy.

9. **Man** Does your agency have any package tours to Hawaii?

   Woman Yes, we have a wonderful seven-day trip for only $945.

   Man I hope that includes airfare.

   Woman No, just hotel.

10. **Woman** We'd like to rent a car for the weekend.

    Man We only have one car left and that's a compact.

    Woman That'll be fine. I'd like full insurance coverage, too.

    Man Full insurance, and a full tank of gas.

11. **Woman** Watch out for that bus! Get back on the sidewalk!

    Man Thank you. Wow! There's a lot of traffic here.

    Woman Let's cross the street at the corner. The cars have to stop for the light there.

    Man I should be more careful.

12. **Man** Let's get there early. I don't want to wait in a long line to get tickets.

    Woman Yes, it's a popular movie. There'll be a lot of people there.

    Man And I want to get good seats— not too close to the screen.

    Woman You sit in the back. I like to sit right up front.

13. **Woman** When the weather's nice, I like to go to that park across the street.

    Man Yes, I like to go there to take a walk through the garden.

    Woman I like sitting on a bench under the trees and reading a good book.

14. **Woman** So how do you like working as a security guard?

    Man The job is hard, but the museum is a great place to work.

    Woman I'd love to be around all those paintings every day. They have great exhibits there.

    Man The school groups are really noisy and you have to tell them all the time, "Don't touch the art."

15. **Man** Where can I find canned vegetables?

    Woman Canned vegetables are in aisle 5, next to the canned soup.

    Man Canned soup? That sounds good. I'll buy some of that to cook for dinner.

    Woman Check out the produce section in the first aisle and our cheeses in the dairy section.

TOEIC Test Practice (page 97)

Questions 1 through 3 refer to the following conversation.

Woman   I'm picking John up this afternoon. His plane gets in at 2:15.

Man   It seems like he's been gone forever. A month at least.

Woman   No, it's just been two weeks. I'll bring him right here to the office so we can go over these papers with him.

Man   Poor guy. I'm sure he'd rather go home and rest.

Questions 4 through 6 refer to the following conversation.

Man   I think I'll try the baked fish.

Woman   I'm getting the seafood stew. If the waiter ever takes our order. We've been waiting, like, an hour.

Man   Calm down. It's only been 15 minutes, and here comes our waiter now.

Woman   All right, I'm calm. I just want to get to the theater before the play starts.

Questions 7 through 9 refer to the following conversation.

Woman   Do you come here much?

Man   Only once a year, but then I get to spend three weeks here.

Woman   Lucky! That's almost a month. I'm only here for a week, and I love it. It's so relaxing to lie on the sand and swim in the sea.

Man   I enjoy the sailing, too. It's a great place to unwind.

Woman   Yes. You can just leave all of your worries on the shore.

Questions 10 through 12 refer to the following conversation.

Man   Will that bus ever come? I've been waiting here since 7:30.

Woman   According to the schedule the next one should be here in exactly six minutes.

Man   That's not too long to wait, then. I hope it's on time. It looks like it's about to rain.

Woman   I hope you have an umbrella. You might be here for a while longer. The only ones who read these schedules are the passengers, not the bus drivers.

Questions 13 through 15 refer to the following conversation.

Woman   The department meeting is today, isn't it?

Man   Actually, it's been changed to Friday.

Woman   When did they decide that? No one told me. I'll bet they changed the location, too.

Man   Well, yes. It's not in the conference room anymore. It's in the company cafeteria. But it starts at the same time—1:50.

Reasons

Strategy Practice: Why (page 101)

1. Man   You are late again, Ms. Boggs.

    Woman   My car wouldn't start and I had to take the bus.

    Man   Try to be on time tomorrow, won't you?

    Woman   I'll come early even if I have to take a taxi.

2. Man   Has it stopped raining?

    Woman   No, it won't stop until Monday.

    Man   No one will come to our picnic then.

    Woman   We can eat indoors.

3. Man   Did you finish the memo?

    Woman   It's on your desk.

    Man   Thanks for staying late. I really appreciate it.

    Woman   Always glad to help.

4. Man   It's five after five. We have to leave in ten minutes.

    Woman   That's not enough time to finish writing this letter.

    Man   Let's just mail it tomorrow, then.

    Woman   All right. Hurrying never pays.

5. **Woman** My pen is out of ink, so I can't sign this memo.
   Man Here. Use my pencil.
   Woman No, it has to be signed in ink.
   Man I'll get you a pen. Blue or black ink?

6. **Man** Can you read this letter for me?
   Woman Did you forget your glasses?
   Man Yes, and I can't see a thing.
   Woman How did you get here? You didn't drive I hope.

7. **Man** The roads are covered with snow. I'm glad I'm not driving.
   Woman They'll probably have to close the highways.
   Man We're smart to take the train in this weather.
   Woman It takes longer, but it's safer.

8. **Man** The car won't start. I think we're out of gas.
   Woman I told you to fill it up. Now we'll have a long walk.
   Man Maybe we can catch a bus from here.
   Woman There aren't any buses here. Let's start walking.

9. **Man** I tried to call you earlier, but your line was busy.
   Woman Yes, I've been on the phone with the doctor.
   Man I hope you're not sick.
   Woman No, I was just trying to make an appointment to see her.

10. **Woman** I'm going to buy some new shoes. These hurt my toes.
    Man You should buy wider shoes then. They're much better for your feet.
    Woman Yes, these shoes are too narrow.

11. **Woman** Could you make these copies before noon, please?
    Man I'm sorry, I can't. The copier is broken and the repair person can't come until tomorrow.
    Woman Tomorrow? That's too late!
    Man Sorry, but that's the story.

12. **Man** We took Mr. Lee to that new restaurant last night.
    Woman Oh, that's right. It was Mr. Lee's birthday dinner, wasn't it?
    Man Yes. That restaurant is a great place for birthdays, and it isn't expensive either.
    Woman I wish I had come.

13. **Woman** I'm sorry Cindy didn't join us for lunch. I wanted you to meet her.
    Man Why didn't she come? Wasn't she hungry?
    Woman She was too busy at work. She just ate a sandwich at her desk.
    Man She works too hard.

14. **Man** I took my new suit back to the store.
    Woman Why did you do that? I liked it. It fit you really well.
    Man I didn't like the color. I exchanged it for a darker one.
    Woman I liked the first one.

15. **Woman** Did you hear that Jack got a raise?
    Man Really? He hasn't been working here very long.
    Woman I know, but he's a hard worker. He deserves to earn more money.
    Man Me, too. And I've been here longer.

TOEIC Test Practice (page 103)

Questions 1 through 3 refer to the following conversation.

   Woman I'm so sorry I missed the meeting. I had a flat tire, and it took me forever to fix it. I'm really getting sick of all these car problems.
   Man I'm sorry you had such a hard time, but you'll be glad to know the meeting went well. It started at 10, right on time for once. I'd be happy to share my notes with you.
   Woman That would be great. Why don't you let me make some copies and I'll give them right back?

Man   Actually, I left them with my secretary to make copies for you. It will only take her a short while to do it, then I'll send them right up to you.

Questions 4 through 6 refer to the following conversation.

Man   We don't have to leave yet. It only takes 15 minutes to drive to the theater from here.

Woman   But I thought we should take the bus instead of driving. It's really hard to find a place to park downtown, and it's expensive, too.

Man   But the parking is free after 6 o'clock, and driving's so much faster than the bus.

Woman   Well, we've got plenty of time to get there. It's only 5:30 now, and the play doesn't start till 7.

Questions 7 through 9 refer to the following conversation.

Woman   I'm having a really bad day today, and on top of everything, I left my wallet at home. Could I borrow a few dollars to get some lunch?

Man   Well, all right, but I need it back soon. How much do you need?

Woman   Eight or ten dollars should be enough. I can get a sandwich and a salad at the café downstairs for that much. I'll pay you tomorrow, I promise.

Man   Look, I'll give you ten, but don't forget to pay me back.

Questions 10 through 12 refer to the following conversation.

Man   Let's not go to that seafood restaurant. It's always so crowded.

Woman   But it's close to the movie theater, and it's so inexpensive. And the food is great.

Man   I agree that the food's not bad, but there are other restaurants near the theater. Anyhow, it's late. We'd better stop talking and get going.

Woman   Oh, we don't have to leave home for another 15 minutes or so. The movie doesn't start for another two hours, so we have plenty of time to eat before then.

Questions 13 through 15 refer to the following conversation.

Woman   Did you get the e-mail about Friday's meeting? It's been canceled.

Man   Yes, I know. The accountant called in sick today, and it looks like she'll be out all week. Of course we can't have the meeting without her.

Woman   That's too bad. I have all my notes ready for my presentation. I've been working so hard on them.

Man   You can still use them. My boss told me that the meeting has been rescheduled for next Wednesday. You'd better write that down. You know what a bad memory you have.

Review: Part 3 (page 106)

Questions 1 through 3 refer to the following conversation.

Man   There'll be 15 people at the meeting tomorrow morning, right?

Woman   Actually, Mr. Kim and his assistant will be there, too, so 17.

Man   The conference room's too small for all those people. It only holds 10 people. The reading room's also too small.

Woman   At least it holds 16 people. Almost big enough. We'll need to use the cafeteria. Why don't you reserve it this afternoon?

Questions 4 through 6 refer to the following conversation.

Woman   Marina's train is supposed to arrive at 9:00.

Man   I called the station. It's delayed because of the snow.

Woman   I hear buses and cars aren't even moving.

Man   They said her train would arrive at 11:30. She'll miss the 10 o'clock meeting. We need some sun or rain to melt this snow.

Questions 7 through 9 refer to the following conversation.

Man   We're leaving for vacation on Monday. We'll be gone two weeks.

Woman   Another vacation? It seems like you just took one last month.

Man   No. I only take three vacations a year. Last month I took a long weekend at the lake.

Woman   Are you going to the beach this time?

Man   No. This time we're going on a cruise. I love being on the water.

Questions 10 through 12 refer to the following conversation.

Woman   Oh. look, they have shrimp on the menu. Only $11. That's not too expensive. You should try it.

Man   I love shrimp, but I can't eat it. I'm allergic.

Woman   Do you like tuna? There's a tuna and rice special for only $17.50.

Man   I'm going to try the spaghetti dinner. It's about the same price as the tuna, $17. Why don't you get that too?

Questions 13 through 15 refer to the following conversation.

Woman   I'm going to the office supply store, the one between the post office and the bank. I need some paper and file folders.

Man   As long as you're going there, could you pick up some marking pens for me? I looked in the supply closet, and all we have left are pencils. Could you get a package of 25?

Woman   All right. I'll get you the pens, but I'll need some cash. Ten dollars should be plenty.

Man   Here's fifteen, just to be sure.

Questions 16 through 18 refer to the following conversation.

Woman   We've changed the location of tomorrow's meeting. It'll be in Conference Room 12.

Man   Thanks for telling me, but I'm not going to be able to make it.

Woman   Really? Why didn't you tell me before?

Man   I'm sorry. I just found out that I have to go out of town today. I'll be working all next week at our New York office.

Questions 19 through 21 refer to the following conversation.

Man   How did your doctor's appointment go?

Woman   It was fine except I got there a little late. I couldn't find a place to park the car.

Man   That's annoying. You got some phone calls while you were out. I left the messages on your door.

Woman   Thank you. Could you make three copies of these notes for me, please? Put them on my desk when you're done.

Questions 22 through 24 refer to the following conversation.

Woman   Here we are—154 State Street. The fare comes to $9.15.

Man   That's a lot more than I expected. It wasn't a long ride.

Woman   We add 15 percent to all the fares after 10 P.M.

Man   Oh, I didn't know that. Well, here's $10. Keep the change.

Questions 25 through 27 refer to the following conversation.

Man   Where's the waiter? We've been waiting for our food for over half an hour.

Woman   I know. They say the food at this restaurant is excellent, but I didn't know the service was so slow.

Man   Well, we may never get to taste the food. We have to leave here by eight if we want to get to the concert on time.

Woman   Last time we were late, they made us wait in the hall until intermission. Remember, we had to watch the concert on that little TV. I don't want to do that again.

Questions 28 through 30 refer to the following conversation.

Woman   See? I got here on time today.

Man   That's great, but you got to work on time every day when you used to drive your car.

Woman   Yes, when I take the bus it takes me an entire hour to get here, but it's a lot more relaxing than driving.

Man   But by car it only took you 40 minutes. We could count on you to be at the office on time every day if you went back to driving.

Woman   Well, I have my cell phone. You can always call me if there's some emergency.

PART 4: TALKS

Advertisements

TOEIC Test Practice (page 113)

Questions 1 through 3 refer to the following advertisement.

Do you want a car, but can't afford a new one? Is your present car safe on the road? Is it always in need of repair? Do people laugh at you when you drive up? Come in and look at our wide selection of previously owned vehicles. Whether you're looking for a four-door sedan or minivan for your family, or a sporty convertible for yourself, we have the car that's right for you.

Buy a used car today and save $1000. That's 5 percent more savings than our competitors can offer. We have all models of cars to choose from. We also have a number of financing options to choose from, so you don't need to worry about running out to get a bank loan before you shop for a car. Come to John's Auto Factory. Located on the corner of Highway 7 and Main. Don't wait. This offer is good only today and tomorrow.

Questions 4 through 6 refer to the following advertisement.

Thinking of refurnishing your office? There's no better time than now! Visit Andre's Warehouse this week and check out our all-time low prices. Our weeklong holiday sale ends Friday at midnight. Prices on desks, chairs, and computer tables have been reduced by 50 percent. All file cabinets are 75 percent off. Nothing will last long at these prices, so hurry on down. We also offer free delivery on purchases over $400. Free delivery is only available for local residents. Mileage charges will apply for delivery outside of this region. A sales manager will be on-site to answer your delivery questions.

Questions 7 through 9 refer to the following advertisement.

People's Store has a back-to-school sale special. Now you can buy two pens and get a third pen free. Buy six pens and pay for only four. Each pen is only thirty-five cents. If you buy more than ten pens, we'll give you a free notebook. This week, 10 percent of all sales at People's Store will be donated to the local Schools-in-Need program. At least four elementary schools in our district are underfunded and facing possible closure. Come in to People's Store this week and support your local schools. Strong communities start with healthy schools.

Questions 10 through 12 refer to the following advertisement.

Do you need health insurance? Are you worried about hospital costs? Are you at least 60 years old? If you have answered "yes" to these questions, call our office for more information. We have insurance plans for you and your family. At Health Insurance Plus we believe that everyone deserves insurance. You shouldn't have to stop traveling or stop living just because of your age or your health condition. Your life has just begun. Put your trust in Health Insurance Plus and look forward to a brighter future.

Questions 13 through 15 refer to the following advertisement.

Does it feel like winter is never going to end? Are deadlines and meetings getting you down? Studies show that skipping even one vacation a year can drastically reduce your life expectancy. What better reason to book a holiday today? Travel Unlimited offers you vacations in the sun. We have three-day, five-day, and seven-day hotel packages starting at $350. That's one whole week of fun in the sun. All meals, hotel charges, and golf lessons are provided. Airfare is not included. Come in this week, and we will waive the booking fee. This offer is only available at the Travel Unlimited agency counter. No online bookings.

Questions 16 through 18 refer to the following advertisement.

Everybody is talking about our city's newest restaurant, the Palm Tree Bistro. We have seafood specials every Friday, and you can enjoy our famous desserts every day of the week. Call 555-4409 to reserve your table today. Special group discounts are offered to parties of eight or more.

Questions 19 through 21 refer to the following advertisement.

Tickets go on sale next Thursday for next month's special performance by the National Orchestra. General admission tickets are available for $55 each, and balcony tickets cost $75. Groups of fifteen or more people get a 10 percent discount. Student and senior citizen discounts are not available for this special performance.

Questions 22 through 24 refer to the following advertisement.

Can't find what you're looking for in your closet these days? Don't fret. It's time to treat yourself to something new. Come into Caroline's, and we'll make you feel brand new again. Don't wait until next week, or you'll miss our end-of-season clothing sale. All

summer clothes, including shorts, sandals, and sun dresses, are 15 to 25 percent off. Ladies' bathing suits are two for the price of one. We're open from 10 A.M. to 10 P.M. Sale ends August 30. All end-of-season sales are exchange only. No cash returns.

Questions 25 through 27 refer to the following advertisement.

Wondering how much time to allow for driving, parking, and finding a ticket booth before you catch that important flight out of the city? Don't rely on a taxi, try the new express bus service to the airport. Buses leave once an hour from the Central Hotel and you arrive at the airport in thirty minutes or less, guaranteed. Leave behind the stress of traffic delays and parking problems. Tickets are only $20. It's the best deal in town. To secure a spot on the bus, reserve and purchase your seat ahead of time by calling 1-800-AIR-9000. This is an automated service. All prepurchased tickets must be paid for with a valid credit card. Tips for the bus driver are appreciated.

Questions 28 through 30 refer to the following advertisement.

If you are interested in plants and flowers, subscribe to *Gardener's Magazine.* Every month we bring you information to improve your garden. Monthly features include, *How to Grow a Healthier Vegetable Garden,* by organic gardener Elaine Fields, and *Tips for Garden Clean-up,* by award-winning author Sherry Brooks. We also highlight a tree, flowering shrub, and herb each month in our *What's In Your Garden?* column written by our own readers. Order your subscription this week and get 15 percent off the usual price. Order a two-year subscription and get 25 percent off. You can order by mail or online.

Weather

TOEIC Test Practice (page 119)

Questions 1 through 3 refer to the following weather report.

Could it already be time to get out the sun block and search for shorts and sunglasses? Well, it may be too early for summer, but warmer weather is finally here. Today the sun is shining and temperatures will be much higher than what you expect for this time of year. The warm weather will continue through tomorrow. There is no chance of rain until early next week, but at this time of year, we know the good weather can't last forever. Our seven-day forecast is showing light snow possible on Wednesday or Thursday.

Questions 4 through 6 refer to the following weather report.

I'm Sara Roberts with your three-day weather forecast. Though it's been a relatively dry week for this time of year, we can expect showers late tonight. There's an 80 percent chance of precipitation tomorrow morning, but the rain is expected to clear by afternoon. Now for the good news. Warm and sunny weather is expected throughout the weekend, taking us right into Sunday evening. Don't miss the chance to go to the beach and enjoy a clear sunset as the weekend comes to a close. Now, back to John with today's sports highlights.

Questions 7 through 9 refer to the following weather report.

There's a slight chance of rain this afternoon, possibly turning to wet snow by evening. There's also a storm warning in effect for tomorrow, so stay tuned to Channel 5's weather news, on the hour every hour. Temperatures will remain cold for the remainder of the day, and with the wind chill we may even reach a record low for March. With the weather watch warning in effect for tomorrow, you're advised not to drive unless absolutely necessary. Walk, take public transit, or better yet, take a day off and stay home.

Questions 10 through 12 refer to the following weather report.

Today was the hottest day on record since 1885, when the city started keeping track of the daily highs and lows. But with today's strong winds it didn't feel as uncomfortable as it might have on a calm summer day. Since this weather isn't typical for a cool fall day, perhaps it means we can get ready for a gentle winter. After last year's harsh winter, I think all of us would welcome milder temperatures this year.

Questions 13 through 15 refer to the following weather report.

This is Angela Booth with your 30-second afternoon weather report. This morning's sunny skies and mild temperatures have turned into a beautiful afternoon. At two o'clock this afternoon, the temperature at the airport was 21 degrees Celsius. The temperature has risen a few more degrees since then, and we can expect things to stay warm throughout the evening. This weather is warm for this time of year, but no one's complaining after the poor weather we've been having this month.

Questions 16 through 18 refer to the following weather report.

Clear skies today will be a welcome relief after yesterday's thundershowers. Although it will be a bit warmer than yesterday, temperatures will remain cool throughout the day. Watch out for more rain and colder temperatures tomorrow, but no snow until next Tuesday. A cold front will be moving in toward the end of next week, so it's almost time to put your rain boots away and get out your warm hats and mittens. Winter's just around the corner.

Questions 19 through 21 refer to the following weather report.

Put away those umbrellas. The clouds are finally gone, so go outside and enjoy the sunshine today. It looks like we have a full week of sun ahead of us, with no more rain expected until after the weekend. Temperatures will remain cool and pleasant until the middle of the week. Wednesday brings us hotter weather. The warmer weather couldn't come at a better time, with the annual town baseball tournament scheduled for next Thursday. The event will take place rain or shine.

Questions 22 through 24 refer to the following weather report.

All local beaches are closed for the weekend due to dangerous winds. In addition to the wind, the weather will remain cloudy all weekend. Temperatures will fall below freezing tonight and there is a slight chance of snow after midnight. If you haven't done so already, now's the time to cover up those precious bedding plants and bring in any bulbs that might not make it through the winter. The last fall pickup for garden waste is this Sunday.

Questions 25 through 27 refer to the following weather report.

Today's high temperature of 75 degrees Fahrenheit is average for this time of year. The record high for this date is 90 degrees and the record low is 55. What is not average is the unusual amount of rain we have had this fall. We were all happy to see today's clear weather and hope the sunshine continues all week.

Questions 28 through 30 refer to the following weather report.

Does it seem like your umbrella is never getting a chance to dry out this May? Well, that's probably because this has been the rainiest spring ever, with a record rainfall last week of five inches. Five inches! That's more rain than we received all summer last year. Rain continues today and through the rest of the week, and cloudy skies are in store for the rest of the weekend. But don't worry. According to our 15-day forecast, summer sunshine and clear skies are just around the corner.

News

TOEIC Test Practice (page 125)

Questions 1 through 3 refer to the following news report.

The Central Water Authority advised all residents today to use less water. There is very little water in the reservoir, and rain is not expected for weeks. For more information, please visit the city government web site. There you will find a list of ways to reduce water consumption, including watering indoor plants with dishwater, and taking showers instead of baths. If you have an important question regarding the water advisory, please type it in the text box provided on the web site. The city government asks that residents not call the offices regarding this matter.

Questions 4 through 6 refer to the following news report.

Patients at City Hospital received holiday gifts today. Children from a local school distributed presents to many of the patients. Keeping in the spirit of the holiday season, the doctors and nurses were given presents as well. A holiday party for hospital patients will take place on Sunday. If you did not have a chance to donate a gift yet, please bring an unwrapped item to floor 7 of the children's ward by Saturday at the latest. Indicate the age and gender appropriateness of your gift. Gifts for adult patients will also be accepted.

Questions 7 through 9 refer to the following news report.

Computer Magazine reported today that the California Computer Company has announced the entry of a new computer. This computer is smaller and faster than other computers currently on the market. Business travelers will find it very useful. The new computer will be available in stores within the next two weeks. To learn more about these innovative systems, log onto *Computer Magazine's* web site and type the phrase *new products* into the keyword search. There you will find more information about the new computer, including more about its unique features.

Questions 10 through 12 refer to the following news report.

All banks and public offices were closed today because of the heavy snowfall. Schools were also closed and will remain closed until next week. Public transit will only be running on major thoroughfares that have been cleared and salted. However, most side roads remain closed, so residents are advised to leave cars in their driveways and stay home from work. If the conditions continue to worsen, the city may have to call in snow clearing crews from surrounding regions. Two of the six trucks that we have to clear snow are currently out of service.

Questions 13 through 15 refer to the following news report.

Malaysia and Canada signed a cultural exchange agreement today. The cultural ministers of both countries attended a concert after the signing. The countries will exchange artists, orchestras, and dance groups. Drama groups are not included in the cultural agreement. It is hoped that a new trade agreement will follow. Relations between Canada and Malaysia have always been strong, and in a recent press conference, both cultural ministers stated that this relationship can only continue to grow.

Questions 16 through 18 refer to the following news report.

This is Jessica Robins with your political news clip of the day. The president left this week on a two-week tour of Asia. He will meet with the heads of state of five different countries, including China, Japan, and South Korea. This is the president's first foreign tour since he took office back in January. The president has received much criticism for not making public appearances at several international conferences in the last few months. His wife is accompanying him on the trip.

Questions 19 through 21 refer to the following news report.

The Venezuelan company, Marisol, a branch of RTV Satellite, announced today that it was laying off 100 employees in its Miami, Florida, office in one week. The company says the laying off of these workers is part of the process to reduce costs. The entire company plans to leave Miami within two years and will relocate to Santo Domingo, the Dominican Republic, a Caribbean island where labor is cheaper. Some of the people who lost their jobs may be eligible to apply for new positions in the company's parent headquarters in Caracas.

Questions 22 through 24 refer to the following news report.

Thousands of people went downtown yesterday morning to see the annual National Day parade. The parade was led by our newly elected mayor and her family. Following the parade, the public enjoyed an afternoon of free concerts in City Park. Nice weather and great music made it a pleasant day for all. If you missed the parade, it will be broadcast tonight on Channel 7 immediately following prime time news. The headliners of the concert, local band, Road Warriors, will be playing a second show tomorrow night at 9:00 P.M. at the downtown coliseum.

Questions 25 through 27 refer to the following news report.

In financial news, an increase in the sales tax was announced yesterday. The tax will go up from 5 percent to 7 percent, the biggest jump we have seen in years. Some local store owners fear this will cause people to buy fewer things. Local mechanic, Ron Hughes,

complained that a 1 percent tax hike ten years ago almost caused him to go out of business. A provincial petition to prevent the rise in sales tax failed to stop the government from passing the bill. The new sales tax will go into effect next month.

Questions 28 through 30 refer to the following news report.

The new high-speed train service to the nation's capital began yesterday. Passengers said they preferred taking the train because it is more convenient than the plane. Three trains a day leave from the downtown train station for the capital. The trip takes two hours and forty-five minutes by train but only one hour by plane. Citizens have been waiting for the new transit system to be completed since construction began on the rails over five years ago. The project was postponed several times over the years due to lack of funding and a labor shortage.

Recorded Announcements
TOEIC Test Practice (page 131)

Questions 1 through 3 refer to the following announcement.

The museum is open every day from 9 A.M. to 6 P.M. and on Thursdays until 9 P.M. The museum is closed on Mondays. Museum visitors are asked to check all coats and bags in the coat room on the ground floor, just next to the front door. A free map of the museum is available in the lobby. If you have difficulty finding an exhibit, please ask the customer service representative at reception for help. Children under 12 must be accompanied by an adult at all times. Thank you for visiting.

Questions 4 through 6 refer to the following announcement.

This is Warren Harolds with your daily employment tip. Pacific Electronics has finally opened at the corner of Todd and Mayfield. The company has openings in the following positions: electricians, plumbers, carpenters, and bricklayers. All interested should apply in person at 614 Todd Street between 7 and 9 A.M. Monday through Friday. Bring a résumé with cover letter and references. Wages start at minimum wage for general laborers. All supervisor and managerial positions have been filled at this time. Pacific Electronics will be doing a second round of hiring in the fall.

Questions 7 through 9 refer to the following announcement.

The Fairlawn Golf Club is open from 5 A.M. to 8 P.M. daily. Only parties of four may play between the hours of 12 P.M. and 7 P.M. Guest passes are not available on the weekends. If you are interested in participating in our annual Senior Tournament, to take place next week, please sign up in the clubhouse. Groups of four will be accepted first. Single participants wishing to be placed in a group will be put on a waiting list until a day or two before the event. Ask to speak with Pro Shop manager Ray Jones for more information.

Questions 10 through 12 refer to the following announcement.

Attention all patrons. In just 15 minutes from now author Cheryl Stone is going to be reading from her best-seller *Managing Your Finances*. All interested please proceed to Room 3 now. This event is free of charge and does not require a library membership. At this time we would also like to remind patrons that the library will be closed during the holiday period. The library will reopen Monday, January 7. You may return all books at that time. You will not be charged a late fee. Your librarians and library volunteers wish you and your family happy holidays.

Questions 13 through 15 refer to the following announcement.

Hello. You have reached the Consumer Complaints Bureau. All our agents are busy at the moment, but your call is important to us. Do not hang up and try again later. All calls will be answered in the order received. Please be patient and stay on the line. To ensure that your question is answered as quickly as possible, please have your bill of sale or proof of purchase in front of you, with the date and location of your purchase circled. We will also be asking for your full name and address, including your postal code.

Questions 16 through 18 refer to the following announcement.

Looking for something to do this week with that special someone? This week the Royal Theater is showing the popular movie *Forever*

Love. This film is set in Paris and stars two of France's award-winning actors, as well as an outstanding supporting cast. The film is in French, but English subtitles will be provided. We have shows at 2, 4, 6, and 8 o'clock. Admission is $8.50. All shows before six o'clock are $5.75. Tickets sell out quickly, so please arrive early. We don't take reservations.

Questions 19 through 21 refer to the following announcement.

This is the office of Dr. Sato. The office is closed for the day. If this is an emergency, please hang up and call 555-6783. To schedule an appointment with the doctor or to speak with a nurse, call back tomorrow between 9 A.M. and 5 P.M. Please be advised that the doctor will be out of the office until the first week of June for his annual vacation. No appointments will be available until then. Thank you.

Questions 22 through 24 refer to the following announcement.

Are you tired of always relying on Mom or Dad or public transit to get you from A to B? If you're over 16 years of age, maybe it's time to think about getting your own license. To apply for a new driver's license, come to the License Office Monday through Friday between 8:30 A.M. and 4:30 P.M. Bring two forms of identification. You will take a written test and a driving test. There will be a fee of $45. The License Office recommends at least 24 hours of classroom lessons before attempting the road test.

Questions 25 through 27 refer to the following announcement.

This is the voice mail of Elizabeth Lee at the *National Times Newspaper*. I will be out of the office all week at a journalists' conference. If you need immediate assistance, please call Mr. Roberts at extension 57. Mr. Roberts will be looking after all of my weekly interviews and assignments while I'm gone. I'll be checking my e-mail daily at an Internet café if you require a personal response from me before the end of the week. However, please be aware that I will not have access to files or contacts on my personal computer.

Questions 28 through 30 refer to the following announcement.

This is the Office Super Store, your store for office furniture. We're open six days a week, Tuesday through Sunday, from 9 A.M. to 9 P.M. This Friday only, we will close at 1 P.M. for our year-end inventory. We'll open again at nine on Saturday. Don't miss our clear-out sale this Sunday. All damaged and floor model stock must go. Some of our furniture will be available at 90 percent off the regular ticket price. The store will remain open past the usual business hours on Sunday if stock remains.

Special Announcements

TOEIC Test Practice (page 139)

Questions 1 through 3 refer to the following announcement.

Good morning, class. My name is Professor Tran, and I will be your biology professor this semester. I've been teaching at York College for over 15 years, and before that I was a student here, just like the rest of you. You may have heard from other students that I am an easygoing teacher who doesn't believe in homework assignments. But, let me warn you, this year things are going to change. This course is an introductory course for students not majoring in science; however, that doesn't mean it's going to be easy. You will be required to study hard in order to pass your exams. Now, I'm going to begin tonight by talking about the scientific method.

Questions 4 through 6 refer to the following announcement.

Welcome aboard Flight 140, nonstop to Hong Kong. All passengers must bring their seat backs to an upright position. Smoking of any kind is not permitted on this flight. Our in-flight movie will begin soon after takeoff, in about 30 minutes. Earphones are available for $5.00 and can be reused on future flights with our airline. If you require a pillow or blanket, please press the call light above you and a flight attendant will come by to assist you.

Questions 7 through 9 refer to the following announcement.

Ladies, this stop on our garden tour will be very short. Please return to the bus in fifteen minutes. We have one more garden to visit before our lunch break, so we must leave on time. Since this stop is so short, it's advisable that we stay together as a group, though if you prefer to wander about on your own, that's also fine. Most importantly, we don't want to leave anyone behind, so if you don't have a watch, please stay close to someone who does.

Questions 10 through 12 refer to the following announcement.

Welcome all passengers. This is the express train to New York. The non-stop trip takes approximately 30 minutes. If you're looking for the local train, which makes four regular stops en route to New York with an estimated travel time of one hour, please walk across the platform to Track B now. As you step onto the express train, please assist young children and elderly travelers and watch for the closing doors. We ask that everyone take a seat unless there are no seats available. Next stop, New York.

Questions 13 through 15 refer to the following announcement.

May I have your attention, please. First I'd like to thank everyone for coming out to our final showing of Shakespeare's *Macbeth*. We've had a great turnout over the last six weeks, and all of the actors and behind-the-scenes crew are sorry to see this production come to an end. Having said that, I'm sorry to announce that Michael Nonis, the lead actor who has been playing Macbeth, is sick tonight. The role of Macbeth for tonight's performance will be understudy Alfred Sato. Thank you and enjoy the show.

Questions 16 through 18 refer to the following announcement.

May I have your attention please. Will the driver of the blue car parked near the front door please move your car? That area is for delivery trucks only. Please move your car to the parking garage. Please be advised that all illegally parked cars will be towed. The towing company in charge of removing vehicles from this lot is advertised on the signpost at the far end of the parking lot. Towing is at the owner's expense. Damage to vehicles may result due to the illegal positioning of your car. While tow truck companies do their best to ensure minimal damage to the vehicle, this is not the store's responsibility.

Questions 19 through 21 refer to the following announcement.

The 10:30 guided tour of the museum will begin in fifteen minutes. All ticket holders please line up at the end of the hall. If you don't have a ticket, please go to the front desk to get one. Tickets are free, but you must have one to participate in the tour. We hope you enjoy your visit today and ask that you please fill out a comment card when you have completed the tour. Comments are anonymous, and you will not be contacted. On your way out, you can also enter to win a free painting from a local artist.

Questions 22 through 24 refer to the following announcement.

Good afternoon, passengers. This is your captain speaking. In about five minutes, we will be passing over Lake Frank. If you look out the left side of the plane, you'll be able to see the lake. The clouds have cleared up and we have beautiful sunny weather now, so you should get a good view. For those of you sitting on the right, just be patient for a minute. You will get a chance to see a better view of the lake as we head slightly east towards the end of this mountain pass. Those seated on the right can also be watching for the volcano that is going to be coming up in about half an hour.

Questions 25 through 27 refer to the following announcement.

Coming up after the news on Radio 2000 we'll have today's weather report, followed by a full hour of classical music. Later this afternoon we'll hear an interview with Ms. Lucinda Park, world-famous violinist, who will discuss her recent concert tour. Ms. Park will also be giving away two free copies of her latest CD, titled *Sounds of Strings*. Keep your dial locked to Radio 2000 and don't miss your chance to be today's lucky caller number 7.

Questions 28 through 30 refer to the following announcement.

Attention all staff. A set of house keys was found in the cafeteria this morning at approximately 10:30 A.M. Please check your wallets, pockets, and purses to make sure you haven't misplaced your keys. If you think the keys are yours, please come to the main office

to identify them. Ask for Mr. Chang. As a reminder, all lost and found items will remain at the main office for 30 days. After this time, items will either be donated to a local charity or disposed of in the trash. Thank you.

Business Announcements

TOEIC Test Practice (page 145)

Questions 1 through 3 refer to the following announcement.

Tonight's dinner honors our colleague Ms. Radice. Ms. Radice will receive the Good Citizen Award for saving the life of our coworker Mr. Chi. Two months ago Ms. Radice went beyond the call of duty of her job by taking a first-aid course. She did this after learning that very few of our employees knew how to administer CPR. A survey of our staff showed that only 1 in 10 of our employees had first-aid certificates. Ms. Radice took the course on her own time and at her own expense. Her initiative paid off by saving a life. To begin our program our director, Mr. Prince, will make a special announcement.

Questions 4 through 6 refer to the following announcement.

While in the clubhouse, all gentlemen must wear a coat and a tie. Ladies must wear a dress or skirt. No informal clothes are allowed in the Clubhouse Dining Room for tonight's anniversary dinner. We thank you for your cooperation in following this dress code. It is important to the members of the clubhouse to keep the tradition of formal dress intact. In doing this, we hope to maintain the reputation of our club as a high-class facility, just as it was when we opened 20 years ago today.

Questions 7 through 9 refer to the following announcement.

If you look at your copy of the meeting agenda, you'll see that we'll be talking about vacation policy as well as the training of new employees. We won't discuss the budget today since our accountant, Mrs. Lopez, is out sick. I will also ask that whoever is in charge of taking the minutes this session makes sure to forward them onto Mrs. Lopez after the meeting adjourns. Please see me after the meeting, and I will provide you with her confidential contact information. And now, without further ado, let's begin with the first item on the agenda.

Questions 10 through 12 refer to the following announcement.

The ABC Food Company is opening a new factory in Asia. We are looking for personnel at all management levels to relocate. If we cannot find enough employees to transfer from within the company, we will be forced to recruit using other means. Despite being a current employee, it is still necessary to apply for the overseas positions. Applicants should send a résumé to our home office. If you have friends or family members who may be interested in a position, please print out an application and have them cite you as a reference.

Questions 13 through 15 refer to the following announcement.

As of today, no food or drinks may be brought into the computer room. We've had to replace three keyboards recently due to hot drinks being carelessly spilled on them. We've also had several problems with sticking keys, likely caused by crumbs getting caught in the keyboard. Please wash your hands after eating before using a computer. Also, please remember that smoking is strictly prohibited while using the computers. Finally, remember to keep the door closed and the fan on at all times.

Questions 16 through 18 refer to the following announcement.

Our speaker this evening is Mr. John Thompson. Mr. Thompson is an accountant with over twenty years' experience, and he also coordinates the annual Small Business Conference at City College. The title of his talk tonight is "What Every Small Business Administrator Needs to Know About Taxes." Following his talk, Mr. Thompson will answer questions in the Great Hall, and coffee and snacks will be served.

Questions 19 through 21 refer to the following announcement.

All employees are advised that repair work on the north elevator was begun this morning and will continue all day. Please use the south elevator or the stairs when exiting the building this afternoon. We expect to have the repairs finished and everything in working order by tomorrow morning. We'd also like to take this opportunity to remind you that the front lobby will be painted next week.

Questions 22 through 24 refer to the following announcement.

In order to show the company's appreciation for the hard work of all our employees, we have started an Employee of the Month program. The Employee of the Month will be chosen according to his or her efficiency and dedication to work. The Employee of the Month will receive an award as well as free lunches in the company cafeteria and a parking space near the front door. The name of the first Employee of the Month will be announced at the end of this week.

Questions 25 through 27 refer to the following announcement.

People have been taking supplies from the supply room without permission. I would like to make it clear that no one may enter the supply room except Mr. Lewis. He's the only one who has the key. All employees who need supplies must give a list to Mr. Lewis two days ahead of time, and he will get the supplies to you. There will be no exceptions to this rule. At no time may any employee enter the supply room unless accompanied by Mr. Lewis himself. If Mr. Lewis is absent either due to illness or a business engagement, he will leave instructions for another manager regarding how to access the supply room.

Questions 28 through 30 refer to the following announcement.

We will choose several employees to send to the international business conference in California at the end of this year. If you are interested in attending the conference, please tell your department head. All department heads will submit a list of interested employees to the Human Resources office at the end of the month. Only those employees who have excelled in their departments and demonstrated an interest in international affairs will be chosen to attend. Please do not contact Human Resources to inquire about the selection. A decision will be posted for all to view in the staff room at the end of the month.

Review: Part 4 (page 150)

Questions 1 through 3 refer to the following weather report.

A severe snowstorm is moving into our area. Snow will begin falling just before midnight. It will continue to fall most of tomorrow, ending early tomorrow evening. Expect a total snowfall of 30 centimeters. Wednesday will be sunny but very cold. We can expect the cold weather to last until at least the end of the month if not halfway through next month. Last year, there were no signs of spring until mid-April despite a milder than average winter.

Questions 4 through 6 refer to the following advertisement.

Walk Well Shoe Store has all the latest shoe styles for men, women, and children. Visit us at our new location on Maine Avenue, across the street from City Center Mall. This month, take advantage of our back-to-school sale. All children's shoes are 25 percent off. Sale ends September 20th. Watch for Walk Well Shoe Store coupons in the next three flyers in your local papers. And remember, there's no tax on children's shoes, so the price you see is the price you get.

Questions 7 through 9 refer to the following message.

You have reached the office of Marlene Rich, assistant to the director. I'm away this week at a conference. I'll be back at my desk on Monday. To leave a message, press 1. To reach the director's office, press 2. To hear a directory of all employee phone numbers, press 3. Thank you for calling, and remember: Keeping a positive attitude throughout the day can improve your life and the lives of those around you. Only three more weeks until spring!

Questions 10 through 12 refer to the following news report.

Construction will begin next month on the new sports arena. In addition to sporting events, the arena will also be used for concerts and theatrical events. It will have restaurants on the ground floor. The location was chosen because it's close to subway stations and parking garages. Construction is expected to take two years.

Questions 13 through 15 refer to the following message.

Thank you for calling the Deluxe Theatre, located inside Maple Tree Mall. Tonight we are showing *In the Small Hours,* featuring sisters Erica and Alicia Kay. We have shows at 7:30, 9:30, and midnight. All shows are $10 general admission or $8 for seniors with identification. Children under 12 will not be admitted. Popcorn and candy are for sale in the lobby. Pick up a copy of this month's features while you're there. You can read the reviews and take the quizzes while you're waiting for the show to start. See you soon!

AUDIOSCRIPT LISTENING COMPREHENSION REVIEW

PART 1 (PAGE 153)

Example:

(A) They're leaving the room.
(B) They're turning on the machine.
(C) They're standing near the table.
(D) They're reading the newspaper.

1. (A) He's closing the door.
   (B) He's carrying a bag.
   (C) He's helping a guest.
   (D) He's waiting by the door.

2. (A) The flight controller is in the tower.
   (B) The teacher is in the schoolyard.
   (C) The worker is at the construction site.
   (D) The farmer is in the bean field.

3. (A) The man is waiting for a plane.
   (B) The waiter is setting the table.
   (C) The rolls are baked at the bakery.
   (D) The trees are being cut down.

4. (A) They're standing in line.
   (B) They're counting their money.
   (C) They're shopping for food.
   (D) They're preparing a picnic.

5. (A) He's looking out the window.
   (B) He's eating in front of the television.
   (C) He's rinsing his fork.
   (D) He's acting on the stage.

6. (A) She's laughing with her friend.
   (B) She's looking at her watch.
   (C) She's sitting on the grass.
   (D) She's cleaning the glasses.

7. (A) They're looking for a place to park.
   (B) They're driving around the block.
   (C) They're buying Otto a mobile phone.
   (D) They're standing beside the car.

8. (A) Passengers must check in early.
   (B) Duty-free items are not taxed.
   (C) Luggage is sold on the corner.
   (D) Baggage comes on the carousel.

9. (A) She's using the telephone.
   (B) She's reading the phone book.
   (C) She's ringing up a sale.
   (D) She's answering the door.

10. (A) They're measuring the painting.
    (B) They're cutting the flowers.
    (C) They're hanging the picture.
    (D) They're covering the wall.

PART 2 (PAGE 159)

Example:

Where is the meeting room?
(A) To meet the new director.
(B) It's the first room on the right.
(C) Yes, at two o'clock.

11. When do you think the man will arrive?
    (A) He'll be here by noon.
    (B) His wife arrived last night.
    (C) I think he arrived on time.

12. What did you do today?
    (A) I usually take the bus.
    (B) I went shopping.
    (C) The radio was playing.

13. Who came to the office first?
    (A) Mrs. Lee arrived before the others.
    (B) I was the last one in line.
    (C) They left the office first.

14. When can Sarah revise the memo?
    (A) She can do it this afternoon.
    (B) She doesn't remember.
    (C) He'll review it tomorrow.

15. No one told me that you called today.
    (A) I didn't leave my name.
    (B) I find it warm in here.
    (C) I told you last week.

16. Where did you leave your briefcase?
    (A) On the train, I think.
    (B) I left work early.
    (C) Yes, it was brief.

17. Who's the new lawyer?
    (A) No, she's studying law.
    (B) They were newly elected.
    (C) She's a friend of mine from law school.

18. How long have you worked for this firm?
    (A) In two weeks.
    (B) Over five weeks.
    (C) Last week.

19. What did you buy?
    (A) I think he's buying a new house.
    (B) We went by the office, but it was closed.
    (C) A coat that was on sale.

20. Where did you go on vacation?
    (A) To Hawaii.
    (B) It starts next week.
    (C) For ten days.

21. What are you doing after work?
    (A) I worked at a bank.
    (B) I'm playing golf.
    (C) Yes, I am.

22. Will you pay by cash or check?
    (A) By check. I don't have enough cash.
    (B) No, he's the cashier.
    (C) We haven't cashed our checks.

23. What is your favorite food?
    (A) The restaurant down the street.
    (B) He prefers fish instead of meat.
    (C) I like anything sweet.

24. When did that secretary join the firm?
    (A) She needs a secretary soon.
    (B) She joined last summer.
    (C) They were married yesterday.

25. The nurse gave me something for the pain.
    (A) No, but I have a pencil.
    (B) I hope it makes you feel better.
    (C) She might if I ask her to.

26. Why are you working late?
    (A) I haven't finished all my work.
    (B) It's too late for me to work.
    (C) I always take a walk at eight.

27. Where's there a public phone?
    (A) No, I think it's closed to the public.
    (B) I usually go there alone.
    (C) There's one in the hallway.

28. I don't hire friends or relatives.
    (A) Do you think you have an ear infection?
    (B) Can't you make an exception?
    (C) Would you tell me which ones to invite?

29. Why are you leaving so early?
    (A) I need to get up earlier.
    (B) I might be late tomorrow morning.
    (C) I have an appointment downtown.

30. How do you turn on the lights?
    (A) We turned it on very slowly.
    (B) Make the first turn on your left.
    (C) The switch is by the door.

31. Why did the manufacturer stop producing this model?
    (A) There were design problems.
    (B) They always stop at the corner.
    (C) She models clothes.

32. I'll send the contracts in an e-mail attachment.
    (A) I wonder why I didn't receive them.
    (B) Never trust Kyle to do your business.
    (C) OK, send them to my work e-mail.

33. Are time sheets due at the end of the month?
    (A) Yes, I asked him.
    (B) No, there's no more time to do it.
    (C) Yes, they must be filled out by the thirtieth.

34. How far is the train station?
    (A) Approximately twenty feet long.
    (B) About fifteen minutes away.
    (C) Five feet tall, I think.

35. Why isn't his number in the directory?
    (A) You should ask the police officer for directions.
    (B) Because he's a new employee.
    (C) Yes, I'd like to have a copy of the directory.

36. Where can we buy a cup of coffee?
    (A) There's a cafeteria next door.
    (B) We're out of clean cups.
    (C) I bought this coffee in Brazil.

37. How did you hear about my promotion?
    (A) There isn't too much here.
    (B) Your secretary told me.
    (C) I don't hear very well.

38. Who turned the copy machine off?
    (A) I turned the coffee machine off.
    (B) It goes off automatically.
    (C) He turned my copy in.

39. Mr. Green canceled my business trip.
    (A) He must've had a good reason.
    (B) He left a tip last time.
    (C) He's speaking at the luncheon.

40. Can you type this letter before you go home?
    (A) Yes, after I go home.
    (B) I let her go home.
    (C) Yes, I'll do it now.

PART 3 (PAGE 160)

Questions 41 through 43 refer to the following conversation.

Woman	Look, I bought a new coat. It's by a famous designer—I forget who. Originally it was $1,525, but now that winter's over, I got it on sale for only $700.
Man	Really? But I liked your old one.
Woman	I did too, but it was too small. And this one is very stylish.
Man	Well, the new one's nice. I like that green color, and at half-off it's a real bargain.

Questions 44 through 46 refer to the following conversation.

Man	Mr. Kim's flight should get in at three. It left at eleven, and it's a four-hour flight.
Woman	Do you want me to get him at the airport in the car, or will he take the subway?
Man	He said he'd take the subway downtown. He'll go right to his hotel, then meet us for dinner later at the restaurant.

Woman	I hope he knows how to get to the restaurant from the hotel. If not, I guess he can always call one of us on our cell phones and ask for directions.

Questions 47 through 49 refer to the following conversation.

Man	Look, there's tuna on the menu. I've been craving tuna for a long time. Oh, but I see it's $35. Why does fish cost so much?
Woman	Well it shouldn't cost that much. That's too expensive for seafood even if it is tuna. Maybe you should try something else.
Man	You're probably right. The shrimp sounds nice, and the price is reasonable. I think I'll have that instead.
Woman	Oh, with lemon and garlic. That does sound good. I think I'll order the same.

Questions 50 through 52 refer to the following conversation.

Man	The train should be here in about five more minutes.
Woman	Good. I've been waiting half an hour. I was getting ready to walk.
Man	Don't do that. It's too far. The train'll be here soon.
Woman	I hope so. I don't like to get home after dark.
Man	I know what you mean. Sometimes when I leave work it's already dark out. It feels like I missed the whole day.

Questions 53 through 55 refer to the following conversation.

Man	Please send this envelope by express mail. It has to arrive as soon as possible.
Woman	All right. I'll do it before lunch, as soon as I've finished typing this report. Do you mind telling me what's in it?
Man	You can take a look if you want. It's just a letter, and I haven't sealed it yet. Don't worry. It doesn't contain any

confidential information. The only reason I'm in a rush to get it out is that I was supposed to send it last week. It's been sitting on my desk for days because I kept forgetting to look up the address.

Woman Oh, just a letter. Well, anyhow, don't worry about it. It'll get there by tomorrow morning.

Questions 56 through 58 refer to the following conversation.

Woman Can we meet in my office on Tuesday morning?

Man I have a dentist appointment then. How about Wednesday?

Woman I'll be at a conference all day. How about Thursday afternoon?

Man That will work out fine. I'll have my secretary send you photocopies of those contracts to look at before we meet.

Woman Great! That will save me from having to read them in front of you. I don't want to waste any of your time.

Questions 59 through 61 refer to the following conversation.

Man Did you hear that Mark's starting a new job next week?

Woman Yes, he told me. His old job just didn't pay him enough.

Man I know. He worked there for 13 years, and in all that time they gave him only one or two raises.

Woman He's lucky to have a new job, then. But if I were he, I'd take a month's vacation before starting it.

Questions 62 through 64 refer to the following conversation.

Man OK, you're sending this envelope to Chicago, right? Does it contain jewelry, cash, or any other valuables?

Woman No, it's just photographs.

Man Fine. That'll be seven dollars for express mail or three dollars regular.

Woman I'll pay for express. That doesn't include insurance, does it? I don't need insurance. They aren't exactly originals.

Man No, it's extra for insurance. We only recommend insuring packages with contents over $50. Anything less than that isn't worth the trouble or expense of tracking.

Questions 65 through 67 refer to the following conversation.

Woman What time would you like your wake-up call tomorrow, sir? Should I arrange it for 8:30 again?

Man No, make it 6:45. I have a breakfast meeting downstairs at seven. It doesn't take me much to get ready in the morning.

Woman All right. And would you like to order dinner in your room tonight? I could have Samuel bring you up a copy of tonight's specials if you like.

Man No, thank you, that won't be necessary. I already ate a few hours ago. I'm going to go relax in the pool now. I'll be down in a minute to pick up a towel.

Questions 68 through 70 refer to the following conversation.

Woman Mrs. Davis called. She says she won't be here until eleven.

Man Her train must have been delayed again.

Woman I think so. Well, as long as she's here no later than one this afternoon.

Man Oh, yes. The meeting starts at one. She has to be here for that.

Woman If for some reason she gets in later than one, we'll have to postpone the meeting until she arrives. It's crucial that Mrs. Davis hears everything the board has to say.

Part 4 (page 163)

Questions 71 through 73 refer to the following talk.

Good morning, class. I'd like to remind you that your midterm exam's just three days away, on Friday. The exam will cover everything we've read in the book up to Chapter 30. Please arrive for the exam on time, and please come prepared. You must write your exam in pen, not pencil, so please bring pens that work. You will not be allowed to look at your textbooks or your notes during the exam, so leave those things at home. Today we'll review some of the material for the exam. Are there any questions?

Questions 74 through 76 refer to the following weather report.

Good evening. This is Bob Jones with the weather update. We'll have cloudy skies tonight, with low temperatures around 11 degrees Celsius. Tomorrow morning brings showers, with rain continuing throughout the weekend, both Saturday and Sunday. High temperatures on both those days will be around 15 degrees Celsius. It looks like we'll have a bit of sunshine early next week, with the rain ending Monday morning. Then we'll have clear skies through Wednesday.

Questions 77 through 79 refer to the following news report.

Two lion cubs were born at the City Zoo early today. The announcement was made this afternoon by Marcia Stuart, the zoo director. According to Stuart, the zoo's lion specialist has created a special habitat for the new babies. During the first weekend of next month, when the babies are old enough for public viewing, the zoo will have a number of special activities to introduce them to the public, including games and educational activities for children. Everyone is invited, so put it on your calendar.

Questions 80 through 82 refer to the following announcement.

Good morning, ladies and gentlemen. This is your captain speaking. Welcome aboard flight 15 from New York to Los Angeles. Our flight should take about five and a half hours, putting us in Los Angeles at noon, just in time for lunch. Flight attendants will be coming around soon to serve beverages to everyone. We also have magazines and pillows and blankets available on request. Enjoy the flight.

Questions 83 through 85 refer to the following advertisement.

Beautiful Interiors Home Store has everything you need to make your home comfortable—sofas, tables, desks, beds, carpets, and more. And we sell it all at a price you can afford. Join us this week for our special anniversary sale. All home office furniture is 30 percent off. Hurry on down. Sale ends Friday. Visit us at our new location at the new City Plaza Mall, right next to the Central Hotel, and very close to the downtown subway station. We're open Tuesday through Sunday. Closed Monday.

Questions 86 through 88 refer to the following message.

You have reached the law offices of Stevenson and Park. Our regular office hours are 7:30 to 4:30, Monday through Friday. To speak with Ms. Stevenson, press 1. To speak with Mr. Park, press 2. To make an appointment, press three for the office assistant. For billing questions, press three also. If this is an emergency and you're calling outside of regular office hours, please hang up and dial 657-555-0983. Thank you.

Questions 89 through 91 refer to the following news report.

Heavy snowfall last night caused several minor traffic accidents and was also the reason for the closing of the Green River Bridge. The bridge had just been opened last month after a year-long reconstruction project. Road conditions are still icy today, and the bridge will remain closed until Wednesday. Most city buses and trains will also be delayed today because of the icy conditions. Warmer temperatures and sunny skies on Tuesday should help melt the ice and clear up the roads.

Questions 92 through 94 refer to the following talk.

Good evening. Our speaker tonight is Dr. James Jones, professor of chemistry at National University. Dr. Jones is a naturalist by hobby, and will speak to us about his recent hiking trip in the Amazon rain forest of Brazil, where he went in search of wild orchids and other exotic flowers. Following the talk, Dr. Jones will answer your questions. Also, if you haven't already, please enjoy his wonderful photographs of his trip on display in the lobby.

Questions 95 through 97 refer to the following talk.

Good morning, everyone. Welcome to the tour of the City Museum of Art. Please line up over here, and have your ticket ready. If you don't have a ticket, get one now. They cost just seven dollars. Don't worry, we'll wait for you. Now then, today we'll look at modern paintings and sculpture in the second floor galleries and works by local artists, including painting and prints, on the third floor. But we'll begin in the main gallery right here on the ground floor, looking at portraits. Is everybody ready? All right, let's go.

Questions 98 through 100 refer to the following announcement.

Attention passengers. This train will be arriving in Central Station in four minutes. This will be the final stop. All passengers must exit the train at Central Station. If you have checked your baggage, please pick it up right outside the gate after exiting the train. All baggage will be brought to the gate within ten minutes of arrival in the station. Have your claim check ready to show to the baggage agent. Any passengers needing assistance disembarking from the train, please ask the conductor for help. Thank you for riding National Railroad.

AUDIOSCRIPT
PRACTICE TEST ONE

PART 1 (PAGE 300)

Example:

   (A) They're leaving the room.
   (B) They're turning on the machine.
   (C) They're standing near the table.
   (D) They're reading the newspaper.

1. (A) The conference is in session.
   (B) The movie is about to begin.
   (C) The concert hall is empty.
   (D) The attendees are standing.

2. (A) They're wading through the water.
   (B) They're filling the tanks with gas.
   (C) They're playing on the field.
   (D) They're walking through the facility.

3. (A) The man is taking a nap.
   (B) The map is in the book.
   (C) The geography book is on the shelf.
   (D) The man is putting a pin in the map.

4. (A) Two purses are next to the chart.
   (B) One man holds a briefcase.
   (C) Both men are standing by the whiteboard.
   (D) The men are laughing.

5. (A) They're meeting at the street corner.
   (B) They're working with computers.
   (C) They're counting their money.
   (D) They're operating heavy equipment.

6. (A) He's closing the doors.
   (B) He's looking in the drawers.
   (C) He's watching the clock.
   (D) He's holding a box.

7. (A) They're sitting on the desk.
   (B) They're eating a piece of cake.
   (C) They're looking at a piece of paper.
   (D) They're using a calculator.

8. (A) The coffeemaker is beside the sink.
   (B) The pots are being washed.
   (C) They're drinking coffee.
   (D) The water left a spot.

9. (A) The shelves are under the table.
   (B) The lamp is above the workbench.
   (C) The technician is at her desk.
   (D) The components are in the showroom.

10. (A) They're buying meat.
   (B) They're having a discussion.
   (C) They're shelving books.
   (D) They're wiping the table.

PART 2 (PAGE 306)

Example:

   Where is the meeting room?
   (A) To meet the new director.
   (B) It's the first room on the right.
   (C) Yes, at two o'clock.

11. Where's the newsstand?
   (A) The news never changes.
   (B) There's one in the lobby.
   (C) I'll stand here.

12. Who is at the door?
   (A) The guests have just arrived.
   (B) The doorman is retired.
   (C) The door is green.

13. What do you need from the store?
   (A) Just some milk and bread.
   (B) The store is open until nine.
   (C) He needs to store his bicycle.

14. Why did your broker call you?
   (A) He suggested I sell my stock.
   (B) He was broke.
   (C) I telephoned my brother.

15. When do you want to eat?
   (A) As soon as we finish lunch.
   (B) Yes, I eat meat.
   (C) Whenever you're hungry.

16. Who received an extra paycheck?
   (A) The customer paid his check.
   (B) I received two paychecks.
   (C) She reviewed the accounts payable.

17. I don't have anything to wear to the retirement party.
    (A) It's in the lobby of the office building.
    (B) You don't have to wear anything fancy.
    (C) He hasn't been with the company that long.

18. Who is on the phone?
    (A) She recently installed a new phone system.
    (B) We have a new telephone.
    (C) The receptionist is talking to a customer.

19. When did they complete the project?
    (A) They bought the complete edition.
    (B) It will take two more years.
    (C) They finished it last night.

20. Why is he leaving the company?
    (A) He was fired.
    (B) The guests had to leave early.
    (C) He lives near the company.

21. Is this the last bus?
    (A) No, there's one more after this.
    (B) Yes, it lasts three hours.
    (C) Yes, the bus goes to the station.

22. Who are you expecting?
    (A) I expect it will rain.
    (B) A package from the office supply store.
    (C) The computer saleswoman is coming at one.

23. Who's that man over there?
    (A) He's my supervisor.
    (B) Yes, he's standing over there.
    (C) The men usually go there for lunch.

24. What is her profession?
    (A) The professor is not here now.
    (B) She's a marketing specialist.
    (C) All of them are professionals.

25. I understand you have a new business partner this year.
    (A) Yes, his name is Chris Burns.
    (B) We've been married for ten years.
    (C) I can explain it again if you like.

26. Where were you this morning?
    (A) They'll come back tomorrow morning.
    (B) You look best in the morning.
    (C) I was in a meeting all morning.

27. We are going to start billing on the first day of the month.
    (A) They sent an invoice on the thirtieth.
    (B) I'd prefer January or February.
    (C) OK, I'll notify our clients.

28. Can we start the meeting now?
    (A) This is a convenient place.
    (B) Yesterday we met all day.
    (C) No, not everyone has arrived yet.

29. Don't forget to make those reservations.
    (A) I thought you were going to make them.
    (B) We'll paint and put new carpets in.
    (C) He always remembers to collect our money.

30. Who wants the newspaper?
    (A) Not me, thank you. I read it already.
    (B) She's a reporter.
    (C) Yes, the copier is out of place.

31. Who is listening to the radio?
    (A) The news comes on at six.
    (B) I am. Is it too loud?
    (C) Yes, we should all listen carefully.

32. What equipment are we missing?
    (A) Our team is short one player.
    (B) We're missing the pump engine and pipes.
    (C) The results of the experiment are lost.

33. Where did you send the letter?
    (A) I'll send it out now.
    (B) I sent it to his office address.
    (C) I wouldn't let her go alone.

34. Whom are you waiting to see?
    (A) I want to see the office manager.
    (B) You waited for an hour.
    (C) The boat is at sea.

35. When will the rain stop?
    (A) The bus will stop at your corner.
    (B) It'll rain tomorrow.
    (C) It's expected to stop tonight.

36. You put the new supplies away, didn't you?
    (A) Yes, I put them in the supply room.
    (B) You can put them anywhere.
    (C) No, I didn't like the new ones.

37. When will the building be finished?
    (A) The architect is Finnish.
    (B) The building has seven stories.
    (C) The contractor says in three months.

38. I'll forward this joke to your personal e-mail address.
    (A) James is the best person to ask.
    (B) Thanks. I can't read jokes at work.
    (C) I thought it was really funny.

39. Why isn't the photocopier working?
    (A) We had our photos taken.
    (B) The electricity is off.
    (C) She copied my work.

40. How large is your staff?
    (A) Yes, we have too much stuff.
    (B) My staff works very efficiently.
    (C) We have twelve people.

PART 3 (PAGE 307)

Questions 41 through 43 refer to the following conversation.

Woman: One new pair of shoes comes to seventeen seventy-five.

Man: I don't have any cash, but here's my checkbook. Will you take a personal check?

Woman: Yes, but I'll need to see a credit card for identification. I'm afraid it's a store policy.

Man: Really? Then I'll just go ahead and pay with the credit card.

Woman: Whichever is easier for you, sir. We accept all major credit cards with a valid expiration date.

Questions 44 through 46 refer to the following conversation.

Man: How long will it take this package to arrive in China?

Woman: Six days by first class and twelve days by second class.

Man: Mail it first class, and insure it for a thousand dollars. It contains jewelry.

Woman: That will be nine dollars for postage and six dollars for the insurance, so your total is fifteen.

Questions 47 through 49 refer to the following conversation.

Woman: The copy machine broke again this morning. That's the fourth time this month.

Man: Don't worry. The repairman will be here tomorrow. He was supposed to come today, but there was a problem with the company truck. He's getting a rental car in the morning, and he hopes to be in first thing in the afternoon to fix the machine.

Woman: But I need these reports copied before the meeting tomorrow. I guess I'll have to go to the photocopy store on the first floor.

Man: It's not there anymore. But there's one across the street. You could go there.

Questions 50 through 52 refer to the following conversation.

Man: It feels like I've been waiting forever. I hope the bus gets here soon.

Woman: Me too. I'm far from home, and it looks like it might rain.

Man: Yes, it's very cloudy, but at least it's not cold. I've been waiting 15 minutes already, so the bus should be here any time now.

Woman: Well, you can never count on this transit system. I wish I lived closer to work so I could just walk home instead.

Questions 53 through 55 refer to the following conversation.

Man: Your vacation starts Tuesday, doesn't it? I envy you. Will you be gone a week this time?

Woman: Two weeks, actually. Can you believe it? We're going to New York.

Man: Really? I thought you liked quiet places like the mountains.

Woman   Actually, we usually go to the beach, but we decided to take a different kind of trip this time.

Questions 56 through 58 refer to the following conversation.

Man   Mr. Kim wasn't at this morning's meeting. I hope he isn't sick.

Woman   No, he's out of town till next week on a business trip.

Man   The meeting didn't go well at all. It started late, and very few people showed up. In fact, out of 15 people only 7 showed.

Woman   I hope things go better at next month's meeting.

Questions 59 through 61 refer to the following conversation.

Woman   I'd like to open a savings account, please.

Man   Certainly. Just fill out this form. You can do it now or bring it back later.

Woman   I can do it now. I'd like to use this $500 check for my initial deposit.

Man   Great. Just sign it on the back, and write the amount on the deposit slip.

Woman   Okay. Deposit slip. Now, which one is that, the pink one or the green one?

Man   Sorry, I should've mentioned that. The deposit slip's always pink. If you're ever in doubt, just look at the bottom left-hand corner of the slip. That will tell you what type of slip it is.

Questions 62 through 64 refer to the following conversation.

Man   We're not driving to work in all this snow.

Woman   You're right. It's dangerous. We'll take the train.

Man   Is today Wednesday? I have a conference call at ten. We have to hurry.

Woman   We'll leave as soon as you've finished eating. The next train leaves in 25 minutes, and that should get us there in plenty of time.

Questions 65 through 67 refer to the following conversation.

Man   We're all sold out of newspapers. Try the hotel across the street.

Woman   Oh, that's all right. I'll take this magazine instead.

Man   That'll be four fifty. Do you want any candy or gum today?

Woman   Just the magazine is fine. I need some reading material while I wait for my dentist appointment. The magazines at the dentist's are always at least a year old.

Questions 68 through 70 refer to the following conversation.

Woman   Do you eat here often?

Man   About once a week. Here, try some bread.

Woman   It's delicious. I could eat here every day. How's the soup here?

Man   It's very good, but I think I'll try the fried chicken today.

Woman   Well, I'm glad you introduced me to this place. It looks like they not only have healthy choices but also decent prices. I'm getting tired of the same old fast-food hamburgers.

PART 4 (PAGE 310)

Questions 71 through 73 refer to the following business announcement.

Today the officers of the company are announcing revisions on longstanding policies regarding health benefits, security procedures, and off-site training programs. The most significant change has been in our wellness program. In the past, employees with illnesses lasting more than four days were required to bring a note from their doctors. Now, no excuse is required regardless of the length of illness.

Questions 74 through 76 refer to the following special announcement.

Stay away from the burning building. I repeat, stay away from the burning building. Firefighters need room to do their job properly. Please stay on the other side of the street so that emergency personnel can get through. Do not interfere with the emergency crew by asking questions or trying to help. Police will have no choice but to apprehend anyone who gets in the way. Keep your children and pets as far from the premises as possible to avoid smoke inhalation.

Questions 77 through 79 refer to the following news report.

The Space Administration has announced its plans to put a canine on Mars. It's more than a dog in space, it's a dog on Mars. What this animal will do there, we can't imagine. Is there even water on that planet? I imagine the space program will provide some tasty treats for the first pet on Mars. It seems like a waste of money to us, but what do we know? This is the first program of its kind, and let's hope it's the last.

Questions 80 through 82 refer to the following news report.

After yesterday's run of bad news, there is finally some good news from the Presidential Palace. The president and his wife became parents for the second time today. A baby boy was born at General Hospital at 5:43 A.M., according to staff doctors. Only the mother will be able to rest; the president must leave immediately to fly to Belgium for a noon meeting. He hopes to return to his wife's side by early evening. When asked if he wanted more children, he said he would like three or four, but no more. Certainly not five.

Questions 83 through 85 refer to the following advertisement.

Do you want to watch television but don't know what's on? You need the program guide *TV Day-by-Day*. We'll give a one-year subscription to *TV Day-by-Day* to the first ten people who buy a new television set today. This offer applies for all models, from black-and-white 10-inch TVs to 42-inch flat screens. Just think, with *TV Day-by-Day* you can cancel the local newspaper that you never get around to reading and save up to $10 dollars a week.

Questions 86 through 88 refer to the following recorded announcement.

You have reached a nonworking number. If you would like to make a call, please hang up and try again. If you would like to check the number you are dialing, please dial 4-1-1 for directory assistance. Don't forget to add the area code to numbers outside the downtown core. Long-distance charges do not apply to local phone calls that require area codes.

Questions 89 through 91 refer to the following weather report.

Last week's rainy weather is behind us. The cool, windy weather that we were expecting last Monday and Tuesday never happened. You must think we don't know what we're talking about. Well, I'll tell you this and I am sure of it. The warm weather that we're experiencing now will continue for the rest of the week. So this Friday and Saturday, get outside and enjoy it. By Sunday, the temperature will drop and rain is once again in our forecast. And lots of it. You can expect up to 4 inches of rain on Sunday and Monday.

Questions 92 through 94 refer to the following announcement.

Don't just sit there playing with your pencil. Push that chair back from your desk. Stand up and walk over to Office Supplies, Inc. No, don't walk. Run. This sale started Tuesday, and we've already run out of many of our sale items. We still have high-quality paper and envelopes remaining. Red, blue, green, and, of course, white. We have all colors but yellow on sale. So don't wait. Today, Friday, you can take an additional 10 percent off of any item. Sale ends tomorrow. See you soon.

Questions 95 through 97 refer to the following news report.

Sparkles Jewelry Store in downtown Shelbyville was robbed last night just before closing. Over $10,000 in cash was taken, but valuables such as jewelry, watches, and computers were left behind. The robbery occurred at 8:55, according to police. Louise Jefferson, the store owner, was the only person present. All customers and staff had already left. Anyone with information about this crime should call police at 222-555-0800.

To leave an anonymous tip online for this or another crime, visit the local police web site.

Questions 98 through 100 refer to the following advertisement.

Please join us at the Sidewalk Café for a meal you won't forget. We're open for lunch and dinner, Tuesday through Sunday. Closed Monday. Think you can eat more than ten giant pancakes in half an hour or less? Take our pancake challenge and get your picture in our infamous photo gallery. Check out our Saturday brunch special—all-you-can-eat pancakes for just six dollars. We're located at 23 River Road, one block from the subway station. Free parking in back.

AUDIOSCRIPT
PRACTICE TEST TWO

PART 1 (PAGE 342)

Example:

  (A) They're leaving the room.
  (B) They're turning on the machine.
  (C) They're standing near the table.
  (D) They're reading the newspaper.

1. (A) The singers are rehearsing on the stage.
    (B) The scientists are analyzing the water.
    (C) The group is sitting around a table.
    (D) The lawyers are speaking before the court.

2. (A) The gardeners are tending the plants.
    (B) The couple is having lunch.
    (C) The cooks are preparing the meal.
    (D) The farmers are growing food.

3. (A) She's having her eyes examined.
    (B) She's speaking into a microphone.
    (C) She's looking through a microscope.
    (D) She's putting the equipment away.

4. (A) The flight attendants serve the meals.
    (B) The passengers board the aircraft.
    (C) The plane is taking off.
    (D) The train is in the station.

5. (A) The writer addresses his mail.
    (B) The shopper looks for a new dress.
    (C) The speaker addresses the audience.
    (D) The loudspeaker is in the back of the room.

6. (A) The statue is being cleaned for display.
    (B) The visitor is admiring the art in the museum.
    (C) The player is getting ready to leave the stadium.
    (D) The trainer is looking for the aquarium.

7. (A) She's conducting an orchestra.
    (B) She's looking for a new hat.
    (C) She's wearing protective clothing.
    (D) She's sewing her own clothes.

8. (A) The train is by the platform.
    (B) The plane is on the runway.
    (C) The passengers wait in the station.
    (D) The rain comes every afternoon.

9. (A) The players are on the field.
    (B) The match is on the table.
    (C) The fruit stand is large.
    (D) The balloon is in the air.

10. (A) They're having supper.
    (B) They're shaking hands.
    (C) They're handing out flags.
    (D) They're writing a book.

PART 2 (PAGE 348)

Example:

  Where is the meeting room?
  (A) To meet the new director.
  (B) It's the first room on the right.
  (C) Yes, at two o'clock.

11. Why does he visit Spain every summer?
    (A) Because he has relatives who live there.
    (B) The springs are so mild there.
    (C) Tourism is their number one industry.

12. How much does this book cost?
    (A) We are not taking reservations right now.
    (B) It's twenty-two dollars.
    (C) It reads quickly.

13. Who left their coffee on my desk?
    (A) I don't know.
    (B) I always have a cup of coffee in the afternoon.
    (C) My desk is so cluttered.

14. Too much staff is working right now.
    (A) We'll start working in a few minutes.
    (B) They're driving, not walking.
    (C) I'll send two people home.

15. When does the express train run?
    (A) It is the fastest.
    (B) We usually go jogging every other day.
    (C) It leaves here on the hour.

16. Could you tell me how to get to the National Museum?
    (A) Take the orange line to subway stop 29.
    (B) It is far away from here.
    (C) It has many priceless pieces of art.

17. I think Marcy is ready to become a store manager.
    (A) Does she have the money to buy it?
    (B) Wasn't Ellen in charge yesterday?
    (C) Do you think she has enough experience?

18. What kind of books do you read?
    (A) I like nonfiction.
    (B) I go to the library.
    (C) I like to read before I go to bed.

19. Why don't we look over these figures?
    (A) I am on a diet.
    (B) I can't do that right now.
    (C) Maybe you can see.

20. Whose shoes are these?
    (A) I find them quite easy.
    (B) We might have to sue them.
    (C) They're mine.

21. Where is the television cable?
    (A) It's on the workbench.
    (B) I like to watch TV when I get home.
    (C) We should be able to help you.

22. What is your personal identification number?
    (A) Our address is 125 North 52nd St.
    (B) It's 3256.
    (C) The personnel department handles employee problems.

23. What did you do with the inventory sheets?
    (A) They're on my desk.
    (B) We haven't made the beds.
    (C) We came up with many new innovations.

24. What kind of dressing would you like on your salad?
    (A) That probably is too big for me.
    (B) I prefer to wear work pants.
    (C) Oil and vinegar will be fine.

25. Can you take me to the airport?
    (A) Most flights leave before 8 P.M.
    (B) Yes, but it will cost you an extra five dollars.
    (C) The air pollution is worst in the summer.

26. Is there anyone who can translate this?
    (A) The order will be transported to another branch.
    (B) No one has a watch.
    (C) Maybe Mr. Baker can.

27. I'm not going to finish the sales report on time.
    (A) Yes, that's the deadline.
    (B) It was five hours late.
    (C) I can give you an extension.

28. Which files did you transfer?
    (A) All the ones that I had.
    (B) The hard drive on this computer is full.
    (C) You don't need to change subways.

29. What did the president say about the new joint venture?
    (A) He didn't say much.
    (B) This connection is not very good.
    (C) The election campaign was a success.

30. I'm still waiting to see the family doctor.
    (A) But your appointment was an hour ago.
    (B) I'll be OK. It's just a mild flu.
    (C) My daughter's still in medical school.

31. Would you mind getting me a cup of coffee?
    (A) I don't drink coffee.
    (B) It's my pleasure.
    (C) We usually drink it with cream and sugar.

32. Do those components come from Asia?
    (A) I don't know how old they are.
    (B) Our opponents are from Japan.
    (C) Most of them are imported from Eastern Europe.

33. How far away is the car rental company?
    (A) It's about two miles down this road.
    (B) All of our automobiles are gone.
    (C) We only sell cars.

34. Can you give me the number for Post Modern Design?
    (A) Our sign was posted last week.
    (B) The address is 2525 North Sherman Avenue.
    (C) The number is 555-9854.

35. Actually, I asked for a return ticket.
    (A) Sorry, I thought you said one way.
    (B) No, I'm not coming back.
    (C) Don't forget to book your trip.

36. Which would Mr. Jenkins prefer, the blue tie or the green one?
    (A) He usually wears slippers.
    (B) Blue, I think. He never wears green.
    (C) I'll try the green one on.

37. When will the applicants get here?
    (A) She applied for that job over two months ago.
    (B) You must apply direct pressure for at least ten minutes.
    (C) They should start arriving around two o'clock.

38. How old is that chair?
    (A) It's only a few years old.
    (B) The chairman is well over sixty years old.
    (C) The table can seat eight people comfortably.

39. Why is your face so red?
    (A) I've been out in the sun too long.
    (B) I walk at a slow pace.
    (C) I read that article this morning.

40. What is your purpose in coming here?
    (A) I wasn't listening.
    (B) I want to interview you.
    (C) You can go whenever you want to.

PART 3 (PAGE 349)

Questions 41 through 43 refer to the following conversation.

Man	I'm bored. Lets go to the movies.
Woman	OK. Do you want to see that comedy at the theater downtown?
Man	That's a good idea. It starts at seven, so we should leave here by six thirty.
Woman	OK, but it's six fifteen now. We'd better hurry.
Man	It's not a big deal if we miss the first 15 minutes. All we'll really miss are the previews for upcoming movies.

Questions 44 through 46 refer to the following conversation.

Man	I'm sorry, Mrs. Kowalski is in a meeting and can't take any calls just now. I can take a message, or I can try to answer your questions.
Woman	That's OK. I'll call later. When's a good time?
Man	You could call later this afternoon or any time tomorrow.
Woman	I'm leaving work early today because I have an appointment. I'll try her first thing tomorrow morning. What time does she usually come in?
Man	She's usually here by 8:30, but it all depends on traffic.

Questions 47 through 49 refer to the following conversation.

Man	I think at least one hundred people are coming to our wedding reception. Or possibly more. Tell the caterer there might be more people coming.
Woman	All right. I'll tell her to be ready for more guests. Now, do we want the fish dinner or the chicken? Or we could go vegetarian.
Man	None of that. I want meat at my wedding. Let's order the steak.
Woman	The steak. OK, I hadn't thought of that. You're right. It's our wedding, and steak is our favorite, so I think that's what we should have. I'll let the caterer know that we've made a decision.

Man   I can have your film ready in an hour, but it'll be half the price if you pick it up tomorrow.

Woman   This afternoon suits me better. I'll pick it up after lunch and pay the higher price.

Man   All right. Now, there are thirty-six photographs on this roll so it comes out to seventeen dollars.

Woman   Seventeen dollars! That's a lot! I guess I haven't brought photos in to be developed for a long time. I usually use my digital camera these days. I hope these pictures turn out for that price.

Questions 53 through 55 refer to the following conversation.

Woman   I spent all day Sunday at the library looking up magazine articles online.

Man   I should've gone with you. I have to do research for a report due Friday.

Woman   I'm sorry I didn't tell you I was going then, but I'm going again tonight. Do you want to come with me this time?

Man   I should, but maybe not. I'm really tired. I'd probably just end up falling asleep in a book or something. Thanks for asking, though.

Questions 56 through 58 refer to the following conversation.

Man   You should put on your boots. It's still snowing.

Woman   Fine idea. I can change into my dress shoes once we get to the dinner.

Man   Are we walking or taking a train?

Woman   Walking? Not in this weather. Anyhow, let's hurry. It's late.

Man   I can see that you don't want to be late tonight, but you really should think about walking

more. Just because it's winter doesn't mean your body doesn't need the fresh air. I'd walk everywhere if I had the time.

Questions 59 through 61 refer to the following conversation.

Woman   All club members are entitled to use all the exercise equipment in this room. If you want to go in the pool, it's right through that door.

Man   Oh, there's a pool? I didn't realize that. Swimming is such great exercise, and it's also refreshing after a long day of work.

Woman   Yes, and our club members say ours is one of the warmest and cleanest pools in town.

Man   OK. Is it all right if I look around for an hour?

Woman   That's fine. Stay as long as you like. We don't close until eight. If you need any more information, I'll be in my office downstairs.

Questions 62 through 64 refer to the following conversation.

Man   This new theater's really nice, and the seats are so comfortable.

Woman   And the ticket prices really aren't bad. They were just one hundred and fifteen dollars a piece.

Man   One hundred and fifteen a piece?! You shouldn't have spent so much. That's way too much money to see a play.

Woman   It's not too much for orchestra seats like these. Please don't lecture me.

Questions 65 through 67 refer to the following conversation.

Man   I got the notebooks and envelopes you wanted. The store was out of those special pens, so I had to order them.

Woman   Really? Will they be here by the end of the week?

Man	The man said two days, so, Wednesday. I ordered five dozen. I hope that's right.
Woman	Yes, that's what I asked for.
Man	Oh, I'm so glad. I must admit, I forgot to write the order down, and I wasn't sure if you wanted five or ten dozen.

Questions 68 through 70 refer to the following conversation.

Woman	Why do you have to be at the office before eight tomorrow? Do you have a breakfast meeting?
Man	No. I have to finish that report before Mr. Park gets back from his trip.
Woman	I thought he came back last night. That's what it says in your daybook. At least, that's what I thought I read.
Man	No, it's always been tomorrow afternoon. Anyhow, if I leave home at 6:30, I should be at the office in time. There shouldn't be too much traffic on a Friday.

PART 4 (PAGE 352)

Questions 71 through 73 refer to the following announcement.

Attention! Attention! Will Mr. Bajarin come to New Air's courtesy desk by the ticketing counter immediately. We have an urgent message for you. That's Mr. Bajarin. If you cannot locate the courtesy desk, please ask the customer service representative from any international airlines desk to help you. An airport security guard should also be able to direct you to our counter. Please advance with your luggage immediately. Thank you.

Questions 74 through 76 refer to the following announcement.

Looking to your left, you will see the first religious building in El Kaban, the Damatian temple. This temple was built to the north of the marketplace on a 50-by-100-meter base. This temple was built in the name of the emperor Damatian who claimed himself to be both emperor and god. During excavations, only the head and an arm of a Damatian statue could be found. Considering the head's

dimension of 1.6 meters, it is estimated that the height of the whole statue was 7 meters.

Questions 77 through 79 refer to the following message.

You have reached the office of Randall Svetlanovich. I am not able to take your call at present. I am either away for lunch or in a meeting. If this is a personal phone call, please try my cell phone number. If you want to leave a message on my voice mail, press 1 now. If you want to speak with the receptionist, please wait and your call will be forwarded to him. Thank you for calling, and I look forward to speaking with you soon.

Questions 80 through 82 refer to the following weather announcement.

It's going to be another beautiful day in Sunny Valley. We have a high pressure system covering our region today, so expect blue skies with only a few light clouds, and temperatures in the 70s. It's a nice day to get outside and have a picnic. Don't forget to apply your sunblock today, as the UV rays are extra strong at this time of year. Doctors recommend sunblock with SPF 30 protection for adults and up to SPF 40 for young children.

Questions 83 through 85 refer to the following news item.

Mr. Joseph Robbins was apprehended by Argentinean authorities yesterday. Mr. Robbins has been sought by the police after fleeing the United States under accusations of tax evasion. Mr. Robbins has been living in Argentina under the alias Ricardo Ruiz and was employed as a florist. Argentinean authorities found out about Ruiz's real identity after receiving information from a local merchant. Mr. Robbins will be returned to the United States next week.

Questions 86 through 88 refer to the following announcement.

I just want to add that the time to be on the bus in the morning is 7:10 A.M. I understand that everyone will be late from time to time, but a few people are making a habit of arriving three to five minutes late every day. Other employees are waiting at other stops on the route after our pickup. They are on time and sometimes are waiting in the rain for a bus that is late. Please be considerate and make it to the bus on time.

Questions 89 through 91 refer to the following advertisement.

Reiser and Sons announces its annual spring weekend sale. Beginning Saturday, we will have reductions on everything . . . that's right . . . everything in the store. Adults' denim shorts and T-shirts have been marked down to only $9.95, with children's sizes a mere $7.98. Everything in our infants' and toddlers' sections is half price. Hundreds of bargains on everything. Sale ends Sunday.

Questions 92 through 94 refer to the following news report.

Heavy rains over the weekend caused major flooding throughout the area. Residents of downtown Riverdale had to leave their homes Saturday afternoon when flood waters rose over one and a half meters high. Everyone was able to evacuate safely, with no reports of accidents or injuries. The rain stopped Monday evening, and residents should be able to return home by Wednesday morning.

Questions 95 through 97 refer to the following message.

Thank you for calling Fly-By-Night Airlines. To hear a schedule of flights to Los Angeles, Honolulu, and Tokyo, press 1. To use our automated system to purchase tickets, press 2. To hear size limits on luggage, press 3. To listen to this month's in-flight movie schedule, press 4. To speak with an operator, please stay on the line.

Questions 98 through 100 refer to the following announcement.

The popular rock band, Heavy Stones, will play an outdoor concert in City Park this Saturday at 7:30. The rain date is Sunday at the same time. Tickets are free but required for entry. Pick up your tickets at City Hall or the public library by Friday. If you aren't familiar with this band, but think you might be interested in attending, visit the Heavy Stones web site. Here you'll be able to listen to sample tracks from their latest album, and read the band's biography.

ANSWER KEYS AND CONVERSION CHARTS

ANSWER KEY
LISTENING COMPREHENSION

PART 1: PHOTO

Photo 1 (page 4)

What Do You See?

A. 1. (N)
    2. (N)
    3. (N)
    4. (Y)
    5. (Y)

B. 1. (?)
    2. (?)
    3. (Y)
    4. (?)
    5. (Y)

Analyze This

1. (?)
2. (?)
3. (?)
4. (N)
5. (N)

Prepositions

1. on
2. next to
3. on
4. at
5. on

Similar Sounds

A. 1. (A)
    2. (B)
    3. (A)
    4. (A)
    5. (B)

B. 1. (A)
    2. (B)
    3. (B)
    4. (A)
    5. (B)

Extra Practice

This is one possible **sample answer**. Your answer may be completely different.

A woman is sitting at her desk, working on her computer. Her hand is on the keyboard, but she isn't typing right now. She is reading the monitor screen. She might be getting ready to print a document. There is a printer to the left of the monitor. We can see the cables that attach the monitor and keyboard to the computer.

Photo 2 (page 7)

What Do You See?

A. 1. (N)
    2. (N)
    3. (Y)
    4. (Y)
    5. (N)

B. 1. (?)
    2. (?)
    3. (Y)
    4. (Y)
    5. (Y)

Analyze This

1. (?)
2. (?)
3. (?)
4. (Y)
5. (N)

Prepositions

1. at
2. in
3. on
4. in, of
5. next to

Similar Sounds

A. 1. (A)
    2. (A)
    3. (B)
    4. (B)
    5. (A)

B. 1. (B)
    2. (A)
    3. (B)
    4. (A)
    5. (B)

Extra Practice

This is one possible **sample answer**. Your answer may be completely different.

Two customers are sitting at a table at an outdoor restaurant. The waitress is writing their order on a pad of paper. The table has an umbrella. It is covered with a clean, white tablecloth, and it has plates and glasses on it. There are a few other customers at the restaurant, but there are also many empty chairs.

Photo 3 (page 10)

What Do You See?

A.		B.	
1.	(N)	1.	(Y)
2.	(N)	2.	(?)
3.	(N)	3.	(Y)
4.	(Y)	4.	(Y)
5.	(Y)	5.	(?)

Analyze This

1. (?)
2. (N)
3. (?)
4. (?)
5. (?)

Prepositions

1. on, of
2. in, of
3. near
4. on
5. behind

Similar Sounds

A.		B.	
1.	(A)	1.	(A)
2.	(A)	2.	(A)
3.	(B)	3.	(B)
4.	(A)	4.	(A)
5.	(B)	5.	(A)

Extra Practice

This is one possible **sample answer**. Your answer may be completely different.

Two men are sitting at a table. They are having a conversation. They are wearing jackets, ties, and white shirts. One of them is wearing glasses, but the other one isn't. One man is holding a pen in his hand. The other man has his hand on a magazine. One man has been drinking water. His water bottle is open, and the cap is on the table. The other man hasn't drunk any water yet. His water bottle is full and the cap is still on it.

Photo 4 (page 13)

What Do You See?

A.		B.	
1.	(Y)	1.	(?)
2.	(N)	2.	(?)
3.	(N)	3.	(?)
4.	(Y)	4.	(?)
5.	(N)	5.	(Y)

Analyze This

1. (?)
2. (N)
3. (Y)
4. (Y)
5. (?)

Prepositions

1. next to
2. on
3. at
4. on
5. around

Similar Sounds

A.		B.	
1.	(A)	1.	(B)
2.	(B)	2.	(A)
3.	(B)	3.	(B)
4.	(A)	4.	(A)
5.	(A)	5.	(B)

Extra Practice

This is one possible **sample answer**. Your answer may be completely different.

A bus is stopped at the corner. Two women are waiting to get on it. One of them is wearing a dark coat and dark pants. The other is wearing light coat and light pants. There are several other people on the sidewalk. They are waiting for the traffic light to turn green so that they can cross the street. It is probably a cold day because all the people in the picture are wearing hats or scarves.

Photo 5 (page 16)

What Do You See?

A.		B.	
1.	(N)	1.	(?)
2.	(N)	2.	(Y)
3.	(Y)	3.	(?)
4.	(N)	4.	(?)
5.	(N)	5.	(Y)

Analyze This

1. (?)
2. (?)
3. (?)
4. (?)
5. (?)

Prepositions

1. beside
2. off
3. on
4. on
5. at

Similar Sounds

A.			B.	
1.	(B)	1.	(B)
2.	(A)	2.	(A)
3.	(B)	3.	(A)
4.	(A)	4.	(B)
5.	(A)	5.	(A)

Extra Practice

This is one possible **sample answer**. Your answer may be completely different.

A jet is sitting on the tarmac. We can see the tail of the jet but not the nose. It is not a very big jet. Everybody in the picture is wearing short-sleeved shirts, so it must be a warm day. Two passengers are getting off the plane. They must be important people because several agents have come out to meet them.

Photo 6 (page 19)

What Do You See?

A.			B.	
1.	(N)	1.	(Y)
2.	(N)	2.	(?)
3.	(N)	3.	(Y)
4.	(Y)	4.	(?)
5.	(Y)	5.	(Y)

Analyze This

1. (?)
2. (?)
3. (N)
4. (N)
5. (N)

Prepositions

1. in
2. behind
3. in, of
4. on
5. by

Similar Sounds

A.			B.	
1.	(A)	1.	(B)
2.	(B)	2.	(A)
3.	(A)	3.	(A)
4.	(B)	4.	(B)
5.	(A)	5.	(A)

Extra Practice

This is one possible **sample answer**. Your answer may be completely different.

The people are waiting in the airport to have their passports examined. They are standing in two lines and there is a barrier between the lines. There are not many people, so the lines are short. Some of the passengers are carrying shoulder bags. They will probably pick up the rest of their luggage after they pass through the passport control. One woman is pushing her baby in a stroller. She is happy that her baby is sleeping quietly. There is one other woman standing in line. The rest are men.

Photo 7 (page 22)

What Do You See?

A.			B.	
1.	(N)	1.	(Y)
2.	(Y)	2.	(Y)
3.	(N)	3.	(?)
4.	(N)	4.	(?)
5.	(N)	5.	(?)

Analyze This

1. (?)
2. (?)
3. (N)
4. (?)
5. (?)

Prepositions

1. in
2. in
3. by
4. to
5. on

Similar Sounds

A.			B.	
1.	(A)	1.	(B)
2.	(B)	2.	(A)
3.	(A)	3.	(A)
4.	(A)	4.	(B)
5.	(B)	5.	(A)

Extra Practice

This is one possible **sample answer**. Your answer may be completely different.

Two men are walking down the street on a rainy night. They are both wearing jackets and ties, so they are probably on the way home from work. They are both carrying umbrellas in their right hands and something else in their left hands. One man has a briefcase and the other is holding a flyer. There are several other people behind them, all carrying umbrellas. It is the end of the workday, and everyone is rushing through the rain to get to the subway station as quickly as possible.

Photo 8 (page 25)

What Do You See?

A. 1. (N)   B. 1. (?)
    2. (Y)   2. (?)
    3. (Y)   3. (Y)
    4. (N)   4. (?)
    5. (N)   5. (?)

Analyze This

1. (?)
2. (N)
3. (N)
4. (?)
5. (Y)

Prepositions

1. of
2. by
3. to
4. on
5. of

Similar Sounds

A. 1. (B)   B. 1. (A)
    2. (A)   2. (B)
    3. (B)   3. (A)
    4. (B)   4. (A)
    5. (A)   5. (B)

Extra Practice

This is one possible **sample answer**. Your answer may be completely different.

Four technicians are on the factory floor, working with a piece of equipment. It is a dangerous place to work, so they have to wear protective suits and protective hats. The piece of equipment is hanging from the ceiling. It is very large and heavy, so the cables that hold it have to be very strong. The piece of equipment is not very hot and not very dirty. Two of the technicians are touching it, but they aren't wearing protective gloves.

Photo Strategy Practice (page 28)

1. (A)   7. (A)
2. (A)   8. (A)
3. (B)   9. (C)
4. (A)   10. (D)
5. (A)   11. (B)
6. (A)   12. (A)

Review: Part 1 (page 35)

1. (B)   5. (A)
2. (A)   6. (C)
3. (D)   7. (A)
4. (C)   8. (C)

PART 2: QUESTION-RESPONSE

Statements (page 40)

Practice A

1. (B)   6. (C)
2. (A)   7. (B)
3. (B)   8. (A)
4. (A)   9. (C)
5. (C)   10. (B)

Practice B

1. Same: hard, yard
   Similar: umbrella, rain
   Opposite: hard, easy
   Sound similar: hard, yard; training, raining
2. Same: got, got; I, I
   Similar context: shoes, They
   Opposite: new, old
   Sound similar: new, news; choose, shoes, news
3. Same: work, work, work; doesn't, doesn't
   Similar: doesn't
   Opposite: doesn't, does
   Sound similar: pen, pencil
4. Same: John, John; seen, seen
   Similar: every day, all week; John, He, he
   Opposite: have, haven't
   Sound similar: weak, week; seen, seems
5. Same: like, like, like
   Similar: nice, friendly
   Opposite: Mary, he
   Sound similar: ice, nice, mice; personally, person
6. Same: find, find; I, I, I
   Similar: my keys, them
   Opposite: can't, can
   Sound similar: kind, find; keys, peas

7. Same: I, I, I
   Similar: meal, food; restaurant,
        eaten, meal
   Opposite: love, don't like
   Sound similar: rest, restaurant
8. Same: how, how, how; know, know; to, to
   Similar: swim, swimsuit
   Opposite: know, doesn't know
   Sound similar: swim, win;
        swim, swimsuit
9. Same: Susan, Susan
   Similar: night, midnight
   Opposite: does, doesn't
   Sound similar: midnight, fight, might;
        plane, flight (fight); plane, plain, train
10. Same: store, store; on, on; is, is
    Similar: Sunday, Monday, day
    Opposite: closed, open
    Sound similar: Sunday, fun day,
        someday; clothes, closed; shore, store

Practice C

1.	(d)	6.	(a)
2.	(g)	7.	(j)
3.	(b)	8.	(f)
4.	(i)	9.	(c)
5.	(e)	10.	(h)

Practice D

Possible answers:
1. You should see a dentist.
2. Let's hire a consultant.
3. You should install software protection.
4. It's too hot to dress up.
5. I'll send it for tomorrow morning delivery.
6. That's a long time to be away from work.
7. There's more in the storage room.
8. We had better increase sales.
9. That's at the other end of the station.
10. Don't worry. This product will last forever.

Practice E

1.	(A)	6.	(A)
2.	(A)	7.	(B)
3.	(B)	8.	(A)
4.	(C)	9.	(C)
5.	(B)	10.	(B)

Practice F

1.	(B)	6.	(B)
2.	(A)	7.	(C)
3.	(C)	8.	(A)
4.	(A)	9.	(B)
5.	(B)	10.	(A)

Who (page 44)

Practice A

1.	(A)	6.	(C)
2.	(C)	7.	(A)
3.	(C)	8.	(B)
4.	(B)	9.	(C)
5.	(A)	10.	(B)

Practice B

1. Same: on, on
   Similar: turn, turned
   Opposite: lights, dark
2. Same: office, office, office, office
   Similar: decisions, decided
3. Same: paper, paper
   Similar: ordered, asked for; put in the
        order, boxes, cartons
   Sound similar: paper, newspaper,
        wrapping paper, copy paper;
        two, twenty-two
4. Same: charge, charge; is, is; of, of
   Similar: advertising, ad
5. Same: memo, memo; going, going
6. Similar: sent, mail
   Sound similar: sent, cents
7. Same: desk, desk; folders, folders
8. Same: meeting, meeting; will, will; be, be
   Similar: meeting, conference
   Sound similar: meeting, eating
9. Same: article, article
   Opposite: read, written
10. Same: last, last; was, was
    Similar: last, lasted; leave, left

Practice C

1.	(i)	6.	(h)
2.	(e)	7.	(g)
3.	(f)	8.	(j)
4.	(d)	9.	(a)
5.	(b)	10.	(c)

Practice D

Possible answers:

1. The famous architect Michelangelo.
2. Kim Khoi.
3. The caterer.
4. My assistant.
5. Mr. Stevenson.
6. Almost everyone in the office.
7. Ms. Browne did.
8. Mr. Park.
9. Ms. Roberts can.
10. Some people from the office.

Practice E

1.	(B)	6.	(A)
2.	(A)	7.	(C)
3.	(C)	8.	(C)
4.	(A)	9.	(B)
5.	(B)	10.	(C)

Practice F

1.	(C)	6.	(B)
2.	(A)	7.	(B)
3.	(B)	8.	(C)
4.	(B)	9.	(C)
5.	(A)	10.	(A)

What (page 48)

Practice A

1.	(A)	6.	(C)
2.	(A)	7.	(A)
3.	(C)	8.	(B)
4.	(B)	9.	(B)
5.	(A)	10.	(A)

Practice B

1. Same: desk, desk, desk; on, on, on; his, his, his
2. Same: street, street; they, they; live, live, live
   Similar: street, Avenue
3. Similar: printer, print; order, ordered
   Sound similar: order, odor
4. Same: briefcase, briefcase
   Similar: cost, sale
   Sound similar: briefcase, briefly; cost, lost
5. Same: work, work, work; are, are
   Sound similar: doing, going
6. Same: store, store
   Sound similar: buy, by
7. Similar: lunch, sandwich, eat
   Sound similar: lunch, much
8. Same: tell, tell
   Sound similar: tell, sell
9. Same: meeting, meeting; at, at
   Sound similar: discuss, bus; will, we'll
10. Same: is, is; bag, bag
    Sound similar: bag, back

Practice C

1.	(d)	6.	(h)
2.	(b)	7.	(f)
3.	(e)	8.	(i)
4.	(a)	9.	(j)
5.	(c)	10.	(g)

Practice D

Possible answers:

1. A fax that just came in for you.
2. I love fish.
3. I went to the theater.
4. My keys.
5. Life in the early 1900s.
6. I usually have dinner with my family.
7. A black dress.
8. A package and three letters.
9. I dropped it and it broke.
10. They visited some museums.

Practice E

1.	(C)	6.	(C)
2.	(A)	7.	(A)
3.	(B)	8.	(B)
4.	(A)	9.	(B)
5.	(A)	10.	(C)

Practice F

1.	(B)	6.	(A)
2.	(A)	7.	(C)
3.	(B)	8.	(B)
4.	(A)	9.	(C)
5.	(C)	10.	(A)

When (page 53)

Practice A

1.	(C)	6.	(A)
2.	(A)	7.	(C)
3.	(C)	8.	(A)
4.	(A)	9.	(B)
5.	(B)	10.	(C)

Practice B

1. Same: France, France
   Similar: leaving, leaves
   Sound similar: France, since; leaving, living
2. Same: over, over
   Similar: meeting, meet
3. Same: check, check, check; we, we, we, we; expect, expect
   Sound similar: our, out; expect, check; thorough, tomorrow
4. Similar: turn, turned
   Sound similar: weather, whether
5. Same: project, project; be, be; finished, finished, finished
   Sound similar: project, predict
6. Same: arrive, arrive
   Sound similar: arrive, drive; plane, plan
7. Same: call, call; him, him, him
   Similar: call, calls
8. Same: lunch, lunch
9. Same: job, job; her, her
   Similar: start, began; job, work
10. Same: machine, machine
    Similar: copy, copies; fixed, repair
    Opposite: fixed, broken

Practice C

1.	(b)	6.	(e)
2.	(j)	7.	(a)
3.	(g)	8.	(h)
4.	(d)	9.	(f)
5.	(c)	10.	(i)

Practice D

Possible answers:
1. After lunch.
2. Next week.
3. Last year.
4. Two years ago.
5. In August.
6. Yesterday at the meeting.
7. In two or three weeks.
8. Next Friday evening.
9. In one year.
10. A week ago.

Practice E

1.	(B)	6.	(A)
2.	(A)	7.	(C)
3.	(A)	8.	(B)
4.	(B)	9.	(B)
5.	(A)	10.	(C)

Practice F

1.	(C)	6.	(A)
2.	(A)	7.	(A)
3.	(B)	8.	(B)
4.	(C)	9.	(C)
5.	(A)	10.	(A)

Where (page 57)

Practice A

1.	(B)	6.	(A)
2.	(A)	7.	(C)
3.	(A)	8.	(A)
4.	(C)	9.	(B)
5.	(B)	10.	(C)

Practice B

1. Sound similar: cafeteria, coffee
   Same: the, the
2. Same: waiting, waiting
   Sound similar: waiting, weigh; left, ten
3. Same: glasses, glasses
   Sound similar: glasses, glass; your, floor
4. Same: phone, phone; is, is, is
   Sound similar: phone, home
5. Same: conference, conference
   Similar: room, rooms
6. Same: hotel, hotel
   Sound similar: hotel, tell
7. Same: your, your; phone, phone
   Similar: leave, left; phone, phones
   Sound similar: cell, sells
8. Similar: work, works
   Sound similar: work, walk, park
9. Same: vacation, vacation
   Sound similar: vacation, vacant
10. Same: dinner, dinner
    Sound similar: dinner, thinner; late, place

Practice C

1.	(b)	6.	(h)
2.	(d)	7.	(g)
3.	(c)	8.	(j)
4.	(e)	9.	(f)
5.	(a)	10.	(i)

Practice D

Possible answers:
1. At the country club.
2. In the hall closet.
3. In the office next to mine.
4. At a used car dealership.
5. In the large file cabinet.
6. On the shelf.

7. From a catalog.
8. At Susan's house.
9. At home.
10. On that table.

Practice E

1.	(A)	6.	(A)
2.	(B)	7.	(C)
3.	(A)	8.	(B)
4.	(B)	9.	(C)
5.	(B)	10.	(A)

Practice F

1.	(C)	6.	(B)
2.	(B)	7.	(A)
3.	(C)	8.	(C)
4.	(C)	9.	(C)
5.	(A)	10.	(B)

Why (page 61)

Practice A

1.	(A)	6.	(A)
2.	(A)	7.	(C)
3.	(B)	8.	(B)
4.	(B)	9.	(B)
5.	(C)	10.	(C)

Practice B

1. Same: you, you; late, late
   Opposite: morning, night
   Sound similar: late, ate, eight
2. Same: she, she; can't, can't; with, with
   Similar: come, came
   Sound similar: she, we; bus, us
3. Sound similar: economics, economy
4. Same: is, is
   Opposite: closed, open
   Sound similar: closed, clothes
5. Same: meeting, meeting
   Similar: meeting, met
   Sound similar: postponed, post
6. Same: office, office, office; the, the
   Sound similar: late, wait; stay, day
7. Same: for, for; job, job
   Sound similar: new, knew; looking,
      booked
8. Same: yet, yet
   Similar: arrived, arrive
   Sound similar: yet, jet; arrived, drive;
      haven't, hasn't
9. Same: here, here
   Sound similar: here, hear
10. Sound similar: cold, old; here, near

Practice C

1.	(i)	6.	(f)
2.	(e)	7.	(j)
3.	(a)	8.	(d)
4.	(g)	9.	(h)
5.	(b)	10.	(c)

Practice D

Possible answers:
1. I just got a promotion.
2. She likes the natural light.
3. There were unexpected problems.
4. The battery is dead.
5. They're in a meeting.
6. The coffeepot is broken.
7. It might rain.
8. He's going to be out of town.
9. I don't like to drive.
10. I ate a big breakfast.

Practice E

1.	(A)	6.	(B)
2.	(A)	7.	(B)
3.	(B)	8.	(A)
4.	(B)	9.	(C)
5.	(A)	10.	(C)

Practice F

1.	(A)	6.	(C)
2.	(B)	7.	(A)
3.	(A)	8.	(A)
4.	(A)	9.	(C)
5.	(C)	10.	(B)

How (page 65)

Practice A

1.	(B)	6.	(B)
2.	(A)	7.	(A)
3.	(C)	8.	(C)
4.	(B)	9.	(B)
5.	(A)	10.	(B)

Practice B

1. Same: have, have
2. Same: new, new
   Similar: computer, computers
3. Same: get home, get home
4. Same: bus, bus, bus; the, the
5. Same: need, need, need; more, more,
      more; file, file
   Similar: file, filed
6. Same: meeting, meeting; last, last

7. Same: soon, soon; you, you
   Sound similar: report, important; soon, room
8. Same: copies, copies, copies
   Similar: copies, copy
   Sound similar: make, take
9. Same: the, the
10. Same: was, was
    Sound similar: your, tour

Practice C

1.	(a)	6.	(h)
2.	(c)	7.	(g)
3.	(e)	8.	(i)
4.	(d)	9.	(f)
5.	(b)	10.	(j)

Practice D

Possible answers:
1. Five hundred dollars.
2. Press the button in the back.
3. Every Sunday morning.
4. One is six years old and the other is ten.
5. As soon as I finish this report.
6. About two and a half hours.
7. It's three blocks away.
8. It's a lot better than my old job.
9. Only three.
10. They were twenty minutes late.

Practice E

1.	(A)	6.	(C)
2.	(B)	7.	(A)
3.	(B)	8.	(C)
4.	(B)	9.	(B)
5.	(B)	10.	(A)

Practice F

1.	(A)	6.	(C)
2.	(B)	7.	(A)
3.	(A)	8.	(B)
4.	(C)	9.	(C)
5.	(A)	10.	(B)

Auxiliaries (page 69)

Practice A

1.	(B)	6.	(A)
2.	(B)	7.	(A)
3.	(A)	8.	(B)
4.	(A)	9.	(B)
5.	(C)	10.	(C)

Practice B

1. Same: before, before; a, a
   Similar: processing, processed, process
2. Same: report, report, report; to the board, to the board
   Similar: report, reported
3. Same: train, train; station, station, station; the, the
   Similar: take, took
4. Same: overnight, overnight, overnight; mail, mail; this, this
   Similar: send, mailed; you, too
   Sound similar: overnight, night
5. Sound similar: contracts, contacted; lawyers, lawyer's
6. Same: meeting, meeting, meeting; the, the
   Similar: tomorrow's, tomorrow
   Sound similar: discuss, bus
7. Same: order, order
   Similar: order, ordered
   Sound similar: supplies, surprise
8. Same: office, office
   Similar: tonight, nights
   Sound similar: tonight, right
9. Same: bank, bank; check, check; take, take
10. Same: long, long, long; here, here

Practice C

1.	(c)	6.	(e)
2.	(i)	7.	(g)
3.	(h)	8.	(b)
4.	(d)	9.	(j)
5.	(a)	10.	(f)

Practice D

Possible answers:
1. Yes, it is.
2. No, I was waiting for him to return from running errands.
3. No, the local.
4. Yes, everything is on schedule.
5. No, the computer they need to use is occupied.
6. Yes, he's in his office.
7. Yes, I got it this morning.
8. No, I've never studied it.
9. No, hers is over there.
10. Everyone except Mrs. Park.

Practice E

1.	(A)	6.	(C)
2.	(B)	7.	(A)
3.	(A)	8.	(A)
4.	(A)	9.	(B)
5.	(A)	10.	(C)

Practice F

1.	(C)	6.	(B)
2.	(A)	7.	(C)
3.	(C)	8.	(B)
4.	(B)	9.	(A)
5.	(A)	10.	(A)

Review: Part 2 (page 73)

1.	(A)	6.	(A)
2.	(C)	7.	(B)
3.	(B)	8.	(A)
4.	(A)	9.	(A)
5.	(C)	10.	(C)

PART 3: CONVERSATIONS

Occupations (page 75)

Vocabulary Practice

1. cook: pots, kitchen, knife
   office worker, secretary: computer, files
2. police officer: parking tickets, law, illegal
   waiter, waitress: dessert, menu
3. teachers: class, exams, students
   mail carrier: mail, packages
4. phone technician: telephone, receiver, cord
   writer: novel, write
5. computer programmer: software, keyboard, monitor
   office worker: files, memo
6. bank teller: money, deposit, withdrawal
   pilot, stewardess, steward: plane, fly
7. waiter: order, tips, customers
   police officer: law, parking tickets
8. accountant: taxes, receivables, total
   construction worker, builder: nails, wood
9. athlete: runner, training, game
   doctor, nurse: sick, hospital
10. doctor: medicine, nurse, hospital
    waiter, waitress: menu, tip
11. musician: instrument, orchestra, notes
    pharmacist, doctor: pills, prescription
12. actor: stage, drama, theater
    mechanic: engine, repair
13. taxi driver: passenger, fare, tip
    politician: campaign, election
14. sales clerk: cash register, change, receipt
    photographer: film, camera
15. journalist: writer, newspaper, reports
    florist, gardener: flowers, seeds

Strategy Practice: Who

1.	(D)	9.	(A)
2.	(B)	10.	(B)
3.	(A)	11.	(B)
4.	(A)	12.	(A)
5.	(C)	13.	(D)
6.	(D)	14.	(C)
7.	(A)	15.	(B)
8.	(B)		

TOEIC Test Practice

1.	(A)	9.	(B)
2.	(C)	10.	(A)
3.	(D)	11.	(B)
4.	(A)	12.	(C)
5.	(D)	13.	(C)
6.	(B)	14.	(B)
7.	(C)	15.	(D)
8.	(C)		

Activities (page 81)

Vocabulary Practice A

Possible answers:

1. cup, spoon, sugar, cream, coffee break
2. film, screen, theater, popcorn
3. door handle, door knob, hinges, push, pull
4. mail, stamps, postal clerk, letters
5. novel, pages, cover, spine
6. number, receiver, dial, answer, cell phone
7. keyboard, monitor, screen, software
8. coin, slot, soda, snacks
9. menu, waiter, waitress, table, drink
10. suit, pants, dress, shirt, dressing room

Vocabulary Practice B

1. He is going to the post office.
2. She is opening the door.
3. He is drinking coffee.
4. They are watching a movie.
5. He is reading a book.
6. She is using a computer.
7. He is ordering food at a restaurant.
8. She is making a phone call.
9. He is buying something from a vending machine.
10. She is buying clothes.

Vocabulary Practice C

1. I'm leaving a friend's home.
2. I'm copying a letter.
3. They're waiting for a bus.
4. He's moving furniture.
5. I'm parking the car.
6. We're paying the bus fare.
7. I'm riding an elevator.
8. She's driving a car.
9. I'm buying a plane ticket.
10. We're eating dinner.
11. She's making a sandwich.
12. I'm picking up the mail.
13. I'm paying the taxi fare.
14. They're washing the floor.
15. She's buying a newspaper.

Strategy Practice: What

1.	(A)	9.	(D)
2.	(B)	10.	(C)
3.	(D)	11.	(A)
4.	(A)	12.	(D)
5.	(A)	13.	(B)
6.	(B)	14.	(D)
7.	(B)	15.	(C)
8.	(A)		

TOEIC Test Practice

1.	(A)	9.	(B)
2.	(C)	10.	(B)
3.	(A)	11.	(B)
4.	(A)	12.	(D)
5.	(C)	13.	(C)
6.	(C)	14.	(A)
7.	(B)	15.	(D)
8.	(C)		

Time (page 88)

Vocabulary Practice

1. How long does the copy machine take to print a hundred pages?
2. When did Ms. Miller join our staff?
3. How long has Mr. DeLorenzo been in the hospital?
4. How often are the floors cleaned?
5. When are we going to the reception?
6. When does the mail usually come?
7. How long did it take to fix the coffee machine?
8. How often did they try to call him?
9. How long will Mr. Gutfreund be gone?
10. When did she mail the package?
11. How long have they been working on this report?
12. When did he send the e-mail message?
13. How often do we have a staff meeting?
14. When did Robert start his new job?
15. How long will it take to paint all these offices?

Strategy Practice: When

1.	(A)	9.	(C)
2.	(C)	10.	(B)
3.	(A)	11.	(B)
4.	(D)	12.	(D)
5.	(A)	13.	(C)
6.	(B)	14.	(D)
7.	(C)	15.	(C)
8.	(B)		

TOEIC Test Practice

1.	(B)	9.	(B)
2.	(D)	10.	(C)
3.	(B)	11.	(C)
4.	(B)	12.	(A)
5.	(A)	13.	(C)
6.	(C)	14.	(B)
7.	(D)	15.	(D)
8.	(D)		

Locations (page 94)

Vocabulary Practice

1. restaurant: order, tip, waiter
   school: teacher, lesson
2. airplane: seat belt, landing, wings
   bank: deposit, bank officer
3. hotel: single room, lobby, reservation
   Asia: Thailand, Malaysia
4. gas station: car, gas, fill up, oil
   restaurant, diner, café: waitress, menu
5. travel agency: package tours, tickets, hotels
   library: library card, bookshelves
6. train station: track, train, platform
   hotel: double room, room service
7. library: book, card, overdue, shelves, periodicals
   gas station: gas, fill up
8. bank: checking account, teller, deposit
   restaurant, diner, café: waiter, tip
9. car rental agency: insurance, rent, cars, reservation
   hospital: patient, nurse
10. import office: products, trade, export
    car: engine, windshield

11. post office: stamps, package, mail
museum, gallery: art, exhibit
12. clothing store: dressing room, hanger, blouse
beach: sand, water
13. park: bench, path, garden
store: can, aisle
14. health club: steam room, swimming pool, exercise equipment
street, road: cars, traffic light
15. kitchen: stove, cabinets, sink
movie theater: screen, tickets

Strategy Practice: Where

1.	(A)	9.	(B)
2.	(B)	10.	(C)
3.	(C)	11.	(C)
4.	(B)	12.	(A)
5.	(C)	13.	(D)
6.	(C)	14.	(B)
7.	(A)	15.	(C)
8.	(A)		

TOEIC Test Practice

1.	(C)	9.	(A)
2.	(B)	10.	(B)
3.	(C)	11.	(B)
4.	(B)	12.	(B)
5.	(C)	13.	(D)
6.	(B)	14.	(C)
7.	(A)	15.	(D)
8.	(D)		

Reasons (page 100)

Vocabulary Practice A

1.	(b)	9.	(h)
2.	(e)	10.	(i)
3.	(a)	11.	(l)
4.	(d)	12.	(o)
5.	(c)	13.	(n)
6.	(g)	14.	(k)
7.	(j)	15.	(m)
8.	(f)		

Vocabulary Practice B

Possible answers:
1. Because she didn't want to drive.
2. Because they don't have enough time.
3. Because the pen was out of ink.
4. Because my shoes are too small.
5. Because she missed her bus.
6. Because it's raining.
7. Because I was talking on the phone.

8. Because she does her job very well.
9. Because she wasn't hungry.
10. Because I lost my glasses.

Strategy Practice: Why

1.	(A)	9.	(A)
2.	(B)	10.	(D)
3.	(A)	11.	(A)
4.	(D)	12.	(D)
5.	(C)	13.	(D)
6.	(B)	14.	(C)
7.	(A)	15.	(B)
8.	(D)		

TOEIC Test Practice

1.	(A)	9.	(D)
2.	(D)	10.	(A)
3.	(C)	11.	(B)
4.	(B)	12.	(B)
5.	(A)	13.	(D)
6.	(D)	14.	(A)
7.	(B)	15.	(B)
8.	(C)		

Review: Part 3 (page 106)

1.	(C)	16.	(B)
2.	(D)	17.	(A)
3.	(A)	18.	(B)
4.	(A)	19.	(B)
5.	(C)	20.	(D)
6.	(C)	21.	(A)
7.	(A)	22.	(B)
8.	(D)	23.	(B)
9.	(B)	24.	(A)
10.	(B)	25.	(D)
11.	(D)	26.	(C)
12.	(D)	27.	(C)
13.	(C)	28.	(A)
14.	(D)	29.	(B)
15.	(B)	30.	(D)

PART 4: TALKS

Advertisements (page 112)

Vocabulary Practice A

1. d
2. c
3. b
4. a

Vocabulary Practice B

1. for sale
2. sale
3. selling

4. On sale
5. to sell
6. sold
7. subscriptions
8. subscribes
9. subscribers
10. advertisements
11. advertisers
12. advertises

TOEIC Test Practice

1.	(A)	16.	(D)
2.	(A)	17.	(D)
3.	(B)	18.	(A)
4.	(D)	19.	(D)
5.	(C)	20.	(D)
6.	(C)	21.	(B)
7.	(B)	22.	(B)
8.	(B)	23.	(B)
9.	(B)	24.	(C)
10.	(D)	25.	(C)
11.	(A)	26.	(C)
12.	(D)	27.	(D)
13.	(D)	28.	(A)
14.	(B)	29.	(C)
15.	(C)	30.	(B)

Weather (page 118)

Vocabulary Practice A

1.	g	6.	b
2.	e	7.	c
3.	d	8.	i
4.	h	9.	f
5.	j	10.	a

Vocabulary Practice B

1. cool/chilly/very breezy/windy/freezing
2. rain
3. cloudy
4. hot/windy
5. clear
6. mild/comfortable
7. freezing
8. blizzard
9. clear
10. typhoons

TOEIC Test Practice

1.	(D)	7.	(A)
2.	(A)	8.	(B)
3.	(C)	9.	(D)
4.	(A)	10.	(A)
5.	(C)	11.	(D)
6.	(A)	12.	(C)

13.	(C)	22.	(D)
14.	(B)	23.	(B)
15.	(D)	24.	(C)
16.	(C)	25.	(C)
17.	(B)	26.	(B)
18.	(C)	27.	(B)
19.	(B)	28.	(A)
20.	(C)	29.	(A)
21.	(B)	30.	(A)

News (page 124)

Vocabulary Practice A

1. game
2. math
3. realtor
4. street
5. pound
6. convenient

Vocabulary Practice B

1. because it is so light
2. because they finally signed the agreement
3. because it hasn't rained
4. because of the snowstorm
5. because of the holiday
6. in order to see the parade
7. because of the increase in sales tax

TOEIC Test Practice

1.	(D)	16.	(B)
2.	(D)	17.	(A)
3.	(C)	18.	(A)
4.	(D)	19.	(A)
5.	(A)	20.	(C)
6.	(A)	21.	(B)
7.	(B)	22.	(C)
8.	(A)	23.	(A)
9.	(C)	24.	(A)
10.	(A)	25.	(B)
11.	(B)	26.	(C)
12.	(C)	27.	(D)
13.	(B)	28.	(C)
14.	(A)	29.	(C)
15.	(B)	30.	(A)

Recorded Announcements (page 130)

Vocabulary Practice A

1. c
2. d
3. e
4. b

5. f
6. a
7. g

Vocabulary Practice B

1. When will the museum close?
2. What should all applicants do?
3. On what days are guests not permitted to play?
4. Why is the library closed?
5. How will calls be answered?
6. Why would someone call this office?
7. How much does an adult ticket cost?
8. What should I do in an emergency?
9. What should I bring when I apply for a license?
10. Why will the store close early?

TOEIC Test Practice

1.	(B)	16.	(A)
2.	(B)	17.	(D)
3.	(B)	18.	(B)
4.	(D)	19.	(D)
5.	(A)	20.	(C)
6.	(B)	21.	(A)
7.	(C)	22.	(B)
8.	(D)	23.	(D)
9.	(D)	24.	(B)
10.	(C)	25.	(C)
11.	(A)	26.	(A)
12.	(A)	27.	(A)
13.	(A)	28.	(B)
14.	(C)	29.	(B)
15.	(C)	30.	(D)

Special Announcements (page 137)

Vocabulary Practice A

1. specialty
2. chemistry
3. express
4. platform
5. freight
6. attentive
7. reviews
8. guide
9. security guard
10. main

Vocabulary Practice B

2. I'm lining up for tickets.
3. I'm getting on the plane.
4. I'm taking a tour.
5. I'm filling the car with gas.
6. I'm getting off at the next stop.
7. I'm waiting for the express train.
8. I love playing golf.
9. I am attending a concert.
10. I'm filling out a lost article form.

TOEIC Test Practice

1.	(A)	16.	(D)
2.	(B)	17.	(B)
3.	(C)	18.	(B)
4.	(D)	19.	(A)
5.	(A)	20.	(A)
6.	(B)	21.	(B)
7.	(C)	22.	(A)
8.	(A)	23.	(C)
9.	(A)	24.	(C)
10.	(D)	25.	(D)
11.	(B)	26.	(B)
12.	(A)	27.	(C)
13.	(D)	28.	(A)
14.	(D)	29.	(C)
15.	(A)	30.	(D)

Business Announcements (page 144)

Vocabulary Practice A

1. food, activities, prizes, families, staff, organize, refreshments, contests
2. comparing, pricing, monitors, keyboards, personal computers, operating systems, technology, modern, software, purpose, memory
3. applicants, qualifications, résumé, interview, questions, candidate, experience, education, reference
4. travel, itinerary, presentations, seminars, participate, meet, guest speaker, group, tickets, topic, seating
5. fill out, stationery, pens, paper, purchase order, invoice, item, total, amount, supplier, phone, tax, shipping, discounts
6. airfare, tickets, holiday, tour, tour guide, visit, sightsee, family, sun, relax, enjoy
7. water, thirsty, clean, use, garbage, keep off, free
8. entrepreneur, proposal, finances, open, business name, hire, staff, office
9. car, space, park, entrance, exit, convenience, elderly, disabled, display, vehicle, ticket, pay

10. paper, write, to do, checklist, organize, number, double check, review, post

Vocabulary Practice B

2. The officer is hiring some new employees.
3. The president drove the staff members to the company picnic.
4. We bought some new computers.
5. We are attending a conference.
6. I wrote a list of names and job titles.
7. She is using the water fountain.
8. She is going to take a vacation.
9. He wants to park near the door.
10. We're starting a new business.

TOEIC Test Practice

1.	(D)	16.	(D)
2.	(C)	17.	(A)
3.	(C)	18.	(C)
4.	(B)	19.	(A)
5.	(A)	20.	(D)
6.	(B)	21.	(D)
7.	(B)	22.	(B)
8.	(C)	23.	(D)
9.	(B)	24.	(A)
10.	(B)	25.	(A)
11.	(C)	26.	(C)
12.	(D)	27.	(C)
13.	(B)	28.	(D)
14.	(B)	29.	(B)
15.	(C)	30.	(C)

Review: Part 4 (page 150)

1. (C)
2. (C)
3. (A)
4. (B)
5. (D)
6. (D)
7. (B)
8. (B)
9. (A)
10. (D)
11. (A)
12. (D)
13. (B)
14. (C)
15. (A)

ANSWER KEY

LISTENING COMPREHENSION REVIEW

PART 1 (PAGE 153)

1. (D) The man is waiting by the open door. Choice (A) is incorrect because he is not touching the door and the door is open. Choice (B) is incorrect because he doesn't have anything in his hands. Choice (C) is incorrect because there are no guests in the photo.

2. (C) The man is working at a construction site. Choice (A) confuses the similar-sounding *controller* and *construction*. Choice (B) confuses *schoolyard* and *lumber yard*, which is associated with construction. Choice (D) confuses the similar-sounding *bean* and *beam*.

3. (B) The waiter is setting the table. Choice (A) confuses the similar sounds *waiting* with *waiter* and *plane* with *place*. Choice (C) is incorrect because although there are rolls on the table, the photo is not of a baker. Choice (D) confuses *trees being cut down* and *the tree branches seen behind the man*.

4. (A) The people are standing in line. Choices (B), (C), and (D) are correct verbs for words like *money, food, picnic* but are not what is happening in the photo.

5. (B) The man is eating at a table in front of the television. Choice (A) uses the verb *looking*, but he's *looking at* the television, not *out* the window. Choice (C) uses the similar-sounding word *rinsing* for *raising*. Choice (D) misidentifies the action.

6. (A) The woman is laughing with her friend. Choice (B) is incorrect because she is wearing a watch but not looking at it. Choice (C) confuses the similar sounds *grass* and *glass.* Choice (D) is incorrect because she may have set up the glasses, but she's not cleaning them.

7. (D) Two people, probably owners of a new car, are standing beside their car. Choice (A) uses words associated with cars, *park.* The car is already parked. Choice (B) misidentifies the action by using words associated with cars, *driving.* Choice (C) tries to confuse you by using the similar-sounding phrase *Otto a mobile* for *automobile.* The distracter further confuses you by using the word *buying.* The man seems to be presenting the woman with a newly purchased car and she is holding the new car manual.

8. (D) Baggage is going around the carousel. Choice (A) confuses *checking in* and *claiming baggage.* Choice (B) associates *duty-free* with *airport.* Choice (C) is incorrect because luggage is *going around the corner of the carousel*, not *being sold on the corner.*

9. (A) The woman is using a public telephone. Choice (B) is incorrect because there are phone books under the phone, but she's not reading them. Choice (C) associates *ringing* with *phone.* Choice (D) confuses *answering the door* and *answering the phone.*

10. (C) Two people are hanging a picture of flowers on the wall. Choice (A) uses the associated word *painting* but misidentifies the action. Choice (B) uses the word *flowers,* which are seen in the watercolor. Choice (D) misidentifies the action but uses the associated word *wall.*

PART 2 (PAGE 159)

11. (A) *By noon* answers *when*. Choice (B) answers *when did she arrive*. Choice (C) is incorrect because he hasn't arrived yet.

12. (B) *I went shopping* answers *what did you do*. Choice (A) answers *how do you get to your destination*. Choice (C) confuses the similar-sounding *playing* and *today*.

13. (A) *Mrs. Lee arrived before the others* answers *who came first*. Choice (B) confuses the opposites *last* and *first*. Choice (C) confuses the opposites *left* and *came*.

14. (A) *This afternoon* answers *when*. Choice (B) confuses the similar-sounding *revise* and *remember*. Choice (C) confuses the similar-sounding *review* and *revise*.

15. (A) This is the reason the speaker didn't receive a message. Choice (B) confuses the similar-sounding *called* and *cold*. Choice (C) has the related word *told* but is not about today's call.

16. (A) *On the train* answers *where*. Choice (B) confuses the similar words *left* and *leave*. Choice (C) confuses the similar-sounding words *brief* and *briefcase*.

17. (C) *A friend* answers *who*. Choice (A) associates *studying law* with *lawyer*. Choice (B) confuses the similar-sounding words *newly* and *new*.

18. (B) *Over five weeks* indicates duration and answers *how long*. Choices (A) and (C) answer *when*.

19. (C) *A coat* answers *what did you buy*. Choice (A) associates *new* with *buy* but answers with *he* and is not in the past tense. Choice (B) confuses the similar-sounding words *closed* and *clothes*.

20. (A) *To Hawaii* answers *where*. Choice (B) answers *when does your vacation start*. Choice (C) answers *how long*.

21. (B) *Playing golf* answers *what are you doing*. Choice (A) confuses the similar words *worked* and *work*. Choice (C) answers the *yes/no* question *are you playing golf after work*.

22. (A) *By check* answers the question by repeating part of the question. Choice (B) associates *cashier* with *pay by cash or check*. Choice (C) confuses the words *cash* (verb) and *cash* (noun).

23. (C) *Anything sweet* answers *what is your favorite food*. Choice (A) associates *restaurant* with *food*. Choice (B) associates *fish* and *meat* with *food* but answers *what is his*, not *your, favorite food*.

24. (B) *Last summer* answers *when*. Choice (A) answers *when does she need a secretary*. Choice (C) answers *when were they married*.

25. (B) The pain medicine should make the speaker feel better. Choice (A) confuses the similar-sounding *pain* and *pen*. Choice (C) is incorrect because the nurse has already offered the pain medication.

26. (A) *I haven't finished all my work* answers *why* with an explanation. Choice (B) confuses *too late to work* and *working late*. Choice (C) confuses the similar-sounding *eight* and *late*.

27. (C) *In the hallway* answers *where*. Choice (A) confuses *open to the public* and *public phone*. Choice (B) confuses the similar-sounding *alone* and *phone*.

28. (B) The respondent is a friend or relative who wants a job. Choice (A) confuses the similar-sounding *hear* (related to *ear*) and *hire*. Choice (C) confuses the related word *invite* with *friends* and *relatives*, but no party is suggested.

29. (C) *I have an appointment* answers *why* with an explanation. Choice (A) confuses the similar words *earlier* and *early*. Choice (B) confuses the opposites *late* and *early* and associates *morning* with *early*.

30. (C) *The switch is by the door* indirectly answers *how*. Choice (A) answers *how did you*. Choice (B) gives directions to a location.

31. (A) *There were design problems* answers *why* with an explanation. Choice (B) repeats the word *stop* but does not answer the question. Choice (C) confuses the similar words *models* (verb) and *model* (noun).

32. (C) The respondent is giving further instructions for the sender. Choice (A) uses the past tense, but the action hasn't happened yet. Choice (B) confuses the similar-sounding *I'll* and *Kyle*.

33. (C) *Yes, they must be filled out by the thirtieth* answers the *yes/no* question *are time sheets due at the end of the month*. Choice (A) is a *yes/no* response but does not answer the question. Choice (B) confuses *time* and *time sheets*.

34. (B) *About fifteen minutes away* answers *how far*. Choice (A) answers *how long*. Choice (C) answers *how tall*.

35. (B) *Because he's a new employee* is the reason he's not listed in the directory. Choice (A) confuses the similar-sounding *directions* and *directory*. Choice (C) repeats the word *directory* but does not answer the question.

36. (A) *A cafeteria next door* answers *where*. Choice (B) confuses *clean cups* with *a cup of coffee*. Choice (C) answers *where did you buy*.

37. (B) *Your secretary told me* answers *how did you hear about*. Choice (A) confuses the similar words *here* and *hear*. Choice (C) answers *how do you hear*.

38. (B) *It goes off automatically* answers *who turned the copy machine off* by offering an alternative to a person doing it. Choice (A) confuses *coffee machine* and *copy machine*. Choice (C) confuses *turned my copy in* and *turn off the machine*.

39. (A) Mr. Green must have had a good reason to cancel the trip. Choice (B) confuses the similar-sounding *trip* and *tip*. Choice (C) is illogical because it is the speaker's trip that is being discussed, not Mr. Green's speech.

40. (C) *Yes, I'll do it now* answers the *yes/no* question *can you*. Choice (A) confuses the opposites *after* and *before*. Choice (B) confuses the similar similar-sounding *let her* and *letter*.

PART 3 (PAGE 160)

9/27

41. (A) This is the reason the man gives for buying a new coat. Choice (B) confuses *two* with *too*. Choice (C) is wrong because, although the color of the new coat is mentioned, the color of the old coat is not. Choice (D) is not true because the woman says that she liked the old coat.

42. (C) The new coat is green. Choice (A) confuses *gold* with the similar-sounding word *old*. Choice (B) confuses *blue* with the similar-sounding word *new*. Choice (D) confuses *white* with the similar-sounding word *like*.

43. (B) The man says he paid $700 for the new coat. Choices (A), (C), and (D) sound similar to the correct answer.

44. (A) The man says that the flight will arrive at 3:00. Choice (B) is confused with *four-hour flight*. Choice (C) confuses *five* with the similar-sounding word *flight*. Choice (D) is the time that the flight left.

45. (D) According to the man, *he didn't mind taking the subway*. Choice (A) is the woman's suggestion. Choice (B) confuses *bus* with the similar-sounding word *us*. Choice (C) confuses *cab* with the similar-sounding word *car*.

46. (C) The woman says *I guess he'll meet us for dinner at the restaurant*. Choices (A), (B), and (D) are other places that Mr. Kim will be during the day, but he won't meet the speakers at any of them.

47. (C) The speakers are looking at a menu so that they can order dinner, so they must be at a restaurant. Choices (A), (B), and (D) are associated with the talk of *tuna*, *fish*, and *shrimp*.

48. (C) The woman says that the tuna costs $35. Choices (A) and (B) sound similar to the correct answer. Choice (D) confuses *for* with the similar-sounding word *forty*.

49. (C) The woman says that she will order shrimp, and the man says that he will get that, too. Choice (A) repeats the word *tuna*. Choices (B) and (D) confuse *rice* and *ice* with the similar-sounding word *nice*.

50. (C) The woman says *When'll the train get here?* Choice (A) is not mentioned. Choice (B) confuses *car* with the similar-sounding word *far*. Choice (D) confuses *plane* with the similar-sounding word *train*.

51. (A) The woman says that she has been waiting half an hour. Choice (B) confuses *hour* with *half an hour*. Choice (C) confuses *noon* with the similar-sounding word *soon*. Choice (D) confuses *5:00* with *five minutes*.

52. (D) The woman says *I don't like to get home after dark.* Choice (A) confuses *store* with the similar-sounding word *more*. Choice (B) confuses *park* with the similar-sounding word *dark*. Choice (C) confuses *work* with the similar-sounding word *walk*.

53. (A) The woman says that she will send the envelope before lunch. Choice (B) confuses *afternoon* with the similar-sounding word *soon*. Choice (C) confuses *tonight* with the similar-sounding word *right*. Choice (D) is when the envelope will arrive at its destination.

54. (B) The woman says that she is typing a report. Choice (A) is confused with the letter that is inside the envelope. Choice (C) is confused with when the woman will send the envelope. Choice (D) is confused with the envelope that the woman will send for the man.

55. (C) The man says that the envelope contains a letter. Choice (A) confuses *book* with the similar-sounding word *look*. Choice (B) confuses *form* with the similar-sounding word *before*. Choice (D) confuses *sweater* with the similar-sounding word *letter*.

56. (A) The woman says *Can we meet at my office . . . ?* Choice (B) is where the man will be on Tuesday. Choice (C) is confused with the woman going to a conference on Wednesday. Choice (D) confuses *hotel* with the similar-sounding word *tell*.

57. (D) The speakers finally agree to meet on Thursday afternoon. Choice (A) is the woman's first suggestion for a meeting time. Choice (B) confuses *Tuesday* with the similar-sounding word *Thursday*. Choice (C) is the man's suggestion.

58. (A) The secretary will send photocopies of contracts. Choice (B) confuses *photographs* with the similar-sounding word *photocopies*. Choice (C) confuses *book* with the similar-sounding word *look*. Choice (D) repeats the word *conference* out of context.

59. (A) The man says that Mark will start his new job next week. Choice (B) sounds similar to the correct answer. Choices (C) and (D) are confused with *take a month's vacation*.

60. (C) The woman explains that Mark wasn't paid enough at his old job. Choices (A) and (B) are not mentioned. Choice (D) is confused with *take a month's vacation*.

61. (A) The woman says that Mark worked there for 13 years. Choices (B) and (D) confuse *14* and *40* with the similar-sounding word *for*. Choice (C) sounds similar to the correct answer.

62. (B) The woman is mailing an envelope by express mail, so they must be in a post office. Choice (A) associates *bank* with *jewelry, cash,* and the discussion of money. Choice (C) associates *stationery store* with *envelope*. Choice (D) associates *photographer* with *photographs*.

63. (C) The woman says that there are photographs in the envelope. Choices (A) and (B) repeat words from the man's question. Choice (D) confuses *press* with the similar-sounding word *express*.

64. (B) The man says that express mail costs seven dollars and the woman says that she will pay for express. Choice (A) is the cost of regular mail. Choice (C) confuses *9* with the similar-sounding word *fine*. Choice (D) confuses *11* with the similar-sounding number *7*.

65. (B) The man asks for a wake-up call, he's offered dinner in his room, and there is a pool, so he must be at a hotel. Choice (A) associates *wake up* and *breakfast* with *home*. Choice (C) associates *breakfast* and *dinner* with *restaurant*. Choice (D) associates *exercise club* with *pool*.

66. (D) The man asks for a 6:45 wake-up call. Choices (A), (B), and (C) sound similar to the correct answer.

67. (C) The man says that he is going to use the pool. Choice (A) is what the woman suggests. Choices (B) and (D) are what he will do tomorrow morning.

68. (D) Mrs. Davis will arrive at 11:00. Choice (A) is the time of the afternoon meeting. Choice (B) confuses *7* with the similar-sounding number *11*. Choice (C) confuses *8* with the similar-sounding word *late*.

69. (C) The woman says her train is delayed. Choice (A) confuses *plane* with the similar-sounding word *train*. Choice (B) confuses *raining* with the similar-sounding word *train*. Choice (D) repeats the word *start* out of context.

70. (B) Both speakers agree that Mrs. Davis has to arrive in time for the one o'clock meeting. Choice (A) confuses *letter* with the similar-sounding word *later*. Choices (C) and (D) confuse *read* and *eat* with the similar-sounding word *meeting*.

PART 4 (PAGE 163)

71. (A) A college professor is telling his students about the upcoming exam. Choice (B) associates *book writer* with the words *write* and *textbook*. Choice (C) associates *student* with the situation of preparing for an exam, but in this case the students are the listeners. Choice (D) associates *doctor* with the word *exam*.

72. (D) The professor explains that the exam is on Friday. Choice (A) confuses *Tuesday* with the similar-sounding word *today*. Choice (B) is not mentioned. Choice (C) confuses *Thursday* with the similar-sounding phrase *three days*.

73. (D) The professor tells the students to bring pens to the exam. Choices (A) and (C) are things that the students are not allowed to bring to the exam. Choice (B) confuses *pencils* with the similar-sounding word *pens*.

74. (B) According to the reporter, the low temperature will be eleven degrees.

Choice (A) confuses *seven* with the similar-sounding number *eleven*. Choice (C) is the temperature over the weekend. Choice (D) confuses *sixteen* with the similar-sounding word *fifteen*.

75. (A) The reporter says *Tomorrow morning brings showers*. Choice (B) confuses *sunny* with the similar-sounding word *Sunday*. Choice (C) is the weather tonight. Choice (D) confuses *windy* with the similar-sounding word *Wednesday*.

76. (C) According to the reporter, the rain will end on Monday morning. Choices (A) and (B) are mentioned in the report as days that will be rainy. Choice (D) is mentioned as a day of clear skies.

77. (B) According to the report, *Two lion cubs were born at the City Zoo early today*. Choice (A) confuses *new lions* with the similar-sounding phrase *zoo's lion*. Choice (C) is something that will happen next month. Choice (D) mentions the director, who made the announcement, but nothing is said about a new director being hired.

78. (B) The zoo director made the announcement. Choice (A) is the person who made a special habitat for the baby lions. Choice (C) associates *publicity* with *public*. Choice (D) associates *activities director* with the special activities planned for next month.

79. (D) The special activities to introduce the lion cubs to the public will take place the first weekend of next month. Choice (A) confuses *two days* with the similar-sounding word *today*. Choices (B) and (C) confuse *next weekend* and *next week* with the *first weekend*.

80. (C) The speaker is on flight 15 to Los Angeles. Choices (A), (B), and (D) are places where one might hear a similar talk, but they aren't *flights*.

81. (C) The speaker says they will arrive at noon. Choices (A) and (B) are confused with *five and a half hours*, the length of the flight. Choice (D) confuses *12:30* with *noon*.

82. (B) The flight attendants will bring beverages to everyone. Choice (A) is confused with the arrival in Los Angeles *just in time for lunch.* Choices (C) and (D) are things passengers can request.

83. (B) The store sells *sofas, tables, desks, beds, carpets, and more.* Choice (A) is confused with the sale on home office furniture. Choice (C) confuses *clothes* with the similar-sounding word *closed.* Choice (D) confuses *cars* with the similar-sounding word *carpets.*

84. (C) The sale ends on Friday. Choice (A) is the day the store is closed. Choice (B) confuses *Thursday* with the similar-sounding word *thirty.* Choice (D) is mentioned as a day the store is open.

85. (A) The store is located in the City Plaza Mall. Choice (B) is wrong because the store is next to a hotel, not down the street from one. Choice (C) is wrong because the store is close to a subway station, not in one. Choice (D) confuses *City Hall* with the similar-sounding phrase *City Plaza Mall.*

86. (A) By pressing 2, a caller can speak with Mr. Park. Since the message is from the law offices of Stevenson and Park, we can assume that Mr. Park is a lawyer. Choice (B) is what happens when a caller presses 3. Choice (C) is what happens when a caller presses 1. Choice (D) is information that is right on the message; the caller doesn't haven't to press any number to hear it.

87. (C) The caller is instructed to press 3 for billing questions. This will connect the caller with the office assistant. The caller will be connected with Choices (A) and (B) by pressing 1 or 2. Choice (D) associates the job of an operator with the phone instructions.

88. (C) Callers with an emergency outside of regular office hours are asked to hang up and dial another number. Choice (A) confuses *press 3* with the previous instructions to press 1, 2, or 3. Choice (B) repeats the phrase *office hours.* Choice (D) repeats the phrase *office assistant.*

89. (B) The bridge was closed because of *heavy snowfall last night.* Choice (A) is something that also happened last night but is not the reason for the bridge closing. Choice (C) repeats the words *heavy* and *traffic.* Choice (D) confuses *construction* with *reconstruction.*

90. (D) According to the report, *the bridge will remain closed until Wednesday.* Choice (A) is when the road conditions are reported to be icy. Choice (B) confuses *tonight* with *last night,* which is when the snow fell. Choice (C) is when the weather will be warmer.

91. (D) Tuesday will have *Warmer temperatures and sunny skies.* Choice (A) is how the weather was last night. Choice (B) confuses *rainy* with the similar-sounding word *train.* Choice (C) confuses *windy* with the similar-sounding word *Wednesday.*

92. (B) James Jones is introduced as a *professor of chemistry at National University.* Choice (A) confuses *medical doctor* with James Jones's title of *doctor,* which probably means he has a doctoral degree in chemistry. Choice (C) associates *travel agent* with James Jones's trip to Brazil. Choice (D) associates *florist* with James Jones's search for *wild orchids and other exotic flowers.*

93. (C) James Jones will talk about his hiking trip in the Amazon. Choices (A) and (B) confuse Dr. Jones's job of chemistry professor with the topic of his talk. Choice (D) repeats the word *trip,* but James Jones took a hiking trip, not a train trip.

94. (A) The speaker says that Dr. Jones will answer questions after the talk. Choices (B) and (D) are confused with the display of photographs in the lobby. Choice (C) is confused with Dr. Jones's search for flowers in the Amazon.

95. (A) The guide says that the tickets cost seven dollars. Choice (B) confuses *eight* with the similar-sounding word *wait.* Choice (C) confuses *ten* with the similar-sounding word *then.* Choice (D) confuses *eleven* with the similar-sounding number *seven.*

96. (D) The guide says *we'll begin in the main gallery . . . looking at portraits.* Choices (A), (B), and (C) are other things the participants will see on the tour.

97. (D) The works by local artists are on the third floor. Choices (A) and (C) are other places in the museaum that the tour participants will visit. Choice (B) confuses *first* with the similar-sounding word *third.*

98. (A) The speaker is addressing passengers on the train, telling them that they are about to arrive in the station. Choice (B) is what passengers with checked baggage should do. Choice (C) uses the word *exit* in a different context. Choice (D) repeats the word *baggage,* but a baggage office is never mentioned.

99. (A) The speaker says that the train wi.. arrive in four minutes. Choice (B) confuses *five* with the similar-sounding word *arrive.* Choice (C) confuses *eight* with the similar-sounding word *wait.* Choice (D) is the amount of time passengers will have to wait for their baggage.

100. (B) Passengers are asked to pick up their baggage right outside the gate. Choice (A) uses the word *check* in a different context. Choice (C) is wrong because all passengers must exit the train at the station. Choice (D) is the suggestion made for passengers who need assistance getting off the train.

PART 5: INCOMPLETE SENTENCES

Word Choice: Nouns (page 170)

1.	(D)	6.	(C)
2.	(C)	7.	(A)
3.	(A)	8.	(D)
4.	(A)	9.	(C)
5.	(C)	10.	(A)

Word Choice: Verbs (page 172)

1.	(B)	6.	(D)
2.	(A)	7.	(D)
3.	(A)	8.	(C)
4.	(C)	9.	(B)
5.	(B)	10.	(A)

Word Choice: Adjectives (page 174)

1.	(B)	6.	(D)
2.	(C)	7.	(A)
3.	(A)	8.	(A)
4.	(B)	9.	(C)
5.	(B)	10.	(D)

Word Choice: Adverbs (page 176)

1.	(B)	6.	(A)
2.	(D)	7.	(A)
3.	(A)	8.	(B)
4.	(B)	9.	(B)
5.	(C)	10.	(D)

Word Choice: Conjunctions (page 178)

1.	(A)	6.	(B)
2.	(C)	7.	(B)
3.	(D)	8.	(C)
4.	(D)	9.	(A)
5.	(A)	10.	(D)

Word Choice: Prepositions (page 180)

1.	(A)	6.	(C)
2.	(C)	7.	(D)
3.	(B)	8.	(C)
4.	(A)	9.	(B)
5.	(A)	10.	(A)

Word Form: Nouns (page 182)

1.	(B)	6.	(D)
2.	(A)	7.	(A)
3.	(C)	8.	(A)
4.	(B)	9.	(D)
5.	(A)	10.	(D)

Word Form: Verbs (page 184)

1.	(C)	6.	(B)
2.	(B)	7.	(C)
3.	(A)	8.	(A)
4.	(D)	9.	(C)
5.	(D)	10.	(C)

Word Form: Adjectives (page 186)

1.	(C)	6.	(D)
2.	(A)	7.	(B)
3.	(D)	8.	(A)
4.	(A)	9.	(D)
5.	(C)	10.	(B)

Word Form: Adverbs (page 188)

1.	(D)	6.	(D)
2.	(C)	7.	(A)
3.	(A)	8.	(B)
4.	(A)	9.	(C)
5.	(C)	10.	(A)

Word Form: Pronouns (page 190)

1.	(A)	6.	(C)
2.	(B)	7.	(B)
3.	(A)	8.	(B)
4.	(C)	9.	(B)
5.	(B)	10.	(D)

Review: Part 5 (page 192)

1.	(B)	11.	(D)
2.	(D)	12.	(A)
3.	(A)	13.	(C)
4.	(A)	14.	(D)
5.	(C)	15.	(B)
6.	(B)	16.	(C)
7.	(D)	17.	(A)
8.	(D)	18.	(C)
9.	(B)	19.	(C)
10.	(B)	20.	(B)

PART 6: TEXT COMPLETION

Reference (page 198)

Practice A

1.	(A)	6.	(B)
2.	(D)	7.	(C)
3.	(C)	8.	(C)
4.	(D)	9.	(B)
5.	(C)	10.	(B)

Verbs (page 199)

Practice A

1.	(A)	6.	(C)
2.	(B)	7.	(D)
3.	(C)	8.	(A)
4.	(D)	9.	(C)
5.	(A)	10.	(D)

Practice B

1.	(A)	6.	(A)
2.	(C)	7.	(C)
3.	(B)	8.	(A)
4.	(D)	9.	(B)
5.	(A)	10.	(C)

Practice C

1.	(C)	6.	(A)
2.	(A)	7.	(B)
3.	(C)	8.	(D)
4.	(A)	9.	(A)
5.	(C)	10.	(A)

Practice D

1.	(A)	6.	(B)
2.	(A)	7.	(B)
3.	(B)	8.	(B)
4.	(A)	9.	(C)
5.	(B)	10.	(A)

Review: Verbs and Reference (page 208)

1.	(D)	7.	(D)
2.	(A)	8.	(A)
3.	(C)	9.	(A)
4.	(C)	10.	(D)
5.	(D)	11.	(B)
6.	(A)	12.	(B)

Modifiers (page 213)

Practice A

1.	(A)	6.	(D)
2.	(B)	7.	(C)
3.	(D)	8.	(B)
4.	(B)	9.	(B)
5.	(D)	10.	(B)

Practice B

1.	(C)	6.	(C)
2.	(B)	7.	(B)
3.	(B)	8.	(C)
4.	(A)	9.	(C)
5.	(D)	10.	(D)

Practice C

1.	(B)	6.	(B)
2.	(B)	7.	(C)
3.	(C)	8.	(D)
4.	(C)	9.	(B)
5.	(C)	10.	(C)

Review: Modifiers and Reference (page 219)

1.	(B)	7.	(D)
2.	(B)	8.	(D)
3.	(A)	9.	(C)
4.	(A)	10.	(C)
5.	(C)	11.	(B)
6.	(D)	12.	(B)

Review: Part 6 (page 223)

1.	(B)	7.	(C)
2.	(C)	8.	(D)
3.	(D)	9.	(A)
4.	(A)	10.	(C)
5.	(B)	11.	(B)
6.	(A)	12.	(A)

PART 7: READING COMPREHENSION

Advertisements (page 229)

Advertisement 1

1.	(B)	7.	(B)
2.	(C)	8.	(A)
3.	(B)	9.	(C)
4.	(A)	10.	(A)
5.	(A)	11.	(C)
6.	–	12.	(A)

Advertisement 2

1.	(B)	6.	(A)
2.	(A)	7.	(A)
3.	(A)	8.	(B)
4.	(B)	9.	(B)
5.	(B)	10.	(B)

Advertisement 3

1.	(A)	7.	(B)
2.	–	8.	(B)
3.	(B)	9.	(C)
4.	(B)	10.	(A)
5.	(A)	11.	(D)
6.	(A)	12.	(D)

Forms (page 237)

Form 1

1.	(A)	7.	(B)
2.	(B)	8.	(D)
3.	–	9.	(C)
4.	(C)	10.	(B)
5.	(A)	11.	(D)
6.	(A)		

Form 2

1.	(B)	7.	(A)
2.	(B)	8.	(D)
3.	(A)	9.	(A)
4.	(A)	10.	(C)
5.	(B)	11.	(D)
6.	(B)		

Form 3

1.	–	7.	(A)
2.	–	8.	(C)
3.	–	9.	(C)
4.	–	10.	(D)
5.	(B)	11.	(B)
6.	(A)		

Letters, E-mail, Faxes, and Memos (page 245)

Letters, E-mail, Faxes, and Memos 1

1.	(B)	7.	(B)
2.	(A)	8.	(A)
3.	(B)	9.	(A)
4.	(A)	10.	(C)
5.	(A)	11.	(A)
6.	(B)	12.	(B)

Letters, E-mail, Faxes, and Memos 2

1.	Bob	7.	(A)
2.	Joyce	8.	(D)
3.	meeting change	9.	(C)
4.	–	10.	(A)
5.	(A)	11.	(D)
6.	(B)		

Letters, E-mail, Faxes, and Memos 3

1.	(A)	9.	(A)
2.	(B)	10.	(B)
3.	(A)	11.	(B)
4.	(B)	12.	(B)
5.	(A)	13.	(C)
6.	(A)	14.	(D)
7.	(B)	15.	(A)
8.	(A)		

Tables, Indexes, and Charts (page 252)

Tables, Indexes, and Charts 1

1.	(A)	5.	(A)
2.	(D)	6.	(B)
3.	–	7.	(C)
4.	–	8.	(B)

Tables, Indexes, and Charts 2

1.	85	7.	(D)
2.	18	8.	(C)
3.	3	9.	(A)
4.	–	10.	(B)
5.	(A)	11.	(B)
6.	(B)		

Tables, Indexes, and Charts 3

1.	(B)	8.	(A)
2.	Emerald Airlines	9.	(A)
3.	6	10.	(C)
4.	–	11.	(C)
5.	–	12.	(D)
6.	(B)	13.	(D)
7.	(A)		

Instructions and Notices (page 259)

Instructions and Notices 1

1.	(A)	7.	(A)
2.	(B)	8.	(B)
3.	(A)	9.	(B)
4.	–	10.	(D)
5.	–	11.	(A)
6.	(A)	12.	(C)

Instructions and Notices 2

1.	(B)	8.	(A)
2.	–	9.	(A)
3.	(A)	10.	(C)
4.	(B)	11.	(B)
5.	(B)	12.	(D)
6.	(A)	13.	(D)
7.	(B)		

Instructions and Notices 3

1.	(A)	7.	(B)
2.	–	8.	(C)
3.	–	9.	(C)
4.	–	10.	(C)
5.	(B)	11.	(D)
6.	(A)	12.	(B)

Review: Part 7 (page 266)

1.	(A)	6.	(B)
2.	(B)	7.	(B)
3.	(B)	8.	(C)
4.	(C)	9.	(A)
5.	(A)	10.	(B)

ANSWER KEY
READING REVIEW

PART 5 (PAGE 270)

101. (B) The singular subject *client* requires a third person singular verb. Choice (A) is first person. Choice (C) is plural. Choice (D) is the simple form.

102. (D) *Friendship* is a noun referring to a thing. Choice (A) is a noun but refers to people. Choices (B) and (C) are adjectives.

103. (B) *In* is used for locations within cities. Choice (A) indicates a time relationship. Choice (C) indicates location nearby. Choice (D) is used with specific times.

104. (B) The past participle *done* is required. Choice (A) is the simple form. Choice (C) is the past tense. Choice (D) is the present tense.

105. (A) The modal *can* indicates ability or willingness in present or future situations. Choices (B) and (C) are past tense. Choice (D) is conditional.

106. (C) *Wise* is an adjective that modifies *advice*. Choice (A) is a noun. Choice (B) is an adverb. Choice (D) is the comparative form of the adjective.

107. (B) *Earn* is a verb meaning *to work for money*. Choice (A) means *the money a person earns*. Choice (C) means *value*. Choice (D) means *money obtained during a period of time*.

108. (C) *Errors* is a noun that means *mistakes*. Choice (A) is a noun that means *chores that involve short trips around town*. Choice (B) is a verb that means *to make bad judgments*. Choice (D) is an adjective that means *irregular*.

109. (C) *And* joins two items equally. Choice (A) indicates a contrast. Choice (B) indicates a choice between items. Choice (D) indicates association.

110. (B) *To* is used with *from* to indicate a range or change of time. Choice (A) is used with specific times but is not paired with *from*. Choices (C) and (D) indicate a deadline or limit on time.

111. (A) *Went* is a main verb in the past tense. Choice (B) is the past participle and must be accompanied by an auxiliary to be part of a main verb. Choice (C) is the simple form of the verb. Choice (D) is the present participle.

112. (B) Adverbs of indefinite frequency may appear between the auxiliary and the main verb. Choices (A), (C), and (D) show the indefinite frequency adverb *always* in inappropriate positions.

113. (C) *Between* indicates position in the space that separates two objects. Choice (A) indicates position within or in the middle of. Choice (B) indicates position nearby. Choice (D) indicates source or direction away.

114. (A) *Job* refers to a specific position. Choice (B) means *a person who works*. Choice (C) means *a small job that may be unrelated to work*. Choice (D) refers to a particular sport.

115. (D) Adverbs of definite frequency may appear at the end of a clause. Choices (A), (B), and (C) are adverbs of indefinite frequency.

116. (B) *Before* organizes events in a time sequence. Choice (A) is an adverb and cannot connect clauses. Choice (C) is not logical; employees would need the lights on while they are in the office. Choice (D) indicates a cause-and-effect relationship.

117. (C) *Since* can indicate a cause-and-effect relationship. Choice (A) indicates a contrast. Choice (B) indicates an unexpected result. Choice (D) means *during*.

118. (B) Adverbs of definite frequency may appear at the end of a clause. Choice (A) is an adverb of indefinite frequency. Choice (C) is a definite frequency adverb but does not make sense as an exercise schedule. Choice (D) is an adjective.

119. (A) *Or* excludes both items. Choices (B) and (D) indicate an unexpected result. Choice (C) indicates a contrast.

120. (D) Adverbs of indefinite frequency may appear between the auxiliary and the main verb. Choices (A), (B), and (C) show the indefinite frequency adverb *always* in inappropriate positions.

121. (B) *Payment* is a noun that refers to money owed for a specific debt. Choice (A) is a noun that refers to salary. Choice (C) is an adjective. Choice (D) is a verb.

122. (C) Someone else will be bringing in the consultant, so the passive *be brought in* is used. Choice (A) is a future form. Choice (B) is the simple form. Choice (D) is the future continuous.

123. (C) Adverbs of definite frequency may appear at the end of a clause. Choices (A), (B), and (D) are adverbs of indefinite frequency.

124. (D) Someone else will organize the files, so the passive *be organized* is used. Choice (A) is the present participle. Choice (B) is the simple form. Choice (C) is a noun.

125. (C) *Near* indicates that items are close to each other. Choice (A) indicates entrance or location within. Choice (B) indicates location opposite but is often paired with *from.* Choice (D) indicates location in the space separating two items.

126. (D) Present tense can indicate habitual or repetitive action. Choice (A) is the present participle. Choice (B) is a noun that refers to people. Choice (C) is the future.

127. (A) *Is hoping* is the present continuous tense. Choice (B) is an adjective. Choices (C) and (D) are nouns.

128. (C) Someone else will leave the spaces open, so the passive *is left* is used. Choice (A) is the past tense. Choice (B) is the simple form. Choice (D) is present continuous.

129. (D) *Have* is used to mean *give* a party. Choices (A), (B), and (C) are not used with *party.*

130. (C) *Decorate* is a verb. Choice (A) is a gerund. Choice (B) is a noun that refers to decorating style. Choice (D) is a noun that refers to individual items.

131. (B) Present real conditions use past tense in the *if* clause. Choice (A) is the present tense. Choice (C) is the future. Choice (D) is the present perfect.

132. (C) *Lives* is a verb used to indicate place of residence. Choice (A) is a noun. Choice (B) is a verb that means *live,* but it is used in scientific contexts. Choice (D) is a noun referring to a person who lives in a place.

133. (B) Present real conditions may use the future tense in the result clause. Choice (A) is the conditional. Choice (C) is the present tense. Choice (D) is the past tense.

134. (A) *On* indicates location on top of. Choice (B) indicates direction away from. Choice (C) means *on behalf of.* Choice (D) indicates possession or origin.

135. (B) *Departs* agrees with the singular subject *plane.* Choice (A) is the present tense plural. Choice (C) is the past tense. Choice (D) is the present participle.

136. (D) *Because* indicates a cause-and-effect relationship. Choice (A) indicates an unexpected result. Choice (B) is a preposition, not a conjunction. Choice (C) is not logical.

137. (A) *Clearly* is an adverb describing how the doctor could see. Choice (B) means *with great control.* Choice (C) means *precisely* or *with delicacy.* Choice (D) means *almost.*

138. (A) Reference to a past tense action requires the past tense. Choice (B) is the present perfect. Choice (C) is the past continuous. Choice (D) is the past perfect.

139. (C) The letter, not Ms. Smith, caused the confusion, so the past participle is used. Choice (A) is the simple form. Choice (B) is a present participle. Choice (D) is the present tense singular.

140. (C) *But* indicates a contrast between items. Choice (A) is usually paired with *or.* Choice (B) indicates a choice between items. Choice (D) indicates a result.

PART 6 (PAGE 274)

141. (D) A *survey* is a research questionnaire sent out to many people. Choices (A), (B), and (C) are things that could be done with office workers but are incorrect in this context.

142. (A) *The remaining 15%* is the subject, correctly followed by the present tense verb *choose.* Choice (B) is the past participle. Choice (C) is a noun. Choice (D) is a present participle.

143. (D) Since the last group of people make their coffee at home, they probably prefer *homemade* coffee. Choices (A), (B), and (C) are adjectives which could also describe coffee.

144. (D) A noun is needed following the possessive adjective *your.* Choice (A) is a verb. Choice (B) is a noun which refers to a person. Choice (C) is a present participle.

145. (D) It is most likely that the result of not paying a phone bill is to have the service *cut off* or *stopped.* Choices (A) and (B) mean to make something bigger, which is the opposite of what is likely to happen. Choice (C) means *make less.*

146. (C) This pronoun refers back to the *you* mentioned in the first part of the sentence. Choices (A), (B), and (D) are not logical.

147. (A) A noun is required as the object of the verb *include.* Choice (B) is a present tense verb. Choice (C) is noun which refers to a person and therefore is not correct in this context. Choice (D) is a present participle.

148. (B) This is a negative imperative form. Choice (A) is an incorrect negative form. Choices (C) and (D) are negative verbs, but they are not imperative.

149. (C) Hotels ask customers to *reserve* a room. Choices (A), (B), and (D) are things that could be done to a room but which don't fit the context.

150. (C) *Lack* means *not having enough.* Not having enough sleep could reasonably cause problems at work. Choice (A) is a verb, but a noun is required here as the subject of the sentence. Choice (B) means *fortune.* Choice (D) means *appearance.*

151. (A) A gerund is required to follow the preposition *in.* Choice (B) is a noun. Choice (C) is a past tense verb. Choice (D) is a present tense verb.

152. (D) *Keep up* means *continue.* Choices (A), (B), and (C) when used with *keep* do not have the correct meaning for the context.

PART 7 (PAGE 279)

153. The e-mail states *Please arrange flights and hotels for me,* so Michelle wants George to (B) *Make hotel and plane reservations.* Choice (A) is incorrect because Michelle is going to Tokyo alone. Choice (C) is incorrect because Michelle wants help with travel arrangements, not travel advice. Choice (D) is incorrect because Michelle asks for a hotel near the airport but not a ride to the airport.

154. (B) *Monday* is the day Michelle plans to begin her trip. Choice (A) is when Michelle wants George to make all the arrangements. Choice (C) is the day she will return. Choice (D) is the date the e-mail was written.

155. Michelle asks for a hotel near the airport, so the correct answer is (C) *Near the airport*. Choice (A) is where Michelle does not want to stay. Choice (B) is the place she will visit, but she will not sleep there. Choice (D) is not mentioned.

156. The ad is for a *sales representative*, so the correct answer is (B) *salesperson*. Choices (A) and (C) are confused with the company product, *computer software*. Choice (D) confuses the need to travel for the job with the job of a travel agent.

157. The ad asks for *3+ years experience*, which means (B) *3 years or more*. Choice (A) confuses the meaning of *3+ years*. Choices (C) and (D) confuse the correct answer with other numbers mentioned.

158. (B) *Involves* mean *includes*; the person who takes this job will have to travel as part of the job. The meanings of choices (A) and (C) are opposite of the meaning of the correct answer. Choice (D) implies that travel is possible but not required.

159. The ad says *Call Mr. Rogers*, so the correct answer is (A) *Make a phone call*. Choice (B) is mentioned but is not the way to apply for the job. Choices (C) and (D) are not mentioned.

160. The letter is signed by the building manager, so the correct answer is (C) *The building supervisor*. Choice (A) confuses the business of the person who receives the letter. Choice (B) is the person who receives the letter. Choice (D) is mentioned but is not the person who wrote the letter.

161. The letter states *You must pay in full by April 15th*, so Mr. Johnson has to (C) *pay three months' rent*. Choice (A) is incorrect because Mr. Johnson has to pay everything he owes, not just one month. Choice (B) is what Mr. Johnson might have to do at the end of the month. Choice (D) is not something that he has to do.

162. All the items on the form are articles of clothing, so the correct answer is (D) *A clothing store*. Choices (A) and (C) confuse *tennis shirts* with *tennis store* and *sports store*. Choice (B) is not mentioned.

163. Since *$15* is the price for shipping, the correct answer is (B) *Sending the order*. Choices (A), (C), and (D) have different prices.

164. Five pairs of socks cost $25, so one pair of socks costs (B) *$5*. Choices (A), (C), and (D) confuse the correct answer with other numbers on the form.

165. (A) *Check* is the method of payment that Mr. Robles chose. Choices (B), (C), and (D) are mentioned on the form but are not marked.

166. *M–F* means (B) *Monday through Friday only* is the correct answer. Choice (A) is incorrect because the instructions give specific times for calling. Choice (C) is incorrect because customers can call only during the week. Choice (D) is incorrect because customers can only call between 9:00 and 5:00 in the day.

167. Credit cards are not accepted for orders by mail but are required for phone and online orders, so the correct answer is (D) *Either by phone or online*. Choices (A), (B), and (C) are incorrect.

168. Phone orders arrive in five days, so the correct answer is (B) *By phone*. Choices (A), (C), and (D) arrive in other amounts of time.

169. (D) *An e-mail address* is the correct answer because it is the only one of the choices not mentioned in the instructions. Choices (A), (B), and (C) are all mentioned.

170. The notice states *There is a $50 fine for violation of this order*, so people who smoke in the building must (A) *Pay $50*. Choice (B) associates *City Police Chief* with *police station*. Choice (C) associates *employee* with *employment*. Choice (D) is not a punishment for smoking but a place where people are allowed to smoke.

171. (D) *On the sidewalk* is the correct answer. Choice (A) is incorrect because smoking is allowed in one room only, not the entire floor. Choice (B) is where smoking is not allowed. Choice (C) associates *office building* with *office*.

172. The memo states *This is the third time this month,* so the correct answer is (C) *Three.* Choices (A), (B), and (D) are incorrect.

173. The memo asks employees to report problems to *Sally Garfield,* so the correct answer is (D) *Tell Sally Garfield.* Choice (A) is incorrect because the memo says *do not attempt to fix it yourself.* Choice (B) is incorrect because the memo says *Do not call a repairperson yourself.* Choice (C) is not mentioned.

174. (C) People are asked to do what the guidelines say, or to *follow* them. The other choices are other possible meanings for *observe,* but they don't fit the context.

175. (D) *April 15th* is the date the new schedule will begin. Choices (A) and (C) are not mentioned. Choice (B) is the date the notice was posted.

176. (D) *6:40 PM* is the correct answer. Choice (A) is the time of the earliest train to Woodmont. Choice (B) is the time of the latest train to Summerside. Choice (C) is the time of the latest train to Marysville.

177. The notice says *Station office hours will remain the same,* so the correct answer is (C) *The station office hours.* Choices (A), (B), and (D) all mention things that will change.

178. (D) Lora, Kyle, Sandy, Tiffany, and Kevin have all requested vacation leave for next month. Choice (A) is the number of people who will take a vacation during the first week of the month. Choice (B) is the number of people who will take a vacation during the fourth week of the month. Choice (C) is the number of people who have had their vacation requests approved for next month.

179. (C) Sandy and Tiffany have had their leave approved for the last week of May. Choice (A) is the person who will do Sandy and Tiffany's work while they are away. Choices (B) and (D) include the person who has not had his vacation request approved.

180. (A) Dan will take his vacation this month, which we see by the date on the e-mail is April. Choice (B) is when many of the other staff members will take their vacation. Choice (C) is when Cynthia wants Kevin to take his vacation. Choice (D) is when Cynthia will take her vacation.

181. (B) Mr. Chang says that he will arrive from Melbourne. Choice (A) is the place that he will arrive at. Choice (C) is the name of his hotel. Choice (D) is where he will go next.

182. (B) Mr. Robertson will pick him up in the company car. Choice (A) is Mr. Chang's suggestion. Choice (C) is how he will get to the office. Choice (D) is not mentioned.

183. (A) Mr. Robertson should arrive half an hour before Mr. Chang's arrival time of 11:00. Choice (B) is Mr. Chang's arrival time. Choice (C) is half an hour before Mr. Chang will arrive at the office, not the airport. Choice (D) is the time Mr. Chang will arrive at the office.

184. (C) Mr. Chang asked to see a copy of the Petersen report, and Ms. McLean asked Mr. Robertson to give it to him. Choices (A) and (B) are things that Mr. Chang will bring with him. Choice (D) is associated with the hotel room.

185. (C) Ms. McLean asks Mr. Robertson to make dinner reservations at the hotel restaurant. Choices (A), (B), and (D) are places that Mr. Chang will visit, but he will not have dinner at any of them Wednesday evening.

186. (B) Mai Le has just become CEO of the Playtime Corporation. Choice (A) is where she used to work. Choices (C) and (D) are where she studied.

187. (D) The article says that she graduated 25 years go. Choice (A) is when she began working at the Playtime Corporation. Choice (B) is confused with the date of the letter. Choice (C) is not mentioned.

188. (A) Alice sent the letter after reading about Mai's promotion in the newspaper. Choice (B) is confused with the fact that they were high school classmates. Choice (C) is confused with Caroline Overall's new business. Choice (D) is confused with a program she started at her company.

189. (D) Alice mentions having met Mai in high school. Choice (A) is confused with the mention of the former company CEO who must have been Mai's old boss. Choices (B) and (C) are confused with the programs that Mai started at her company.

190. (A) Alice says that Mai's former boss, who is the ex-CEO Caroline Overall, will attend the dinner. The other choices are people who were invited to the dinner but cannot attend.

191. (D) According to the memo, he needs to learn to perform his job duties adequately. Choice (A) is a plausible reason but is not mentioned. Choice (B) is confused with the fact that he will take classes, but the classes are not at a university. Choice (C) is associated with the mention of the co-workers who have already taken classes at the institute.

192. (A) Mr. Amadeo recommends 105A, which is Introduction to Database I. Choices (B) and (D) are other courses on the schedule. Choice (C) looks similar to courses on the schedule but doesn't actually appear there.

193. (D) Mr. Caldwell will take 105A, which is offered on Monday and Wednesday, and either 101B or 106A, both of which are offered on Tuesday and Thursday, so he will study Monday, Tuesday, Wednesday, and Thursday.

194. (A) The memo says that the company will pay for the entire tuition, so Mr. Caldwell himself will pay nothing. Choice (B) is the cost of one class. Choice (C) is the cost of two classes and is the amount the company will pay. Choice (D) is the cost of three classes.

195. (A) Class number 110A is the only business writing course offered at the institute. Choices (B), (C), and (D) are different courses.

196. (D) According to the instructions, a full refund is guaranteed during the first 30 days, and Peter says that they have had the printer five days longer than that. Choice (A) is the number of days past the refund date that they have had the printer. Choice (B) is five days less than the refund limit. Choice (C) is the number of days in the refund limit.

197. (C) This is the problem that Peter states. Choice (A) is confused with the two hours Peter spent on the phone. Choice (B) is not correct because Peter says that a new ink cartridge did not solve the problem. Choice (D) can't be correct because they have had the printer for only 35 days.

198. (A) Peter plans to return the printer to the company, and the instructions say that the purpose of this is repairs. Choice (B) is confused with the refund that is offered during the first 30 days. Choice (C) is not mentioned. Choice (D) is confused with the person with whom Peter spoke on the phone.

199. (B) According to the instructions, the company will not pay for the postage to return a printer to the company, so Mary will have to buy stamps. Choices (A), (C), and (D) are things which, according to the instructions, the company provides with the printer.

200. (C) In his e-mail, Peter complains that New Century products always break down. Choice (A) is incorrect because Peter says that the prices are great. Choice (B) is incorrect because Peter is mailing the printer to the company for repairs. Choice (D) is incorrect because the only cost of returning the printer is the shipping, and no one mentions that this is too high.

Answer Key
Practice Test One

Part 1 (page 300)

1. (A) The conference is in session. Choice (B) confuses a *movie* and a *conference*. Choice (C) confuses *concert hall is empty* and *conference room is full*. Choice (D) is incorrect because the attendees are sitting, not standing.

2. (D) They're walking through the facility. Choice (A) confuses the similar-sounding words *wading* and *walking*. Choice (B) uses the associated words *tanks* and *gas*. Choice (C) uses the associated word *field*.

3. (D) The man is putting a pin in the map. Choice (A) confuses the similar-sounding words *nap* and *map*. Choice (B) is incorrect because the map is on the wall, not in a book. Choice (C) associates *geography book* with *map*.

4. (C) Both men are standing by the whiteboard, probably discussing the figures. Choice (A) confuses the similar-sounding words *purses* and *persons*. Choice (B) is incorrect because one of the men is holding an eraser, not a briefcase. Choice (D) is incorrect because neither man is laughing.

5. (B) The men are working with computers. Choice (A) confuses the similar *street corner* and *corner of the desk*. Choice (C) confuses the similar-sounding words *money* and *monitor*. Choice (D) is incorrect because computers are not considered heavy equipment.

6. (B) He's looking through one of the drawers. Choice (A) confuses the similar-sounding words *door* and *drawer* and the opposites *closing* and *opening*. Choice (C) confuses the words *watch* (verb) and *watch* (noun) and associates *watch* with *clock*. Choice (D) is incorrect because he's looking through the drawer, not holding a box.

7. (C) The woman and man are looking at a piece of paper. Choice (A) is incorrect because they're sitting at the desk, not on the desk. Choice (B) confuses *piece of cake* and *piece of paper*. Choice (D) confuses the similar-sounding words *piece of paper* and *calculator*.

8. (A) The coffeemaker is beside the sink. Choice (B) is incorrect because the coffeepots are in use, and there are no pots in the sink. Choice (C) confuses *drinking coffee* and *making coffee*. Choice (D) confuses the similar-sounding words *spot* and *pot* and associates *water* with *sink*.

9. (B) The lamp is above the workbench. Choice (A) is incorrect because the shelves are above the table, not under it. Choice (C) is incorrect because no one is at the desk. Choice (D) confuses *showroom* and *workroom*.

10. (B) They're having a discussion. Choice (A) confuses the similar-sounding words *meat* and *meeting*. Choice (C) is incorrect because they have books in front of them, but they are not shelving the books. Choice (D) is incorrect because they're leaning on, not wiping, the table.

Part 2 (page 306)

11. (B) *In the lobby* answers where. Choice (A) associates *news* with *newsstand*. Choice (C) confuses the words *stand* (verb) and *stand* (noun).

12. (A) *The guests* answers *who*. Choice (B) associates *doorman* with *door*. Choice (C) repeats the word *door* but answers *what*.

13. (A) Milk and bread can be purchased at the store. Choice (B) answers *until what time is the store open*. Choice (C) confuses the words *store* (verb), meaning *to place or put something away for later*, and *store* (noun), meaning *a retail establishment*.

14. (A) *He suggested I sell my stock* answers *why* by providing an explanation. Choice (B) confuses the similar-sounding words *broke* and *broker*. Choice (C) associates *telephoned* with *call* and confuses the similar-sounding words *brother* with *broker*.

15. (C) *Whenever you're hungry* answers *when*. Choice (A) associates *lunch* with *eat* but is not likely because the speakers probably wouldn't want to eat again right after eating lunch. Choice (B) confuses the similar-sounding words *meat* and *eat*.

16. (B) *I received two* answers *who*. Choice (A) associates *paid* and *check* with *paycheck*. Choice (C) confuses the similar-sounding words *reviewed* with *received* and *payable* with *paycheck*.

17. (B) The event does not require fancy (extra special) clothing. Choice (A) confuses *wear* and *where*. Choice (C) uses the related idea of being with the company for a long time and *retirement party* but does not address the concern about clothing.

18. (C) *A customer* answers *who*. Choice (A) associates *phone system* with *phone*. Choice (B) repeats the word *phone* but does not answer the question.

19. (C) *Last night* answers *when*. Choice (A) confuses the words *complete* (adjective) and *complete* (verb). Choice (B) is incorrect because they already finished the project.

20. (A) *He was fired* answers *why*. Choice (B) answers *who is leaving*. Choice (C) confuses the similar-sounding words *live* and *leave*.

21. (A) *No, there's one more after this one* answers the *yes/no* question. Choice (B) confuses the similar-sounding words *lasts* and *last*. Choice (C) repeats the word *bus* but answers *where*.

22. (C) *The computer saleswoman* answers *who*. Choices (A) and (B) answer *what*.

23. (A) *He's my supervisor* answers *who*. Choice (B) repeats the phrase *over there* but answers *where*. Choice (C) repeats the word *there* but does not answer the question.

24. (B) *She's a marketing specialist* answers *what is her profession*. Choice (A) confuses the similar-sounding words *professor* and *profession*. Choice (C) confuses the similar-sounding words *professionals* and *profession*.

25. (A) The new partner is Chris Burns. Choice (B) confuses the related ideas of *business partner* and *marriage partner*. Choice (C) uses the related word *explain*, though no new understanding is required.

26. (C) *In a meeting* answers *where*. Choice (A) answers *when*. Choice (B) does not answer the question.

27. (C) The clients need to be told about the change. Choice (A) is illogical because the change is going to take place in the future. Choice (B) confuses the related words *January or February* with *month*, but no opinion is requested.

28. (C) *No, not everyone has arrived yet* answers the *yes/no* question with a reason for not starting the meeting. Choice (A) answers *where*. Choice (B) answers *when*.

29. (A) The respondent thought the speaker was responsible for the task. Choice (B) confuses the similar-sounding words *renovations* and *reservations*. Choice (C) uses the related word *remember*, but the reminder is about making reservations, not collecting money.

30. (A) *Not me, thank you* is a polite response to the question. Choice (B) associates *reporter* with *newspaper*. Choice (C) does not answer the question.

31. (B) *I am* answers *who*. Choice (A) associates *news* with *radio*. Choice (C) confuses the similar words *listen* with *listening*.

32. (B) *The pump engine and pipes* answers *what equipment is missing*. Choice (A) associates *team* with *equipment* and *short* with *missing* by using the words out of context. Choice (C) confuses the similar-sounding words *experiment* and *equipment* and associates *lost* with *missing*.

33. (B) *To his office address* answers *where*. Choice (A) answers *when*. Choice (C) confuses the similar-sounding words *let her* and *letter*.

34. (A) *The office manager* answers *who.* Choice (B) answers *how long.* Choice (C) confuses the *sea* and *see.*

35. (C) *It's expected to stop tonight* answers *when.* Choice (A) answers *what will stop.* Choice (B) answers *when will it rain.*

36. (A) *Yes, I put them in the supply room* answers the *yes/no* question. Choice (B) answers *where can I put the supplies.* Choice (C) does not answer the question.

37. (C) *In three months* answers *when.* Choice (A) confuses the similar-sounding words *Finnish* and *finished.* Choice (B) repeats the word *building* but does not answer the question.

38. (B) This person's business e-mail account is not for personal use. Choice (A) uses the repeated root *person,* but James is not the topic of this conversation. Choice (C) uses the related word *funny,* but it is in the wrong tense. The joke hasn't been forwarded yet.

39. (B) *The electricity is off* answers *why* by providing a reason. Choice (A) associates *photos* with *photocopier.* Choice (C) associates *copied* with *photocopier.*

40. (C) *Twelve people* answers *how large is your staff.* Choice (A) confuses the similar-sounding words *stuff* and *staff.* Choice (B) repeats the word *staff* but does not answer the question.

PART 3 (PAGE 307)

41. (A) The man is buying a new pair of shoes. Choice (B) confuses *pear* with word *pair.* Choice (C) confuses *book* with *checkbook.* Choice (D) confuses *newspaper* with the similar-sounding phrase *new pair.*

42. (B) The woman says that the shoes cost $17.75. Choices (A), (C), and (D) are numbers that sound similar to the correct answer.

43. (B) The man says that he will pay with a credit card. Choice (A) is incorrect because the man says that he doesn't have cash. Choice (C) confuses *traveler's check* with *personal check.* Choice (D) is one way the man considers paying.

44. (A) The man decides to mail the package first class, which takes six days. Choices B and C are not mentioned. Choice (D) is how long the package would take by second class.

45. (C) The man says that the package contains jewelry. Choice (A) uses the word *China* out of context. Choice (B) is confused with the method of payment the man considers using. Choice (D) uses the word *class* in a different context.

46. (C) The man will pay for postage and insurance, which adds up to $15. Choice (A) is the cost of insurance alone. Choice (B) is the cost of postage alone. Choice (D) is the value of the contents of the package.

47. (B) The man says that the repairperson will come tomorrow. Choice (A) is when the machine broke. Choices (C) and (D) are confused with *the fourth time this month.*

48. (A) The woman says that she has to get reports copied. Choice (B) confuses *photographs* with the similar-sounding word *photocopies.* Choice (C) associates *repair bill* with *repairperson.* Choice (D) associates *meeting agenda* with *meeting.*

49. (C) The woman says that there is a photocopy store across the street. Choice (A) is the former location of a photocopy store. Choice (B) uses the word *fourth* out of context. Choice (D) confuses *door* with the similar-sounding word *floor.*

50. (B) The man says *I hope the bus gets here soon.* Choice (A) confuses *car* with the similar-sounding word *far.* Choices (C) and (D) confuse *train* and *plane* with the similar-sounding word *rain.*

51. (B) The man says that it's cloudy. Choice (A) is what the woman thinks might happen later. Choice (C) is incorrect because the man says that it's not cold. Choice (D) confuses *hot* with the similar-sounding word *not.*

52. (A) The man says that he has been waiting 15 minutes. Choices (B), (C), and (D) are numbers that sound similar to the correct answer.

53. (B) The woman says that her vacation begins on Tuesday. Choice (A) confuses *Monday* with the similar-sounding word *mountains*. Choice (C) is not mentioned. Choice (D) confuses *Thursday* with the similar-sounding word *Tuesday*.

54. (D) The woman says that her vacation will last two weeks. Choice (A) confuses *two days* with the similar-sounding word *Tuesday*. Choice (B) is the man's guess. Choice (C) confuses *eight* with the similar-sounding word *wait*.

55. (D) The woman says that she will spend her vacation in New York. Choice (A) confuses *lake* with the similar-sounding word *like*. Choice (B) is where the woman usually spends her vacation. Choice (C) is the man's guess.

56. (D) The woman says that Mr. Kim is out of town on a business trip. Choice (A) is the man's guess. Choice (B) confuses *downtown* with the similar-sounding phrase *out of town*. Choice (C) repeats the word *late*.

57. (B) The man says that seven people showed up at the meeting. Choice (A) confuses *two* with the similar-sounding word *few*. Choice (C) confuses *eleven* with the similar-sounding word *seven*. Choice (D) is the number of people that were supposed to show up.

58. (D) The man mentions *next month's meeting*. Choice (A) is confused with *this morning*. Choice (B) confuses *two* with the similar-sounding word *few*. Choice (C) is when Mr. Kim will return from his trip.

59. (A) The speakers discuss opening a savings account and making a deposit, so they must be in a bank. Choice (B) associates *$500* and *check* with buying something in a store. Choice (C) is not mentioned. Choice (D) confuses *accountant* with *savings account*.

60. (B) The woman says she has a *$500 check*. Choice (A) confuses *four* with *for*. Choice (C) confuses *eight* with the similar-sounding word *great*. Choice (D) confuses *nine* with the similar-sounding word *sign*.

61. (C) The man asks the woman to sign the check on the back. Choices (A) and (D) are mentioned in the conversation, but nobody says anything about signing them. Choice (B) confuses *letter* with the similar-sounding word *later*.

62. (A) The man says that there is too much snow to drive. Choice (B) confuses *rain* with the similar-sounding word *train*. Choice (C) confuses *hot* with the similar-sounding word *not*. Choice (D) confuses *windy* with the similar-sounding word *Wednesday*.

63. (B) The woman says that they will take the train. Choice (A) associates *car* with *driving*, which the man says they won't do. Choice (C) confuses *walk* with the similar-sounding word *work*. Choice (D) is not mentioned.

64. (C) The man says that he has a conference call at 10:00. Choice (A) confuses *meeting* with the similar-sounding word *eating*. Choice (B) uses the word *conference* out of context. Choice (D) is incorrect because the man will have to get on the train well before 10:00 in order to be at work on time for the conference call.

65. (C) The man says that there is a hotel across the street. Choice (A) confuses *another street* with *across the street*. Choice (B) is not mentioned. Choice (D) uses the word *right* in a different context.

66. (B) The woman decides to buy a magazine. Choice (A) is what the woman wanted to buy, but the man says they're sold out. Choices (C) and (D) are other things the man offers for sale.

67. (C) The man says that the magazine costs $4.50. Choices (A), (B), and (D) are numbers that sound similar to the correct answer.

68. (D) The speakers are in a place where they go to eat sometimes, so they must be in a restaurant. Choice (A) associates *home* with *eat*. Choice (B) associates *bakery* with *bread*. Choice (C) associates the different kinds of food mentioned with a *grocery store*.

69. (C) The man says he eats there once a week. Choice (A) is how often the woman would like to eat there. Choices (B) and (D) are not mentioned.

70. (C) The man says he will try the fried chicken. Choice (A) is what the woman asks about. Choice (B) confuses *rice* with the similar-sounding word *fried*. Choice (D) associates *sandwiches* with *bread*.

PART 4 (PAGE 310)

71. (A) Company employees would listen to this business announcement on company policy. Choice (B) confuses *doctors* with *doctor's note*. Choices (C) would probably not be interested in this announcement. Choice (D) repeats the word *officer*.

72. (C) Company policy on the need for doctor's notes has been revised. Choice (A) is what the policy was about. Choices (B) and (D) are not mentioned.

73. (D) Employees are no longer required to get a doctor's note for illnesses lasting more than four days. Choices (A), (B), and (C) are contradicted by the phrase *no longer required*.

74. (D) A building is on fire and firefighters have to have room to work. Choice (A) confuses *people need a hotel room* and *firefighters need room to work*. Choice (B) associates *going home* and *stay away*. Choice (C) confuses *personnel office* with *emergency personnel*.

75. (B) Emergency personnel must get through to deal with the fire. Choice (A) associates *office* with *building* and confuses *office personnel* and *emergency personnel*. Choice (C) is not mentioned. Choice (D) confuses the similar-sounding words *file* and *fire*.

76. (B) People are asked to stay *on the other side of the street*. Choices (A) and (D) use the word *room* in a different context. Choice (C) confuses *beside* with the similar-sounding word *side*.

77. (B) The Space Program is mentioned. Choice (A) confuses the similar-sounding words *race* and *space*. Choice (C) confuses the similar-sounding words *tasting* and *tasty*. Choice (D) uses *waste* in a different context.

78. (A) A dog (canine) is the only animal mentioned. Choices (B), (C), and (D) are not mentioned.

79. (A) This is the first time the program will send an animal to Mars. Choices (B), (C), and (D) are contradicted by *this is the first . . .*

80. (C) The president is described as being a parent. Choice (A) describes the president's wife. Choice (B) associates *doctor* with *hospital*. Choice (D) confuses a *general* and *General Hospital*.

81. (A) The president and his wife have become parents *for the second time*, so they have two children. Choices (B), (C), and (D) are confused with the numbers in *5:43*, the time that the baby was born and the numbers of children born in the future.

82. (B) The baby was born at 5:43 A.M. today. Choices (A), (C), and (D) are contradicted by 5:43 A.M.

83. (B) Televisions are being sold. Choice (A) confuses *selling a watch* and *watching television*. Choice (C) associates *calendar* with *Day-by-Day*. Choice (D) is what is being offered as a free gift.

84. (D) They'll give a one-year subscription. Choice (A) confuses *ten days* and *the first ten people*. Choice (B) is contradicted by a *one-year subscription*. Choice (C) confuses *ten months* and *ten people*.

85. (B) The first ten people who buy a television set will get the special offer. Choice (A) confuses *one person* and *one-year subscription*. Choices (C) and (D) are contradicted by *the first ten people*.

86. (C) The caller has reached a nonworking number. Choices (A) and (B) are contradicted by *a nonworking number*. Choice (D) confuses *the caller hung up* and *hang up and try again*.

87. (D) The caller is told to hang up and try again. Choice (A) confuses *give up* and *hang up*. Choice (B) associates *get another job* and *nonworking*. Choice (C) is contradicted by *hang up*.

88. (A) The announcement says *if you would like to check the number you are dialing*. Choice (B) uses the word *check* out of context. Choice (C) repeats the words *dialing* and *assistance*. Choice (D) repeats the word *number*.

89. (C) The warm weather will continue for the rest of the week. Choices (A) and (B) are what the weather is expected to be by Sunday. Choice (D) *windy* is what the weather was.

90. (A) By Sunday, temperatures will drop and rain is likely. Choices (B), (C), and (D) are mentioned in other contexts.

91. (C) The speaker says *Expect up to four inches*. Choice (A) confuses *two* with *to*. Choice (B) is not mentioned. Choice (D) confuses *24 inches* with the similar-sounding phrase *to four inches*.

92. (C) High-quality paper and envelopes are on sale. Choices (A) and (B) are mentioned in a different context. Choice (D) is not mentioned.

93. (B) All colors but yellow are available. Choices (A), (C), and (D) are all available.

94. (D) Saturday is the last day of this sale. Choices (A), (B), and (C) are contradicted by Saturday being the last day.

95. (B) Sparkles Jewelry Store was robbed. Choice (A) confuses *clothing* with the similar-sounding word *closing*. Choice (C) repeats the word *computer,* which was something not taken from the store. Choice (D) repeats the word *watch,* which was also something not taken from the store.

96. (D) The robbery occurred at 8:55. Choices (A), (B), and (C) are numbers that sound similar to the correct answer.

97. (D) The store owner was the only person present. Choice (A) is mentioned in the report but not as being present at the time of the robbery. Choices (B) and (C) are people who left the store before the robbery.

98. (A) The advertisement says that the café is closed Monday. Choices (B) and (D) are confused with *open Tuesday through Sunday*. Choice (C) is the day of the brunch special.

99. (B) The brunch special is all-you-can-eat pancakes for $6.00. Choice (A) confuses *birthday cake* with the last syllable of *pancakes*. Choice (C) confuses *steak* with the similar-sounding word *pancake*. Choice (D) confuses *pans* with the first syllable of *pancakes*.

100. (D) The advertisement says that the café is located *one block from the subway station*. Choice (A) is confused with *River Road*. Choice (B) is confused with *parking in the back*. Choice (C) confuses *bus station* with *subway station*.

PART 5 (PAGE 313)

101. (A) *To* indicates direction toward. Choices (B) and (D) indicate location. Choice (C) indicates manner.

102. (B) *Will be* requires the past participle *shortened*. Choice (A) is an adjective. Choice (C) is a present participle. Choice (D) is a noun.

103. (A) The subordinating conjunction *after* joins two clauses. Choices (B) and (C) indicate a cause-and-effect relationship. Choice (D) is a coordinate conjunction.

104. (C) Someone else will mail the paychecks, so the passive *be mailed* is used. Choice (A) is the simple form of the verb. Choice (B) is the present tense. Choice (D) is the present participle.

105. (A) A past action that occurs before another past action requires the past perfect tense. Choice (B) is the present tense. Choice (C) is the present perfect. Choice (D) is the present continuous.

106. (B) The adjective *successful* modifies year. Choice (A) is an adverb. Choice (C) is a singular noun. Choice (D) is a plural noun.

107. (D) The coordinate conjunction *and* joins two verbs. Choices (A) and (B) are subordinating conjunctions. Choice (C) is a coordinating conjunction but excludes both items.

108. (C) The noun *home* serves as an object of *heading*. Choices (A), (B), and (D) are adjectives.

109. (B) *By* indicates association with. Choice (A) indicates association but is not used with *accompanied*. Choice (C) indicates direction toward. Choice (D) indicates direction away.

110. (A) The adjective *foolish* modifies *decisions*. Choice (B) is a noun referring to a person. Choice (C) is a noun referring to behavior or attitudes. Choice (D) is a verb.

111. (B) *On* is used with days of the week. Choice (A) is used with specific times. Choice (C) indicates a time limit. Choice (D) indicates direction away.

112. (B) The present tense indicates habitual action. Choice (A) is the present tense but does not agree with the singular *owner*. Choice (C) is the present participle. Choice (D) is the past tense.

113. (D) *Assist* means *help*. Choice (A) means *to be present at*. Choice (B) means *to make presumptions about*. Choice (C) means *to give a duty to*.

114. (B) Adverbs of definite frequency may appear at the end of a verb phrase. Choices (A), (C), and (D) are adverbs of indefinite frequency.

115. (C) *At* is used with specific times. Choice (A) indicates direction toward. Choice (B) indicates direction from. Choice (D) indicates purpose.

116. (B) *Seems* is present tense, indicating the same time frame as *have available*. Choice (A) is the past perfect. Choice (C) is the present continuous. Choice (D) is the future tense.

117. (A) Adverbs of indefinite frequency may come between the auxiliary and the main verb. Choices (B), (C), and (D) show the indefinite frequency adverb *always* in inappropriate positions.

118. (B) The adjective *popular* describes the new schedules. Choices (A) and (C) are verbs. Choice (D) is a noun.

119. (B) *On* is used with dates. Choice (A) indicates purpose. Choice (C) indicates direction toward. Choice (D) indicates directions away.

120. (C) The subordinate conjunction *when* joins two clauses in a time relationship. Choice (A) is a preposition. Choice (B) indicates cause and effect. Choice (D) is a subordinating conjunction but means *during*.

121. (B) *Borrow* means *to take something with the agreement that it will be returned to the owner after use*. Choice (A) refers to something that has been borrowed. Choice (C) means *allow to borrow*. Choice (D) means *to transmit or transfer something to another person*.

122. (A) Adverbs of indefinite frequency may occur between the auxiliary and the main verb. Choices (B), (C), and (D) show the indefinite frequency adverb *never* in inappropriate positions.

123. (C) *Or* provides a choice between items. Choice (A) is a coordinate conjunction paired with *or*. Choice (B) includes both items. Choice (D) indicates a contrast between items.

124. (D) Adverbs of indefinite frequency may occur between the auxiliary and the main verb. Choices (A), (B), and (C) show the indefinite frequency adverb *ever* in inappropriate positions.

125. (A) Present unreal conditions use past tense in the *if* clause. Choice (B) is the present tense. Choice (C) is the future tense. Choice (D) is conditional.

126. (C) Adverbs of definite frequency may appear at the end of a clause. Choices (A), (B), and (D) are adverbs of indefinite frequency.

127. (B) Someone else will open the boxes, so the passive *be opened* is used. Choice (A) is the present participle. Choice (C) is the simple form. Choice (D) is present tense singular.

128. (C) The directors are the ones who will understand the problem, so the simple form *understand* is used. Choice (A) is the present participle. Choice (B) is the past tense. Choice (D) with *will* forms the future continuous.

129. (B) *Since* is a subordinating conjunction that indicates a cause-and-effect relationship. Choice (A) indicates an unexpected result. Choice (C) indicates a contrast. Choice (D) must appear in the effect clause.

130. (D) Someone else will deposit the checks, so the passive *be deposited* is used. Choice (A) is the simple form. Choice (B) is the present tense singular. Choice (C) is the present participle.

131. (B) A present real condition may use the future tense in the result clause. Choice (A) is the present tense singular. Choice (C) is the past tense. Choice (D) is the present continuous.

132. (D) *Entrance* is a noun modified by the adjective *side*. Choice (A) is the simple form of the verb. Choice (B) is the past tense. Choice (C) is the past participle.

133. (D) *Will be checking out* is the future continuous. Choice (A) cannot be followed by the past participle of the verb. Choice (B) is not logical; guests who have checked out would not be asked to contact the front desk. Choice (C) cannot be followed by the past participle.

134. (B) *Millionaire* is a noun referring to a person. Choices (A) and (C) are nouns referring to money. Choice (D) is an adjective.

135. (A) Present real conditions may use present tense in the *if* clause. Choice (B) is the future tense. Choice (C) is the past perfect. Choice (D) is the simple verb.

136. (D) Situations in the present may be described by the present tense. Choice (A) *shall* indicates an intention for future action. Choice (B) is the future perfect. Choice (C) is the present continuous.

137. (C) *Knowledgeable* is an adjective that describes the company president. Choice (A) is the present participle. Choice (B) is a noun. Choice (D) is the present tense singular verb.

138. (B) *Has been working* is the present perfect continuous form. Choice (A) *has* must be used with *worked* to form the present perfect. Choice (C) is the present tense. Choice (D) is the future tense.

139. (D) Present unreal conditions use the conditional form in the result clause. Choice (A) is the future tense. Choice (B) is the simple form. Choice (C) is the past tense.

140. (A) Someone else picked up the suitcases, so the past participle *picked up* is used. Choice (B) is the present participle. Choice (C) is the present tense. Choice (D) is passive.

PART 6 (PAGE 317)

141. (A) *Move* is a verb of motion followed by the adverb *there*, referring to a place at a distance from the speaker. Choices (B) and (D) are pronouns for things. Choice (C) refers to the current location of the speaker.

142. (B) *Residential* refers to a neighborhood where people live, away from businesses, which is what Boris says he is looking for. Choice (A) refers to factories. Choice (C) means *full of influence*, which is not a likely way to describe a neighborhood. Choice (D) refers to stores.

143. (C) An infinitive verb is required to follow the main verb plan. Choice (A) is a base form. Choice (B) is a present participle. Choice (D) is a future verb.

144. (C) The notice addresses the reader directly, so the second-person form is required. Choice (A) is a first-person form and is confused with the word *we*, used as the subject of the sentence. Choices (B) and (D) are third-person forms.

145. (B) A motel guest can dial a phone number to contact someone at the front desk. Choices (A), (C), and (D) are words that could be used with numbers but not with phone numbers.

146. (D) *Complimentary*, meaning *free*, is an adjective form used to describe *breakfast*. Choice (A) is a verb meaning *to say kind words*. Choice (B) is the past tense form of the verb. Choice (C) is the present participle.

147. (D) *Easily* is an adverb describing how the guests will hear. Choice (A) is a noun. Choice (B) is an adjective. Choice (C) is a comparative adjective.

148. (C) *Need* is followed by the infinitive form of the verb. Choice (A) is the base form. Choice (B) is present tense. Choice (D) is the present participle.

149. (A) *Fees* are prices, which is what this sentence is asking about. Choices (B), (C), and (D) are words that are related to rentals, but they don't fit the sentence.

150. (A) *Retailer* means *seller*. Choices (B), (C), and (D) are related to the topic of cars but do not have the correct meaning for the context.

151. (A) *Ourselves* refers back to the subject of the sentence *We*. Choices (B) and (C) refer to the word *you*. Choice (D) refers to the word *it*.

152. (B) *Safety* refers back to the topic of the previous sentence about making sure that roads are not dangerous and customers feel secure. Choices (A), (C), and (D) are other things that car sellers may care about but don't fit the context of the sentence.

Part 7 (page 323)

153. (B) Bus riders would need to know about changes in bus routes. Choice (A) associates *weather* with *rain*. Choice (C) assumes that city workers take buses. Choice (D) associates *bus repair people* with *bus routes*.

154. (B) The bus routes will be changed due to the parade. Choice (A) confuses *being used in the parade* and *changing routes to get around the parade*. Choice (C) is not mentioned. Choice (D) confuses *going out of service* and *changing routes*.

155. (B) In the event of rain, the parade will take place shortly after 3:00 P.M. Choice (A) is when the parade is originally scheduled. Choices (C) and (D) are contradicted by the parade being held shortly after 3:00 P.M.

156. (C) Ordering supplies is the subject of the memo. Choice (A) associates *accounts* with *accounting department*. Choice (B) associates *office furniture* with *office supplies*. Choice (D) associates *computers* with *typed requests*.

157. (A) Only typed requests will be accepted. Choices (B) and (C) are contradicted by *only typed requests will be accepted*. Choice (D) is what happens to approved requests.

158. (D) Requests that are accepted will be forwarded to the Accounting Department. The other options do not fit the context.

159. (C) Approved requests will be sent onto the Accounting Department. Choice (A) is what would happen to handwritten and unsigned requests. Choice (B) associates *purchasing* with *ordering*. Choice (D) is not mentioned.

160. (C) A letter up to 25 grams can be sent to South Africa, a country in Africa, for ¥130 (130 yen). Choice (A) is the cost of sending a postcard. Choice (B) is the cost of sending an aerogramme. Choice (D) is the cost of sending a letter weighing more than 25 grams to Africa.

161. (B) An aerogramme sent to anywhere in the world costs ¥90. Choice (A) is the cost of sending a postcard. Choice (C) is the cost of sending a letter up to 25 grams to Zone 2. Choice (D) is the cost of sending a letter weighing between 25 and 50 grams to Zone 1.

162. (A) A letter weighing 25 grams or less costs ¥110 to Europe. Choice (B) would cost ¥190. Choice (C) is not stated in the chart. Choice (D) is incorrect because the weight (up to 25 grams) is specified.

163. (D) Since the bulletin refers to train reservations, train passengers would probably be most interested in reading it. Choice (A) confuses the similar-sounding words *plane* and *train*. Choice (B) confuses the similar-sounding words *car* with *cart* and the words *car* (automobiles) with *car* (train). Choice (C) associates *bus* with *coaches*.

164. (B) Reservations are required for all first-class compartments. Choice (A) is incorrect because only trains with first-class cars, which require reservations, have dining cars. Choices (C) and (D) are mentioned as coaches not requiring reservations.

165. (B) Dining cars are in trains that have first-class cars. Choices (A), (C), and (D) are contradicted by *trains that do not have first-class cars will not have a dining car.*

166. (B) Any extra bags may be checked. The other options do not fit the context.

167. (C) Mr. Goodwin probably lives in Australia since his company's address is in Australia. Choices (A), (B), and (D) are countries he will visit next summer.

168. (A) Mrs. Mangala exports jewelry. Choice (B) is what Mr. Goodwin probably manufactures. Choice (C) associates *textiles* with *fashions*. Choice (D) is not mentioned.

169. (D) A line is a type of product. The other options do not fit the context.

170. (D) Since Mrs. Mangala's business is in Sri Lanka, the jewelry will probably be exported from there. Choice (A) is where Mr. Goodwin is going. Choice (B) is where the jewelry would be exported to. Choice (C) is where Mr. Goodwin is going.

171. (A) Mr. Goodwin's London associates were very pleased with the quality of Mrs. Mangala's gems. Choices (B), (C), and (D) are not mentioned.

172. (C) The directions are for waterproofing. Choices (A) and (B) confuse *protection from dirt and dust* with *remove all dust and dirt from shoes*. Choice (D) confuses *drying out* and *let dry*.

173. (B) The directions say to repeat application one more time. Choice (A) is contradicted by the phrase *one more time*. Choice (C) confuses *six times* with *six inches* and *six months*. Choice (D) confuses *eight times* and *eight inches*.

174. (D) The application will last for six months. Choices (A), (B), and (C) are contradicted by *six months*.

175. (C) The total number of teachers in the survey is 43. Choice (A) is the number of teachers who said the reason for lack of computer education was because it was too expensive. Choices (B) and (D) are contradicted by *43*.

176. (D) More teachers gave expense as a reason than any other reason listed. Choices (A) and (B) have lower numbers than the *too expensive* reason. Choice (C) is the reason given the least often.

177. (C) Only eight teachers said they feared computers. Choices (A), (B), and (D) all have a higher number of respondents.

178. (A) Mr. Ng must have written an essay in order to win the Essay Competition award. Choices (B) and (C) are not mentioned. Choice (D) confuses *announced the winner* and *announced his retirement*.

179. (B) The winner was announced last night. Choice (A) confuses *last year* and *Hotel Manager of the Year*. Choices (C) and (D) are contradicted by *last night*.

180. (D) Mr. Ng wants to make it possible for others to achieve success by themselves. Choice (A) is selfish attitude. Choices (B) and (C) refer to Mr. Ng's analogy that a manager is like a parent.

181. (B) There is a matinee and an evening performance on Saturday. Choice (A) is the number of performances on other days. Choice (C) is the number of days of the week that there are performances. Choice (D) is not mentioned.

182. (A) The ad is for a live performance of a play by Shakespeare. Choice (B) is contradicted by *live performance*. Choice (C) is not a performance. Choice (D) is confused with *orchestra seats*.

183. (B) According to the ad, a group of at least 15 people can get a 10 percent discount, and Mr. Stein says his department has just enough people to qualify for it. Choice (A) is the size of the discount. Choice (C) is the size of the larger discount. Choice (D) is the number of people needed to get the larger discount.

184. (A) Mr. Stein wants tickets for opening night, which, according to the ad, is March 12. Choices (B) and (C) are not mentioned. Choice (D) is the last night of the play.

185. (D) Mr. Stein suggests that everybody take the subway to the theater after work. Choice (A) associates *bus* with *bus lines*. Choice (B) associates *car* with *parking garage*. Choice (C) associates *foot* with *walking distance*.

186. (D) Mr. Schmidt wrote to ask about liability if his debit card is stolen. Choices (A) and (C) repeat the word *account*. Choice (B) repeats *credit card*.

187. (D) Mr. Schmidt has been a customer at the bank *for over 15 years*. Choice (A) is the amount of time he has to report a stolen debit card. Choice (B) is the amount of time he has had his debit card. Choice (C) confuses the meaning of *over 15 years*.

188. (B) Mr. Schmidt says he didn't see the information he needed in the booklet *Rules for Personal Accounts at Union Bank,* but Ms. Ugarte point out that the information actually is there and tells him the page number. Choices (A), (C), and (D) are items that are associated with banking information but are not the correct answer.

189. (A) Elena Ugarte replied to Mr. Schmidt's letter, which was addressed to the Customer Service Office. Choices (B), (C), and (D) are positions at a bank but are not the correct answer.

190. (B) Ms. Ugarte enclosed a copy of page 39 of *Rules for Personal Accounts at Union Bank,* the document Mr. Schmidt mentioned in his letter. Choice (A) is associated with the topic of Mr. Schmidt's question. Choice (C) is confused with the $50 liability for stolen debit cards. Choice (D) confuses *photograph* with *photocopy.*

191. (C) Mr. Takubo is helping Ms. Choi find an apartment to rent, so he is a real estate agent. Choice (A) is not correct because Mr. Takubo mentions the landlord as a different person. Choice (B) is Ms. Choi's profession. Choice (D) is not mentioned.

192. (D) Ms. Choi says the most important thing is a convenient location. Choice (A) is incorrect because Ms. Choi says that she does not need a large space. Choice (B) is not mentioned. Choice (C) is incorrect because Ms. Choi says she wants something reasonably priced.

193. (D) Ms. Choi says she hopes to spend about $2,000, and Mr. Takubo says the office is $500 more than that. Choice (A) is the difference between Ms. Choi's preferred rent and the actual rent. Choice (B) is $500 less than Ms. Choi's preferred rent. Choice (C) is Ms. Choi's preferred rent.

194. (C) Ms. Choi says she needs something by the end of the month, and Mr. Takubo says the office will be available when she needs it. Choice (A) is not mentioned. Choice (B) is when Mr. Takubo wants to show the office. Choice (D) is confused with the *end of the month*.

195. (C) Mr. Takubo states that he wants to meet Ms. Choi at 11:00. Choice (A) is confused with the office address. Choice (B) is confused with the office suite number. Choice (D) is not mentioned.

196. (D) Joe is applying for the advertised position, which is customer account representative. Choice (A) associates *accountant* with *Accounting Department*. Choice (B) associates *software engineer* with *computer software*. Choice (C) is Ms. Ahmad's job.

197. (A) The ad asks for a résumé. Choice (B) is confused with the responsibilities of the job, which is handling billing problems. Choice (C) confuses a letter of recommendation with a cover letter. Choice (D) associates college diploma with the desirability of a college degree.

198. (C) Joe's letter states that he has worked for a mail order company for several years. Choice (A) is where Joe worked in the past. Choice (B) is confused with Joe's field of study. Choice (D) is where the current job opening is available.

199. (D) The ad asks for two years' experience as a customer service representative, and Joe says he has been at his current job as a customer service representative for three years more than that. Choice (A) is the number of years of experience required for the new position. Choice (B) is the number of years of experience Joe has beyond the requirement. Choice (C) is the number of years Joe worked at his previous job.

200. (D) Joe states that his degree is in French. Choice (A) associates *computer science* with *computer software*. Choice (B) confuses *communications* with the *communication skills* required for the job. Choice (C) uses the word *accounting* in a different context.

Answer Key
Practice Test Two

Part 1 (page 342)

1. (C) A group of people is sitting around a table. Choice (A) is incorrect because the people are at a table, not on stage. Choice (B) is incorrect because there is no water on the table. Choice (D) is incorrect because the people are speaking around the table, not before the court.

2. (B) The man and woman are having lunch. Choice (A) is incorrect because there are no plants in the restaurant, and we don't see any gardeners. Choice (C) might be true but is not what we see in the photo. Choice (D) associates *food* with *restaurant*.

3. (C) The laboratory technician is looking through a microscope. Choice (A) uses the associated words *eye* (for *looking*) and *examined*. Choice (B) uses the similar-sounding word *microphone*. Choice (D) uses the associated word *equipment*.

4. (B) The passengers are boarding the plane. Choice (A) will probably happen once the plane reaches cruising altitude. Choice (C) is incorrect because the pilot has to wait for all the passengers to board before taking off. Choice (D) confuses the similar-sounding words *train* and *plane*.

5. (C) The speaker is addressing the audience. Choice (A) confuses *addresses* (writes an address) and *addresses* (gives a talk). Choice (B) confuses the similar-sounding words *dress* and *address*. Choice (D) confuses *speaker* (thing that produces sound) and *speaker* (lecturer).

6. (B) There is one visitor in a gallery at a museum. Choice (A) uses the associated word *statue*. Choices (C) and (D) misidentify the person and the location.

7. (C) The scientist is wearing protective clothing. Choice (A) confuses *conducting an orchestra* and *conducting an experiment*. Choice (B) confuses *looking for a new hat* and *wearing a hat*. Choice (D) is incorrect because she is wearing protective clothing, not sewing clothes.

8. (A) The train is by the platform. Choice (B) confuses the similar-sounding words *plane* and *train* and confuses *runway* with *platform*. Choice (C) is incorrect because there are no passengers in the station. Choice (D) confuses the similar-sounding words *rain* and *train*.

9. (A) The players are on the field. Choice (B) confuses *match* (to light cigarettes) and *match* (sporting event). Choice (C) confuses *(fruit) stand* and *stands* where fans sit. Choice (D) confuses the similar-sounding words *balloon* and *ball*.

10. (B) The men are shaking hands. Choice (A) is incorrect because they're sitting at a table, but they're not eating dinner. Choice (C) confuses *handing out flags* and *shaking hands*. Choice (D) associates *the open books on the table* with *writing a book*.

Part 2 (page 348)

11. (A) *Because he has relatives who live there* answers *why*. Choice (B) associates *spring* with *summer*. Choice (C) associates *tourism* with *visit*.

12. (B) *It's twenty-two dollars* answers *how much*. Choice (A) associates *reservation* with *book*. Choice (C) answers *how easily can the book be read*.

13. (A) *I don't know* answers the question. Choices (B) and (C) do not answer the question.

14. (C) It isn't busy enough to have so many employees at work. Two people can go home. Choice (A) repeats the word *working,* but the speaker is concerned about the amount of people who are already working. Choice (B) confuses the similar-sounding words *walking* and *working.*

15. (C) *It leaves here on the hour* answers *when does the train run.* Choice (A) associates *express* with *fastest.* Choice (B) associates *run* with *jogging* by using the words in a different context.

16. (A) *Take the orange line to subway stop 29* gives directions by subway to the National Museum. Choices (B) and (C) do not answer the question.

17. (C) The respondent is questioning Marcy's readiness for the promotion. Choice (A) uses the related word *buy,* but Marcy is an employee, not a customer. Choice (B) relates the word *in charge* with *manager,* but the conversation is about the future, not the past.

18. (A) *I like nonfiction* answers *what kind.* Choice (B) associates *books* with *library.* Choice (C) does not answer the question.

19. (B) *I can't do that right now* is a way of refusing the suggestion to look over the figures. Choice (A) associates *figures* with *diet* by using the words in a different context. Choice (C) associates *look* with *see.*

20. (C) *They're mine* answers *who owns the shoes.* Choice (A) confuses the similar-sounding words *these* and *easy.* Choice (B) confuses the similar-sounding words *shoe* and *sue.*

21. (A) *On the workbench* answers *where is the cable.* Choice (B) does not answer the question. Choice (C) confuses the similar-sounding words *cable* and *able.*

22. (B) *It's 3256* is the most logical PIN. Choice (A) confuses *an address number* with *a PIN.* Choice (C) confuses the similar-sounding words *personal* with *personnel* and associates *employees* with *personnel.*

23. (A) *They are on my desk* answers *what happened to the inventory sheets.* Choice (B) associates *sheets* with *beds.* Choice (C) confuses the similar-sounding words *inventory* and *invention* by associating it with *innovation.*

24. (C) *Oil and vinegar will be fine* is the choice the respondent makes for salad dressing. Choices (A) and (B) associate *dressing* with *clothes* by using the words in a different context.

25. (B) *Yes, but it will cost you an extra five dollars* is the response of the taxi driver. Choice (A) does not answer the question. Choice (C) confuses *airport* with *air pollution.*

26. (C) *Maybe Mr. Baker can* answers *who can translate the document.* Choice (A) confuses the similar-sounding words *transport* and *translate.* Choice (B) associates *translate* and *watch.*

27. (C) The respondent is offering more time to get the job done. Choice (A) relates the word *deadline* with *on time,* but no specific time is mentioned Choice (B) suggests that the deadline has already passed, which is incorrect.

28. (A) *All the ones that I had* answers *which files have been transferred.* Choice (B) associates *files* with *computer.* Choice (C) associates *transfer* with *subway.*

29. (A) *He didn't say much* answers *what did the president say.* Choice (B) associates *joint* with *connection.* Choice (C) associates *president* with *election campaign.*

30. (A) The respondent is surprised that the speaker is still waiting. Choice (B) offers a reason a person would want to see a doctor, but the respondent is not the person waiting. Choice (C) relates the word *daughter* with *family* and *medical school* with *doctor* but does not relate to the speaker's problem.

31. (B) *It's my pleasure* is a polite response to the request *to get a cup of coffee.* Choices (A) and (C) do not answer the question.

32. (C) *From Eastern Europe* answers *where did the components come from.* Choice (A) associates *old* with *age* and confuses the similar-sounding words *age* and *Asia.* Choice (B) confuses the similar-sounding words *components* and *opponents.*

33. (A) *About two miles down the road* answers *how far is it.* Choices (B) and (C) do not answer the question.

34. (C) *The number is 555-9854* is an appropriate response to the request. Choice (A) confuses *Postmodern* with *posted.* Choice (B) offers an address instead of a phone number.

35. (A) The respondent originally heard the wrong request and made a mistake when issuing the ticket. Choice (B) confuses who is doing the traveling. Choice (C) is illogical because the speaker is at the ticket window making travel arrangements now.

36. (B) The speaker thinks Jenkins would prefer blue since he never wears green. Choice (A) associates *tie* with *shoe* and *slippers* by confusing *tie* (verb) and *tie* (noun). Choice (C) repeats the words *green* and *one* and uses the similar-sounding words *try* and *tie.*

37. (C) *Around two o'clock* answers *when will they get here.* Choices (A) and (B) confuse *applicant* with *applied* and *apply* and do not answer the question.

38. (A) *Only a few years old* answers *how old is that chair.* Choice (B) confuses *chair* and *chairman.* Choice (C) associates *chair* with *table.*

39. (A) *I've been out in the sun too long* answers *why* by providing a reason. Choice (B) confuses the similar-sounding words *face* and *pace.* Choice (C) confuses *red* with *read.*

40. (B) *I want to interview you* answers *what is your purpose for being here.* Choice (A) does not answer the question. Choice (C) confuses the opposites *go* and *come.*

PART 3 (PAGE 349)

41. (B) The man suggests going to a movie and the woman agrees. Choice (A) is confused with the location of the movie theater. Choice (C) associates *play* with *theater.* Choice (D) associates *jokes* with *comedy.*

42. (C) The man says that he feels bored. Choice (A) confuses *sick* with the similar-sounding word *six.* Choice (B) uses the word *good* in a different context. Choice (D) confuses *worried* with the similar-sounding word *hurry.*

43. (B) The man says that they should leave by 6:30. Choice (A) is the time now. Choice (C) is the time the movie starts. Choice (D) confuses *eleven* with the similar-sounding word *seven.*

44. (D) The man says that Mrs. Kowalski is in a meeting. Choices (A), (B), and (C) are all words that sound similar to *meeting.*

45. (D) The man says that he can't interrupt Mrs. Kowalski. Choices (A) and (C) are what the man offers to do. Choice (B) is what the man has already done.

46. (C) The woman says she'll try tomorrow morning. Choice (A) confuses *noon* with *afternoon.* Choice (B) is one of the man's suggestions. Choice (D) confuses *tomorrow afternoon* with *later this afternoon.*

47. (B) The man says there will be *at least 100 people.* Choice (A) confuses *less* with the similar-sounding word *least.* Choice (C) confuses *300* with the similar-sounding phrase *at least 100.* Choice (D) confuses *four* with *for.*

48. (D) This is what the man asks the woman to do. Choice (A) is related to *we might add more people to the list,* but he doesn't ask the woman to do this. Choice (B) is wrong since they are planning their wedding, so we can assume the man (or woman) has already done this. Choice (C) is wrong because they are discussing the caterer as a third person.

49. (D) The man says that he wants steak. Choices (A), (B), and (C) are suggestions made by the woman.

50. (C) The woman says that she will return after lunch, which is the afternoon. Choice (A) is when the man says the film can be ready. Choice (B) confuses *before lunch* with *after lunch*. Choice (D) is a possibility the man suggests.

51. (D) The woman is leaving film to be developed into photographs. Choice (A) confuses *ice* with the similar-sounding word *price*. Choice (B) uses the word *suit* in a different context. Choice (C) confuses *sweater* with the similar-sounding word *better*.

52. (C) The man says that the price is $17. Choices (A) and (B) sound similar to the correct answer. Choice (D) is the number of photographs on the roll of film.

53. (A) The woman says she spent all day Sunday at the library. Choice (B) confuses *Monday* with the similar-sounding word *Sunday*. Choice (C) confuses *Tuesday* with *tonight*. Choice (D) is when the man's report is due.

54. (B) The woman looked for articles online. Choice (A) is what the man has to do. Choice (C) confuses *searched* with the similar-sounding word *research*. Choice (D) is wrong because the woman read the magazine articles on the computer, not in actual magazines that could be taken home.

55. (C) The man says he feels tired. Choice (A) confuses *hot* with the similar-sounding word *not*. Choice (B) confuses *fine* with the similar-sounding word *time*. Choice (D) is how the woman feels.

56. (C) The man suggests that the woman put on boots because of the snow. Choice (A) is what the woman says they should do. Choice (B) confuses *thinner* with the similar-sounding word *dinner*. Choice (D) is confused with *change into dress shoes*.

57. (A) The man says that it's snowing. Choice (B) confuses *rain* with the similar-sounding word *train*. Choice (C) uses the word *fine* in a different context. Choice (D) confuses *hot* with the similar-sounding word *not*.

58. (C) The woman says that she can change her shoes when they get to the dinner. Choice (A) confuses *work* with the similar-sounding word *walk*. Choice (B) confuses *show* with the similar-sounding word *snow*. Choice (D) associates *shoe store* with *shoes*.

59. (C) The speakers mention exercise equipment, a pool, and members, so they must be in a health club. Choice (A) uses the word *office* in a different context. Choice (B) confuses *clothes* with the similar-sounding word *close*. Choice (D) associates *exercise equipment store* with *exercise equipment*.

60. (A) The man says that he will stay for an hour. Choices (B) and (C) confuse *four* with *for*. Choice (D) is the time the club closes.

61. (C) The woman says that the man should look for her in her office if he wants more information. Choice (A) confuses *call* with the similar-sounding word *all*. Choice (B) confuses *book* with the similar-sounding word *look*. Choice (D) confuses *online* with the similar-sounding word *fine*.

62. (D) The speakers are in a theater and the man says *That's way too much money to see a play*. Choice (A) associates *concert* with *orchestra* by confusing the meaning of *orchestra seats*. Choice (B) uses the word *lecture* in a different context. Choice (C) associates *movie* with *theater*.

63. (C) The woman says that the tickets cost $115 a piece. Choices (A), (B), and (D) are numbers that sound similar to the correct answer.

64. (C) The man says that the woman shouldn't have spent so much money on the tickets, so he is probably angry. Choices (A) and (B) are confused with the similar-sounding word *bad*. Choice (D) uses the word *comfortable* in a different context.

65. (A) The man had to order pens because the store was out of them. Choice (B) confuse *pencils* with the similar-sounding word *pens*. Choice (C) and (D) are the things that the man got at the store.

66. (B) The man says that he ordered five dozen pens. Choices (A) and (C) confuse *four* with *for*. Choice (D) repeats *five*.

67. (B) The man says that the order will arrive on Wednesday. Choice (A) confuses *Tuesday* with the similar-sounding phrase *two days*. Choices (C) and (D) are confused with *by the end of the week*.

68. (C) The man says that he has to finish a report. Choice (A) repeats the word *breakfast*. Choice (B) repeats the word *meeting*. Choice (D) is confused with Mr. Park's returning from a trip.

69. (C) The man says that Mr. Park will return tomorrow afternoon. Choices (A) and (D) are confused with the *last night*, which is when the woman thought Mr. Park had returned. Choice (B) is when the man wants to arrive early at the office.

70. (C) The man says that he plans to leave at 6:30. Choices (A) and (D) are confused with *before 8:00*, which is when the man wants to arrive at the office. Choice (B) is confused with *6:30*.

PART 4 (PAGE 352)

71. (D) This announcement would be heard at an airport. Choices (A) and (B) associate *ticketing counter* with *movie theater*. Choice (C) is not likely.

72. (A) Mr. Bajarin has a message. Choice (B) associates *urgent* with *risk*. Choice (C) confuses *attention* with *paying attention*. Choice (D) confuses *New Air* with *air pollution*.

73. (C) The announcement asks Mr. Bajarin to go to the courtesy desk to get his message. Choice (A) uses the word *desk* in a different context. Choice (B) associates *ticket* with *ticketing counter*. Choice (D) confuses *fresh air* with the name of the airline *New Air*.

74. (A) The building is extremely old. Choice (B) is not mentioned. Choices (C) and (D) are not the reasons the building is important.

75. (C) The total size was estimated from the size of the remaining head. Choice (A) is incorrect because an entire statue does not exist. Choices (B) and (D) are not mentioned.

76. (C) This announcement is heard on a tour bus because of *Looking to your left*. Choices (A), (B), and (D) are incorrect because it would be impossible to look at a temple site from a museum, classroom, or church.

77. (B) Randall Svetlanovich is not in, and this is his recorded message. Choices (A) and (D) are incorrect because the call can be forwarded to the receptionist. Choice (C) is incorrect because the caller can leave a message on the voice mail.

78. (B) The message says that the caller can leave a voice mail message. Choice (A) uses the word *present* in a different context. Choice (C) uses the word *mail* in a different context. Choice (D) is not mentioned.

79. (B) The message says *If you want to speak with the receptionist, please wait*. Choice (A) is not mentioned. Choice (C) confuses *e-mail* with *voice mail*. Choice (D) repeats *voice mail*.

80. (B) The skies are blue. Choice (A) describes the pressure system. Choice (C) is incorrect because *cloudy* means having more than a few light clouds. Choice (D) refers to the locale of Sunny Valley.

81. (A) A high pressure system is covering the region. Choices (B) and (D) are mentioned but are not covering the region. Choice (C) associates *Sunny Valley* with *sun*.

82. (D) The report says that the temperature will be in the 70s. Choices (A), (B), and (C) sound similar to the correct answer.

83. (C) Robbins was charged with tax evasion. Choices (A), (B), and (D) are not crimes Robbins was charged with.

84. (A) The Argentinean authorities found Ruiz from a tip received from a local merchant. Choices (B), (C), and (D) are not mentioned.

85. (D) Robbins is being returned to the United States next week. Choice (A) is what he did to hide from the police. Choice (B) is incorrect because he was accused of the crime in the United States. Choice (C) is incorrect because Robbins was working as a florist to hide from police.

86. (C) This announcement concerns late employees. Choice (A) is mentioned but is not the focus of the announcement. Choice (B) is not mentioned. Choice (D) confuses *being late for the bus* with *the bus being late*.

87. (D) Some employees are late every day. Choices (A) and (B) refer to the three to five minutes they are late. Choice (C) confuses *7:10* and *ten times*.

88. (B) Employees at other stops wait longer for the bus. Choice (A) is incorrect because it is other employees, not the bus driver, who wait in the rain. Choice (C) is not mentioned. Choice (D) is not a problem and is not caused by late employees.

89. (A) It is a clothing store. Choices (B) and (C) are not consistent with the information given. Choice (D) associates *infants* and *toddlers* with *baby furniture store*.

90. (B) The sale runs two days, Saturday and Sunday. Choice (A) confuses *half-price* with *half a day*. Choice (C) confuses *spring sale* and *all spring*. Choice (D) associates *annual* with *all year*.

91. (A) Infants' and toddlers' clothes are half price. Choice (B) is not mentioned. Choices (C) and (D) are prices for other items in the store.

92. (D) People had to leave their homes because of floods. Choice (A) associates a broken pipe with floods, but the report says that rain, not a broken pipe, was the cause of the floods. Choices (B) and (C) are wrong because the report says that there were no accidents or injuries.

93. (D) The report says that the water was *over one and a half meters high*. Choices (A), (B), and (C) sound similar to the correct answer.

94. (C) The rain stopped Monday evening. Choice (A) is when people had to leave their homes. Choice (B) confuses *Sunday* with the similar-sounding word *Monday*. Choice (D) is when people will be able to return to their homes.

95. (A) This is a message from an airline company giving information about flights. Choice (B) associates *movie theater* with *tickets* and *movie schedule*. Choice (C) associates *flights, tickets,* and *luggage* with *travel*. Choice (D) associates *operator* with *phone company*.

96. (B) The message says *To use our automated system to purchase tickets, press 2*. Choice (A) is what happens if the caller presses 4. Choice (C) is what happens if the caller presses 1. Choice (D) is confused with hearing about *size limitations on luggage*, which is what happens if the caller presses 3.

97. (B) The message says to stay on the line in order to speak to an operator. Choice (A) will give the caller a recorded flight schedule. Choice (C) associates *ticket agent* with *purchase tickets*. Choice (D) confuses going *online* with *stay on the line*.

98. (D) The announcement says that the concert will be in City Park. Choice (A) confuses *parking lot* with *park*. Choices (B) and (C) are the places where people can pick up tickets.

99. (C) The announcement says that the rain date is Sunday. Choice (A) is the last day to pick up tickets. Choice (B) is the official day of the concert. Choice (D) confuses *Monday* with the similar-sounding word *Sunday*.

100. (A) The tickets are free. Choice (B) confuses *three* with the similar-sounding word *free*. Choices (C) and (D) sound similar to *7:30*, the time the concert starts.

PART 5 (PAGE 355)

101. (C) *Although São Paulo* is the correct subordinate phrase showing an unexpected result. Choice (A) lacks a subordinate conjunction. Choice (B) has the incorrect subordinate conjunction *if* that would need to show some condition. Choice (D) includes the relative pronoun *which*, making the pronoun *it* redundant.

102. (B) *Direct link* needs the indefinite article *a*. Choice (A) has two verbs in the same clause agreeing with the noun, *exists* and *is*. Choice (C) also has two verbs in a relative clause with only one subject. Choice (D) would make the sentence a subordinate clause with no independent clause and no article with the noun phrase *direct link*.

103. (B) The passive *will be checked* is the correct answer because luggage is the theme of the sentence. Choices (A), (C), and (D) are active voice.

104. (A) Mr. Moliere came here at a particular time in the past. Choices (B) and (C) are present perfect and a particular time reference is made by *two weeks ago*. Choice (D) is simple present.

105. (C) *That a product is sold in large quantities* is the noun phrase that is the subject of the sentence. Choices (A), (B), and (D) would all have redundant verbs in the same clause for the noun *product*.

106. (D) *Such a nice person* is the correct word order. Choice (A) has the wrong word order. Choice (B) has the wrong word order and the wrong meaning of *so*. Choice (C) lacks the indefinite article *a*.

107. (B) *Faced with* means *to encounter*. Choices (A), (C), and (D) are not logical.

108. (B) *Depends on* is the two-word verb that means *determined by*. Choices (A), (C), and (D) are not logical.

109. (D) *Thrown* is the past participle that correctly modifies *cigarettes*. Choice (A) is present continuous. Choice (B) is present perfect. Choice (C) is the simple present.

110. (B) *Knew* is the correct second conditional verb. This sentence is untrue/imaginary in the present. Choice (A) is incorrect because there is no need for the modal *would*. Choice (C) is the simple present. Choice (D) is the present perfect.

111. (A) *Or* is a conjunction indicating a choice between items. Choice (B) joins clauses, not words. Choices (C) and (D) indicate a contrast between items.

112. (B) The sensory verb *saw* requires the unmarked simple present of the verb *run* as its objective complement. Choice (A) is the simple past. Choice (C) is the third-person simple present. Choice (D) is the past perfect.

113. (D) *Even if* strengthens the condition to show that in spite of the plumber's ability to fix the toilet, he still will not fix it. Choices (A) and (C) show a cause-and-effect relationship with an intended outcome. Choice (B) is a transition word showing opposition and an unexpected result.

114. (C) *Covered* is the correct past participle. *Laborers* is the passive recipient of *cover*. Choice (A) is the present participle. Choice (B) is the simple present. Choice (D) is a noun.

115. (B) *Despite* is a preposition showing unexpected results. Choices (A), (C), and (D) are conjunctions and must be followed by a clause.

116. (C) *Had waited* is the correct third conditional. It is untrue/imaginary in the past. Choice (A) is the present perfect. Choice (B) is the second conditional or simple past. Choice (D) is the simple present.

117. (D) *Finish* is correct because the simple present tense is used in an adverbial time clause. Choices (A) and (B) both use *will,* which is impossible in an adverbial time clause. Choice (C) is the present continuous.

118. (C) The causative verb *had* takes the simple form of *pick up.* Choice (A) is the present participle. Choice (B) is the infinitive. Choice (D) is the simple past.

119. (A) The adverb *already* shows that something happened before this time. Choice (B) should be used in a question or negative sentence. Choice (C) shows that something has not happened until now. Choice (D) shows that a situation continues to exist from the past until now.

120. (B) *Obligation* takes the adjective *contractual.* Choice (A) is a noun. Choice (C) is the plural noun. Choice (D) is the present participle.

121. (A) *Knows* is the correct simple present verb for the subject *who.* Choice (B) is the present continuous. Choice (C) is the present perfect. Choice (D) is the plural present continuous.

122. (B) *Yet* is the correct adverb to show that something has not happened until now. Choices (A) and (D) are midsentence adverbs. Choice (C) shows that a past situation has changed.

123. (D) The subject *product* takes the adjective *national.* Choice (A) is an adverb. Choice (B) is not the idiomatic adjective. Choice (C) is a noun.

124. (B) *Because* is a cause-and-effect conjunction that shows an expected result. Choice (A) is a conjunction that means *in addition to.* Choice (C) is a conjunction that shows contrast. Choice (D) shows that one clause is the result of the other.

125. (C) *Turn into* means that the road becomes an interstate highway. Choices (A), (B), and (D) all have different meanings from the intended meaning.

126. (A) *Quarterly* is the correct definite adverb of frequency. Choices (B), (C), and (D) are indefinite adverbs of frequency.

127. (D) The verb should be passive present perfect: *have been terminated. This year* needs the present perfect because of a particular time in the past up until now. Choices (A) and (B) are both active, and *people* is not the agent of *terminate.* Choice (C) is past perfect.

128. (A) *And* is a conjunction that joins two equal parts of speech. Choice (B) joins clauses, not words. Choice (C) is a conjunction that indicates a choice between two items. Choice (D) is an adverb.

129. (B) *Had had* is the correct third conditional showing an untrue/imaginary situation in the past. Choice (A) is a real conditional. Choice (C) is the past continuous. Choice (D) is the present perfect.

130. (C) *Should* is used to show a possible condition in the future. Choice (A) is simply a modal showing a degree of certainty in the present. Choices (B) and (D) are subordinate conjunctions that would make *condition* agree with *get* instead of *should.*

131. (B) *Until* is a subordinate conjunction that shows the firefighters will wait to that time and no longer. Choice (A) is a coordinate conjunction that means *in addition to.* Choice (C) needs to be followed by *if* or *through.* Choice (D) is a subordinate conjunction that shows an expected result.

132. (C) The noun *slip* requires the noun used as an adjective *withdrawal*. Choice (A) is the simple present form of the verb. Choice (B) is the present participle. Choice (D) is the past participle.

133. (A) *But* is a conjunction that shows contrast. Choice (B) means *in addition to*. Choice (C) is a conjunction that indicates a choice between items. Choice (D) is an adverb.

134. (C) The verb *forget* takes the gerund when the action has happened. Choice (A) is the infinitive. Choice (B) is the simple past tense of the verb. Choice (D) is the simple present tense of the verb.

135. (D) The paired conjunction *not only . . . but also* requires the verb to come before the subject. Choice (A) has the wrong word order. Choices (B) and (C) cannot be used with *but* beginning the second clause.

136. (B) The verb *offered* takes the infinitive. Choice (A) is the present participle. Choice (C) is the past infinitive. Choice (D) is preposition plus gerund.

137. (B) The time clause *by the end of March* requires the verb to be future perfect. Choice (A) is the simple present. Choice (C) is the future continuous. Choice (D) is the present perfect.

138. (A) The verb *mind* takes the gerund. Choice (B) is the infinitive. Choice (C) is third-person simple present. Choice (D) is preposition plus gerund.

139. (D) The simple past is needed because the two actions are independent of each other. There is no notion of "during." Choice (A) is the simple present. Choice (B) is the past perfect. Choice (C) is the present perfect.

140. (B) *Would not listen* fulfills the second clause of the second conditional; it is untrue/imaginary in the present. Choices (A) and (D) are illogical. Choice (C) is the third conditional.

PART 6 (PAGE 359)

141. (A) The base form of the verb is needed to complete the infinitive beginning with *to*. Choice (B) is an adjective. Choice (C) is a noun. Choice (D) is a verb that looks similar to *comply* but that has a completely different meaning.

142. (B) This pronoun refers back to the subject of the sentence *We*. Choices (A), (C), and (D) cannot be used in this context.

143. (D) A person might close a bank account because of an experience that wasn't satisfactory. Choices (A), (B), and (C) would not be reasons to close an account.

144. (C) The message talks about the furniture and equipment in the office, which describe its general condition. Choices (A), (B), and (D) are very specific qualities and are not discussed in the message.

145. (C) A gerund is required to follow the preposition *for*. Choice (A) is a base form verb. Choice (B) is an infinitive verb. Choice (D) is a future verb.

146. (B) She was not able to, or *could not*, find the software. Choices (A), (C), and (D) are modals that don't have a correct meaning for this context.

147. (B) There is an open spot on the committee, which means that someone has left it or resigned from it. Choices (A), (C), and (D) cannot be correctly used in this context.

148. (D) A noun is needed in this subject position of the clause. Choice (A) is a verb. Choice (B) is an adjective. Choice (C) is an adverb

149. (B) Customers trust the company because it protects their information from theft. This is likely to make sales grow, or *increase*. Choices (A) and (D) mean *stopped*. Choice (C) means *decreased*.

150. (C) *Rail* refers to *train*, which is the kind of travel Sigmund is writing about. Choice (A) refers to plane travel. Choice (B) refers to car travel. Choice (D) refers to boat travel.

151. (D) The expression *free of charge* means that no money will have to be paid. Choice (A), (B), and (C) cannot be correctly used with this expression.

152. (B) *Bored* is a participial adjective describing a feeling. Choice (A) is a verb. Choice (C) is a participial adjective describing the cause of a feeling. Choice (D) is a noun.

PART 7 (PAGE 365)

153. (C) Yamitomo is a music company. Choices (A) and (B) associate *electronics* and *computer* with *compact discs* and *CD-ROM*. Choice (D) associates *moving* with *carrier*.

154. (D) Excellence, diversity, and innovation are the themes of the passage. Choice (A) is not mentioned. Choice (B) is incorrect because Yamitomo sells, not develops, analog cassettes. Choice (C) is mentioned but is not the focus.

155. (C) Electronics wholesalers would be interested in this magazine. Choice (A) is the companies that advertise. Choice (B) is too specific. Choice (D) confuses *the offer of a free magazine* with *magazine publishers*.

156. (C) Magazines are offered. Choices (A), (B), and (D) are all in the magazines offered in the advertisement.

157. (A) This letter was written to show appreciation. Choices (B) and (C) are mentioned in the letter but are not the reason for it being written. Choice (D) is incorrect because the letter is written to existing members of the 25-Year Club.

158. (C) The writer wants to ensure that the 25-Year Club will grow in membership in the years to come. Choices (A), (B), and (D) are all mentioned but are not the writer's hope.

159. (B) This letter would be most likely to appear in a company newsletter. Choice (A) would not be necessary. Choice (C) is too specific. Choice (D) is too informal and in the wrong context.

160. (D) The most noticeable characteristic of the river is the deep orange color of the water. Choices (A) and (B) are mentioned but are not the most noticeable. Choice (C) associates *rate of flow* with *spewing from*.

161. (C) The silting of Lake Maracaibo has increased the risk of flooding. Choice (A) is contradicted by *fishing grounds have been destroyed*. Choices (B) and (D) are not mentioned.

162. (B) Reservations should be sent to the Hall of World Cultures of Knotty Pines. Choices (A), (C), and (D) are not mentioned.

163. (A) *Potential society members* refers to those who are interested in joining the society. Choice (B) is who should contact the Hall of World Cultures of Knotty Pines. Choices (C) and (D) are not mentioned.

164. (B) The chart lists the values and increases and decreases in mining equipment shipments. Choice (A) is incorrect because there is no listing of present stocks of the equipment. Choice (C) is incorrect because there are no prices for individual pieces of equipment. Choice (D) is incorrect because there is no mention of sales.

165. (B) Mineral-processing equipment decreased by 4 percent. Choices (A), (C), and (D) are all decrease statistics for other types of mining equipment.

166. (A) Portable crushing machinery had a 25-percent increase. Choices (B), (C), and (D) all saw decreases.

167. (D) NGJ International is sponsoring the event. Choice (A) has certified the event. Choice (B) is the site of the event. Choice (C) is the focus of the event.

168. (A) Baltimore has a specific address that one should write to for an application package. Choices (B) and (C) do not have specific addresses. Choice (D) is not mentioned.

169. (B) Oil and gas executives would be interested in a trade fair for oil and gas equipment. Choice (A) associates *politicians* with *the U.S. Department of Commerce*. Choice (C) associates *environmentalists* with *oil* and *gas*. Choice (D) associates *trade negotiators* with *trade fair*.

170. (A) DynaBold is an automated teller machine (ATM) manufacturer. Choices (B) and (C) associate *investment* and *bank* to references in the passage. Choice (D) associates *security expertise* with *security service*.

171. (D) DynaBold created the first modular ATM that could be upgraded without changing the housing. Choice (A) confuses *modular ATM* with *modular homes*. Choices (B) and (C) associate *investment* and *bank* to the references in the passage.

172. (B) The service organization responds to problems 24 hours a day, 365 days a year. Choices (A), (C), and (D) are improvements, not maintenance.

173. (D) Consumers would be most interested in this information. Choices (A) and (B) are people who should be on the committee. Choice (C) is not the intended audience.

174. (A) Drug advisory committees should advise. Choice (B) is incorrect since there is no mention of profit. Choice (C) confuses *consumer* in the passage with *consumer advocate*. Choice (D) confuses *being evaluated by the Ministry of Health* with *evaluating the Ministry of Health*.

175. (D) Consulting is closest in meaning to advisory. These consulting committees give advice. The other options do not fit the context.

176. (B) Availability of over-the-counter drugs would be a possible topic because it involves an impact on the consumer. Choices (A), (C), and (D) are not the foci of these committees.

177. (D) This passage would probably appear in a travel guidebook to be read before one's journey. Choices (A), (B), and (C) are all not specific enough.

178. (A) If staying in a country for several weeks, it is worthwhile to register at one's embassy. Choices (B), (C), and (D) are all associated with references to *passport, passport photos,* and *hotel* mentioned in the passage.

179. (A) The traveler should seek out the proper official and request that the passport be stamped. Choice (B) wouldn't help in getting the passport stamped. Choice (C) confuses *go to the embassy* and *register at the embassy*. Choice (D) wouldn't be able to help.

180. (C) Passport holders must make certain that their passports are stamped. The other options do not fit the context.

181. (C) The letter is addressed to *Neighborhood Business,* but not to any one business in particular. Choice (A) is incorrect because local attorneys probably received the letter, but other businesses probably received it as well. Choice (B) is incorrect because the letter is not addressed specifically to that business. Choice (D) is incorrect because the letter is addressed to *Neighborhood Business* and states *we offer a convenient location close to your business.*

182. (D) Robert and Oscar Lumpkin signed the letter from Lumpkin's Computer Center, so we can assume they are the business owners. Choice (A) is confused with the business of the person who wrote the memo. Choices (B) and (C) associate *software* and *computer manufacturers* with the name of the business, but they are incorrect because the letter states that the purpose of the business is to sell computer supplies and repair computers.

183. (A) The letter states that the Computer Center sells *refurbished*, or restored, computers. Choice (B) is associated with the name of the business, but the letter says nothing about this. Choice (C) is wrong because the letter says that the center repairs computers, not printers. Choice (D) is wrong because the letter says that the center sells *new*, not recycled, ink cartridges.

184. (B) The letter says that the computer supply store is *on the same block as we are*, and we know from the letter that the computer supply store is on Chestnut Street. Choice (A) is the location of the stationery store. Choice (C) is confused with the name of the stationery store. Choice (D) is confused with the name of the computer supply store.

185. (C) Myra wants 5 ink cartridges and 10 packages of paper and asks Yoshi to be sure to get the 10 percent discount. Choice (A) is the price of 5 ink cartridges with the discount. Choice (B) is the price of 5 ink cartridges without the discount. Choice (D) is the price of 5 ink cartridges and 10 packs of paper without the discount.

186. (C) Ms. Degenaro is seeking a position as an accountant. Choices (A), (B), and (D) are things that one might do when seeking a job but are not the stated purpose of the letter.

187. (D) This is the opening Mr. Sachimoto mentions in his letter. Choice (A) is the type of job Ms. Degenaro wants. Choice (B) is the job she had before entering graduate school. Choice (C) is the type of company she worked for.

188. (A) Mr. Sachimoto says that he went to the same graduate school as Ms. Degenaro, which, according to her letter, is Pitt. Choice (B) is the college where Ms. Degenaro got her bachelor's degree. Choice (C) is confused with the name of the company she worked for. Choice (D) is confused with the name of the city where she lives.

189. (C) Mr. Sachimoto says that his assistant's name is Ms. Rogers. Choice (A) is confused with the department that has a job opening. Choice (B) is associated with Ms. Degenaro's description of her work experience. Choice (D) is confused with the company where Mr. Sachimoto works.

190. (C) The documents that Ms. Degenaro mentioned in her letter are her college transcripts. Choices (A) and (D) are things that she has already sent to Mr. Sachimoto. Choice (B) is not mentioned.

191. (B) Akiko will be in Melbourne on May 13th and 14th.

192. (D) This is the date on the itinerary. Choices (A), (B), and (C) are dates that she will be in other cities.

193. (A) According to the itinerary, Mr. Andrews works for BelAir although, according to the e-mail, he used to work for Holiday, Inc. Choice (B) is where Mr. Andrews used to work. Choice (C) is where Ms. Chang works. Choice (D) is where Akiko works.

194. (C) Akiko asks Tamako to send the photos to her at the conference, which is in Darwin. Choices (A), (B), and (D) are the other cities that Akiko will visit.

195. (B) Akiko will call Tamako from Ms. Chang's office. She will be there on May 19th. Choices (A), (C), and (D) are other dates on the itinerary.

196. (D) Luiz's letter states that he is going to Greendale to work on a project. Choice (A) is what he will do after the project is finished, but it is not the primary reason for his trip. Choice (B) isn't correct because Luiz wants to rent, not buy, a place to live. Choice (C) is something he might do while in Greendale, but it isn't mentioned and isn't the primary reason for the trip.

197. (D) Luis states in the letter that he will spend three months in Greendale. Choice (A) is the time he will spend traveling at the end of his stay. Choices (B) and (C) aren't mentioned.

198. (B) Luis wants to spend no more than $1,500, and Roberto says that the suites are $300 less than that. Choice (A) is the difference between the actual price and the price mentioned by Luis. Choice (C) is the price mentioned by Luis. Choice (D) is $300 more than the price mentioned by Luis.

199. (C) Roberto says that the hotel suites are in the North End of the city. Choices (A), (B), and (D) describe the location of Luis's office.

200. (D) Luis says that he plans to take a vacation at the beach, and Roberto says that he will go with him. Choice (A) is confused with the purpose of Luis's visit. Choices (B) and (C) are things that Roberto might do, but they are not mentioned in the letter.

PRACTICE TEST CONVERSION TABLE

Match the number of correct answers with the corresponding Practice Score. Add the two Practice scores together. This is your estimated total Practice Score.

Number Correct Listening = Practice Listening Score _____

Number Correct Reading = Practice Reading Score + _____

Total Estimated Practice Score _____

PRACTICE TEST ESTIMATED CONVERSION CHART

# CORRECT	LISTENING	READING
0	5	5
1	5	5
2	5	5
3	5	5
4	5	5
5	5	5
6	5	5
7	10	5
8	15	5
9	20	5
10	25	5
11	30	5
12	35	5
13	40	5
14	45	5
15	50	5
16	55	10
17	60	15
18	65	20
19	70	25
20	75	30
21	80	35
22	85	40
23	90	45
24	95	50
25	100	60
26	110	65
27	115	70
28	120	80
29	125	85
30	130	90
31	135	95
32	140	100
33	145	110
34	150	115
35	160	120
36	165	125
37	170	130
38	175	140
39	180	145
40	185	150
41	190	160
42	195	165
43	200	170
44	210	175
45	215	180
46	220	190
47	230	195
48	240	200
49	245	210
50	250	215

# CORRECT	LISTENING	READING
51	255	220
52	260	225
53	270	230
54	275	235
55	280	240
56	290	250
57	295	255
58	300	260
59	310	265
60	315	270
61	320	280
62	325	285
63	330	290
64	340	300
65	345	305
66	350	310
67	360	320
68	365	325
69	370	330
70	380	335
71	385	340
72	390	350
73	395	355
74	400	360
75	405	365
76	410	370
77	420	380
78	425	385
79	430	390
80	440	395
81	445	400
82	450	405
83	460	410
84	465	415
85	470	420
86	475	425
87	480	430
88	485	435
89	490	445
90	495	450
91	495	455
92	495	465
93	495	470
94	495	480
95	495	485
96	495	490
97	495	495
98	495	495
99	495	495
100	495	495